lali
B

ENGLISH IN ACTION

THIRD EDITION

TEACHER'S GUIDE

NATIONAL GEOGRAPHIC
LEARNING

BARBARA H. FOLEY
ELIZABETH R. NEBLETT

Australia • Brazil • Mexico • Singapore • United Kingdom • United States

National Geographic Learning,
a Cengage Company

***English in Action* Level 3 Teacher's Guide: Third Edition**
Barbara H. Foley, Elizabeth R. Neblett

Publisher: Sherrise Roehr

Executive Editor: Sarah Kenney

Managing Development Editor: Claudienma Mimó

Senior Development Editors: Brenden Layte and Lewis Thompson

Associate Development Editor: Katie Davis

Assistant Editor: Becky Long

Media Researcher: Leila Hishmeh

Director of Global Marketing: Ian Martin

Product Marketing Managers: Dalia Bravo and Joy MacFarland

Sr. Director, ELT & World Languages: Michael Burggren

Production Manager: Daisy Sosa

Content Project Manager: Beth Houston

Manufacturing Customer Account Manager: Mary Beth Hennebury

Composition: MPS North America LLC

Cover/Text Design: Lisa Trager

Art Director: Brenda Carmichael

Cover Image: ©Jean Pierre Lescourret/ Getty Images

ISBN: 978-1-337-90608-1

National Geographic Learning
20 Channel Center Street
Boston, MA 02210
USA

Locate your local office at **international.cengage.com/region**

Visit National Geographic Learning online at **ELTNGL.com**
Visit our corporate website at **www.cengage.com**

Printed in China
Print Number: 01 Print Year: 2018

ACKNOWLEDGMENTS

The authors and publisher would like to thank the following reviewers and Advisory-Panel members:

Karin Abell
Durham Technical Community College, Durham, NC

Angela Addy
Passaic County Community College, Passaic, NJ

Beth Anglin
Bucks County Community College, Newtown, PA

Irma Baack
Harper College, Schaumburg, IL

Teresita Bautista
Paramount Adult Education, CA

Rod Bennett
Emily Griffith Technical College, Denver, CO

Anne Bertin
Union County College, New Jersey

Patricia Bone
Montgomery College, Rockville, MD

Carlo Buzzi
North Shore Community College, Danvers, MA

Julia Cantu
MiraCosta College, Oceanside, CA

Fang Chen
Central New Mexico Community College, Albuquerque, NM

Kathryn Clark
Daytona State College, Daytona Beach, FL

Lin Cui
William Rainey Harper College, Palatine, IL

Andre DeSandies
Union County College, New Jersey

Lois Eisenber
Bucks County Community College, Newtown, PA

Linda Foster
Hillsborough County, FL

Tracy Fung
Palomar College, San Marcos, CA

Litsa Georgiou
Union County College, New Jersey

Deborah Greene
Sharon Technical College, Hollywood, FL

Jill Harold
University of North Texas, Denton, TX

Harriet Hirschfeld
Bucks County Community College, Newtown, PA

Katherine Hiscock
Portland Adult Education, Portland, ME

Lorraine Hromalik
Bowers/Whitley Adult Community School, Tampa, FL

Liz Hughes
Rosie's Place, Boston, MA

Dawn Humphry
University of Arkansas Cossatot Community College, Nashville, AR

Kim Johnson
Palomar College, San Marcos, CA

Christopher Kilmer
Emily Griffith Technical College, Denver, CO

Eileen Krai
Bucks County Community College, Newtown, PA

Caron Lieber
Palomar College, Fallbrook, CA

Mayra Lopez
MiraCosta College, Oceanside, CA

Melissa Lutz
University of Arkansas Cossatot Community College, De Queen, AR

Diann Mandile
Emily Griffith Technical College, Denver, CO

Cheo Massion
College of Marin, Kentfield, CA

Lynn Meng
Union County College, New Jersey

Gregor Mieder
Metropolitan State University, Denver, CO

Susan Moser
Portland Community College, Portland, OR

Susana Murillo
Palomar College, San Marcos, CA

Karen Nelson
Pittsburg State University, Pittsburg, KA

Sergei Paromchik
Hillsborough County Public Schools, Tampa, FL

Claudia Pena
Houston Community College, Houston, TX

Dinah Perren
Palomar College, Oceanside, CA

Kandyce Pinckney
Emily Griffith Technical College, Denver, CO

Howard Pomann
Union County College, New Jersey

Nicole Powell
SUNY Orange, Bloomingburg, NY

Tami Richey
Palomar College, San Marcos, CA

Julie Roberts
Georgia Piedmont Technical College, Doravilla, GA

Christi Stilley
CARIBE Refugee Program, Tampa, FL

Gail Voorhes
Palomar College, Ramona, CA

Huaxin Xu
Union County College, New Jersey

Rochelle Yanike-Hale
Portland Adult Education, Portland, ME

Beth Zarret
Bucks County Community College, Newtown, PA

Miriam Zemen
Montgomery College, Silver Spring, MD

CONTENTS

CONTENTS

Welcome to the third edition of **ENGLISH IN ACTION!**

*Walkthrough shows content from Level 3, Unit 4

REAL-WORLD CONTENT from National Geographic to foster Critical Thinking and 21st Century Skills

NEW A thought-provoking visual at the beginning of each unit allows learners to engage in purposeful classroom discussions.

NEW focus on **WIOA** and **College and Career Readiness Standards** to equip learners with the essential skills they need to succeed in the real world.

NEW Video and reading activities showcase National Geographic footage and readings, making students' language learning experience interesting and relevant.

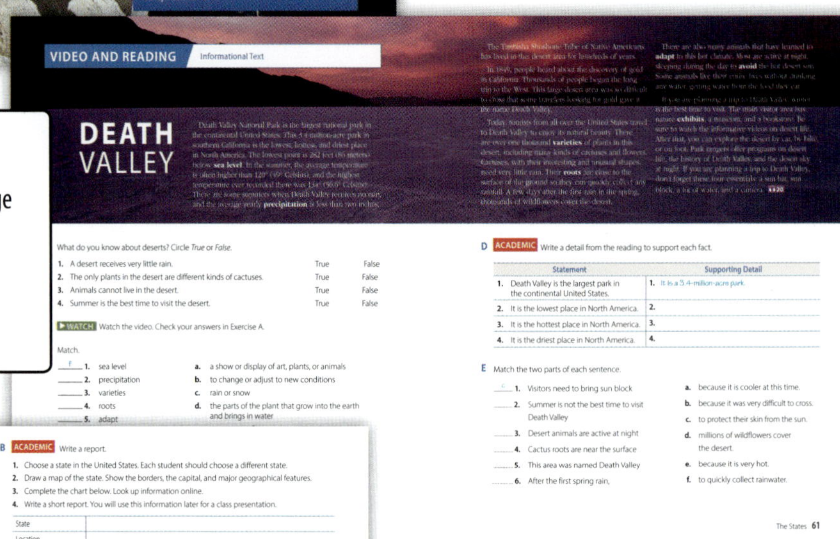

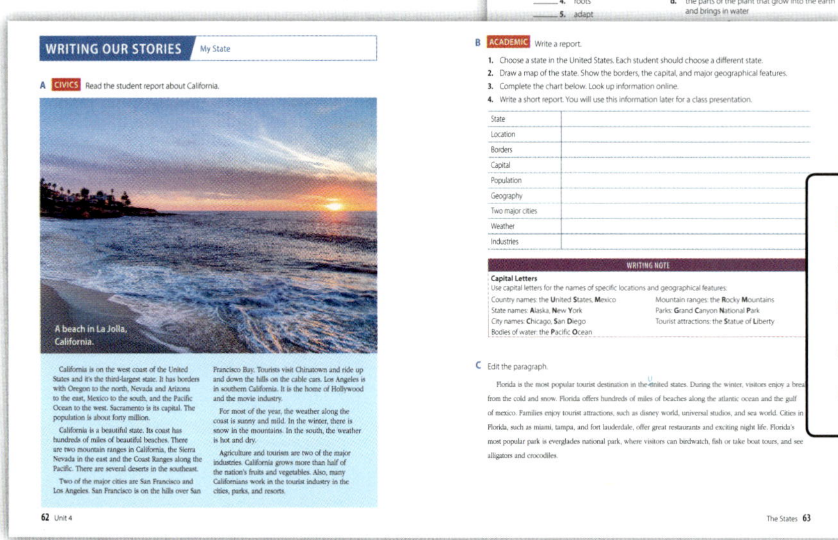

UPDATED *Writing Our Stories* activities allow learners to master the **process of writing** with guided practice that empowers them to improve their own writing.

English in Action, Third Edition

PLANNING CURRICULUM To Meet WIOA Goals and CCRS

UPDATED The ***Big Picture* section** allows learners to practice all skills around a story or conversation, motivating them to apply new grammar and vocabulary.

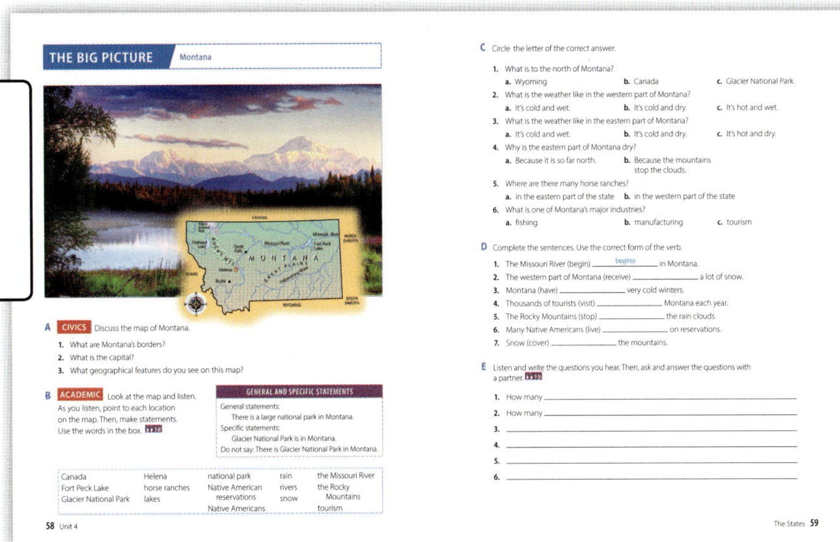

THE BIG PICTURE Montana

A CIVICS Discuss the map of Montana.

1. What are Montana's borders?
2. What is the capital?
3. What geographical features do you see on this map?

B ACADEMIC Look at the map and listen. As you listen, point to each location on the map. Then, make statements. Use the words in the box.

GENERAL AND SPECIFIC STATEMENTS
General statements:
There is a large national park in Montana.
Specific statements:
Glacier National Park is in Montana.
Do not say: There is Glacier National Park in Montana.

Canada Fort Peck Lake Glacier National Park	Helena horse ranches lakes	national park Native American reservations Native Americans	rain rivers snow	the Missouri River the Rocky Mountains tourism

58 Unit 4

C Circle the letter of the correct answer.

1. What is to the north of Montana?
 a. Wyoming b. Canada c. Glacier National Park
2. What is the weather like in the western part of Montana?
 a. It's cold and wet. b. It's cold and dry. c. It's hot and wet.
3. What is the weather like in the eastern part of Montana?
 a. It's cold and wet. b. It's cold and dry. c. It's hot and dry.
4. Why is the eastern part of Montana dry?
 a. Because it is so far north. b. Because the mountains stop the clouds.
5. Where are there many horse ranches?
 a. in the eastern part of the state b. in the western part of the state
6. What is one of Montana's major industries?
 a. fishing b. manufacturing c. tourism

D Complete the sentences. Use the correct form of the verb.

1. The Missouri River (begin) _____ in Montana.
2. The western part of Montana (receive) _____ a lot of snow.
3. Montana (have) _____ very cold winters.
4. Thousands of tourists (visit) _____ Montana each year.
5. The Rocky Mountains (stop) _____ the rain clouds.
6. Many Native Americans (live) _____ on reservations.
7. Snow (cover) _____ the mountains.

E Listen and write the questions you hear. Then, ask and answer the questions with a partner.

1. How many _____
2. How many _____
3. _____
4. _____
5. _____
6. _____

The States 59

UPDATED The ***Active Grammar* activities**, a hallmark to this series, are directly related to the theme of the unit, allowing learners to gain language skills for college and the workplace.

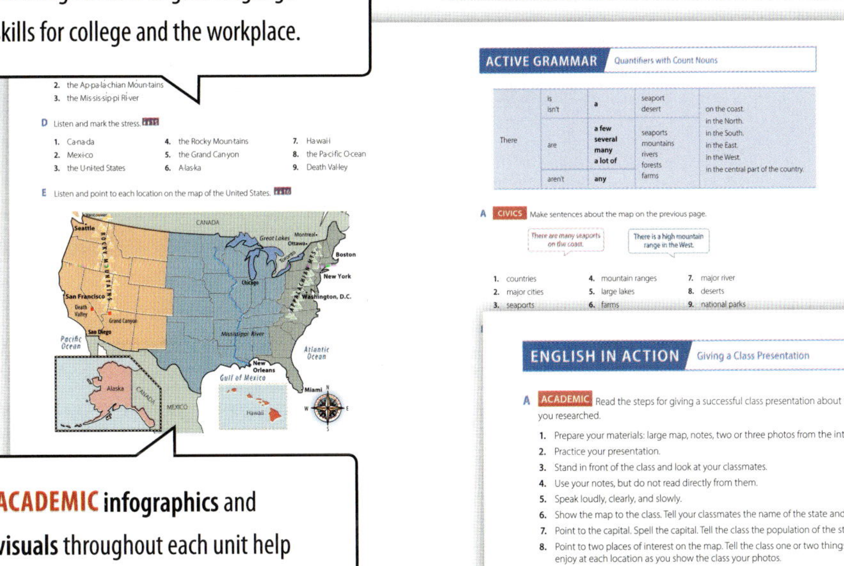

2. the Ap·pa·la·chian Moun·tains
3. the Mis·sis·sip·pi Ri·ver

D Listen and mark the stress.

1. Ca·na·da
2. Mex·i·co
3. the U·ni·ted States
4. the Rocky Moun·tains
5. the Grand Can·yon
6. A·las·ka
7. Ha·wai·i
8. the Pa·ci·fic O·cean
9. Death Val·ley

E Listen and point to each location on the map of the United States.

ACTIVE GRAMMAR Quantifiers with Count Nouns

There	is isn't	a	seaport desert	on the coast.
	are	a few several many a lot of	seaports mountains rivers forests farms	in the North. in the South. in the East. in the West. in the central part of the country.
	aren't	any		

A CIVICS Make sentences about the map on the previous page.

There are many seaports on the coast.

There is a high mountain range in the West.

1. countries
2. major cities
3. seaports
4. mountain ranges
5. large lakes
6. farms
7. major river
8. deserts
9. national parks

ACADEMIC infographics and **visuals** throughout each unit help learners to build the skills they need for college and career readiness.

The **HALLMARK** ***English in Action*** sections provide learners with practice that promotes workforce, academic, and life skills, and allows them to successfully transition into the real world.

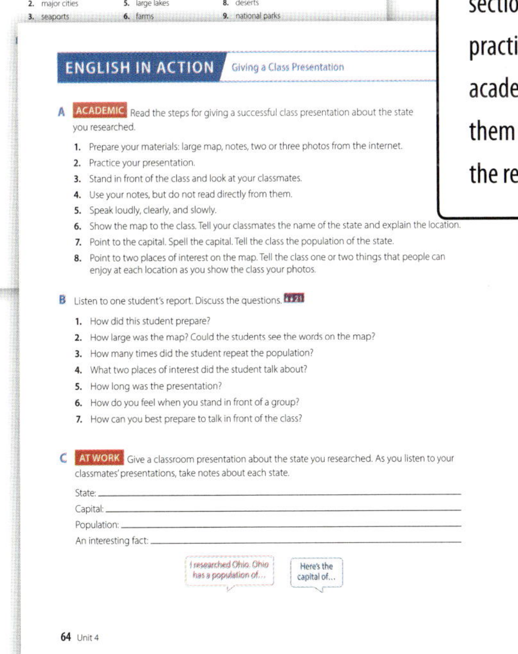

ENGLISH IN ACTION Giving a Class Presentation

A ACADEMIC Read the steps for giving a successful class presentation about the state you researched.

1. Prepare your materials: large map, notes, two or three photos from the internet.
2. Practice your presentation.
3. Stand in front of the class and look at your classmates.
4. Use your notes, but do not read directly from them.
5. Speak loudly, clearly, and slowly.
6. Show the map to the class. Tell your classmates the name of the state and explain the location.
7. Point to the capital. Spell the capital. Tell the class the population of the state.
8. Point to two places of interest on the map. Tell the class one or two things that people can enjoy at each location as you show the class your photos.

B Listen to one student's report. Discuss the questions.

1. How did this student prepare?
2. How large was the map? Could the students see the words on the map?
3. How many times did the student repeat the population?
4. What two places of interest did the student talk about?
5. How long was the presentation?
6. How do you feel when you stand in front of a group?
7. How can you best prepare to talk in front of the class?

C AT WORK Give a classroom presentation about the state you researched. As you listen to your classmates' presentations, take notes about each state.

State: _____
Capital: _____
Population: _____
An interesting fact: _____

I researched Ohio. Ohio has a population of...

Here's the capital of...

64 Unit 4

English in Action, Third Edition

ENGLISH IN ACTION | Supports Teachers and Adult Learners for Greater Achievement

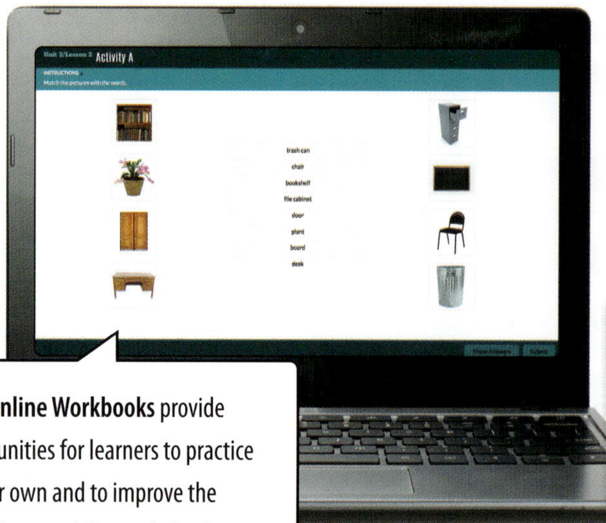

NEW Online Workbooks provide opportunities for learners to practice on their own and to improve the digital literacy skills needed to be successful in the 21st century.

The **NEW Classroom Presentation Tool** includes digital versions of the student book and workbook with interactive games, answer keys, and integrated audio and video.

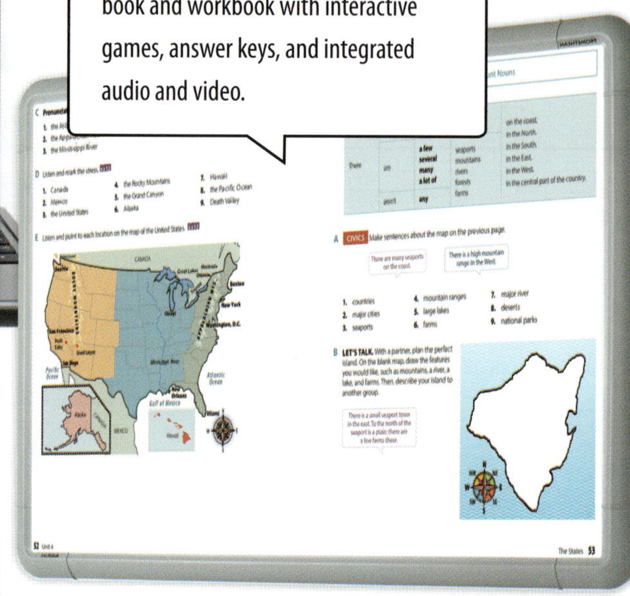

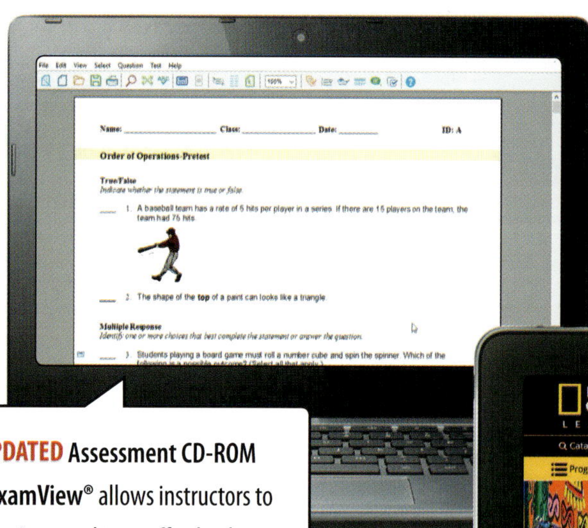

The **UPDATED Assessment CD-ROM with ExamView®** allows instructors to create quizzes and tests effortlessly.

NEW companion sites provide additional resources such as correlations for teachers and access to the audio program for learners.

AUDIO AVAILABLE VIA MOBILE PHONE

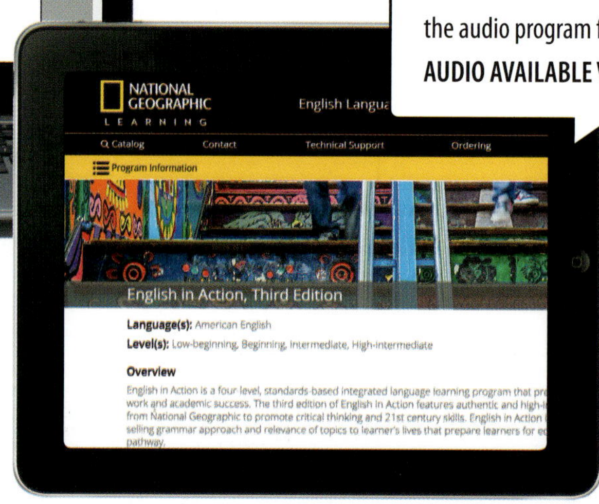

ABOUT THE AUTHORS

Elizabeth Neblett

Elizabeth Neblett teaches ESL full-time at Union County College in Elizabeth, New Jersey. She has presented workshops on teaching at many TESOL conventions and has done workshops on how to use *English in Action* throughout Mexico. She has co-authored *English in Action, Grammar in Action*, Books 2–3, and *Basic Grammar in Action*. She has also written a series of ESL novellas.

Barbara Foley

Five years ago, I had planned on taking early retirement after thirty-eight years of teaching ESOL at Union County College in New Jersey. My "retirement" lasted five months before I found myself back in the classroom, directing an ESOL program for refugees. Interacting with adult learners and participating in their journey in a new language and a new culture is a special experience. I thank my students for sharing their stories, their insights, their struggles, and their achievements these many years. It has enriched my life and my world.

TEACHER'S GUIDE CONTENTS

UNIT 1 THE FIRST WEEK

First-year students move into Victoria College, in Toronto, Canada.

ACADEMIC Take notes; interpret graphs; take a survey

AT WORK Introduce yourself and others; read and interpret visuals; identify strengths and weaknesses

CIVICS Understand classroom expectations

CCRS Level A: R 1, 2, 5, 7; W 2, 5; L 1, 6; Level B: R 1, 2, 5, 6, 7; W 2, 4, 5; L 1, 3, 6; Level C: R 1, 2, 7; W 2, 4, 5, 9; L 1, 3, 6; Level D: R 1, 2, 7; W 2, 4, 5, 9; L 1, 3, 6; Level E: R 1, 2, 7; W 2, 4, 5, 9; L 6

ELPS Level 1 Standards 1, 2, 3, 7, 8, 9, 10; Level 2 Standards 1, 2, 3, 7, 8, 9, 10; Level 3 Standards 1, 2, 3, 7, 8, 9, 10; Level 4 Standards 1, 2, 3, 7, 8, 9, 10; Level 5 Standards 1, 2, 3, 7, 8, 9, 10

CIVICS 13-1; 13-2; 50-6

CASAS 0.1.2; 0.1.5; 4.1.2; 4.1.8; 4.1.9; 4.4.3; 7.1.1; 7.1.2; 7.4.4; 7.7.3

IN THIS UNIT

In Unit 1, students will:

- Practice taking notes, interpret graphs, and conduct a survey
- Practice simple present affirmative statements, *There is / There are*, and prepositions of location
- Write an introductory narrative

ABOUT THE PHOTO

The photo shows students at Victoria College in Toronto, Canada, moving into their dorm at the beginning of the semester. Explain to students that *dorm* is short for *dormitory*, a building provided by the college/university where students live together and usually share a room with another student. Most adult students will live at home with their families, but if appropriate, ask if students live in a dorm and if they share a room with another student. In the US, many students also live *off campus*, in apartments near the college/university. Ask: *Where do students in your country usually live—at home, in dorms, or off campus?*

As a class, discuss students' experiences living together with other people. On the board, draw a two-column chart and ask students to list the positives and negatives of living with another person.

Ask students to identify some of the things the students are bringing with them in the dorm. (refrigerator, microwave oven, musical instrument, clothing, etc.) Encourage students to answer using *There is / There are*, which they will review and practice in Unit 1.

Preview the unit topic by telling students that one of the things they probably do several times during the first week at a new school or a new job is to introduce themselves to people they meet. Ask: *When you introduce yourself to a new person, what information do you give them about yourself?* (name, where you're from, how long you've been at the school/job, what class(es) you're taking/what your job is, etc.)

A

- Have students look at the photo and make predictions about the passage. Ask: *Who is he? What is his job? Where is he now? Where does he live?*
- Ask students to read the passage all the way through without stopping. Then, read the passage aloud to the class.
- Ask questions about the passage, such as: *What's his name? Where does he go to school? What class does he take? How many students are in his class? When is his class? Who is his teacher? Where is her office?*

B

- Ask students to read the sentences and fill in the blanks. Tell students that they can complete the sentences with information about a different class and teacher if they want.
- Then, invite one or two volunteers to read their sentences aloud. Correct any mistakes in grammar or pronunciation.
- Ask the other students questions about the volunteers' information. Ask: *What's his / her name? What class is he / she taking? When is his / her class? Who is his / her teacher?*

C 2

- Read the Writing Strategy aloud to the class.
- Play the audio and ask students to listen without taking notes.
- Play the audio a second time and have them take notes about Kenji's life. Remind students that they should write key words, not sentences.

ACADEMIC

Note taking is a key academic skill that can help students when preparing and studying for tests.

A Read.

Hi. My name is Kenji, and I'm a student at the University of California, San Diego. I'm a student in the English language program. I'm taking Listening and Pronunciation in Room 142. There are ten students in my class, four men and six women. We are from five different countries. Our class meets on Mondays, Wednesdays, and Fridays from 10:30 a.m. to 12:30 p.m. My teacher is Ms. Burak. Her office is in Room 12.

B Complete the sentences about yourself. Answers will vary.

1. My name is ____________________.
2. I'm a student at ____________________.
3. I'm taking ____________________ in Room ______.
4. There are ______ students in my class, ______ men and ______ women.
5. I have class on ____________________ (days).
6. My teacher is ____________________. His / Her office is in Room ______.

C **ACADEMIC** Listen to Gloria interview Kenji about his life in the United States. Take notes. Then, compare your notes with a partner. 2 Answers may vary.

WRITING STRATEGY

When you take notes, you write a few words to help you remember important information. You do not write full sentences.

2 Unit 1

MORE ACTION

For more practice with simple present statements, make some false sentences about the passage in Exercise A and ask students to correct you. For example:

T: *His name is Koji.*

S: *No, his name is Kenji.*

Kenji:	new student
Japan	doesn't work
six months	not married
	21 years old
mother, father, sister	swims 4-5 times per week
studies English	photography and rock music
lives in student dorms	laptop

D Look at your notes. Answer the questions about Kenji.

1. What country is Kenji from? He's from Japan.
2. How long has he been in the United States? He has been in the United States for six months.
3. Why is he in the United States? He studies English in college.
4. How many people are in his family? Four. He has a mother, father, and sister.
5. Where does he live? He lives in the student dorms.
6. Is he a new student? Yes, he is.
7. Does he work? No, he doesn't.
8. Is he married? No, he isn't.
9. How old is he? He's 21.
10. How often does he swim? He swims four or five times a week.
11. What other interests does he have? He likes photography and music.
12. What kind of music does he like? He likes rock music.
13. What kind of computer does he have? He has a laptop.
14. How will he meet other students at college? What do you think?
    Answers may vary. He will meet other students in class, in the dorm, and at the pool.

CULTURE NOTE

Americans usually do not ask about age or religion when they first meet a person. They do not talk about their salary with strangers or friends, and sometimes not even with family.

D

- Have students work in pairs and take turns asking each other the questions. Students should compare their notes and answers with their partners'.
- If necessary, play some or all of the audio again to clarify any difficult questions.
- Call on one or two students to read aloud their answers. Ask the class to correct any mistakes.
- Then, ask students to close their books and ask each other as many questions about Kenji as they can remember.

CULTURE NOTE

Read the Culture Note and explain that, in the United States, it is considered impolite to ask about a person's age, religion, or salary if you do not know them well. Ask students if this is the same or different in their culture.

CIVICS

Explain that Americans consider it rude to ask about things that are "too personal." For Americans, age, religion, and salary are considered too personal to ask about. Ask students to identify things that are too personal to ask about in their own cultures. List students' answers on the board. Ask: *How would you feel if someone asked you about something on this list? What would you think about a person who asked you one of these things?*

MORE ACTION

For more practice with note taking, invite one or two students to write their notes from Exercise C on the board. Ask the class to make suggestions for improvements. Then, give a short talk about yourself and ask students to take similar notes about your life. Afterwards, students can work in pairs to ask and answer questions about you.

ACTIVE GRAMMAR: Simple Present: Affirmatives

A

- Read the sentences in the grammar charts. Ask students to explain the differences between the three charts. (Each chart uses a different subject pronoun.)
- Ask: *What is different about the verbs in the first sentence of each chart?* (The verb *be* has three different forms—*am, is, are*.) *How are the verbs* lives *and* works *in the second chart different from the other verbs in the other charts?* (They both end in *s*.)
- Have students read and complete the sentences in Exercise A individually.
- Ask students to compare answers in pairs. Then, call on individual students to read their answers. Correct any mistakes.

B

- Have students read the notes. Ask a few questions about Pierre. *How old is he?* (32) *Where is he from?* (Haiti) *What are his interests?* (soccer and guitar)
- Have students write ten sentences about Pierre. Then, ask volunteers to write some of their sentences on the board. Invite the class to correct any mistakes.

ACTIVE GRAMMAR Simple Present: Affirmatives

I **am** a student.	She **is** a student.	They **are** students.
I **live** in New York.	She **lives** in New York.	They **live** in New York.
I **work** part time.	She **works** part time.	They **work** part time.
I **have** a computer.	She **has** a computer.	They **have** computers.

A Complete the sentences.

1. Eva and Mariola (be) ___are___ sisters.
2. They (study) ___study___ English at Summit Adult School.
3. Eva (work) ___works___ full time.
4. Mariola (have) ___has___ two small children.
5. They (go) ___go___ to school two nights a week.
6. Eva (drive) ___drives___ to school.
7. She (pick up) ___picks up___ Mariola on the way to school.
8. On the way to school, they (talk) ___talk___ about their families.

B In your notebook, write ten sentences about Pierre. **Answers will vary.**

Name:	Pierre Dorval
Age:	32
Country:	Haiti
Years in US:	Four
School:	Bay Adult School; Intermediate level; Mondays and Wednesdays, 9:00 a.m to 12:00 p.m.
Marital Status:	Married, one son
Occupation:	Waiter; West Hotel; six nights a week
Interests:	Soccer and guitar
Computer:	Yes
Music:	Jazz and rock

TEACHING TIP

To give students more practice with finding and correcting their own mistakes, have students reread their own sentences from Exercise B and look for mistakes. Explain that editing is an important skill that will help them improve their writing.

C **LET'S TALK.** Interview a classmate. Take notes. *Answers will vary.*

1. What's your name? ______
2. What country are you from? ______
3. Is your family here in the United States? ______
4. How many people are in your family? ______
5. How long have you been in the United States? ______
6. Where do you live? ______
7. Are you a new student in this school? ______
8. How do you get to school? ______
9. Do you have a driver's license? ______
10. Are you married? Do you have any children? If so, how many? ______
11. Do you work? Where do you work? What do you do? ______
12. What are your interests? ______
13. What kind of music do you like? ______
14. Do you have a computer? ______

D AT WORK **LET'S TALK.** Introduce your partner to the class.

I'd like you to meet Gloria. She's from Guanajuato, Mexico. She lives here in Los Angeles. She's . . .

CULTURE NOTE

To introduce a person, say:

I'd like to introduce (*name*).
I'd like you to meet (*name*).
This is my friend, (*name*).

CULTURE NOTE

Ask students to identify scenarios in which they need to introduce themselves or others. (new coworker, new student, new neighbor, etc.) Ask: *What information is helpful when you meet a new person?* (name, where the person is from, how long the person has been in the US/at the job/at school, etc.) Remind students that it is sometimes considered rude not to introduce a new person.

TEACHING TIP

Ask students to take the time to learn how to correctly pronounce their partner's name before introducing them in front of the class. Encourage students to help each other with pronouncing and spelling their names.

C

- Have students read the questions silently and think about the answers they will give.
- Ask students to work in pairs and interview each other. Remind them to take notes, not to write complete sentences.

D

- Point out the language used for introductions in the Culture Note and in the speech bubble. Ask several students to practice each line.
- Call on volunteers to use their notes from Exercise C to introduce their partner to the class. Tell students that they do not have to use all of their notes when introducing their partner—they can pick the information they think the class would find most interesting.
- Encourage other students to ask questions about each person who is introduced.
- Then, have students form groups of four and take turns introducing their partners to the other two students.

AT WORK

Encourage students not to be shy about requesting or facilitating introductions on the job. It will help them appear confident and invested in the team and will set a good tone for group work. A good introduction will include eye contact and a handshake; repeating the person's name (*Nice to meet you, Gloria.*) is a good strategy to help remember.

ACTIVE GRAMMAR: *There is / There are* and Prepositions

A

- Ask students to read the sentences in the grammar chart aloud. Ask: *What is the subject of each sentence?* (library and restrooms) *Why does the first sentence use* isn't *and the second sentence use* aren't? (Because *library* is singular and *restrooms* is plural.)
- Model the correct pronunciation of *There is* and *There are*.
- Use the map to explain the meaning of the prepositions *at the end of, in, on, next to,* and *across from*.
- Allow time for students to complete the sentences individually. Then, check the answers as a class.

B

- Ask students if there are any rooms or facilities in your school that are not in the list.
- Write any additions on the board and have students complete the exercise. Move around the room and answer questions about any unfamiliar words.

ACTIVE GRAMMAR *There is / There are* and Prepositions

There	**is** **isn't**	a library	**in** this building. **in** this school. **on** this floor.
	are **aren't**	restrooms	

More information in Appendix A.

A ACADEMIC Complete the sentences about the school map. Use the prepositions in the box.

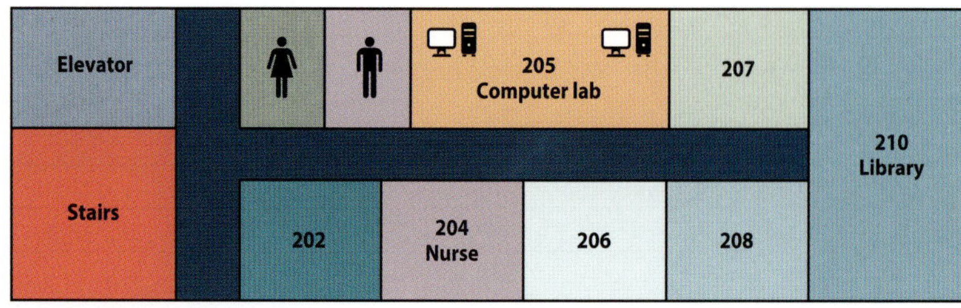

at the end of the hall
in Room 201
on the second floor
next to the stairs
across from Room 202

1. The library is ___at the end of___ the hall.
2. The nurse's office is ___in___ Room 204.
3. There is an elevator ___next to___ the stairs.
4. The women's restroom is ___across from___ Room 202.
5. The library is ___on___ the second floor.
6. The stairs are ___at the end of___ the hall.
7. The men's restroom is ___next to___ the women's restroom.
8. There are a few computers ___in___ the library.
9. There is also a computer lab ___on___ this floor.
10. There are many computers ___in___ the computer lab.

B Circle the rooms and facilities in your school. Answers will vary.

ATM	copy machine	library	swimming pool
bookstore	counselor's office	nurse's office	theater
cafeteria	day care center	restrooms	tutoring center
computer lab	gym	student center	water fountains

MORE ACTION

Ask students to work in pairs to draw a small map of your school or classroom building. After students have finished creating their maps, have them work with another pair of students and use their maps to explain the location of different facilities in the school or building to each other.

Then, draw a map of the school or building on the board and ask one or two students to fill in the locations as directed by the other students.

C **LET'S TALK.** Use *there is* and *there are* to describe the facilities at your school.

> There's a tutoring center in the library.

D Answer the questions about your school. **Answers will vary.**

1. Is this school in a city?
2. Is this school large?
3. Is this school open in the evening?
4. Are there many students in this school?
5. Are there many computers in this classroom?
6. Is there a library in this building?
7. Is the library open today?
8. Is there a water fountain on this floor?
9. Are there any restrooms on this floor?
10. Is there a cafeteria in this building?
11. Is the cafeteria's food good?
12. Is there a bookstore in this building?
13. Are the books expensive?
14. Are the students friendly?
15. Are the students from many different countries?

> Is there a library in this building?
> Yes, there is.
> No, there isn't.

> Is this school small?
> Yes, it is.
> No, it isn't.

> Are there any restrooms on this floor?
> Yes, there are.
> No, there aren't.

> Are the students friendly?
> Yes, they are.
> No, they aren't.

E **Pronunciation: Sentence stress** Listen and repeat. Then, listen again and underline the stressed words. 3

1. The cafeteria is on the first floor.
2. The nurse's office is across from the elevator.
3. The bookstore is in the student center.
4. The computer lab is on the third floor.
5. There is a copy machine in the library.
6. The restrooms are next to the stairs.

> The important words in a sentence receive stress. We say these words a little more clearly and give them a little more emphasis.

TEACHING TIP

Read the note next to Exercise E aloud and check that students understand the meaning of the word stress. Explain that there are stressed and unstressed words in every sentence. Stressed words sound a little longer, clearer, and stronger than unstressed words, while unstressed words sound quieter and reduced because they are not as important as the stressed words in a sentence. Demonstrate the difference between stressed and unstressed words by reading some of the sentences from Exercise E and exaggerating the stressed (underlined) words.

C

Ask students to work in pairs and make sentences about your school using the prepositions in the list on the previous page.

D

- Read the questions and answers in the boxes. Then, write some phrases with locations on the board and have students ask and answer questions using the phrases and *There is / There are*. For example:

T: *Nurse's office, this building*

S1: *Is there a nurse's office in this building?*

S2: *No, there isn't.*

T: *Restrooms, this floor*

S1: *Are there any restrooms on this floor?*

S2: *Yes, there are some restrooms next to the computer lab.*

- Call on volunteers to ask additional questions. Have different students in the room answer them.
- Have students complete the exercise individually. Remind them to answer the questions by using *There is* and *There are*.

E 3

- Play the audio, pausing after each sentence so students can repeat.
- Play the audio again so that students can underline the stressed words.
- Check the answers as a class. Then, have students practice saying the sentences with a partner.

ACTIVE GRAMMAR: Quantifiers

A

- Have students read the sentences in the illustration. Remind them to look at the pictures for clues to the meaning of each sentence.
- Then, read the sentences aloud, one by one, and ask if the sentences are true about your class. Ask students to change the sentences that aren't true so that they are true about your class. For example:
  A couple of the students in this class have blonde hair. None of the students is (or *are*) *absent today.*
- Point out that some of the sentences in the illustration are about more than one person. Ask: *Which sentences in the box are singular, and which are plural?* (Singular: 5-6, Plural: 1-4)
- Explain to students that the last sentence in the box is about no one (*none = not one*). *None of* is used with a singular verb in the example, but it can also be used with plural verbs (see the Teaching Tip at the bottom of the page).
- Ask students to complete Exercise A independently. Then, check answers as a class.

ACTIVE GRAMMAR Quantifiers

1. **All of** the students study English.

2. **Many of** the students have computers.

3. **Some of** the students work.

4. **A couple of** the students are married.

5. **One of** the students wears glasses.

6. **None of** the students has a cat.

A Circle the correct verb.

1. Many of us **is** / **are** from Spanish-speaking countries.
2. Ten of the students **work** / **works** part time.
3. Most of the students **have** / **has** computers.
4. One of the students **take** / **takes** the train to school.
5. None of us **live** / **lives** in a dormitory.

WORD PARTNERSHIPS	
a couple a few all most none one some ten	of us of them of the students

MORE ACTION

Ask students to make five true sentences about the class using different quantifiers from the Word Partnerships box. Invite them to write their sentences on the board. Survey the class to see if the sentences are true or not.

TEACHING TIP

Explain that *none of* can be used with both singular and plural verbs. For example:

None of the students understands the assignment. (singular)

None of the students are here. (plural)

Tell students that the plural is more commonly used with *none of* in conversation, but that it is correct to use the singular and plural with *none of* when speaking and writing.

B AT WORK The graph shows how students in one class get to school. Look at the graph and answer the questions.

1. How many students are in the class? 23
2. How do most students get to school? They drive.
3. How many students take the bus? 6
4. How many students walk? 4

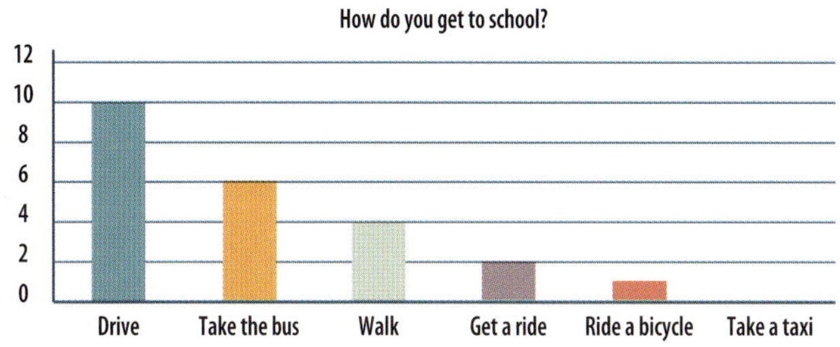

C Write five sentences about the graph in Exercise B. Answers will vary.

1. Ten of the students drive ________ to school.
2. Six of the students take the bus ________ to school.
3. A few of the students walk ________ to school.
4. A couple of the students get a ride to school.
5. One of the students rides a bicycle to school.
6. None of the students takes / take a taxi to school.

D ACADEMIC **LET'S TALK.** Survey your classmates. Then, complete the graph. In your notebook, write five sentences about the information. Use *all of us*, *many of us*, *some of us*, and so on. Answers will vary.

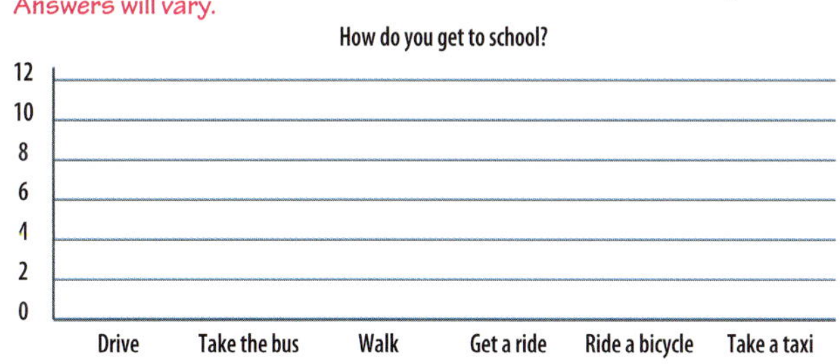

B

- Have students study the graph and answer the questions individually. Explain any information in the graph that students do not understand.
- Check the answers as a class.

C

- Ask students to write the sentences individually. Remind them to use the quantifiers from Exercise A on the previous page.
- Invite volunteers to write their answers on the board.
- Ask the other students to correct any mistakes.

D

- Divide the class into six groups. Assign each group one of the categories in the graph to survey the other groups about.
- Then, draw the graph on the board. Ask a volunteer from each group to come to the board and complete the graph with the correct information for their group's category.
- Have students return to their groups and write five sentences in their notebooks about the information in the graph. Have volunteers from each group read their sentences aloud.

ACADEMIC

In case students aren't familiar with reading bar graphs, explain that it's a visual representation of information, usually numbers. The horizontal axis (x) usually lists the types of information being compared, while the vertical axis (y) shows the values for each thing being compared. Labels on the axes help the reader know what each bar represents.

TEACHING TIP

Another way to conduct the survey in Exercise D is to put students in pairs or small groups and ask them to write the names of other classmates in their notebook. Then, they will move around the classroom and ask other students how they get to school, marking the answers next to each student's name. Finally, students will rejoin their partners or groups and pool their information in order to complete the graph.

THE BIG PICTURE: Classroom Expectations

A

- Have students read the statements about classroom expectations in other countries. Ask students if they think the statements are true for your class.
- Ask students to think about which statements they agree and disagree with.
- Invite students to take turns making statements comparing school in their home countries with school in the United States. To promote discussion, it may be helpful to write topics on the board, such as *attendance, classroom behavior,* and *homework*.

THE BIG PICTURE Classroom Expectations

A Classroom expectations vary from country to country. Read each statement. Circle the information that is true for your country.

1. In some countries, students can arrive a few minutes late for class.
2. In some places, students call the teacher "Teacher," not by his or her name.
3. In some countries, textbooks are free.
4. In many countries, students sit quietly, listen to the teacher, and take notes.
5. In most countries, students raise their hands to ask or answer a question.
6. In some countries, students stand when they speak.
7. In some places, students can bring a cup of coffee into the classroom.
8. In most places, students have to turn off their cellphones before class.
9. In some countries, students have many hours of homework.
10. In some countries, students can copy each other's homework.
11. In a few countries, students do group projects and assignments.

B CIVICS Listen to each statement. Circle *True* if the statement is true for your class. Circle *False* if it is false for your class. 4 Answers will vary.

1.	True	False	**7.**	True	False
2.	True	False	**8.**	True	False
3.	True	False	**9.**	True	False
4.	True	False	**10.**	True	False
5.	True	False	**11.**	True	False
6.	True	False	**12.**	True	False

C Write three more expectations in your classroom. Answers will vary.

1. ______________________________

2. ______________________________

3. ______________________________

D Ask your teacher these questions about your school and your class.

1. Where is your office?
2. Can I email you? What is your email address?
3. Does this school have a computer lab? Can I get a student account?
4. May I bring a computer to class?
5. Is there a library in this school? How do I get a library card?
6. Do we have homework every night?
7. What should I do if I don't understand something?
8. What are we going to study in this class?
9. Are there other classes I can take at this school?
10. What should I do if I am absent?
11. What is the school calendar? Do we have any vacation days?

E Write three more questions about your school or class. Then, ask your teacher the questions.

____

____

____

B 4

- Play the audio, pausing after each statement. Have students listen to the statements and complete the exercise individually or with a partner.
- Discuss the answers as a class. If a statement is not true for the class, have students rewrite the statement so that it is true.

C

- Call on individual students to read their sentences to the class. Ask the class if they agree or disagree.
- Make a list of sentences on the board.

D

- Invite students to take turns asking you the questions. As you answer each one, explain the meaning of any words in the question that students don't understand.
- Tell students that they may wish to copy some of the information about your school and/or class into their notebooks.

E

- Give students time to write more questions individually or with a partner.
- Ask students to read their questions aloud.
- Answer each question, explaining any new words in either the question or the answer.

CIVICS

The activities on this spread may naturally lend themselves to a comparison of classrooms in the US and students' home countries. The teacher-student relationship, for example, may be somewhat less formal than in some students' countries. You could also point out that, in the US, the government takes an active interest in ESL curriculum and its ability to improve students' success in the workforce. Many programs must document student accomplishments to receive federal funding.

TEACHING TIP

When a particularly useful piece of information comes out of any student-generated question activity, write key items on the board. For example, if a student asks, *What TV shows are good for learning English?* you could write the names, TV networks, and times of these programs on the board for students to copy into their notebooks.

READING: Personal Narrative

A

- Ask students to read the four paragraphs straight through without stopping. Explain that they may not understand everything, but that they should try to learn one or two things about each person.
- Write the four names on the board and call on volunteers to tell one or two things they learned about each person. Every time a student mentions a problem, write the name of the problem on the board under the name of the correct person. For example, *Lian—pronunciation.*
- Elicit specific problems by asking questions such as: *What is difficult for Ravi?* When you finish, you should have a list of all the problems on the board: *Ravi—no one corrects him; grammar. Maria Luisa—lives in a neighborhood where English isn't spoken; can't find ways to practice English. Lian— nervous when speaking English; pronunciation. Ketsia—vocabulary.*
- Then, ask students to read the paragraphs again and underline the problems that each student is having. Tell them to use the list on the board for help. Review the answers as a class.

ABOUT THE PHOTO

JR is a Parisian photographer that has taken portraits of people and displayed them in installations in public places and exhibits around the world. JR has also directed short films and documentaries.

READING Personal Narrative

A Underline the problem(s) each student is having with English.

READING NOTE

Comparing the text to your experiences

As you read, compare the information in the reading to your own experiences.

English Is Frustrating!

Ravi

I work 50 hours a week as a taxi driver, so I talk to people all day. They understand me, but I know I make a lot of mistakes. No one corrects me. My vocabulary is strong. Grammar is my problem. For example, I don't use the simple past. I always say, "I drive him to the office this morning" instead of "I drove him to the office this morning." I'm trying to change little by little.

Maria Luisa

I live in an area where everyone speaks Spanish. I can speak Spanish with my neighbors and friends, at the supermarket, at the bank, and at the post office. I don't work, so it's really difficult to find ways to practice English.

Lian

I understand the grammar and the readings in my class. I think my writing is good, but I'm very nervous when I speak English. I don't want to make any mistakes because people will think that I'm not smart. Also, my pronunciation isn't good. When I speak, people often say, "What? Say that again."

Ketsia

I have been in the United States for one year. I'm studying hard and I'm learning grammar, but the vocabulary is difficult. When I listen, I don't understand many of the words. When I try to read, there are two or three new words in every sentence. I feel bad about it. 5

12 Unit 1

ACADEMIC

Explain to students that comparing their own experiences to what they read about makes them active readers. They are engaging with the text in an active way and are more likely to understand and remember what they read.

MORE ACTION

Extend this reading activity by making sentences about the people on this page and asking students to identify who the sentences are about. For example, *This person finds vocabulary difficult.* (Ketsia)

B Read the suggestions for learning English. Add one more suggestion. Answers will vary.

1. Watch one TV show in English every day.
2. Listen to songs in English. Sing along.
3. Try to speak English when you go out in the community.
4. Use the internet or an app. There are many English learning tools online.
5. Don't worry about mistakes. It's natural to make mistakes when you are learning a language.
6. Use English language learning computer programs in your computer lab.
7. Find a study partner. Work together one or two days after school.
8. Make a friend from your school who doesn't speak your language. Meet once a week after class for conversation practice.
9. Read the newspaper in English.
10. Be kind to yourself. Understand that learning another language takes time.
11. Keep an English journal. Write a mistake you made while speaking. Then, write the sentence correctly. Also, write new words and sentences you hear.
12. ______________________________

C Give each student on the previous page two or three suggestions from the list in Exercise B. Write the numbers of the suggestions on the lines next to their names. Answers may vary.

Ravi	4	10	11
Maria Luisa	1	2	7
Lian	3	7	8
Ketsia	4	6	9

D AT WORK Write two of your strengths in learning English. Write two of your difficulties. Which suggestions can you try? Answers will vary.

My Strengths	My Difficulties
______________	______________
______________	______________

1. I'm going to ______________________________.
2. I'm going to ______________________________.

Many words used in English come from other languages. Yoga and sushi are two examples. What words from your language are used in English?

B

- Ask students to read the list and circle the numbers of the suggestions they have tried or would like to try.
- Call on volunteers to read the sentences out loud. After each sentence, ask the other students to raise their hands if they think it is a good idea for learning English.
- Record which suggestions are the most popular and ask students to try one of them in the next week.
- Ask students to give additional examples, such as specific TV shows or websites they like to watch or use.

C

- Have students work individually or with a partner as they write two or three suggestions for each person mentioned in the reading on the previous page. Tell students that they can use the same suggestion for more than one person.
- Review the answers as a class.

D

- Ask students to complete this exercise independently and share their responses with a partner.
- Conduct a class discussion of what students plan to do to improve their English.

AT WORK

As you approach Exercise D, point out to students that being aware of one's own strengths and weaknesses is important professionally. It's a good idea to be able to discuss them somewhat openly at work in the interests of moving forward (they might be asked to do this in a performance review, for example). Encourage students to be solutions-oriented when discussing their weaknesses/areas for development, as they are asked to do in Exercise D, and remind them not to take critical feedback personally.

MORE ACTION

Extend the activities on this page by making a poster with suggestions for learning English. Divide the class into groups and assign each group a skill, such as reading, writing, or pronunciation.

ACADEMIC

English has always borrowed words to express ideas or objects that don't have a native equivalent. Ask students if they know words from their own languages that have been borrowed into English. Ask if students think there are words from their own languages that *should* be borrowed into English to express ideas for which there is no English word.

WRITING OUR STORIES: An Introduction

A

- Ask students to read the writing model to themselves first, but not to read the blue note boxes. Explain that it isn't important for them to understand every single word in the passage, but they should try to understand the main ideas in each paragraph.
- When students finish reading, invite them to ask about anything in the passage that they didn't understand. Ask the class if they find any details about Sandra's life in the United States interesting.
- Read the blue boxes aloud to the class. Have students point in their books to the part of the composition that each box refers to.

ABOUT THE PHOTO

Museo del Oro, Bogota, Colombia

This fascinating museum is a very popular destination in Bogota. It houses more than 55,000 artifacts (made with gold and other materials) representative of the pre-Columbian peoples that inhabited Colombia.

Through different permanent exhibits, visitors can learn about ancient mining techniques and the relevance and uses of gold and other metals in pre-Hispanic culture.

WRITING OUR STORIES An Introduction

A Read Sandra's story. She is introducing herself to her teacher and class.

Start your story on the front of the paper.

Give your story a title. Write the title in the middle of the line.

Buses arrive at the Museo del Oro (Gold Museum) bus stop in Bogota, Colombia.

Skip a line between the title and the story.

Indent each paragraph.

Hello

My name is Sandra and I am from Bogota, Colombia. I came to the United States five years ago. My sister, Gloria, is here with me, but my mom and dad and my six brothers all live in Colombia. I miss them a lot, but we email each other all the time.

I work full time at a small printing company. I do several jobs at this company. Sometimes, I do data entry. At other times, I help customers at the counter.

I don't have much free time, but I enjoy music, especially rock and romantic music. On Saturday afternoons, I play tennis with the tennis club at my school.

Right now, I'm studying English. I plan to major in communications and work in the TV industry. I have many dreams. Someday, I would like to live in Florida and have a family.

Put your name and the date at the top or bottom of your composition.

Sandra Martinez, September 10

MORE ACTION

Extend this activity by having students write questions about the information in the passage. Then, students can work in pairs to ask and answer the questions.

B Look at Sandra's composition and complete her notes.

My Family	My Work	My Interests	My Future
Gloria	printing company	music:	communications
six brothers	full time	-rock	TV industry
Mom and Dad	data entry	-romantic	Florida
	help customers	tennis club	family

C Correct the mistakes with the articles, and the singular and plural nouns.

1. I have two ~~brother~~ brothers and three ~~sister~~ sisters.
2. I work in a clothing store.
3. I'm a cashier.
4. I'm a student at an adult school.
5. I'm taking four ~~class~~ classes.
6. I have a computer.
7. I work part time, twenty ~~hour~~ hours a week.
8. I came to the United States two ~~year~~ years ago.

WRITING NOTE

Singular and Plural Nouns

1. Use an article with a singular noun.
2. Use *an* with nouns that begin with a vowel sound: *a, e, i, o,* and sometimes *u*.
3. Do not use *a* or *an* before proper names: *Tom, California*.
4. Plural nouns usually end in *-s* or *-es*. Some irregular plurals are *men, women,* and *children*. Do not use *a* or *an* with a plural noun.

WRITING NOTE

Look carefully at the correct composition format. Refer to it when you write a composition.

D ACADEMIC Organize your ideas in the chart. Then, write a story to introduce yourself to your teacher and your class. For help, refer to the writing model on the previous page. Answers will vary.

My Family	My Work	My Interests	My Future

E In small groups, share your stories. Ask each other questions.

B

- Point out that there are four columns of notes in the chart under Exercise B, and four paragraphs in Sandra's story. Explain that the words in each column represent the ideas that Sandra included in each paragraph of her story.
- Have students complete the notes independently. Then, ask volunteers to read their notes aloud to the class.

C

- Read the Writing Note about singular and plural nouns to the class.
- Ask students to correct the mistakes on their own and then compare answers in pairs.
- Discuss the answers as a class and ask students to match the mistakes with the relevant grammar rule from the Writing Note.

D

- Give students time to work on their charts.
- Walk around the room and provide help as needed.
- Students can start writing in class and complete their stories for homework.
- Remind students to follow the format of the model on the previous page.

E

After students share their stories with their groups, have volunteers read their stories aloud to the class. Encourage students to ask questions.

MORE ACTION

Have students trade their stories with a partner and check that the composition follows the rules listed in the blue note boxes on the previous page. Students may find it helpful to label their own composition with key words such as *title, name and date,* and *paragraph indent* to use for future reference.

ACADEMIC

Point out the organizational rubrics in B and D to students. Tell students that taking time to organize their thoughts in a chart or other outline can help their time management and organization of their writing. Writing from an outline is a useful skill to develop for English class as well as other subjects.

ENGLISH IN ACTION: Studying with a Textbook

A

- Explain that the purpose of this exercise is to determine what kinds of interesting and useful information can be found in this textbook.
- Read the text in the blue box aloud to the class. Ask: *Why would it be helpful to know where the information is located?*
- Do the first two questions together as an example.
- Ask students to work in groups to answer the other questions.
- Call on volunteers to read their answers aloud and see if the other students agree.

B

- Explain that the purpose of this exercise is to improve students' study skills.
- Read the sentences or ask students to read them aloud. Ask students to circle the strategies they already use and put a star next to the ones they would like to try.
- Have students work in pairs to add one more suggestion to each list.
- Call on volunteers to read their suggestions aloud or come to the board to make a list.

ENGLISH IN ACTION Studying with a Textbook

A Look through this textbook and complete the information. Then, share your answers with the class. Answers may vary.

1. There are ______ pages in this textbook.
2. Look at the table of contents. There are ______ units in this textbook.
   Two topics in the textbook are ____________ and ____________.
3. There is a grammar chart section that begins on page ______.
4. If I need spelling rules, I can look on page ______.
   Write the third person simple present of these verbs:
   fix ____________ wash ____________
   cry ____________
5. I can look up the irregular form of past verbs on page ______.
   Write the simple past of these verbs:
   break ____________ fly ____________ teach ____________

When you open a new textbook, it's a good idea to look through the book quickly. You can see how the book is organized and where helpful information is located.

B Discuss the study suggestions. Add more suggestions. Answers will vary.

1. Grammar
   - Look at the charts and examples.
   - Write some of your own sentences using the new grammar.
   - Review any mistakes you made in class or in your homework. Write the sentences correctly.
   - ____________________
2. Speaking
   - Practice conversations from the unit with a partner.
   - ____________________
3. Listening
   - Listen to the audio several times. Write some of the sentences.
   - ____________________
4. Vocabulary
   - In a notebook or on your cellphone, write two or three words each day that are new to you.
   - Look up the words in a dictionary or ask someone the meaning. Write each new word in a sentence.
   - ____________________

TEACHING TIP

Some students may have trouble understanding the Roman numeral numbering system used for information at the beginning of the book. Write the applicable Roman numerals on the board and explain that these are used for special content at the beginning of textbooks, such as the table of contents, instructions for the teacher, and information about the authors of the textbook. Tell students that the main textbook information usually starts on page 1.

MORE ACTION

Ask students to think about writing a list of goals for learning English. Explain that making short-term goals each week will help with their long-term goal of learning English.

Give some examples of short-term goals. For example, *Write five new words in my vocabulary notebook every day.*

Allow some time for students to work on writing goals for the next week. Review the goals at the end of the week.

UNIT 2

LIFE IN THE UNITED STATES

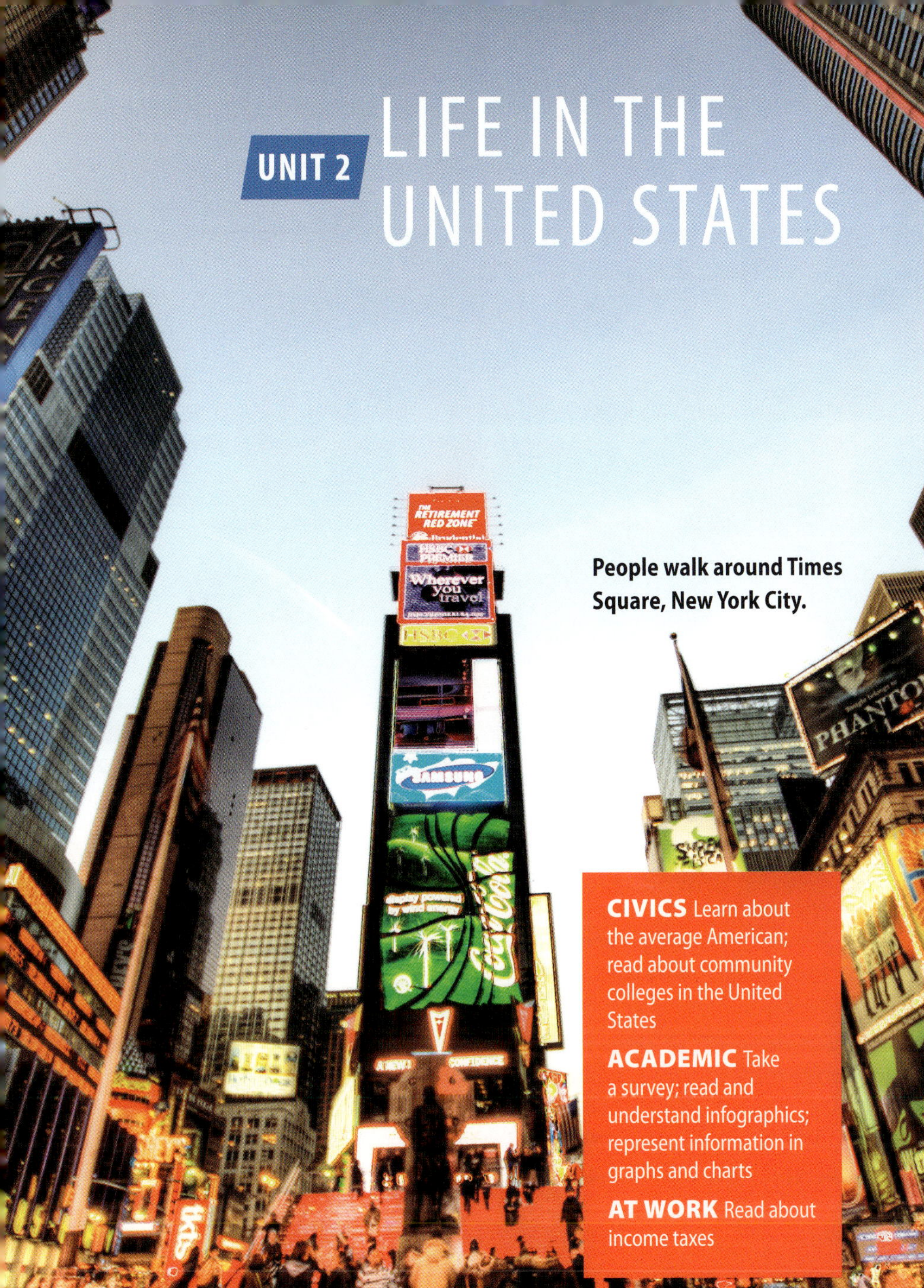

People walk around Times Square, New York City.

CIVICS Learn about the average American; read about community colleges in the United States

ACADEMIC Take a survey; read and understand infographics; represent information in graphs and charts

AT WORK Read about income taxes

CCRS Level A: R 1, 2, 5; W 2; L 1; Level B: R 1, 2, 5, 6; W 2, 4; L 1, 3, 6; Level C: R 1, 2, 7; W 2, 4, 9; L 1, 3, 6; Level D: R 1, 2, 5, 7; W 2, 4, 9; L 1, 3; Level E: R 1, 2, 5, 7; W 2, 4, 9

ELPS Level 1 Standards 2, 3, 9, 10; Level 2 Standards 1, 2, 3, 7, 9, 10; Level 3 Standards 1, 2, 3, 7, 9, 10; Level 4 Standards 1, 2, 3, 7, 9, 10; Level 5 Standards 1, 2, 3, 7, 9, 10

CIVICS 11-2, 11-3, 11-5, 11-10, 14-4

CASAS 0.1.2; 0.1.5; 0.2.1; 0.2.4; 2.8.2; 2.8.3; 6.7.2; 6.7.3; 6.7.4

IN THIS UNIT

In Unit 2, students will:

- Read infographics about the average American
- Practice simple present with time expressions and adverbs of frequency
- Learn about community colleges in the US
- Write a description of the average person in their country

ABOUT THE PHOTO

Located in the heart of Manhattan on a famous theater strip, Times Square, New York City, is one of the most famous urban locations in the United States. Known for its bustling streets full of performers, bright lights, and ubiquitous advertisements, Times Square is at once visually overwhelming and iconic for that very fact. Every aspect of the square must conform to strict, gaudy regulations—even the subway entrance is lit up in the bright lights of Broadway.

To review the present tense, ask students what people do in Times Square and what they can find there (using *there is/there are*). Ask: *What do people do in Times Square? What kinds of things are there?* Possible answers: *People go to see shows. Tourists take pictures. There are many theaters. There are many restaurants.* Ask questions to see if you can get students to guess the time of year and time of day in the photo. It's likely evening, due to the crowd, and the coats people are wearing would indicate a colder month.

A

- Ask questions about the photo. For example:

  Describe the people you see. How old are they? What are they wearing? What are they doing? Where are they?

- Ask students to read the statements silently. Answer any questions they may have about vocabulary. Then, have students circle their answers.
- Read the answers aloud to the class and have students check their answers. Ask if any information surprised them. For example, were they surprised that the average American changes jobs every four years?
- Encourage students to discuss differences between these facts about American culture and similar facts about their own culture.

On July 4, Americans celebrate their independence with parades, concerts, and fireworks.

A CIVICS Read about the average American. Guess and circle the information.

1. The average American lives in **a house / an apartment / a condo**.
2. The typical American family has **one child / two children / three children.**
3. About a third of people eat breakfast **at home / at work / on the go**.
4. The average person drinks **one / two / three** cup(s) of coffee a day.
5. Most Americans **take a bus / walk / drive** to work.
6. The average American consumes **5 / 50 / over 150** pounds of sugar in one year.
7. The average family has **one / two / three** TV(s).
8. Most Americans check their phones **30 / 50 / 80** times a day.
9. The average American changes jobs every **four / seven / ten** years.
10. The average person moves **five / eight / eleven** times in his or her lifetime.

1. a house **2.** two children **3.** on the go **4.** two **5.** drive **6.** over 150 **7.** two **8.** 80 **9.** four **10.** eleven

MORE ACTION

If there are students from several different cultural groups in the class, make a chart on the board comparing information about the different cultures. Ask students about popular foods, the average marrying age, and other topics, like clothing and hobbies, that are relevant to their cultural group. You can list topics down the left side of the chart and list the names of the countries or groups as column heads across the top.

B Circle or complete the statements about your life. Then, read your sentences to a partner.
Answers will vary.

1. I live in **a house / an apartment / a condo**.
2. My family has **one / two / three /** ______________ child / children.
3. I eat breakfast **at home / at work / on the go**.
4. I **take a bus / walk / drive /** ______________ to work.
5. I eat **one / two / three /** ______________ hamburger(s) a week.
6. My family has **one / two / three /** ______________ TV(s).
7. I check my phone **30 / 50 / 80 /** ______________ times a day.

C Listen and complete the chart. Then, compare Charlie to the average American male. 6

Charlie	The Average American Male
32 – single	gets married at 27
is 6' 2" tall	is 5'10" tall
weighs 210 pounds	weighs 195 pounds
likes (circled) / **doesn't like** his job	likes his job
works ten hours a day	works eight hours a day
earns $70,000 a year	earns $43,056 a year
lives in a / an apartment	lives in a house
walks or takes the bus to work	drives to work
has (circled) / **doesn't have** a pet	has a pet

The average American male gets married at 27. Charlie is 32, and he is single.

B

- Ask students to complete the statements individually and then discuss their answers with a partner.
- Ask students to report to the class on how their partner's lifestyle compares with that of an average American.

C 6

- Read the instructions and explain the first note under Charlie's name. Say: *Charlie is 32 years old, and he's single. That means he's not married. According to the information in the chart, the average American male gets married at 27. Charlie is single later in life than the average American male.*
- Play the audio and have students take notes while listening. Pause the audio after each bit of information so students have time to write their notes.
- Encourage students to fill in as much of the chart as they can using their notes. Then, play the audio again without stopping and have students complete the rest of the chart.
- Go over the answers as a class, playing the audio again as necessary.
- Ask volunteers to compare one aspect of Charlie's life to that of the average American male.

MORE ACTION

For additional writing practice, have students write some of the comparisons from Exercise C in complete sentences.

ACTIVE GRAMMAR: Simple Present

A

- Read aloud the statements in the charts at the top of the page.
- Ask students questions about how the verb forms are used. For example:

  T: *Which pronouns in the affirmative sentences are followed by verbs ending in s?*

  S: He *and* it.

  T: *Which pronouns in the negative sentences are followed by* don't?

  S: I, you, we, *and* they.
- Have students complete Exercise A individually.
- Then, call on students to read aloud their answers. Correct any mistakes.

B

- Read the questions aloud to the class or ask volunteers to read the questions. Read the note to the right of the exercise and explain that students should use those phrases to answer the questions.
- Set a time limit for students to complete this task. Then, ask volunteers to report to the class on what they found out about their partner.

ACTIVE GRAMMAR Simple Present

Affirmative Statements	
I You We They	work. eat breakfast.
He She It	work**s**. eat**s** breakfast.

Negative Statements		
I You We They	**don't**	work. eat breakfast.
He She It	**doesn't**	work. eat breakfast.

The simple present describes routines and activities that happen every day, every week, every month, and so on.

A AT WORK Complete with the correct form of the verb. Some of the verbs are negative.

1. April 15th (or around that date) is tax day in the United States. People (need) ___need___ to file their income taxes by that date.
2. Most states also (have) ___have___ a state income tax, but a few states (have) ___don't have___ any state income tax.
3. If a person (make) ___makes___ a high income, that person usually (pay) ___pays___ more taxes.
4. Some people (owe) ___owe___ a lot in taxes, but some people (owe) ___don't owe___ anything. For example, if a person's income is under $10,000, she (pay) ___doesn't pay___ anything.
5. If a person (overpay) ___overpays___ his taxes, the government (send) ___sends___ him a refund. More than 80% of all taxpayers (receive) ___receive___ a refund.

B Interview a classmate. How are your days similar? How are they different? Answers will vary.

	You	Your Partner
1. Do you eat breakfast every day?		
2. Do you work full time?		
3. Do you take public transportation to school?		
4. Do you use a computer every day?		
5. Do you cook for your family?		
6. Do you have classes every day?		
7. Do you go to bed before midnight?		

Yes, I do.
No, I don't.

TEACHING TIP

When monitoring pair work or group work, take notes of mistakes. Read them aloud at the end of the activity and ask students to identify and correct any mistakes. To avoid embarrassing students, do not attribute sentences with mistakes to any particular student.

AT WORK

Tell students that tax day is April 15th provided the 15th is a business day (not on the weekend). Point out to students that they can see taxes deducted from their wages on their paycheck. You may want to bring in a sample paystub to show them and point out federal, state, social security, and other deductions.

C Pronunciation: Final *-s* Listen and repeat. 7

/s/	/z/	/iz/
likes	owns	watches
wants	drives	uses
takes	studies	dances

D Circle the sound you hear. 8

1. /s/ (/z/) /iz/
2. (/s/) /z/ /iz/
3. (/s/) /z/ /iz/
4. /s/ /z/ (/iz/)
5. /s/ (/z/) /iz/
6. (/s/) /z/ /iz/
7. /s/ /z/ (/iz/)
8. /s/ (/z/) /iz/
9. /s/ (/z/) /iz/

E STUDENT TO STUDENT

Student 1: Turn to Appendix C. Read the sentences in Set A.

Student 2: Look at the picture. Listen and write the sentences under *Josh* or *Sam*.

Then, change roles. Student 2, turn to Appendix C and read the sentences in Set B. Student 1, write the sentences under *Josh* or *Sam*. **Answers in Appendix C.**

Josh	Sam
1. ______	1. ______
2. ______	2. ______
3. ______	3. ______

C 7

- Explain that the three symbols at the top of the chart are the sounds heard in words that end in *s*. The sounds come from the *s* at the end of each word.
- Point to and say the three different sounds at the top of the chart and have students repeat each one. Draw out or repeat each sound: *SSSSSS*, *ZZZZZZ*, and *EZ, EZ*.
- Play the audio and have students repeat the words.

D 8

- Review the three final *s* sounds. Then, play the audio and ask students to circle the sound they hear in each word.
- Play the audio a second time and have students check their work.
- Review the answers with the class. If several students get the same answer wrong, replay that section of the audio so they can listen again.

E

- Read the instructions and model the exercise with one pair of students.
- Set a time limit for the exercise.
- Check the answers as a class.

MORE ACTION

For further pronunciation practice, ask students to make a chart with three columns. Have students write the three different *s* sounds at the top of each column. Dictate the verbs from the chart in Exercise C in random order. Students should write the verbs in the three columns according to their final sound.

Then, draw the chart on the board and invite volunteers to write the answers under the appropriate sounds. You could also conduct this exercise by using new words ending in *s*.

ACTIVE GRAMMAR: Singular and Plural Subjects

A

- Ask students to read the sentences in the grammar charts to themselves.
- Have students close their books. Read each sentence in the boxes aloud, saying *beep* for the verb. Students need to say the missing verb. For example, *The average person [beep] a cellphone.*
- Have students complete the sentences in Exercise A individually.
- Then, review the answers as a class.

WORD PARTNERSHIPS

Read the phrases in the box. Make a few true statements about the class using the phrases. For example:

Half of the students in our class are men.

More than half of the women in our class are wearing jeans.

Ask students to write their own statements about the class using the phrases in the box. Then, ask volunteers to read their sentences aloud. Have other students correct the sentences as necessary.

B

- Point to the graphs and ask two students to describe the topic of each graph.
- Dictate the sentences in Appendix D, saying each sentence two or three times at normal speed.
- Ask volunteers to write the answers on the board.

ACTIVE GRAMMAR Singular and Plural Subjects

Singular Subject	
The average person The average man The average woman The man The woman	**has** a cellphone. **drives** to work. **works** full time.

Plural Subject	
Most Americans Most people Fifty percent of people	**have** a cellphone. **drive** to work. **work** full time.

A Complete the sentences. Use the correct form of the verb.

1. The average adult (exercise) ____exercises____ twenty minutes a day.
2. Most full-time workers (receive) ____receive____ a paid vacation.
3. The average teenager (take) ____takes____ a summer class.
4. Most Americans (drive) ____drive____ to work.
5. The average person (sleep) ____sleeps____ 6.5 hours a night.
6. Women (do) ____do____ 70 percent of the housework in a family.
7. The average person (use) ____uses____ a computer every day.

WORD PARTNERSHIPS	
50 percent half about half more than half fewer than half	of the students of the men of the women

B Listen and write the sentences that you hear. Your teacher will turn to Appendix D.

Do you wear a seat belt?

1. The average person wears a seat belt.
2. 10% of people don't wear a seat belt.

Do you rent or own your home?

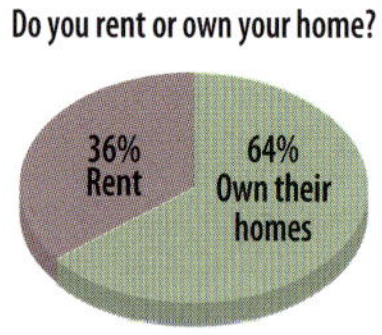

3. The average person lives in a house.
4. More than half of Americans own their homes.
5. Many people rent their homes.

MORE ACTION

Have students carry out a class survey on eating or drinking habits with a partner. First, ask them to select the topic for their survey. Then, have them interview the other students and collect their information. Finally, ask pairs to present their findings in the form of a pie chart or a bar graph.

C ACADEMIC **LET'S TALK.** Work with a partner. Write sentences about each chart.

Answers may vary.

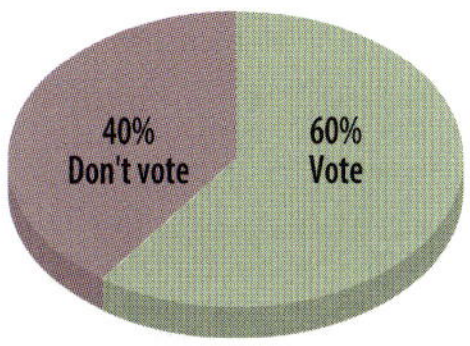

1. What percentage of Americans vote in national elections?
   a. 60% of Americans vote in national elections.
   b. 40% of people don't vote in national elections.

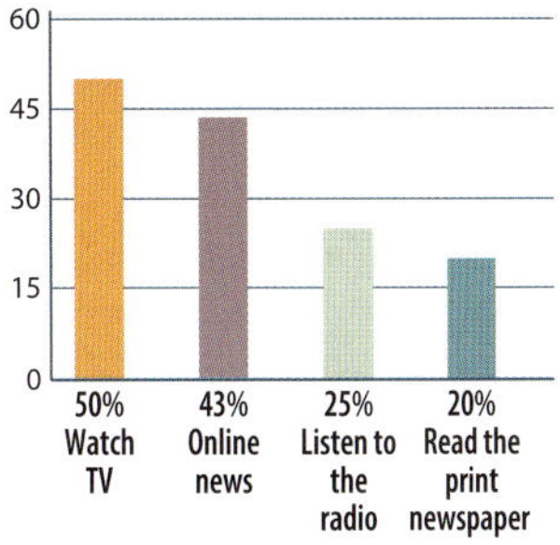

2. How do most Americans get their news?
   a. Most Americans watch TV to get their news.
   b. About 40% of Americans read the news online.

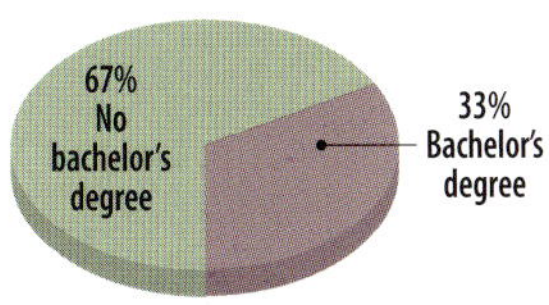

3. Do most Americans have a bachelor's degree?
   a. Most Americans do not have a bachelor's degree.
   b. 33% of Americans have a bachelor's degree.

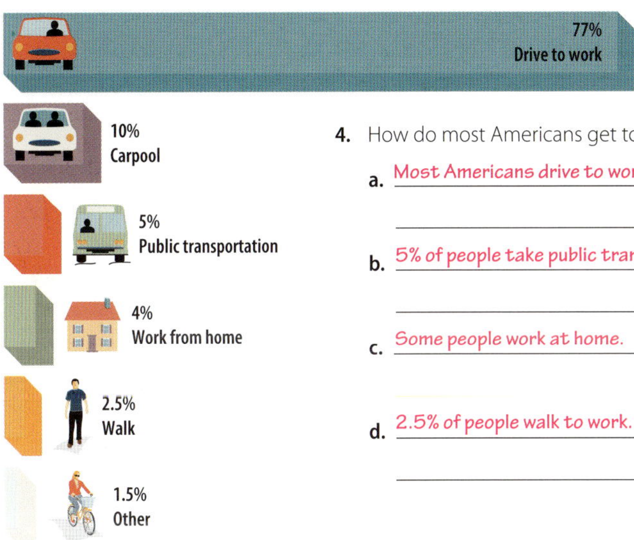

4. How do most Americans get to work?
   a. Most Americans drive to work.
   b. 5% of people take public transportation.
   c. Some people work at home.
   d. 2.5% of people walk to work.

C

- Ask students to identify the topic of each graph.
- Read the question for each graph aloud.
- Have students work together in pairs to write sentences for each graph.
- Ask volunteers to read their answers aloud or write them on the board. Discuss possible alternative answers.
- Ask students if they can think of any reasons for these statistics. For example: *Why doesn't everyone wear a seat belt? Why don't more people carpool?*
- Ask students if they think these statistics are the same in their home country. Have them make similar sentences about their home country.

ACADEMIC

Exercise C requires students to read infographics, including a pie chart and a bar graph. Explain these graphics to students. The pie chart shows percentages out of 100; the bar graph compares amounts of things, but not necessarily out of a total of 100. The example in question 2, for example, tallies to more that 100%, showing that many people get their news from more than one source.

MORE ACTION

Conduct a survey of the class using the questions from Exercise C. Write the questions on the board and then ask the class the questions, keeping tally of how many students in the class answer affirmatively. For example:

T: *How many of you wear a seat belt?*
10/14 (Ten out of fourteen students wear a seat belt.)

Then, have students write statements about the survey results using the phrases from the previous page.
For example:
More than half of the students in our class wear a seat belt.
Have students share their sentences with the class.

Life in the United States 23

ACTIVE GRAMMAR: Time Expressions

A

- Review the meaning of each expression in the grammar chart at the top of the page.
- Give some statements and ask students to pick the best time expression for each statement. For example, *I go to the dentist in January and July.* (two times a year)
- Ask students to complete the sentences in Exercise A individually.
- Invite volunteers to read aloud their answers to the class. Ask other students to raise their hand if they have the same sentence.

B

- Explain that *How often* questions are used to find out how frequently a person does something. Practice the formation of questions with *How often* using different items than those in the exercise.
- Have students ask their partners questions about the topics and take notes on their partner's answers.
- Ask volunteers to report to the class on their partner and how similar or different they are from their partner. Make sure that students use the third person (*he / she*) when talking about their partner's activities.

ACTIVE GRAMMAR Time Expressions

every morning	once a week	on the weekend	in the summer
every day	twice a month	on Sundays	in the winter
every night	three times a year		

Time expressions are usually placed at the end of a sentence.

A Complete the sentences about yourself. Use time expressions. Answers will vary.

1. I study English ________________.
2. I go to work ________________.
3. I work overtime ________________.
4. I go to the dentist ________________.
5. I take a vacation ________________.
6. I sleep late ________________.
7. I buy new clothes ________________.
8. I pay my bills ________________.
9. I get a haircut ________________.
10. I check my phone ________________.

B Talk with a partner. How often do you do each activity listed?

I go dancing every weekend.

I go dancing once a year!

1. go dancing
2. eat out
3. call my family abroad
4. order a pizza
5. do the laundry
6. eat at a fast-food restaurant
7. exercise
8. go to a party
9. text my friends
10. check my email
11. go to the beach
12. watch TV

ACTIVE GRAMMAR Adverbs of Frequency

always	100%
usually	
often frequently	
sometimes	
hardly ever rarely	
never	0%

Put adverbs of frequency before most verbs.
I **often** walk in the park.
He **never** takes a taxi.
Put adverbs of frequency after the verb *be*.
I am **never** late for work.
She is **rarely** sick.

A Put the words in the correct order.

1. always / homework / do / I / my I always do my homework.
2. tired / in the morning / He / always / is He is always tired in the morning.
3. her / She / rarely / sister / calls She rarely calls her sister.
4. class / is / interesting / usually / This This class is usually interesting.
5. drives / He / always / too fast He always drives too fast.
6. weather / is / Florida / usually / in / The / beautiful The weather in Florida is usually beautiful.
7. wear / They / their / always / seat belts They always wear their seat belts.

B Talk about yourself. Use an adverb of frequency in each sentence. Add two sentences of your own. Answers will vary.

I always eat breakfast.

I never eat breakfast. I'm not hungry in the morning.

1. I eat breakfast.
2. I am polite.
3. I am homesick.
4. I get headaches.
5. I think about my future.
6. I am worried.
7. I go to bed early.
8. I do my homework.
9. I am late for class.
10. I take a taxi.
11. I am busy.
12. I lose my keys.
13. ______________
14. ______________

ACTIVE GRAMMAR: Adverbs of Frequency

A

- Explain that adverbs of frequency describe how often you do something.
- Read the list of adverbs in the first grammar chart and give some example sentences.
- Give prompts for students to make sentences. For example:
  T: *ride the bus, usually, I*
  S: *I usually ride the bus.*
- Have students complete Exercise A individually.
- Then, ask them to find a partner and correct his or her work.
- Ask volunteers to write their answers on the board.

B

- Ask students to complete the answers individually and then compare their answers with a partner.
- Monitor their work and provide assistance as needed.
- Give feedback to the class on common errors with adverbs of frequency, such as putting the adverb in the wrong place in the sentence.
- Ask volunteers to read aloud their sentences for items 13 and 14.

TEACHING TIP

When asking students to correct their mistakes, ask them to try to identify the type of mistake first. For example, is it a mistake in spelling, word order, or subject-verb agreement? If they cannot find the error, you can use these terms to give them a hint.

THE BIG PICTURE: An American Family

A 🎧9

- Before playing the audio, invite students to comment on and ask questions about the pictures. You may wish to have students ask and answer the questions. For example:

  S1: *What is Mrs. Shaw doing?*

  S2: *She's using a computer. Maybe she's working.*

- If necessary, ask leading questions to get students talking about the pictures.

  For example:

  T: *Look at the third picture. What can you tell me about the family?*

  S: *They have a dog and a cat. They live in a house. Mrs. Shaw is going to have a baby.*

- Now, play the audio and have students take notes as they listen.
- Play the audio a second time and ask students to fill in the blanks.
- Play the audio a third time so students can check their answers.
- Review the answers as a class.

THE BIG PICTURE An American Family

A Listen. Under the pictures, write the missing information about the Shaw family. 🎧9

1.

Mr. Shaw: Hours: 7:30 a.m. – 3:00 p.m. Salary: $60,000

Mrs. Shaw: Hours: 9:00 a.m. – 5:00 p.m. Salary: $80,000

2.

Mr. Shaw: 20 minutes

Mrs. Shaw: 40 minutes

3.

$ 175,000

4.

5.

6.

B Read about the average American family. Then, compare with the Shaw family.

1. Most husbands earn more than their wives.
   Mrs. Shaw earns more than Mr. Shaw.
2. Most workers drive to work.
   Mr. Shaw drives to work. Mrs. Shaw takes the train.
3. The average family has one pet.
   The Shaws have two pets, a dog and a cat.
4. The average household is a mother and father and two children.
   Mr. Shaw's parents live with them.
5. The average family takes a vacation twice a year.
   The Shaws take a vacation once a year.
6. Most families have two TVs.
   The Shaws have two TVs.

C Complete with the correct form of the verb. Some of the verbs are negative.

1. Mr. Shaw (drive) doesn't drive a minivan.
2. Mr. Shaw (work) works close to home.
3. Mrs. Shaw (take) doesn't take public transportation to work.
4. Mr. and Mrs. Shaw (have) have one child.
5. Mr. and Mrs. Shaw (live) don't live in an apartment.
6. Andy's parents (work) don't work part time.
7. Mrs. Shaw (work) doesn't work at a college.
8. The family (eat) eats out once a week.
9. Andy (have) doesn't have a pet bird.
10. The Shaws and the grandparents (live) live in the same house.

The word **family** is singular, but people often use **they** to talk about family.
The **family** eats out on Friday night.
They like Chinese or Italian food.

B

- Replay the audio from Exercise A and tell students to review their notes as they listen. Then, ask students to complete Exercise B individually.
- Call on volunteers to read their answers aloud or write them on the board.

C

- Read the note to the right of the exercise aloud to the class. Explain that *family* is singular, but since a family is made up of multiple people, the plural pronoun *they* is often used in the place of *family*.
- Set a time limit for students to complete the exercise.
- Review the answers as a class. For each sentence, ask students to identify if the subject is singular or plural. If they stumble on item 8, remind them that *family* is singular, although it describes a group of people. (Singular: 1–3, 7–9; Plural: 4–6, 10)

MORE ACTION

Ask students to write a paragraph in their notebook comparing themselves and their family to the facts about the average American family in Exercise B.

VIDEO AND READING: Informational Text

CIVICS

If your students are enrolled in ESL through a non-profit, encourage them to research community colleges in your area. Community college is a great and affordable option that can support their continued development in English as well as their other career and professional goals. Often times a representative from the college will be happy to visit adult ed centers and give a presentation on the resources the college can offer.

CULTURE NOTE

Tell students that community colleges are some of the largest higher education institutions in the US, with many servicing tens of thousands of students. According to a recent study, here are some numbers: College of Southern Nevada, 43,000; Houston Community College, 63,000; Northern Virginia Community College, 76,000; Miami Dade College, over 100,000.

TEACHING TIP

Ask students to research community colleges in your town or city using the internet or the library. You may want to assign specific topics to each student or group of students—for example, information about credit and non-credit classes, tuition, and financial aid. In the next class, have students report on what they found out.

VIDEO AND READING Informational Text

The Average Community College Student

About 40 percent of all college students in the United States attend community colleges. Community colleges are schools that offer two-year associate degrees and certificates and licenses in a large number of careers, such as paralegal, office assistant, and information technician. The 1,103 community colleges in the United States also **train** students for new jobs and offer courses in many subjects, including English as a second language.

Most community colleges have open admissions; they **accept** almost all students who apply. Thirty-six percent of the students are the first ones in their families to attend college. Most students need one or more **basic skills** courses in reading, writing, or math to prepare them for college-level classes. Sixty-two percent of full-time students work, so full-time schedules are difficult. More than 60 percent of all students attend school part time. The tuition at a community college is more **affordable** than at a four-year school. The average tuition is $3,570 a year, and more than half of the students receive some financial aid. Many of the students who begin at a community college **transfer** to a four-year college for their junior and senior years.

Emily is a typical community college student. She attends school part time. As a young woman, she is part of the 56 percent of all community college students who are women. She is 28 years old, the average age of a community college student. Emily's parents and her older brother graduated from high school, but she is the first person in her family to begin college.

Emily works full time in the admissions office in the county hospital. Her **goal** is to become a registered nurse. She is taking pre-nursing courses and has been accepted to the nursing program. Many of the nurses in the United States receive their degrees from community colleges.

Emily is a second-semester student. During her first semester, she needed to take a course in basic math. This semester, she is taking three courses. In the fall, Emily will attend school full time and work on the weekends. She applied for financial aid and is going to receive $1,500 a semester next year.

Most students take three years or more to **complete** their degrees at a community college. Emily hopes to have her nursing degree by the time she is 31. 10

Pasadena City College, in Pasadena, California, offers 114 associate degree programs and serves over 29,000 students.

A Discuss these questions.

1. Where do you study—at a community college, an adult school, a high school, or another kind of school?
2. What community college is nearest to your home? What programs does it offer?

B Circle the correct word or phrase.

1. The program will train him to be a **police officer** / **student**.
2. The school **accepts** many **students** / **classes** each semester.
3. The student needed a **basic skills** course in **reading** / **financial aid**.
4. The tuition at an **affordable** school is **reasonable** / **expensive**.
5. Some students transfer from a two-year college to a **four-year college** / **job**.
6. Emily's goal is to **become a nurse** / **apply to college**.

READING NOTE

Finding Examples

A reading often gives facts about a topic. Then, it tells a story to give specific examples.

C **CIVICS** Read the facts about community college students. Find examples in the reading to show that Emily is a typical community college student.

1. Community college students are often the first ones in their families to attend college.
   Emily's parents and brother didn't go to college.
2. Most students need one or more basic skills courses.
   Emily needed to take a course in basic math.
3. Most students work full or part time.
   Emily works full time at the county hospital.
4. More women than men attend community college.
   Fifty-six percent of community college students are women.
5. More than half of the students receive some financial aid.
   Emily is going to receive $1,500 in financial aid next semester.

D **▶ WATCH** Watch the video about diversity in Queens, New York. How does this compare to diversity in your school?

A

- Ask students to read the passage on the previous page straight through without stopping. Explain that they may not understand everything, but they should try to understand the main ideas.
- Ask some general comprehension questions about the passage. For example: *What kinds of classes can you take at a community college? How much is the average community college tuition?*
- Ask students to answer the discussion questions with a partner.
- Ask some questions about new vocabulary. For example: *What is tuition? What is financial aid? What are basic skills courses?*

B

- Ask students to complete the exercise individually.
- Call on volunteers to read their answers aloud in complete sentences. Then, ask other students if they agree with each answer.

C

- Read the Reading Note aloud. Then, read the first item and the sample answer from Exercise C.
- Suggest that students underline the relevant sentence in the passage for each question before writing their answers.
- Go over the answers as a class.

D ▶ WATCH

- Play the video. Ask students to take notes while they watch the video.
- Ask students to compare diversity in Queens with diversity at school, using their notes and what they recall about the video. Encourage students to cite examples that show similarities and differences.

MORE ACTION

Review the vocabulary in Exercise B by making flashcards with an example sentence on one side and the missing word on the other side. The example sentence should have a blank for the vocabulary word. For example, *The tuition is not expensive. It is* ______________. (Answer: affordable) Hand out the cards and ask students to test each other on the vocabulary words.

WRITING OUR STORIES: The Average Brazilian

A

- Ask students to read the passage silently. Explain that it isn't important for them to understand every single word, but they should try to understand the main ideas in each paragraph.
- When students finish reading, invite them to ask about anything they don't understand.
- Ask what differences there are between the average Brazilian and the average American.
- Ask students what facts they found surprising. What facts are different for their own countries? What things are the same?

ABOUT THE PHOTO

With a landscape consisting of tropical beaches and lush mountains, Rio de Janeiro is a very popular tourist destination, where visitors can hike trails with scenic views, visit old churches and museums, and lounge on iconic beaches like Ipanema and Copacabana.

Rio's Carnaval, a five-day festival that attracts thousands of visitors every year, is one of the world's most famous celebrations.

WRITING OUR STORIES The Average Brazilian

A Read.

People enjoy a beach day in Rio de Janeiro, Brazil.

1 My family is from Brazil. Brazil is the largest country in South America and one of the largest countries in the world. The people of Brazil speak Portuguese.

2 Brazilians are outgoing, expressive people. When we meet, we kiss each other on both cheeks. Men pat one another on the back or give each other a hug. When we speak with a friend, we often touch or hold hands.

3 Families are the center and heart of our lives. Families usually live in the same city or in the same area of the city. Often, many members of a family live on the same block! We see each other almost every day. On the weekends, the younger cousins go out in groups together. There are few childcare centers because aunts and uncles and grandparents help care for the babies and younger children.

4 The main meal is lunch, in the early afternoon, between 12 and 2 p.m. We eat a lot of rice and beans and we know how to cook them many different ways. Lunch also includes meat or fish and a vegetable or a salad. On Sundays, the whole family often eats together. There is a lot of talking, laughing, and enjoying each other's company.

5 We enjoy sports, especially volleyball, basketball, and tennis. But the most popular sport is *futebol* (*soccer* in the United States). We think that our teams and players are the best in the world. Brazil has won the World Cup five times.

6 One of our favorite activities is going to the beach. The beaches are free. We put down our blankets, take out our suntan lotion, and turn on our stereos—loud! People walk along the beach selling food, drinks, hats, jewelry, and many other things. As the day continues, we begin to dance and it becomes like a party on the beach. We stay at the beach until late at night. Brazilians enjoy celebrations and parties. When you visit our country and receive your first invitation to a party, remember to come at least an hour late. In Brazil, we are very relaxed about time.

MORE ACTION

Extend Exercise A by going around the class and having each student ask a question about the passage. The other students in the class will answer. The only rule is that a question cannot be repeated. For example:

S1: *How do Brazilians greet each other?*

S2: *They kiss each other on the cheek, pat each other on the back, or hug.*

Another way to extend this activity is to ask students to work in pairs. One student closes the book while the other student asks questions about the passage. Then, they can switch roles.

WRITING NOTE

Adding Details

In a composition, each paragraph has one topic or idea. To make a story more interesting, include many details and examples about the topic.

B Write the topic of each paragraph in the reading.

1. introduction
2. greetings
3. families
4. food / meals
5. sports
6. the beach / other activities

C **LET'S TALK.** In groups, talk about the lives of average people in your country. Take notes. Some topics you can discuss are:

greetings	education
families	holidays
sports	weekend activities
food	religion
transportation	work

In my country, most young people like to go to the beach when they are on vacation.

D Write a composition about the lives of average people in the country you are from. Choose three or four topics to write about. Give many details and examples. Use your notes from Exercise C.

E **CIVICS** Correct the mistake with the underlined verb. If the verb is correct, write *correct*.

1. Most Americans drives to work. drive
2. Many Americans take public transportation. correct
3. Most American women doesn't get married before age 25. don't get
4. The average American have a computer. has
5. The average American doesn't eat a large breakfast. correct
6. Most American families has one or two children. have
7. Americans eats their main meal in the evening. eat

B

Read the Writing Note aloud to the class. Explain that a topic is the subject of a paragraph or reading. Tell students that the first paragraph of a reading is usually the introduction to the main topic of the entire reading.

C

- Tell groups to pick a few topics from the list or make up their own topics to discuss.
- Assign a representative in each group to take notes as students talk.
- Have each group give a report to the class about the lives of average people in their country using the group's notes.

D

Students can start writing in class and complete this task for homework.

E

If students need help completing this exercise, have them refer back to the grammar charts on page 22 (Singular and Plural Subjects).

TEACHING TIP

Students enjoy hearing about life in other countries. Make copies of several student paragraphs from Exercise D for the class to read or invite two or three students to read their stories aloud. Encourage comments and questions from other students.

For example:

S1: *In my country, most teenagers play sports, too. What sports are popular in your country?*

S2: *In my country, students don't wear uniforms. What color are the school uniforms in your country?*

ENGLISH IN ACTION: Taking a Survey

A

- Read the instructions and ask for three volunteers—one student who will ask the questions, one student who will count the answers, and one student who will write the answers on the board.
- Hand the exercise over to the class and see how they manage to complete the task.
- At the end, you may decide to give feedback on how well the class conducted the exercise.

B

- Ask students what answers from Exercise A would be best represented by a pie chart and which answers would be best represented by a bar graph.
- Divide the class into five groups and assign each group one of the questions from Exercise A. Each group should decide on what kind of infographic they are going to create for their question.
- After groups have finished, have one or two representatives from each group come to the board and draw their group's graph. Have the rest of the class evaluate the accuracy and clarity of each graph and determine whether the answers are well represented by the type of graph selected by the group.

ACADEMIC

Remind students of the pie charts and bar graphs they saw earlier in the unit. Would either of these be useful for showing some of the information?

ENGLISH IN ACTION Taking a Survey

A ACADEMIC Take a class survey. Write the information about your class. Answers will vary.

- One student is the leader and will read each question to the entire class.
- Students will raise their hands to show their answers to each question.
- Two students are the counters. They will count each answer, including their own.
- Write the answers in your book.

1. Number of students in our class: ____________
2. Seat belts
   Who wears a seat belt? ____________
   Who doesn't wear a seat belt? ____________
3. Work
   Who works part time? ____________
   Who works full time? ____________
   Who doesn't work? ____________
4. How many hours do you watch TV?
   Who doesn't watch TV? ____________
   Who watches TV one hour a day? ____________
   Who watches TV two hours a day? ____________
   Who watches TV three hours a day? ____________
   Who watches TV four or more hours a day? ____________
5. What country are you from?

Country	Number of Students
____________	____________
____________	____________
____________	____________
____________	____________
____________	____________
____________	____________
____________	____________

B ACADEMIC In small groups, draw four charts to show the results of your class survey. Use the information from Exercise A.

MORE ACTION

Ask students to give examples of subjects in school that often use pie charts or bar graphs (for example, scientific information, population charts, and so on). Ask what kind of information these graphs are used to present. What are the benefits of presenting information in a graph versus writing it out in sentences? If possible, bring in examples of infographics from a textbook or news article and ask students to describe the information in their own words.

UNIT 3 WORKING AND SAVING

These men compare sections of counterfeit, or fake, one-hundred dollar bills to a sample of a real bill.

ACADEMIC Identify and retell key details; recall information

AT WORK Describe occupations; ask and answer questions about employment and the workplace

CIVICS Learn about and discuss how to pay for college; understand money-saving tips; write an email to customer service

CCRS Level A: R 1, 2, 4, 5; W 6, 7, 8; L 1, 2, 6; Level B: R 1, 2, 4, 6; W 4, 6, 7, 8; L 1, 2, 3, 6; Level C: R 1, 2, 4; W 4, 6, 7, 8, 9; L 1, 2, 3, 6; Level D: R 1, 2, 3, 4; W 4, 6, 7, 8, 9; L 1, 3, 6; Level E: R 1, 2, 3, 4; W 4, 6, 7, 8, 9; L 6

ELPS Level 1 Standards 1, 2, 3, 4, 5, 7, 8, 9, 10; Level 2 Standards 1, 2, 3, 5, 7, 8, 10; Level 3 Standards 1, 2, 3, 5, 7, 8, 10; Level 4 Standards 1, 2, 3, 5, 7, 8, 10; Level 5 Standards 1, 2, 3, 5, 7, 8, 10

CIVICS 01-5; 14-3; 33-11; 47-1; 48-1; 48-3; 48-9; 51-2; 52-4; 52-8

CASAS 0.1.2; 0.1.5; 0.2.1; 0.2.4; 1.3.3; 1.5.2; 4.1.8; 2.8.7; 7.4.4; 7.7.3; 7.7.4

IN THIS UNIT

In Unit 3, students will:

- Practice the present tense with *wh-* questions
- Learn about some financial systems in the US
- Read about some financing college
- Write an email to customer service

ABOUT THE PHOTO

The design of US currency, like that of many other nations, is intentionally complex to prevent counterfeit (fake) bills from entering into circulation. Many of the details that prove authenticity are too small to be seen easily, and everything from the type of paper and ink to the hidden watermarks are tightly controlled by the US mint.

Students may find an analysis of some bills and coins interesting, so depending on what you have on hand, give them a bit of background on the people and places featured, which they may rarely have a chance to explore. Start by asking them: *What do you think this picture is of?* They might have trouble arriving at "money," so you can give it away if need be. *Which bill is this? The $1, $5, $10, or $100?* ($100) *Who is on the bill?* (Ben Franklin. Explain that Franklin is a founding father, but not a president and that he signed the Declaration of Independence). Then take out whatever you have in your wallet, within reason, and repeat the process. For reference: $1 Bill: George Washington; $5 Bill: Abraham Lincoln; $10 Bill: Alexander Hamilton; $20 Bill: Andrew Jackson. Repeat for coins if appropriate.

A

- Ask students about a time when they began a new job. Was there a lot to learn? How did they learn it? Who taught them? Did they learn "on the job," or was there a training session?
- Ask students what they know about the job of a baker. Do they know anyone who bakes as their job, or who bakes at home for fun? Then, have them look at the photo and identify any baked goods they recognize, helping with any new vocabulary (*quiche, coffee cake, blueberry, rolls, peach*).
- Ask students to complete Exercise A individually and then check their answers with a partner. Explain any new vocabulary.

B

- Read the discussion questions to the class.
- Set a time limit for students to discuss the questions with a partner.
- Walk around the class as students are talking and take note of additional vocabulary they need.
- Finally, ask each pair their answers and opinions for each question. For example, do they like to bake? Why? Discuss the answers as a class.

A baker stands behind shelves of baked goods.

A **AT WORK** Complete the sentences about bakers using the present.

1. A baker (train) ___trains___ in bakeries, grocery stores, and restaurants.
2. Some bakers (study) ___study___ for one to two years at culinary or technical schools.
3. Other bakers (learn / sometimes) ___sometimes learn___ on the job.
4. Bakers in training (prepare) ___prepare___ breads, pies, cookies, and other baked goods.
5. A baker (use) ___uses___ mixers to prepare dough.
6. A new baker (learn) ___learns___ the basics and correct sanitation procedures.
7. Bakers (work) ___work___ part time or full time.
8. Many bakers (work / often) ___often work___ weekends and holidays.

B Discuss these questions.

1. Do you know how to bake? If you do, what do you like to bake?
2. Do you have a favorite bakery? Where is it?
3. What kind of baked goods do you like to eat?

TEACHING TIP

Encourage students to record new vocabulary in their notebooks. They can create their own example sentence in English, or, if necessary, translate the word into their own language. To encourage students to keep a vocabulary notebook, you may want to do this as a class activity a couple of times or until students feel comfortable doing it on their own.

AT WORK

The restaurant industry in the US is carefully regulated by the Department of Health and must follow OSHA's safety regulations. Invite students who work in the food or restaurant industry to share some of the requirements of their jobs. Ask them about safety and sanitation requirements and any special training they go through before they start work.

ACTIVE GRAMMAR Present: *Yes/No* Questions

Do	I you we they	**work** **learn** **have**	full time? on the job? long hours?	Yes, I **do**. Yes, you **do**. Yes, we **do**. Yes, they **do**.	No, I **don't**. No, you **don't**. No, we **don't**. No, they **don't**.
Does	he she			Yes, he **does**. Yes, she **does**.	No, he **doesn't**. No, she **doesn't**.
	it	**taste**	good?	Yes, it **does**.	No, it **doesn't**.

A Read the conversation. Then, practice it with a partner.

Jack: Do you like your job?
Andrea: Yes, I do. I'm a baker.
Jack: Really? Do you work full time or part time?
Andrea: I work part time right now.
Jack: Do you work on weekends?
Andrea: Yes, I do. Weekends are very busy at the bakery.

B **LET'S TALK.** Walk around the classroom and ask the following questions about jobs. If a student answers "Yes," write that student's name. If a student answers "No," ask another student the question. Answers will vary.

	Questions	Student's Name
1.	Do you have a job?	______
2.	Do you work full time?	______
3.	Do you like your job?	______
4.	Do you work weekends?	______
5.	Do you have benefits?	______
6.	Do you like your coworkers?	______
7.	Do you feel tired at the end of the day?	______
8.	Do you have to sign in at work?	______
9.	Do you want to find a different job?	______

ACTIVE GRAMMAR: Present: *Yes / No* Questions

A

- Call on students to read the questions from the grammar charts aloud. Then, call on other students to answer the questions.
- Point out that the first word in a *yes / no* question is a verb, and that only the auxiliary verb is repeated in the short answer.
- Call on two students to read the conversation in Exercise A.
- Then, have students work in pairs, first reading the dialog and then substituting their own information.

B

- Model the exercise with one or two students. Show how to ask a question, make a note of the reply, and move on to another student.
- To encourage students to talk to as many students as possible, you may want to set a rule that students can ask each student only one question.
- Conclude the exercise by reading each question aloud and having students call out the names of students who answered affirmatively for that question.

TEACHING TIP

Walk around and listen as students complete Exercise B, or consider doing this activity alongside students so they feel less inhibited about making mistakes.

C

- Point out the photo and the explanation about what a radiation therapist does. Depending on your class and your perception of the sensitivity level of your students, you might ask if anyone has any experience with this type of equipment or therapy.
- Check that students understand all of the vocabulary in the chart.
- Ask students to complete the task individually. Then, call on volunteers to read aloud their answers.
- Then, practice some additional questions and answers with the class. For example:

  T: *Jenny, does Kendra work at a hospital?*

  S1: *Yes, she does.*

  T: *Manny, do Mario and Lana work full time?*

  S2: *No, they don't.*

C **AT WORK** Complete the questions about radiation therapists.

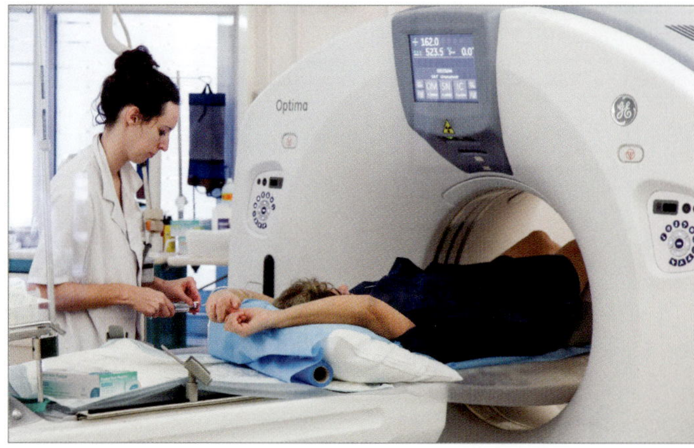

A **radiation therapist** uses radiation to treat patients with cancer and other diseases.

	Kendra	Mario and Lana
Education	has a bachelor's degree	have associate degrees
Place of work	works at a hospital	work at an outpatient center
Full time / Part time	works full time	work part time
Specialty	specializes in breast cancer	specialize in skin cancer
Salary	earns $102,500	earn $45,100 each
Savings	saves $1,000 a month	save $1,200 a month each

1. _Does_ Kendra _have_ a bachelor's degree? _Yes, she does._
2. _Do_ Mario and Lana _have_ bachelor's degrees? _No, they don't._
3. _Do_ Mario and Lana _have_ associate degrees? _Yes, they do._
4. _Do_ Mario and Lana _work_ at a hospital? _No, they don't._
5. _Does_ Kendra _work_ part time? _No, she doesn't._
6. _Do_ Mario and Lana _work_ part time? _Yes, they do._
7. _Do_ Mario and Lana _specialize_ in skin cancer? _Yes, they do._
8. _Does_ Kendra _specialize_ in skin cancer? _No, she doesn't._
9. _Does_ Kendra _have_ a good salary? _Yes, she does._
10. _Do_ Mario and Lana _save_ a lot of money each month? _Yes, they do._

AT WORK

Tell students that there are many paths to a career in the medical fields in the US. While some jobs require bachelor's degrees and beyond, others require 2-year associate degrees or that students complete certificate programs.

ACTIVE GRAMMAR Present: *Wh-* Questions

What Where When Why How How often How much How many hours	**do**	I you we they	**work?** **study?** **save?**
	does	he she	
		it	**last?**

A bank teller.

A Match the questions and answers about Liza, a bank teller.

i	**1.** Where does a bank teller work?	**a.** At 6:30 a.m.
g	**2.** What does a bank teller do?	**b.** Yes, she does.
a	**3.** What time does Liza get up?	**c.** A dress or a suit.
e	**4.** How does she get to work?	**d.** At 9:00 a.m.
c	**5.** What does she wear to work?	**e.** She takes the bus.
d	**6.** What time does the bank open?	**f.** She earns $31,000 a year.
h	**7.** What benefits does she get?	**g.** A teller handles cash and helps customers.
j	**8.** What time does the bank close?	**h.** Medical benefits.
f	**9.** How much does she earn?	**i.** A bank teller works at a bank.
b	**10.** Does she like her job?	**j.** At 4:00 p.m.

B Write questions about a bank security guard. Ask and answer the questions with a partner. Use your imagination to answer the questions. **Answers will vary.**

1. Where ______________________________?
2. How many hours ______________________________?
3. What time ______________________________?
4. How much ______________________________?
5. What ______________________________?

ACTIVE GRAMMAR: Present: *Wh-* Questions

A

- Call on students to read questions from the grammar chart aloud. Then, call on other students to answer the questions.
- Point out the difference between *wh-* questions and *yes / no* questions. In *wh-* questions, the first word is a question word and the verb comes second.
- Have students complete Exercise A individually.
- Then, ask volunteers to read aloud their answers. Write the answers on the board and go over them as a class.

B

- Elicit one or two questions. For example: *What is his / her name? What does he / she do?*
- Set a time limit for students to ask and answer the questions in pairs.
- Walk around and make note of words or grammar that are difficult for students.
- Read some questions or answers with mistakes aloud and ask students to correct them as a class.

MORE ACTION

For further practice with *wh-* questions in the third person, invite students to ask a partner questions about themselves and their family. Then, call on volunteers to present their conversations to the class.

C 11

- Play the audio without stopping and have students take notes while they listen.
- Play the audio again and have students complete the chart in their books.
- Check the answers as a class.

D

- Have students complete the exercise individually. Tell them to look at the grammar chart on the previous page if they need help forming the questions.
- Check the answers as a class.

E

- Ask students what they spend money on regularly.
- Have students work in pairs and read the conversation together.
- Give students time to write their conversations together. Encourage them to use topics in addition to those listed in the word box.
- As students perform their conversations for the class, write a list of items on the board that students spend their money on. Then, discuss the list with the class and ask whether students are surprised by any items or how much money students spend on them.

C ACADEMIC Listen and take notes about how Laura spends money each day. Laura works at a bakery and would like to save more of her paycheck. Add up the total. 11

Expenses	Amount
Coffee and donut	$4.00
bus - morning	$2.00
lunch	$8.00
soda	$1.00
bus - afternoon	$2.00
lottery ticket	$1.00
Total	$18.00

D Complete the questions about Laura's daily expenses.

1. What does Laura buy at the coffee shop? A coffee and a donut
2. How far does she live from work? About a mile
3. Why does she take the bus to work? Because she gets up late
4. How much does she spend for lunch? About $8.00
5. What does she buy from the vending machine? A soda
6. How much does she spend for the bus? $4.00 a day
7. What does she buy on her way home? A lottery ticket
8. Does she have a budget? No, she doesn't have a budget.

E Read the conversation. Then, write a conversation about some of your daily or weekly expenses. Use some of the ideas in the word box. Present your conversation to the class.

A: Do you know how you spend your money?
B: Not really.
A: How do you get to work?
B: I drive. I spend about $20 a week on gas.
A: How much do you spend a day on lunch?
B: I usually spend six or seven dollars.
A: What else do you buy every day?
B: I always get a cup of coffee on my way to work.

bus / train
childcare
clothes
coffee
gas
lottery tickets
lunch

MORE ACTION

Ask students to take the list of things they buy regularly from Exercise E and think of ways to save money on these items. For example, if students ate dinner at a restaurant one less time a week, they could save at least several dollars each week.

For homework, ask students to write a paragraph about what they buy every week and how much they spend on it.

ACADEMIC

Tell students that taking notes while they listen to audio is a great way to help them with comprehension. They are likely to find this same exercise format on exams, and it is also a useful skill to develop for other academic and professional pursuits.

F **LET'S TALK.** Write questions about Marta and Ryan's activities and expenses. Then, work in a group and ask and answer your questions. **Answers will vary. Possible answers shown.**

1. apartment
2. rent: $1,000 a month

3. three times a week
4. from 6:00 to 7:00

5. college / part time
6. Tuesday and Thursday

7. a salesman
8. gas: $3,000 a year

9. every Saturday night
10. Thai

11. savings: $100 a month

1. *Where do they live?*
2. *How much do they pay for rent?*
3. How often *does Marta go to the gym?*
4. How long *does she exercise?*
5. Does *Ryan go to college part time or full time?*
6. When *does he have class?*
7. What *does he do?*
8. How much *does he spend on gas a year?*
9. How often *do Ryan and Marta go out to dinner?*
10. What kind of food *do they usually have?*
11. How much *money do they save a month?*

F

- Ask students about the apartment and car expenses and whether they think they are high or not.
- Read the caption under the first picture and the sample answer.
- Allow a few minutes for students to complete the questions individually.
- Then, ask students to work in groups and compare their questions. Have students ask and answer all the questions with their group.
- Check the answers as a class. Make sure to listen for the third person -*s* on the appropriate items. The answers to the questions are:

1. They live in an apartment.
2. They pay $1,000 a month.
3. She goes three times a week.
4. She exercises from 6:00 to 7:00.
5. He goes to school/college part time.
6. He has class on Tuesday and Thursday.
7. He is a salesman.
8. He spends $3,000 a year.
9. They go out every Saturday night/once a week.
10. They usually have Thai.
11. They save $100 a month.

MORE ACTION

Have students work with a partner and discuss how much they pay each month for the items in the pictures. Ask volunteers to role-play their conversations for the class.

ACTIVE GRAMMAR: *Who* Questions

A

- Point out the difference in form between subject and object questions with *who*. In subject questions, *who* is followed by the main verb. For example, *Who washes the dishes? Henri does*. In object questions, *who* is followed by the auxiliary verb and then the subject. For example, *Who does she call the most? She calls her sister the most*.
- Give some further examples of *who* questions and ask students to identify if they are subject or object questions.
- Have students form groups. Tell students to ask and answer all the questions in Exercise A. Then, have them write a sentence or two about the group's responses. For example:

  S1: *Who has young children?*

  S2: *I do.*

  S3: *I do.*

  S1: *I don't.*

  Students could then write:

  Two students have young children. One student doesn't have young children.

B

- Read the first and second questions and answers aloud. Students can continue working in groups to complete the task.
- Have students check their answers with another group.

ACTIVE GRAMMAR *Who* Questions

When *who* is the subject of a sentence, it is always singular.		When *who* is the object of a sentence, it can be singular or plural.	
Who works at City Bank? **Who saves** money every month?	**Liza** does. **Henry and Ivan** do.	**Who** does he drive to work? **Who** do they send money to?	He drives **his brother** to work. They send money **to their parents**.

A LET'S TALK. In a group, answer the questions. Then, make sentences about your group.

1. Who has young children?
2. Who lives in an apartment?
3. Who has a mortgage?
4. Who banks online?
5. Who buys lottery tickets?
6. Who downloads music?
7. Who works at night?

B Write questions with *Who* about each statement.

1. Molly drives her daughter to school.
   Who does Molly drive to school ?
2. Nidia wants to be a nurse.
   Who wants to be a nurse ?
3. Josh saves $100 a week.
   Who saves $ 100 a week ?
4. Carlos calls his girlfriend every night.
   Who does Carlos call every night ?
5. Martin sends money to his brother every month.
   Who does Martin send money to every month ?
6. Sofia belongs to a health club.
   Who belongs to a health club ?
7. Wendy works the night shift.
   Who works the night shift ?

TEACHING TIP

An alternative way of doing Exercise A is to ask students to appoint a secretary for the group who keeps a record of all the answers. (Students can take turns asking the questions.) Then, after answering all the questions, they can work together to write the sentences.

ACTIVE GRAMMAR *Yes / No* Question Review: *Am / Are / Is / Do / Does*

Yes / No* Questions with *be		
Am	I	**tired**? **a student**? **at school**?
Are	you we they	
Is	he she	
	it	**cheap**?

Yes / No* Questions with *do			
Do	I you we they	**work**	in a bank? at night?
Does	he she		
	it	**cost**	a lot?

When asking a *Yes / No* question, use *be* with adjectives and nouns. Use *do / does* with verbs other than *be*.

A Complete the questions with *Am, Are, Is, Do,* or *Does.*

1. __Do__ you have a credit card?
2. __Does__ he spend a lot of money?
3. __Am__ I careful with my money?
4. __Is__ she sometimes late with her bills?
5. __Does__ he work full time?
6. __Is__ gas expensive?
7. __Do__ you shop at the mall every weekend?
8. __Do__ they pay taxes?
9. __Are__ you good at saving money?
10. __Does__ your family compare prices?

B With a partner, ask and answer the questions.

Do you work in a bank?

No, I don't.

1. you / work in a bank? **Do you work in a bank?**
2. you / get up early in the morning? **Do you get up early in the morning?**
3. you / a serious student? **Are you a serious student?**
4. your teacher / from the United States? **Is your teacher from the United States?**
5. this class / difficult? **Is this class difficult?**
6. you / talkative? **Are you talkative?**
7. your teacher / give a lot of homework? **Does your teacher give a lot of homework?**
8. you / always do your homework? **Do you always do your homework?**

MORE ACTION

For further practice with *yes / no* questions, write a list of subject pronouns on the board (*I, you, he, she, it, we, they*). Then, point to a pronoun and prompt students to make a question.

For example:

T: (points to the word *he* on the board) *work in a bank*

S: *Does he work in a bank?*

ACTIVE GRAMMAR: *Yes / No Question Review: Am / Are / Is / Do / Does*

A

- Read the questions in the grammar charts aloud. Point out the adjectives used after the verb *be* in the first chart. Ask students to name other words that would work for those questions. (happy, a doctor, at the gym)
- Remind students that the base form of the verb in the second chart stays the same no matter which pronoun it is used with. It is only in statements that the base form takes an *s* or *es* after *he, she*, and *it.*
- Read the first three items of Exercise A aloud.
- Ask students to explain how to identify the correct answer. (Look for the verb, the subject, or an adjective.)
- Have students complete the task individually. Then, ask volunteers to read aloud their answers.

B

Model one or two questions with a pair of students. Then, ask students to complete the task in pairs.

THE BIG PICTURE: The Internship

A

- Ask if any students have ever had an internship. Where did they work? What did they do there? What did they think of the experience? What benefits do they think an internship brings?
- Ask other students in the class if they agree.
- Guide a discussion about the vocabulary in Exercise A.

B 12

- Have students read the sentences and try to predict the answers.
- Play the audio once and have students listen only.
- Play the audio again and have students fill in the answers. If necessary, pause the audio periodically so that students have time to write their answers.
- Have students compare their answers with a classmate's.
- Review the answers with the class.

THE BIG PICTURE The Internship

A Discuss the meanings of these words with your class.

3D design	animation
character	design
internship	technology

An **internship** is a program for beginners in an occupation at an organization. An internship may last a summer, a semester, or a year. **Interns** are often students or recent graduates.

B Listen to Mia's story. Then, complete the information about Mia's background and internship. 12

1. Mia is a student at a university in ___Pennsylvania___.
2. She is studying design, ___art___, and ___technology___.
3. She wants to design ___animation___ for ___video___ games.
4. She has experience with computer ___animation___ and 3D ___design___.
5. She has a paid ___full-time___ internship. She will work 40 hours a week.

TEACHING TIP

You may want to use Exercise B as an opportunity to encourage students to use their vocabulary notebooks. Ask them to make a new page under the heading *Internships* and then write new vocabulary from this lesson either as a list or as a word web.

CULTURE NOTE

Tell students that many companies require you to be a current student in order to be an intern. The internship is treated like a class, with the amount of academic credit received depending on the number of hours spent at the internship. For this reason, while some internships are paid, in many cases they are not, and the credit earned toward graduation earned is considered payment.

6. Her pay is ___$3,200___ a month.

7. Her ___tuition___ at the university is very expensive.

C ACADEMIC Write questions about Mia.

1. Why ___does Mia need to save money___?

   She needs to save money because tuition is expensive.

2. How ___does Mia feel___?

   She feels excited.

3. Who ___does she work with___?

   She works with a team of people.

4. What ___does she buy___ every morning?

   She buys coffee and breakfast.

5. Where ___does she stop on the way to work___?

   She stops at a coffee shop on the way to work.

6. What ___does she usually do___ at night?

   She rents a movie or goes out with the other interns.

7. ___Answers will vary. Question should start with "Does she…"___?

   Yes, she does.

D Write three more questions about Mia. Ask a classmate your questions. Answers will vary.

1. ______
2. ______
3. ______

E **LET'S TALK.** With a small group of students, list other ways that Mia can save money.
Answers will vary.

1. ______
2. ______
3. ______
4. ______

C

- Read the answer (second line) in item 1 with the class and then read the sample question in blue (the answer students are expected to produce). Point out that students do not need to hear the audio to generate the answer: they can deduce the question being asked by the answer.
- Tell them items 1–6 have specific answers, but item 7 is open-ended: they can invent something.
- Give them a few minutes to let them work on their own. Then, have them work in pairs to check each other's work.
- Briefly review the answers as a class, making sure to emphasize the correct use of the auxiliary verb.
- Ask volunteers to provide their suggestions for item 7.

D

- You may consider playing the audio again to help students brainstorm.
- Give students a few minutes to write their own suggestions, circulating the class to answer questions.
- Put students in pairs and have them ask each other their questions.

E

- In small groups, have students brainstorm ways to save money. Let them know that they are welcome to record more than four suggestions.
- Have groups share their ideas with the class. Encourage groups and individuals to share strategies they use in their own lives.
- For additional discussion, provide them with some other examples and ask them if they think those suggestions are good strategies. For example: never spend a $5 bill (always save it); put $1 in your savings when you break a rule (missing class, cheating on a diet).

ACADEMIC

The task in Exercise C requires students to use their critical thinking skills to deduce the question from the answer. If your students are preparing for any standardized tests, it is a good idea to expose them to some of these less straight-forward question formats. Other examples include True/False activities with a "Not Given" option; paraphrasing activities; questions about a speaker/author's attitude or intentions.

READING: A Brief Guide

A

- Have the students discuss the two questions in groups of three for two minutes.
- Ask for volunteers to share their answers. For an example of how much college in the US can cost, point out the photo and the photo caption to the class.
- Ask students to suggest answers, take notes on the board and emphasize any particularly strong suggestions or themes that will come up in the reading.

B

- Give students time to read the article on their own. Then, play the audio or call on individual students to read a paragraph at a time. Answer any questions about unfamiliar vocabulary as they go.
- Invite students to make comparisons between the information in the reading and their own institution.

CIVICS

College in the United States is notoriously expensive, but there are a lot of resources to help students finance an education. In addition to financial aid, scholarships, and federal and private loans, encourage students to look into tuition reimbursement or work sponsorship. Depending on the area where students live, some fields, such as medicine, may have other less expensive pathways to a degree. For example, many hospitals in need of specialized technicians will partner with community colleges to (1) get students into the workforce as soon as possible and (2) finance the necessary degree. Local community colleges will often be able to provide guidance on such opportunities, if students are open to considering different fields.

READING A Brief Guide

A Discuss these questions.

1. How much does college cost? Do all colleges cost the same?
2. How do students pay for college?

B **CIVICS** Read and discuss the information about paying for college.

Paying for College

College in the United States is very expensive. However, there are several ways to pay for tuition and fees. To access many of the financial aid opportunities available, students do not need to be US citizens: these opportunities are also open to permanent residents and refugees. High school students can speak with a counselor. People who have finished high school can contact the college that they want to attend. Here are a few options that help students pay for college:

Federal Grants

Many students are eligible for federal grants. Some grants are need-based and help low-income students. Other grants are merit-based and are for students with high grades. Students do not need to pay back grants. They must attend school at least part time. Students can apply for federal grants online.

Scholarships

A scholarship is money that a student receives based on need, high grades, athletic ability, or other criteria. Colleges, local organizations, and businesses give scholarships. Ask the financial aid office or go online to find a list of scholarships that are available.

Tuition Reimbursement

Many businesses help their workers pay for college. In most cases, an employee registers and takes a class at a college. When the employee passes the course, usually with a C grade or better, the employer pays back all or part of the tuition. Check your company's benefits and policies.

Federal Student Loans

The federal government offers student loans with low interest rates. Students do not need to pay back the loan until they finish college. They must pay back the money with interest whether they finish college or not. Students can apply for a federal loan online. 13

David Tenorio chose to study engineering at Harvey Mudd College instead of attending Harvard University.

C Check the information that applies for each type of financial assistance.

Type of Assistance	Students with Need	Students with Good Grades	Federal Program	Must Pay Back
Grants	✓	✓	✓	
Scholarships	✓	✓		
Tuition Reimbursement		✓		
Student Loans	✓		✓	✓

D Read and discuss the information about student loan repayment.

After students finish or stop attending college, they must start paying back their student loans plus interest. The standard repayment plan is for ten years, one payment a month, 120 payments in all.

Karla, Josh, and Deanna all borrowed money to attend college at a 4.45% interest rate.

Karla borrowed $6,000. She attended college for a year but stopped attending after that.

Josh borrowed $10,000 to attend a two-year college.

Derek borrowed $50,000 to attend a four-year college.

	Karla	Josh	Derek
Total amount borrowed	$6,000	$10,000	$50,000
Interest amount at end of loan	$1,462	$4,873	$12,183
Total amount to pay back	$7,462	$14,873	$62,183
Monthly payment for ten years	$62	$207	$518

E Answer the questions about the loan information in the chart above.

1. What is the interest rate on each loan? 4.45%
2. Does Karla have to pay back her loan? Yes, she does.
3. What is her monthly payment? $62
4. How much did Josh borrow? $10,000
5. How much is his monthly payment? $207
6. How much did Derek borrow? $50,000
7. What is the total amount he has to pay back? $62,183
8. How much is his monthly payment? $518

F **LET'S TALK.** In a group, agree or disagree with the following statements. Give your reasons.

1. If you don't have enough money, do not apply to college.
2. You should check how much money different careers pay.

C

- Give students 2–5 minutes to complete Exercise C on their own.
- Review the answers as a class, pausing to clarify any confusion by directing attention to the appropriate location in the text.

D

- Give students three minutes to read the paragraph and chart.
- Ask volunteers to read the paragraph and each line of the chart out loud, pausing to answer any questions and support correct pronunciation.

E

- Have students work on Exercise E individually first.
- Then, put them in pairs to compare answers. Circulate the room to make sure everyone is on track, or review answers as a class.

F

- Put students in groups of 3–4 to discuss the two statements. Designate one person (perhaps a quieter student) to take notes. Let the note taker know they will share the opinions.
- Circulate the room to make sure that everyone in the group participates. Then, invite the notetaker to share some of their groups' ideas. Allowing students who are more apprehensive about speaking aloud in class (or simply quieter by personality) to speak from notes may help assuage some nerves.

WRITING OUR STORIES: Email to Customer Service

A

- Ask students to volunteer reasons why someone might call or write to customer service. If they have trouble getting started, provide suggestions: to make a purchase (no); to ask a question about a return policy (yes); to check on a delivery (yes); to shop (no); to complain (yes).
- Have students discuss the questions in Exercise A briefly as a class.

B

- Call on students to read the email out loud section by section, pausing to answer any questions.
- Point out the different elements of the letter, such as the opening and the closing. Point out to students that this is a formal piece of writing, and that, even if they are complaining, they should use clear, correct, and polite language.

WRITING OUR STORIES | Email to Customer Service

A Discuss these questions. Have you ever sent an email to a business? Why did you send it?

B Read the following email to customer service.

To: customerservice@online*shop.com — Put the recipient's email here. **Recipient** is another word for the person who receives the message.

Subject: Order #187653-445 — If you have a complaint or a return, include the order number.

To Whom It May Concern: — If you do not have a name, type *To Whom It May Concern:*

On January 5th, I ordered 12 rolls of paper towels for $28.97 and 2 boxes of 13-gallon kitchen trash bags for $23.30. The order total was $52.27 plus shipping and handling. The order arrived on January 8th, and I received only 6 rolls of paper towels and only 1 box of trash bags, but I was charged the full amount. Please credit my account, or send me the remaining part of my order. Please credit my credit card for any shipping and handling. Attached are the original order (#187653-445) and the packing slip that was in the box.

Thank you for your attention to this matter. If you need additional information, I can be reached at this email address or at (555) 555-1212.

Sincerely, — End your email with *Sincerely.*

Charles Anton — Include your full name.

CULTURE NOTE

As shoplifting and other types of petty theft have become more common, return policies have become stricter. Encourage students to know the return policy before they make important purchases and to keep track of receipts. They should not assume they can return a product without a receipt for cash; many retailers only offer store credit.

C Answer the questions. **Answers may vary.**

1. Who wrote the email? Charles Anton
2. When did he buy the products? January 5
3. Did he buy the products from a store? No, he didn't.
4. Why is he sending an email to the company? He didn't receive his full order.
5. What does he want the company to do? He wants the company to credit his account or send the remaining part of his order.
6. Did he attach anything to the email? Yes, he attached the original order and the packing slip that was in the delivery box.

WRITING NOTE	
Use capitals for:	
the names of streets	the names of cities
the names of states	the first letter in every line of an address

D CIVICS Write an email to a company. Use one of the suggestions below or think of another reason.

1. You want to return a product.
2. Your credit card company made a mistake on your bill.
3. The cellphone company charged you for services you did not use.
4. You want to thank a business for excellent service.
5. You want to order a product or request information.
6. You purchased an object online, but it broke before you received it and you want a full refund.

WRITING NOTE

Emails to Customer Service

1. Use a clear subject.
2. Start your message with a greeting.
3. Make sure the email is brief and clear.
4. Use proper spelling, punctuation, and capitalization. Do not write the entire message using capital letters.
5. Mention any attachments that you send with the message.

C

- Allow students a few minutes to answer the questions on their own, then have them compare answers in pairs. Circulate the class to check their work.
- Review the Writing Note as a class. Review the rules of capitalization briefly. Emphasize to students that the rules should be followed in a letter like this.
- Ask students to volunteer other appropriate uses of capitalization: the pronoun *I*; months of the year and days of the week; proper nouns.

D

- Have volunteers read the suggestions for the topic out loud.
- Review the second Writing Note with students. Encourage them to look back at the writing model on the previous page and notice if these conventions are present.
- Give students about twenty minutes to complete their writing. If they are short on time, you may also assign this for homework.
- Review common errors with the class, being careful not to draw attention to any individual, and point out good uses of the conventions that have been highlighted.

CIVICS

It's common in informal writing (text messages, social media posts) to not follow the correct rules of capitalization. However, in formal communication, such as a message to customer service, or any writing to a teacher or boss, all of the formal conventions should be followed. Perhaps equally importantly, capitalization for emphasis (writing entire words in capitals to show that they writer is "screaming") is extremely inappropriate in any formal communication. Learning the rules of polite formal communication (polite even when making a complain) will be helpful for students as they interact with various systems and institutions in the US.

ENGLISH IN ACTION: Money-Saving Tips

A

- Call on volunteers to read sections of the article out loud, pausing for questions.
- Put students in pairs to discuss the words in bold and make sure they understand the meaning.
- Ask pairs to write a sample sentence (a new one) with each of the terms in bold that demonstrates the meaning of the term. Give them an example: *A great* ***tip*** *for learning English is to watch TV in English*. Ask for a few examples to make sure students understand the meaning.

B

- Talking about budgets can be sensitive as students may not want to share their pay, so be aware of this and let students know that you will only be looking at the format of the sheets—not real information.
- Post what students bring in around the classroom. Give them time to circulate and think about which ones are easy to use.
- Vote on the best one. Have the students explain their choices.

ENGLISH IN ACTION Money-Saving Tips

A Read the article. Then, discuss the meanings of the words in bold with a partner.

In 1980, Omar got his first job. His monthly salary was $800. His parents told him, "Put 10 percent of your paycheck away for your future." Omar put $80 in the bank each month. Over the years, Omar's salary continued to rise, and he continued to save 10 percent of his salary. His next employer had a 401(k) plan. Omar continued to save 10 percent of his salary and his employer added 3 percent. When Omar retired last year, he had $475,000 in his 401(k) retirement plan!

How do people save money? Omar's **system** was simple—put 10 percent of every paycheck into a retirement plan. Here are some savings **tips** from money experts.

1. **Keep a budget.** This is the first step in any savings plan. How much money comes in every month? Where does it go? For a few months, keep a **record** of your expenses—car payments, gas, phone, rent, utility bills, food, and eating out. Don't forget about the large yearly **expenses** like car insurance.

2. **Make a plan.** Decide what you are saving for. A car? A house? Retirement? How much money do you need for each?

3. **Use your credit card wisely.** When you use credit cards, pay them off as soon as possible. If you pay $1,200 in credit card interest a year, that is $1,200 you could save.

4. **Buy used.** It is possible to buy lightly used items for half or less of the original price. Stop at garage sales and look for furniture and children's items. There are websites for used items in excellent condition. Car dealers offer late-model used cars with one-year warranties. These cars often have low mileage.

5. **Cut your spending.** Try to figure out how to **cut** your expenses. If you have a cellphone, can you drop your landline? Can you refinance your mortgage? Can you get a better price on car insurance? Do you need two cars?

Saving money is a family **effort**. Sit down with your partner and talk about money. As you start to save, you will feel more secure and satisfied as your dollars start to grow.

B CIVICS Search online for a basic budget worksheet. Use the keywords below. Print and bring several worksheets to class. Compare the worksheets and decide which is the most useful.

free budget worksheet	basic budget planner	basic budget form

CIVICS

Budgeting is important, especially if you are a renter, as there are many conventions landlords follow when choosing tenants. Ideally, living expenses (rent) will be around 25% of household (not individual) income. The thinking is that this amount allows for other expenses like utilities, a car, and childcare, as well as some savings. It becomes difficult to get approved for an apartment if the rent is 40–50% of household income.

UNIT 4 THE STATES

A national park service worker at Mt. Rushmore, South Dakota.

ACADEMIC Read and understand maps; categorize nouns; find supporting details; write a report; prepare a presentation; make observations

AT WORK Listen to and give a presentation

CIVICS Identify land features in a map of the United States; learn about Montana, California, and the Death Valley National Park

CCRS Level A: R 1, 2, 5, 7; W 2, 5, 7, 8; L 1, 5; Level B: R 1, 2, 5, 6, 7; W 2, 4, 5, 7, 8; L 1, 2, 7; Level C: R 1, 2, 7; W 2, 4, 5, 7, 8, 9; L 1, 2, 3, 5; Level D: R 1, 2, 7; W 2, 4, 5, 7, 8, 9; L 1, 3; Level E: R 1, 2, 7; W 2, 4, 5, 7, 8, 9

ELPS Level 1 Standards 2, 3, 5, 9, 10; Level 2 Standards 1, 2, 3, 5, 7, 9, 10; Level 3 Standards 1, 2, 3, 5, 7, 9, 10; Level 4 Standards 1, 2, 3, 5, 7, 9, 10; Level 5 Standards 1, 2, 3, 5, 7, 9, 10

CIVICS 10-3; 10-4; 10-8; 50-7

CASAS 0.1.2; 0.1.5; 0.1.8; 2.2.5

IN THIS UNIT

In Unit 4, students will:

- Talk about geographical features and places in the United States
- Practice count and noncount nouns
- Make statements and questions with determiners *much, many,* and *enough*
- Write a report

ABOUT THE PHOTO

The Mount Rushmore National Memorial is a famous monument in South Dakota. Carved into the granite face of a mountain, the sculpture features four US presidents: George Washington, Thomas Jefferson, Theodore Roosevelt, and Abraham Lincoln. In this humorous photo, a National Parks worker appears to be on the brink of being inhaled as he rappels down Lincoln's nose.

Preview the topics in this unit by asking students *yes/no* questions on the photo. Explain the monument to them and tell them: *This photo is in South Dakota. What do you know about South Dakota? Is it near the ocean?* (No) *Does it have mountains/forests?* (yes) *Does it have big cities with skyscrapers?* (No). You may want to give examples of mountains, skyscrapers, oceans by name to support comprehension.

To activate students' background knowledge on the fifty states, see if students can name some places with these features. Ask: *Where can you see skyscrapers?* (New York, Chicago) *The ocean?* (California, Hawaii) *Mountains?* (Colorado, New Hampshire) *Forests?* (Vermont, Washington). Sample answers may change based on your students' frame of reference.

If any of the other features listed on the next page are particularly relevant to your community (*desert, river, canyon,* etc.), elicit examples of those: *Here in our town/state, we have X. What other states have X?*

A

- Encourage students to use their dictionaries, either print or on their phones.
- Review by going over the terms visible in the photo as a class.

B

- Read the features in the list aloud. Ask students to repeat each one.
- Ask questions, such as: *What's the difference between a plain and a mountain? What is another word for* seaport*? Where do you find a seaport? What is a glacier?*
- Encourage students to ask questions about anything they don't understand and to make comments on the land formations in the picture.
- Invite them to discuss which of these geographical features are present in their own countries or the city / area in which they currently live.

C

- Read the statements aloud.
- Answer any questions students may have about new vocabulary.
- Then, have students circle their answers and check them with a partner.

Palouse Falls State Park, Washington.

A Check the words you see in the photo. Look up the words you don't know.

B Give an example of each of these geographical features in the United States: a lake, a river, a mountain range, a seaport, an island, and a canyon.

C Circle *True* or *False* about your city. Answers will vary.

1.	We can see mountains from our school.	True	False
2.	This city / town is on a river.	True	False
3.	If I drive for an hour, I can see the Atlantic or the Pacific Ocean.	True	False
4.	This city is the capital of the state.	True	False
5.	There is a desert near here.	True	False
6.	This city / town is near a lake.	True	False
7.	There is a large forest near here.	True	False
8.	This city / town is also a seaport.	True	False

TEACHING TIP

Bring in a large map of the United States, or use the one at the back of the student book. Name some geographical features in the US, such as the Great Salt Lake and the Mississippi River, and ask students to find them on the map. Then, ask students to tell you which features they have visited or would like to visit.

ACTIVE GRAMMAR Count Nouns: Singulars and Plurals

Count nouns are people, places, or things that we can count individually (one by one).
Count nouns can be singular or plural.
Expressions with *one of the*, *every*, and *each* before the noun take a singular verb.
Every state **has** a capitol building.
Expressions with *a few of the*, *some of the*, *many of the*, *all of the*, etc., take a plural verb.
All of the states **have** capitol buildings.

A Write *S* next to the nouns that take a singular verb, and *P* next to the nouns that take a plural verb.

1. S a desert		**6.** S one of the cities		**11.** S each of the farms	
2. P mountains		**7.** S a mountain range		**12.** P all of the states	
3. S a forest		**8.** P a few of the parks		**13.** P millions of tourists	
4. P rivers		**9.** S every national park		**14.** S every state	
5. P seaports		**10.** P many of the people		**15.** P several of the islands	

B Circle the correct forms of the verbs.

1. A plain is / **are** a large area of flat land.
2. A range is / **are** a group of mountains.
3. Canyons **is** / are long, deep cracks in the earth's surface.
4. Glaciers **is** / are large rivers of slow-moving ice.
5. Every major city has / **have** a lot of traffic.
6. Many rivers **begins** / begin in the mountains.
7. Millions of tourists **visits** / visit national parks every summer.
8. Every dairy farm produces / **produce** milk.
9. Every state has / **have** interesting places to visit.
10. All the states **has** / have interesting places to visit.
11. Each farm grows / **grow** many kinds of vegetables.
12. All road maps **shows** / show cities and highways.
13. Most cities **has** / have skyscrapers.

One World Trade Center is a skyscraper in New York City.

MORE ACTION

For further practice with singular and plural count nouns, give students the beginning of sentences and ask them to complete the sentences in pairs. For example:

All cities… (have a city hall.)

Many mountains… (have snow in winter.)

Every state… (has a capital.)

ACTIVE GRAMMAR: Count Nouns: Singulars and Plurals

A

- Review the information in the grammar chart with the class.
- Read out some of the words or phrases from Exercise A in random order. Ask students to raise their right hand if the noun is plural and their left hand if the noun is singular.
- Have students complete Exercise A individually.
- To review the answers, call on different students to give an answer and explain it. For example:

S1: Desert *is a singular noun. It has* a *in front of it and doesn't end in* -s.

S2: One of the cities *is a singular noun.* Cities *is plural, but the phrase* one of the *is singular. The phrase is referring to only one city.*

B

Have students work on the exercise individually and then check their answers in pairs. Remind students to look at the grammar chart if they need help determining what expressions are singular or plural.

CIVICS

Let any students who may be intending to take the citizenship test know that this unit contains information that will be useful. The interview can include questions on the states and US geography. **Civics** labels within the unit will draw attention to material of particular relevance.

C 🎧14

- Write the three place names on the board, placing bullets between syllables as shown in the exercise.
- Explain that the bullets divide each word into syllables, and each word has one syllable that is stressed. Then, play the audio. Ask volunteers to tell you which syllable is stressed in each word.
- Mark the stressed syllables on the board. Point to each item and have the class repeat it using the correct stress pattern.

D 🎧15

- Point to the words on the board from Exercise C. Call attention to the stress marks and ask students to use this kind of mark as they complete the exercise.
- Play the first two items in the audio and have students mark the stress in their books. Have them check each other's work.
- Then, play the entire audio and ask students to put stress marks on all the place names.

E 🎧16

- Play the audio. Ask students to listen and point to each place as they hear it.
- Play the audio a second time if students have difficulty finding each location on the map.

CIVICS

Point out that the names of many states and geographical features are derived from the indigenous languages of Native Americans (and that that is why some of them look so unfamiliar). Point to these places on a map (Hawaii, Massachusetts). Other places used to be part of Mexico and have Spanish names (Colorado, Texas). Yet others were part of French territory and have French names! (Vermont)

C **Pronunciation: Syllables and stress** Listen and repeat. 🎧14

1. the At·lán·tic Ó·cean
2. the Ap·pa·lá·chian Móun·tains
3. the Mis·sis·síp·pi Rí·ver

D Listen and mark the stress. 🎧15

1. Cá·na·da
2. Méx·i·co
3. the U·ní·ted Státes
4. the Róck·y Móun·tains
5. the Gránd Cán·yon
6. Á·las·ka
7. Ha·wái·i
8. the Pa·cí·fic Ó·cean
9. Déath Vál·ley

E Listen and point to each location on the map of the United States. 🎧16

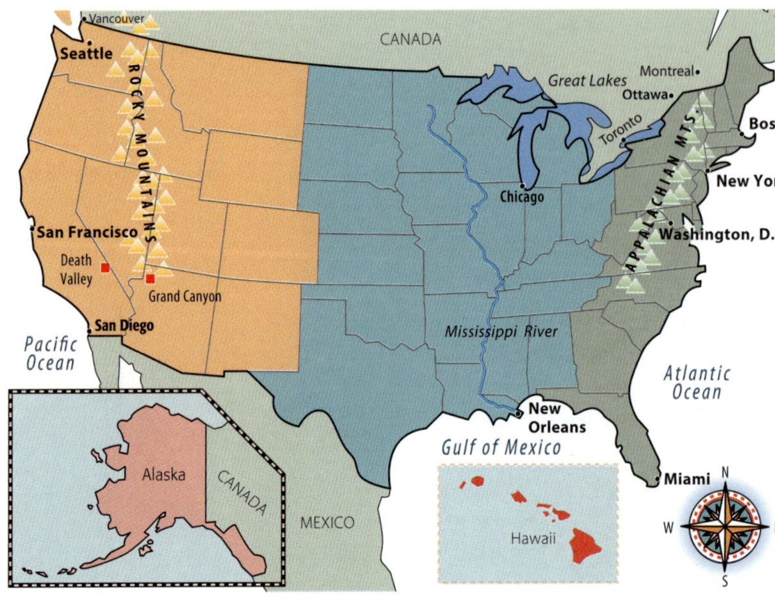

MORE ACTION

Ask students to identify the location of their own state and city or town on the map in Exercise E. Then, ask them for names of places they have visited or lived in. If you have a wall map in your classroom, invite students to come to the map and show others where they have visited or lived.

ACTIVE GRAMMAR Quantifiers with Count Nouns

There	is isn't	**a**	seaport desert	on the coast. in the North. in the South. in the East. in the West. in the central part of the country.
	are	**a few** **several** **many** **a lot of**	seaports mountains rivers forests farms	
	aren't	**any**		

A CIVICS Make sentences about the map on the previous page.

> There are many seaports on the coast.

> There is a high mountain range in the West.

1. countries
2. major cities
3. seaports
4. mountain ranges
5. large lakes
6. farms
7. major river
8. deserts
9. national parks

B **LET'S TALK.** With a partner, plan the perfect island. On the blank map, draw the features you would like, such as mountains, a river, a lake, and farms. Then, describe your island to another group.

> There is a small seaport town in the east. To the north of the seaport is a plain; there are a few farms there.

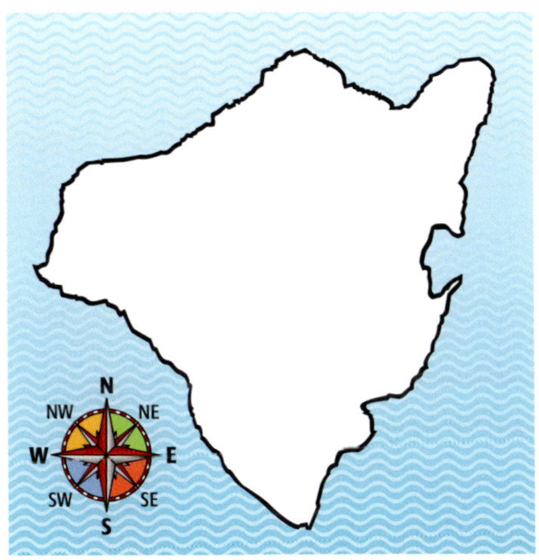

TEACHING TIP

Bring in pictures of islands or geographical features that students can use for inspiration when planning their perfect island.

ACTIVE GRAMMAR: Quantifiers with Count Nouns

A

- Explain to students that a quantifier goes directly before the noun it modifies. Ask students to explain how many of each item the quantifiers in the grammar chart are describing.

  a=one

  a few=three or four

  several=five or more

  many=more than several

  a lot of=same as *many*

  any=one or more

- Have two students read the text in the speech bubbles. Then, have students complete Exercise A independently.
- Invite volunteers to read their answers or write them on the board.
- Ask the other students to decide if the sentences are true and to correct any grammatical mistakes.

B

- Draw an island on the board and ask students to tell you what geographical features to add and where they should go.
- Ask students to work in pairs to complete their maps.
- Have each pair present descriptions of their islands. Ask pairs how their islands differed from other students' maps.

ACTIVE GRAMMAR:
Count and Noncount Nouns

A

- Review the explanation of count and noncount nouns in the grammar chart.
- Ask students for additional examples for each category. For example: Count nouns—river, shoe, website Noncount nouns—clothing, cereal, poverty
- Ask why it is important to know if a noun is count or noncount. (Because you need to know if the verb is singular or plural.)
- Explain the meaning of any unknown words in Exercise A. Remind students that some words can be both count and noncount nouns depending on the context in which they are used, so those words should be written in both columns.
- Have students write the words in the correct columns.
- As you review the answers with the class, ask students to give a simple explanation for each answer. For example:
  S: Industry *is a noncount noun.*
  T: *Why?*
  S: *It's not a single thing. It's a general category.*
  T: *Industry can also be a count noun. We can talk about one industry. Can you think of an industry?*
  S: *The auto industry.*
  T: *What about another industry?*
  S: *The tech industry.*
  T: *Right! The auto industry and the tech industry are two* ***industries*** *that make a lot of money in the US.*

ACTIVE GRAMMAR Count and Noncount Nouns

Count nouns are items that we can count individually (one by one): lake—lakes. They can be singular or plural.
Noncount nouns cannot be counted. They are always singular.
1. Liquids or gases: water, oil, oxygen, rain
2. Items that are too small or too numerous to count: sand, corn, rice
3. General categories: traffic, scenery, music, tourism
4. Ideas: information, beauty, work
Note: Some words can be both count and noncount: crime—crimes, industry—industries.

A ACADEMIC Write the words under the correct column in the chart.

country	mountain	ranch	tourism
crime	museum	river	tourist
factory	noise	seaport	traffic
farm	pollution	skyscraper	unemployment
industry	rain	snow	university

Count Nouns	Noncount Nouns
industry	industry
mountain	pollution
tourist	unemployment
country	crime
crime	noise
factory	rain
farm	snow
museum	tourism
ranch	traffic
river	
seaport	
skyscraper	
university	

WORD PARTNERSHIPS	
air water noise	pollution

MORE ACTION

For further practice with count and noncount nouns, ask students to make sentences using the words in Exercise A. You can make this into a team quiz by having each team come up with five count nouns and five noncount nouns and use them in sentences that are either true or false. For example: Snow *is a count noun.* (Answer: false.) The other teams can guess if the sentences are true or not.

ACTIVE GRAMMAR Quantifiers with Noncount Nouns

There	is	**no** **a little** **a lot of**	traffic pollution rain crime industry	in this city. in my country. in the United States.
	isn't	**any** **much**		

A Complete the sentences. Use *there is, there isn't, there are,* or *there aren't*.

1. ___There are___ a lot of factories in the city, so ___there is___ a lot of pollution.
2. ___There is___ a lot of traffic in the city, so ___there is___ a lot of noise.
3. ___There are___ a lot of large companies in the city, so ___there isn't___ much unemployment.
4. ___There is___ a large seaport near the city, so ___there is___ a lot of traffic in the bay.
5. ___There are___ many museums, restaurants, and shows, so ___there is___ a lot of tourism.
6. ___There are___ many police officers, so ___there isn't___ much crime.

B Talk about the city or town that your school is in.

> There are a few colleges and universities near here.

> There is a lot of tourism in this city.

1. colleges and universities
2. tourism
3. factories
4. crime
5. museums
6. ethnic restaurants
7. traffic
8. nightclubs
9. unemployment
10. fast-food restaurants
11. noise
12. hospitals

MORE ACTION

For further practice with quantifiers, ask students to write a description of your city or state in their journal for homework.

ACTIVE GRAMMAR: Quantifiers with Noncount Nouns

A

- Ask some students to make sentences using the words in the grammar chart.
- Ask the other students to decide if the sentences are grammatically correct.
- Ask students to work on Exercise A independently.
- Review the correct answers with the class. Ask if these sentences are true about your city.

B

- Ask students to work in pairs or groups. Set a time limit and remind students to use quantifiers as they discuss the topics.
- Invite volunteers to report to the class about their discussion and find out if the other students agree.
- After discussing, have students come to the board and list the topics in groups of quantifiers (which items there are a lot of in your city or area, which items there are a few of, which items there aren't any of, and so on).
- Ask volunteers to add items to the lists of quantifiers based on what is true for your city or area. Provide a mix of count and noncount prompts as necessary: stores, museums, concerts, sports teams, bad weather, job opportunities, money.

ACTIVE GRAMMAR: *How many / How much*

A

- Review the grammar chart.
- Ask students to explain when to use *How many* or *How much*. (*How many* is used with count nouns, while *How much* is used with noncount nouns.)
- Then, have students ask you questions about the city or state you come from. Give prompts to help students make questions. For example:
  T: *snow*
  S1: *How much snow is there in your city?*
  T: *parks*
  S2: *How many parks are there in your state?*
- Have students form groups of three or four. If possible, ask them to sit with students from different countries.
- Have students complete the questions from Exercise A with their group and then discuss the topics of the questions. Ask a representative from each group to report to the class on any interesting facts they found out.

B

- Model the first item with a pair of students.
- Ask students to complete the task in pairs.

ACTIVE GRAMMAR *How many / How much*

How many	museums parks	are	there	in your city? in your country?
How much	snow traffic	is		

A **LET'S TALK.** Complete the questions. Use *How much* or *How many*. Then, in small groups, talk about the countries you come from. If possible, each student should be from a different country.

1. What country are you from?
2. How many skyscrapers are there in your country?
3. How much tourism is there in your country?
4. How much traffic is there in your country?
5. How many immigrants are there in your country?
6. How many farms are there in your country?
7. How much snow is there in your country?
8. How many mountain ranges are there in your country?
9. How much crime is there in your country?
10. How many universities are there in your country?

I'm from Japan. There are many skyscrapers in my country.

B **STUDENT TO STUDENT.** Ask and answer questions about Canada and Mexico. Use *How much* and *How many*.

Student 1: Turn to Appendix C. Ask your partner about Canada. Complete the chart.

Student 2: Ask your partner about Mexico. Complete the chart below.

	Mexico	Canada
Tourism	a lot	a lot
Desert regions	two	one
Mountains	many	many
National parks	67	47
Snow	very little	a lot
Ski resorts	one	many
Official languages	one	two

How much tourism is there in Mexico?

There is a lot of tourism in Mexico.

TEACHING TIP

When doing information gap activities like the one in Exercise B, it is helpful to have students sit opposite each other, rather than side by side, as that makes it harder for them to see each other's information.

MORE ACTION

Ask students to name the item or give an example of some of the more well-known categories for each country in Exercise B.

Tourism: Cancun, Quebec

Deserts: Sonora, Okanagan

Mountains: Rockies, Sierra Madre

Languages: French and English, Spanish

ACTIVE GRAMMAR *Too many, too much, not enough*

There	is	**too much** **not enough**	rain. industry.
	are	**too many** **not enough**	fast-food restaurants. parks.

We often use *not enough* and *too many / too much* to talk about problems or to complain.

not enough = less than you want or need

There are**n't enough** farms in that country. There is**n't enough** food.

too many, too much = more than you want or need

There are **too many** cars on the road. There is **too much** traffic.

A Listen to the complaints about world problems. Complete the sentences. Use the words in the box. 17

aren't enough	are too many	isn't enough	is too much

1. There isn't enough rain.
2. There aren't enough jobs.
3. There are too many homeless people.
4. There isn't enough food for everyone.
5. There is too much snow.
6. There is too much traffic.
7. There isn't enough public transportation.
8. There are too many plastic bottles.

B ACADEMIC **LET'S TALK.** In a group, make a list of five things you like and five things you don't like about the area where you live. Answers will vary.

There are a lot of good restaurants.

There is too much crime.

Things we like	Things we don't like
1.	1.
2.	2.
3.	3.
4.	4.
5.	5.

MORE ACTION

For homework, ask students to write a paragraph about the town or state they live in and say what things they like and dislike about it.

ACTIVE GRAMMAR: *Too many, too much, not enough*

A 17

- Review the explanation of *too many, too much,* and *not enough* and read the sentences in the grammar chart.
- Then, give prompts to help students make example sentences.
  For example:
  T: *cars, too*
  S1: *There are too many cars.*
  T: *rain, not enough*
  S2: *There isn't enough rain.*
- Ask students to read the sentences in Exercise A and say what some possible answers could be.
- Play the audio once all the way though.
- Play the audio again and pause after each question so students can fill in their answers.
- Check the answers as a class.

B

- Ask the class what things they like about their town or state and what things they dislike.
- Start a list of these things on the board. Then, ask students to make their own lists in groups. Make sure students write items in complete sentences like the examples in the speech bubbles.
- Have a volunteer from each group read their group's sentences to the class.

THE BIG PICTURE: Montana

A

- Discuss the answers to the three questions with the class.
- Encourage students to ask questions and comment on any other aspects of the map.
- Ask if any students have been to Montana and what they thought about it.

B 18

- Check that students understand the meaning of the words in the word box. Model the pronunciation if needed.
- Play the audio and ask students to listen and point to the features on the map in Exercise A that the audio describes.
- Then, play the audio again and invite students to take notes to help them construct their statements about Montana.
- Ask students to write a mix of general and specific statements about Montana using the words in the box.
- Call on volunteers to take turns reading their statements.

ACADEMIC

As they move through their academic careers, students will be expected to digest various information graphics, including maps. An information graphic requires students to do more than read words to understand it. Encourage them to take time to evaluate both the visuals and the words as they look at these graphics (and/or numbers, if applicable).

THE BIG PICTURE Montana

A CIVICS Discuss the map of Montana.

1. What are Montana's borders? *north - Canada; east - North Dakota and South Dakota; south - Wyoming; west - Idaho*
2. What is the capital? *Helena*
3. What geographical features do you see on this map? *mountains, rivers, lakes, plains, glaciers*

B ACADEMIC Look at the map and listen. As you listen, point to each location on the map. Then, make statements. Use the words in the box. 18

GENERAL AND SPECIFIC STATEMENTS

General statements:
There is a large national park in Montana.
Specific statements:
Glacier National Park is in Montana.
Do not say: There is Glacier National Park in Montana.

Canada	Helena	national park	rain	the Missouri River
Fort Peck Lake	horse ranches	Native American reservations	rivers	the Rocky Mountains
Glacier National Park	lakes	Native Americans	snow	tourism

TEACHING TIP

You may want to use this opportunity to review note-taking skills and give examples of how to take notes from the audio. Students should try to focus on key words and not write full sentences.

C Circle the letter of the correct answer.

1. What is to the north of Montana?
   a. Wyoming   **(b.)** Canada   **c.** Glacier National Park
2. What is the weather like in the western part of Montana?
   (a.) It's cold and wet.   **b.** It's cold and dry.   **c.** It's hot and wet.
3. What is the weather like in the eastern part of Montana?
   a. It's cold and wet.   **(b.)** It's cold and dry.   **c.** It's hot and dry.
4. Why is the eastern part of Montana dry?
   a. Because it is so far north.   **(b.)** Because the mountains stop the clouds.
5. Where are there many horse ranches?
   (a.) in the eastern part of the state   **b.** in the western part of the state
6. What is one of Montana's major industries?
   a. fishing   **(b.)** manufacturing   **c.** tourism

D Complete the sentences. Use the correct form of the verb.

1. The Missouri River (begin) ___begins___ in Montana.
2. The western part of Montana (receive) ___receives___ a lot of snow.
3. Montana (have) ___has___ very cold winters.
4. Thousands of tourists (visit) ___visit___ Montana each year.
5. The Rocky Mountains (stop) ___stop___ the rain clouds.
6. Many Native Americans (live) ___live___ on reservations.
7. Snow (cover) ___covers___ the mountains.

E Listen and write the questions you hear. Then, ask and answer the questions with a partner. 19

1. How many rivers are there in Montana?
2. How many Native American reservations are there?
3. How much snow is there in the Rocky Mountains?
4. How much industry is there in Montana?
5. How much tourism is there?
6. How much traffic is there in Montana?

C

- Have students answer the questions from memory.
- Then, play the audio from Exercise B again so they can check their answers.

D

- Ask students to complete the sentences independently.
- Then, call on volunteers to read their answers.

E 19

- Play the first item of the audio only and go over the answer with the class.
- Then, play the rest of the audio, pausing after each question so students have time to write in their notebooks.
- Have students work in pairs asking and answering the questions. Have each pair present an answer to the class.

CIVICS

Remind students that some knowledge of US geography, including naming bordering countries or giving an example of a river or mountain range, may be included in the citizenship interview.

MORE ACTION

Have students work with a partner to research information about a state that interests them. Then, have them write and ask each other questions about that state. Ask volunteers to present their conversation to the class.

VIDEO AND READING: Informational Text

A

- Have students look at the picture on pages 60 and 61 that go with the reading. Ask: *What do you see in the picture?* (hills, the sky, bare ground) *What do you NOT see?* (plants, water, life)
- Ask them what facts they already know about deserts.
- Discuss the statements, but don't give the answers. Have students answer the statements after reading the passage.

B ▶ WATCH

- Play the video one time with the sound off. Have students take notes on things they see.
- Play it again with the sound on. Then move through the activities in the video worksheet at the back of this book.

C

- Have students complete this exercise after reading the passage and viewing the video.
- Point out that these vocabulary items are the bold words in the passage. If students are still unclear about any definitions after reading the passage, have them work on the exercise with a partner.

DEATH VALLEY

Death Valley National Park is the largest national park in the continental United States. This 3.4-million-acre park in southern California is the lowest, hottest, and driest place in North America. The lowest point is 282 feet (86 meters) below **sea level**. In the summer, the average temperature is often higher than 120° (49° Celsius), and the highest temperature ever recorded there was 134° (56.6° Celsius). There are some summers when Death Valley receives no rain, and the average yearly **precipitation** is less than two inches.

A What do you know about deserts? Circle *True* or *False*.

1.	A desert receives very little rain.	(True)	False
2.	The only plants in the desert are different kinds of cactuses.	True	(False)
3.	Animals cannot live in the desert.	True	(False)
4.	Summer is the best time to visit the desert.	True	(False)

B ▶ WATCH Watch the video. Check your answers in Exercise A.

C Match.

f **1.**	sea level	**a.**	a show or display of art, plants, or animals
c **2.**	precipitation	**b.**	to change or adjust to new conditions
g **3.**	varieties	**c.**	rain or snow
d **4.**	roots	**d.**	the parts of the plant that grow into the earth and brings in water
b **5.**	adapt	**e.**	to stay away from
e **6.**	avoid	**f.**	at the same height as the sea or ocean
a **7.**	exhibit	**g.**	kinds or types

READING NOTE

Supporting Details

When an article makes a statement, it usually gives specific information to support the statement.

The Timbisha Shoshone Tribe of Native Americans has lived in this desert area for hundreds of years.

In 1849, people heard about the discovery of gold in California. Thousands of people began the long trip to the West. This large desert area was so difficult to cross that some travelers looking for gold gave it the name Death Valley.

Today, tourists from all over the United States travel to Death Valley to enjoy its natural beauty. There are over one thousand **varieties** of plants in this desert, including many kinds of cactuses and flowers. Cactuses, with their interesting and unusual shapes, need very little rain. Their **roots** are close to the surface of the ground so they can quickly collect any rainfall. A few days after the first rain in the spring, thousands of wildflowers cover the desert.

There are also many animals that have learned to **adapt** to this hot climate. Most are active at night, sleeping during the day to **avoid** the hot desert sun. Some animals live their entire lives without drinking any water, getting water from the food they eat.

If you are planning a trip to Death Valley, winter is the best time to visit. The main visitor area has nature **exhibits**, a museum, and a bookstore. Be sure to watch the informative videos on desert life. After that, you can explore the desert by car, by bike, or on foot. Park rangers offer programs on desert life, the history of Death Valley, and the desert sky at night. If you are planning a trip to Death Valley, don't forget these four essentials: a sun hat, sun block, a lot of water, and a camera. 20

D ACADEMIC Write a detail from the reading to support each fact.

Statement	Supporting Detail
1. Death Valley is the largest park in the continental United States.	**1.** *It is a 3.4-million-acre park.*
2. It is the lowest place in North America.	**2.** The lowest point is 282 feet below sea level.
3. It is the hottest place in North America.	**3.** The highest temperature ever recorded here was 134°.
4. It is the driest place in North America.	**4.** There are some summers when Death Valley receives no rain. The average yearly precipitation is less than two inches.

E Match the two parts of each sentence.

c **1.** Visitors need to bring sun block

e **2.** Summer is not the best time to visit Death Valley

a **3.** Desert animals are active at night

f **4.** Cactus roots are near the surface

b **5.** This area was named Death Valley

d **6.** After the first spring rain,

a. because it is cooler at this time.

b. because it was very difficult to cross.

c. to protect their skin from the sun.

d. millions of wildflowers cover the desert.

e. because it is very hot.

f. to quickly collect rainwater.

MORE ACTION

Have students quiz each other about the content of the passage by creating questions based on the passage. Students can quiz each other on vocabulary and comprehension. Have students work in pairs.

D

- Read the Reading Note at the bottom of the previous page aloud to the class. Ask students to scan the passage quickly and give an example of a supporting detail. (For example: *In the summer, the average temperature in Death Valley is often higher than 120 degrees.* This detail supports the statement that Death Valley is the hottest place in North America.) Tell students that numbers are a common supporting detail.
- Review the instructions and point out the sample answer.
- Have students complete the exercise individually.
- Then, review the correct answers by having a different student write each supporting detail on the board.

E

- Ask students to complete the exercise independently.
- Then, have students go back to the passage and underline sentences that helped them answer the questions. Tell them to write the appropriate question number next to the part of the passage that answers each question.
- Review the answers as a class.

ACADEMIC

Remind students that the use of supporting details is not just important for reading comprehension; it is also an important feature to include in their own writing, whether they are writing a description or opinion. It is also a skill with cross-curricular value that they should aim to develop in their reading and writing endeavors in other subject areas.

WRITING OUR STORIES: My State

A

- Ask students to look at the photo. Ask them what they see and ask them what else they know about California. Students may mention beaches, the Pacific Ocean, bordering states (or countries), cities, and other geographical features they know.
- Read the caption, emphasizing the proper pronunciation of *La Jolla* (/lə 'hoiə/).
- Then, read the report to the class or have students read it on their own.
- Ask some simple comprehension questions, such as: *Are there any beaches in California?* (Yes, there are hundreds of miles of beaches in California.) *Where are the deserts?* (They're in the southeast.)
- Ask students to identify the topic of each paragraph. (1. Location, capital, and population 2. Geography 3. Cities 4. Weather 5. Industries)

ACADEMIC

The order of the topics in the reading in A is the same as the order of the topics in the chart in B. Encourage students to look to the reading on California as a model and really follow the steps in B to develop their process writing skills. This will help them produce a more organized, thorough, and focused piece. if they follow through with an editing step as in C, their writing will also have fewer errors. Feel free to encourage a peer edit, as a new set of eyes can often be helpful.

WRITING OUR STORIES | My State

A CIVICS Read the student report about California.

A beach in La Jolla, California.

California is on the west coast of the United States and it's the third-largest state. It has borders with Oregon to the north, Nevada and Arizona to the east, Mexico to the south, and the Pacific Ocean to the west. Sacramento is its capital. The population is about forty million.

California is a beautiful state. Its coast has hundreds of miles of beautiful beaches. There are two mountain ranges in California, the Sierra Nevada in the east and the Coast Ranges along the Pacific. There are several deserts in the southeast.

Two of the major cities are San Francisco and Los Angeles. San Francisco is on the hills over San Francisco Bay. Tourists visit Chinatown and ride up and down the hills on the cable cars. Los Angeles is in southern California. It is the home of Hollywood and the movie industry.

For most of the year, the weather along the coast is sunny and mild. In the winter, there is snow in the mountains. In the south, the weather is hot and dry.

Agriculture and tourism are two of the major industries. California grows more than half of the nation's fruits and vegetables. Also, many Californians work in the tourist industry in the cities, parks, and resorts.

TEACHING TIP

Discuss with students some possible resources for finding information for their report. If possible, accompany them to the library to locate books or websites that will help them. You might also help them to identify keywords that will help them when searching online.

B **ACADEMIC** Write a report.

1. Choose a state in the United States. Each student should choose a different state.
2. Draw a map of the state. Show the borders, the capital, and major geographical features.
3. Complete the chart below. Look up information online.
4. Write a short report. You will use this information later for a class presentation.

State	
Location	
Borders	
Capital	
Population	
Geography	
Two major cities	
Weather	
Industries	

WRITING NOTE

Capital Letters

Use capital letters for the names of specific locations and geographical features:

Country names: the **U**nited **S**tates, **M**exico

State names: **A**laska, **N**ew **Y**ork

City names: **C**hicago, **S**an **D**iego

Bodies of water: the **P**acific **O**cean

Mountain ranges: the **R**ocky **M**ountains

Parks: **G**rand **C**anyon **N**ational **P**ark

Tourist attractions: the **S**tatue of **L**iberty

C Edit the paragraph.

Florida is the most popular tourist destination in the united states. During the winter, visitors enjoy a break from the cold and snow. Florida offers hundreds of miles of beaches along the atlantic ocean and the gulf of mexico. Families enjoy tourist attractions, such as disney world, universal studios, and sea world. Cities in Florida, such as miami, tampa, and fort lauderdale, offer great restaurants and exciting night life. Florida's most popular park is everglades national park, where visitors can birdwatch, fish or take boat tours, and see alligators and crocodiles.

B

- Read through the instructions with the class.
- Then, have students choose a state. Make a list of the states students have chosen so that each student has a different state.
- Have students look at the chart. Tell them that their report should focus on those topics. If you have time, take students to the library to conduct research.
- Remind students that they will present their reports and will need to draw a large map of their state. Have them read the steps listed in the English in Action section for this unit (next page) so they can start planning for their presentation.

C

- Read the locations in the Writing Note and ask which words are not capitalized (articles and prepositions). Explain that it is important to capitalize place names because they are proper nouns that are different from regular nouns. Capitalizing locations is a way of making them stand out from the rest of the text.
- Set a time limit for students to find and correct the mistakes. You may want to introduce an element of competition by asking who can find the most mistakes.
- Invite volunteers to come to the board and each write a sentence from the paragraph with their corrections.

MORE ACTION

Another way to practice capitalization of names is to use the text in Exercise A on the previous page as a dictation. After writing the sentences, students can check their work against the book and correct their capitalization at the same time. Alternatively, you can dictate sentences about places in your town or city and then correct students' capitalization.

ENGLISH IN ACTION: Giving a Class Presentation

A

- Explain that the purpose of this exercise is to practice giving a class presentation.
- Read the steps aloud to the class.
- Explain that students will need notes for their presentation. They will not read from their reports directly. They will have to look at the audience and speak directly to them when giving their presentation.
- Have students prepare their notes and practice their presentations in pairs or in small groups.
- Move around the room and provide support and encouragement.

B 21

- Play the audio and discuss the content of the presentation.
- Use the discussion questions to highlight the skills of giving a good presentation that you discussed earlier.

C

- Invite students to come to the front of the class to give their presentation.
- While listening to each student, the other students should fill out the information in the chart.
- Encourage students to ask questions, especially if there is anything that they did not hear or understand.
- You may want to make audio or video recordings of the presentations for giving feedback later.

ENGLISH IN ACTION Giving a Class Presentation

A ACADEMIC Read the steps for giving a successful class presentation about the state you researched.

1. Prepare your materials: large map, notes, two or three photos from the internet.
2. Practice your presentation.
3. Stand in front of the class and look at your classmates.
4. Use your notes, but do not read directly from them.
5. Speak loudly, clearly, and slowly.
6. Show the map to the class. Tell your classmates the name of the state and explain the location.
7. Point to the capital. Spell the capital. Tell the class the population of the state.
8. Point to two places of interest on the map. Tell the class one or two things that people can enjoy at each location as you show the class your photos.

B Listen to one student's report. Discuss the questions. 21 *Answers will vary.*

1. How did this student prepare?
2. How large was the map? Could the students see the words on the map?
3. How many times did the student repeat the population?
4. What two places of interest did the student talk about?
5. How long was the presentation?
6. How do you feel when you stand in front of a group?
7. How can you best prepare to talk in front of the class?

C AT WORK Give a classroom presentation about the state you researched. As you listen to your classmates' presentations, take notes about each state. *Answers will vary.*

State: ______________________________

Capital: ______________________________

Population: ______________________________

An interesting fact: ______________________________

I researched Ohio. Ohio has a population of…

Here's the capital of…

AT WORK

Discuss with your class why giving and listening to presentations are much more than just using language skills. Good presentation skills are important for conveying information clearly and engaging the audience—and making your point. These skills include being confident, speaking clearly and slowly, looking at the audience, and using visual aids. Students may use these skills even if they are not giving a formal presentation to be more effective communicators. You may want to prepare a list of criteria for giving a good presentation with your class or design a poster with guidelines for how to give a good presentation. Good listening and note taking skills are important for following along in meetings at work, and keeping track of information for later use.

UNIT 5 TECHNOLOGY

A photographer uses a camera with flash bulbs to take a photo in the 1930s.

ACADEMIC Give and follow directions; identify the topic of a paragraph; identify key details in a text

AT WORK Understand the impact of technology on a business

CIVICS Discuss how technology has changed everyday life; read and understand signs

CCRS Level A: R 1, 2, 3, 5; W 2, 6; L 1; Level B: R 1, 2, 6; W 3, 4; L 1, 2, 3; Level C: R 1, 2; W 4, 6, 9 ; L 1, 2, 3; Level D: R 1, 2; W 4, 6, 9; L 1, 2, 3; Level E: R 1, 2; W 4, 6, 9; L 2

ELPS Level 1 Standards 2, 3, 9, 10; Level 2 Standards 1, 2, 3, 7, 10; Level 3 Standards 1, 2, 3, 7, 10; Level 4 Standards 1, 2, 3, 7, 10; Level 5 Standards 1, 2, 3, 7, 10

CIVICS 12-2; 36-7; 47-1; 47-2; 47-4; 47-7; 48-1; 48-3; 48-9; 50-13

CASAS 0.1.2; 0.1.5; 0.2.1; 0.2.4; 7.4.4; 7.7.1; 7.7.2; 7.7.3; 7.7.4; 7.7.5; 7.7.6

IN THIS UNIT

In Unit 5, students will:

- Discuss technology and its effect on our lives
- Practice the present continuous
- Give clear directions on how to use technology

ABOUT THE PHOTO

Technology is always changing. This photo shows an early predecessor of the camera feature we all now take for granted built into our phones. The lightbulbs (flash bulbs) in this photo were a huge advancement at the time, as prior to 1929, flash powder, a highly flammable substance, was used to create artificial light. This unstable substance actually resulted in the deaths of photographers preparing the flash.

Ask students about their technology usage and their knowledge of older devices, previewing *Who* subject/object questions. Ask: *Who takes pictures with their phone? Who takes pictures with a camera? Who has a landline at their house? Who only has a cellphone/smartphone? Who prints pictures? Who keeps digital copies? Who likes to talk on the phone? Who prefers to send text messages? Who do you talk to? Who do you send messages to?*

Ask students what else they do with their phone, drawing comparisons between the smartphone and older analog devices. Possible subjects for discussion: calendars and appointments; access to music and video; access to the news; dictionaries and support with English. You may also choose to ask them about generational differences with technology use if they are enjoying the discussion.

A

- Have students label the pictures in their books.
- Ask volunteers to read their answers aloud. Correct pronunciation as necessary.
- Ask students to explain what each of these items is used for. Prompt them to match items to functions. *Which things can you play music on?* (smartphone, tablet) *Which ones can help you improve your health?* (fitness tracker) *Which do people use at work?* (laptop, smartphone) *Which can you use to play games?* (game console, virtual reality headset)
- Ask students what other electronic devices they own and what those items are used for. Write the names of the items on the board for students to copy in their notebooks.

B

- Answer any questions students have about vocabulary.
- Ask students to complete the sentences individually and then work in pairs to compare their answers.
- Ask volunteers to share their answers for sentences 4-9 with the class. Then, invite students to ask each other questions about what kind of technology they use regularly.

A Label the electronic equipment.

fitness tracker	laptop	tablet
game console	smartphone	virtual reality headset

1. smartphone

2. tablet

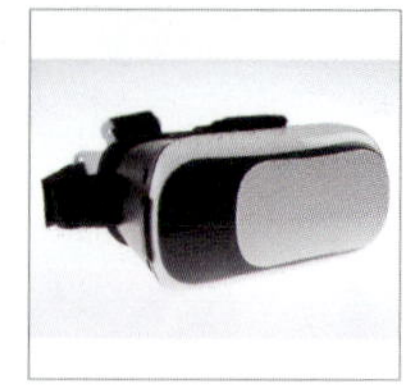

3. virtual reality headset

4. fitness tracker

5. laptop

6. game console

B Complete the sentences. Then, discuss your answers. **Answers will vary.**

1. I **have / don't have** a laptop.
2. I **have / don't have** internet access at home.
3. The school **has / doesn't have** a computer lab for students.
4. I spend about ______ hours a day on social media.
5. I have the following electronic device(s): ______________________________
____
6. I'd like to buy the following electronic device(s): ______________________
7. I can use the following software: ______________________________
8. My favorite social media site is ______________________________
9. My favorite app is ______________________________

TEACHING TIP

As you discuss this topic with the class, write any new vocabulary that comes up on the board (for example, *game console* and *memory card*). At the end of the class, ask students to copy the list into their vocabulary notebooks. Review the words at the beginning of the next class.

CULTURE NOTE

It may be helpful to remind students to be responsible with their use of social media. Let them know that their digital footprint can leave a lasting impression. For example, employers may check this information when evaluating candidates. Encourage students to use privacy settings to protect personal information and discourage posting photos or comments they would be embarrassed to share in class.

66 Unit 5

ACTIVE GRAMMAR Present Continuous

I	**am**	(not)	send**ing** an email.
You	**are**		order**ing** a pizza.
He She	**is**		mak**ing** reservations.
It	**is**		work**ing**.
We They	**are**		play**ing** a video game.

1. The present continuous talks about an action that is happening now.
   He **is using** his computer.
2. The present continuous talks about an action that is temporary.
   He **is living** with his brother.
   (He expects to move soon.)

A Complete the sentences. Use the present continuous form of the verb.

1. Li-Ping (write) _is writing_ to her brother. She (email / not) _is not emailing_ him. She (text) _is texting_ him.
2. Raul (take) _is taking_ a virtual tour of an art museum. He (look) _is looking_ at paintings by Picasso and Dalí.
3. Mr. and Mrs. Chan (visit) _are visiting_ their friends in the city. They (stay / not) _are not staying_ in a hotel. They (stay) _are staying_ with their friends.
4. Lauren (learn) _is learning_ a new software program. She (take / not) _is not taking_ the course at her company. She (attend) _is attending_ a local college.

B CIVICS Read each sign. Imagine that a person is breaking the rules. What is he or she doing?
Answers will vary.

1. 

He is taking a photo.

2. 

She is talking on a cellphone.

3. 

He is walking on the grass.

4. 

She is throwing something away.

5. 

He is smoking.

6. 

She is eating in the computer lab.

7. 

He is playing loud music.

8. 

She is littering.

That man isn't paying attention to the sign. He is taking a photo.

MORE ACTION

For further practice with the present continuous, prepare a set of sentences that describe actions. Write the sentences on note cards or strips of paper. Invite volunteers to take a sentence and mime the activity for the class (play charades). The other students will try to guess what he or she is doing. For example:

You are watching TV.

You are eating a pizza.

You are reading a newspaper.

ACTIVE GRAMMAR: Present Continuous

A

- Call on individual students to make affirmative and negative sentences using the words in the grammar chart.
- Read the grammar note aloud and give examples of each type of use of the present continuous, asking students to identify the meaning. For example: *He's watching TV.* (happening right now) *He's learning Italian.* (temporary action)
- Have students complete Exercise A individually.
- Ask students to read their sentences aloud. Review the answers as a class.
- Then, ask students to identify which sentences describe something that is happening now and which describe something temporary.

B

- Point to the first sign and read the speech bubble aloud.
- Have students work in pairs to complete the exercise.
- Ask pairs to read their answers. Encourage pairs with different answers to read their descriptions also.

CIVICS

Ask students where they would expect to see these signs. Sample answers:

No photos: a museum
No cell phones: a library
Keep off the grass: a private home
Please recycle: a park
No smoking: hospitals, airports
No food or drink: computer lab (given), a museum
No loud music: an apartment building
Please don't litter: a city street, a highway

ACTIVE GRAMMAR:
Present Continuous:
Yes / No Questions

A

- Review the information in the grammar charts.
- Ask: *What type of word comes first in each question?* (the verb *be*) *What comes second?* (the subject) *How do you know which form of the verb* be *to use?* (It has to agree with the subject.)
- Have students ask and answer *yes / no* questions about their classmates by giving prompts. For example:
  T: *Talk on her cellphone / Maria*
  S1: *Is Maria talking on her cellphone?*
  S2: *No, she isn't.*
- Call on two students to read the speech bubbles for Exercise A.
- Then, have students ask and answer the questions with a partner.

B 22

- Explain that students will write questions based on what they hear happening in the audio.
- Play the audio for the first item and read the sample answer aloud.
- Then, play the rest of the audio, pausing after each question to allow time for students to write their answers.
- Review the answers as a class.

ACTIVE GRAMMAR Present Continuous: *Yes / No* Questions

Am	I	tak**ing** a photo?
Are	you	send**ing** an email?
Is	he	read**ing** a book?
Is	she	listen**ing** to music?
Is	it	work**ing**?
Are	we	study**ing**?
Are	they	mak**ing** reservations?

Yes, you **are**.	No, you **aren't**.	No, you're not.
Yes, I **am**.	No, I'm **not**.	
Yes, he **is**.	No, he **isn't**.	No he's not.
Yes, she **is**.	No, she **isn't**.	No, she's not.
Yes, it **is**.	No, it **isn't**.	No, it's not.
Yes, we **are**.	No, we **aren't**.	No, we're not.
Yes, they **are**.	No, they **aren't**.	No, they're not.

A Ask and answer the questions with a partner.

Are we sitting in the classroom?

Yes, we are.

1. we / sit in the classroom?
   Are we sitting in the classroom?
2. you / speak your native language?
   Are you speaking your native language?
3. we / speak English?
   Are we speaking English?
4. teacher / take a break?
   Is the teacher taking a break?
5. you / look out the window?
   Are you looking out the window?
6. it / rain?
   Is it raining?
7. students / take a test?
   Are the students taking a test?
8. we / look at our books?
   Are we looking at our books?
9. we / sit in the back of the classroom?
   Are we sitting in the back of the classroom?
10. you / drink water?
    Are you drinking water?

B Listen to each speaker. Ask questions and guess what he or she is doing. Then, listen again and compare your questions with a partner's. 22 *Answers may vary.*

1. Is he taking a photo?
2. *Is he / she using his / her GPS?*
3. *Is he / she listening to the weather forecast?*
4. *Is she making hotel reservations?*
5. *Is she ordering Chinese food?*
6. *Is he leaving a message?*
7. *Is she renting a car?*

MORE ACTION

Bring in pictures from newspapers or magazines that show people in different situations (for example, advertisements or pictures from an article). Have students work in pairs, taking turns asking and answering questions about each picture.

TEACHING TIP

If you notice students making spelling errors, briefly review spelling rules for the continuous form, including dropping the final *-e* (*tak**e*** → *tak**ing***) and doubling consonants following a short vowel (*stop* → *sto**pp**ing*).

ACTIVE GRAMMAR Present Continuous: *Wh-* Questions

What	**am**	I	do**ing**?
Which movie	**are**	you	order**ing**?
How	**is**	it	work**ing**?
Where	**are**	they	go**ing**?

You're check**ing** prices.
I'm order**ing** *Space Age*.
It's work**ing** well.
They are go**ing** to the lab.

The present continuous can be used to talk about specific future plans.

I'**m leaving** at 2:00.

A Complete the questions. Answers may vary.

Conversation 1

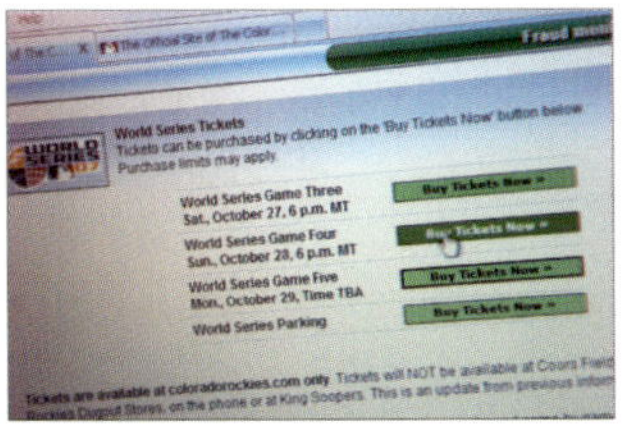

A: What website $\underset{1}{\text{is}}$ he $\underset{2}{\text{looking at}}$?

B: He's looking at a sports ticket website.

A: What $\underset{3}{\text{is}}$ he $\underset{4}{\text{doing}}$?

B: He's buying a ticket to the World Series.

A: When $\underset{5}{\text{is}}$ he $\underset{6}{\text{going}}$?

B: He's going on October 28th.

Conversation 2

A: What $\underset{1}{\text{is she doing}}$?

B: She's shopping for shoes.

A: What site $\underset{2}{\text{is she using}}$?

B: She's using Online Shop.

A: What kind of shoes $\underset{3}{\text{is she looking for}}$?

B: She's looking for shoes for work.

A: How many pairs $\underset{4}{\text{is she buying}}$?

B: She's buying two pairs of shoes.

B Listen to the conversation. Then, practice it with a partner. 23

A: What are you doing?
B: I'm writing a report.
A: What software are you using?
B: I'm using Write Now.
A: How's it coming?
B: Very slowly. And it's due tomorrow.

TEACHING TIP

Another way of using the audio in Exercise B is to use it as a dictation. Or, you can divide the class into two groups, with each side repeating either the A or B lines of the conversation. Then, ask students to try to repeat the conversation in pairs from memory.

ACTIVE GRAMMAR: Present Continuous: *Wh-* Questions

A

- Ask students to read some of the questions and answers from the grammar charts aloud.
- Ask: *What type of word comes first in each question?* (the question word) *What comes second?* (the verb *be*) *What comes third?* (the subject) *What comes last?* (the rest of the verb) *How do you know which form of the verb* be *to use?* (It has to agree with the subject.)
- Read the grammar note and give example sentences contrasting the present continuous and the future. Ask students to identify the difference in meaning for each. For example:
  I'm going now.
  (This is happening now.)
  I'm going tomorrow.
  (This is going to happen in the future.)
- Have students complete Exercise A individually.
- Then, invite volunteers to read lines from the conversations aloud for the class. Review the answers as a class.

B 23

- Play the audio. Pause after each line so that students can repeat.
- Ask students to say which words are stressed in each sentence.
- Have students practice the conversation with a partner.

C 🎧 24

- Explain that *wh-* questions have a rising, then falling, intonation.
- Point out the intonation lines for sentences 1 and 2. Model the first two questions, drawing a line on the board to represent your intonation as you do so. Explain that the upward spike in the line comes from the stressed word in the question.
- Play the audio and pause after each question. Have the class repeat in unison.
- Have students practice pronouncing the questions with a partner.

D

- Have students ask a few questions about the picture. Remind them to use the question words from the chart on the previous page.
- Have students work individually to write their questions.
- Then, have students work in groups to ask and answer each other's questions.

C Pronunciation: *Wh-* questions Listen and repeat. 🎧 24

1. Where is he going?
2. Who are you texting?
3. What is she studying?
4. Who is she calling?
5. What are you listening to?
6. Which game is she playing?
7. What are you ordering?
8. Which site are you using?

Wh- questions have a rising / falling intonation.

D LET'S TALK. In your notebook, write ten questions about the people in the picture. Then, in a group, ask and answer the questions. **Answers will vary.**

What is Ahmed printing?

MORE ACTION

For further practice with *wh-* questions, have students work in pairs to write one question about the picture in Exercise D. Ask students to write their sentence on a piece of paper and give it to the next pair of students. Each pair will ask and answer the question in their notebooks before passing it along to the next pair.

70 Unit 5

ACTIVE GRAMMAR Present Continuous: *Who* Questions

When *Who* is the subject of a sentence, it is always singular.	
Who is buying a computer?	Laura **is**.
Who is fixing the computer?	Henry and Ivan **are**.
When *Who* is the object of a sentence, it can be singular or plural.	
Who is Max calling?	He **is** calling his sister.
Who are Ali and Kim talking to?	They **are** talking to their friends.

A Answer the questions. Use your imagination. **Answers will vary.**

1. Who is taking a photo? Mark is.
2. Who is he taking a photo of? His daughter

3. Who is writing an email? Jessica is.
4. Who is she writing to? Her professor

5. Who is driving? Paul is.
6. Who is taking a trip? Margo and Paul are.

B **LET'S TALK.** Two or three students will act out each situation for the class. Ask two *Who* questions about each situation.

1. Student 1 is giving a book to Student 2.
2. Student 1 is taking a photo of two students.
3. Student 1 is helping Student 2 with homework.
4. Student 1 is inviting Student 2 to a party.
5. Student 1 is texting Student 2.
6. Three students are talking to the teacher.

Who is Lynn giving a book to?

Who is giving a book to Martha?

ACTIVE GRAMMAR: Present Continuous: *Who* Questions

A

- Read the questions in the grammar chart out loud.
- Ask students to make additional examples of each type of *who* question. Give prompts with different verbs. For example:
  T: *Who / Sarah / write to*
  S1: *Who is Sarah writing to?* (object)
  T: *Who / talking on the phone*
  S2: *Who is talking on the phone?* (subject)
- Ask students to look at the photos in Exercise A and describe what is happening in each.
- Then, ask students to complete the exercise. Check the answers as a class.

B

- Point out the photo and ask students what is happening in the picture.
- Read the two speech bubbles aloud and explain that students need to write two types of *who* questions about each situation—one using *who* as the subject, and one using *who* as the object.
- Have students work in pairs to write the questions and then act out the situations.

ACTIVE GRAMMAR: Nonaction Verbs

A

- Explain that nonaction verbs (intransitive verbs) describe feelings, senses, beliefs, and possession. (They do not usually describe actions.) Write these four categories on the board and ask students to identify the verbs in the box with each category. (Feelings: *feel, hate, like, love, prefer*; Senses: *forget, hear, know, look, need, remember, see, seem, smell, sound, taste, understand*; Beliefs: *agree, believe, think;* Possession: *belong, cost, have, own*)
- Read the second grammar chart, which contains exceptions to the rule about not using nonaction verbs in the present continuous. Give additional examples as necessary.
- Have students complete Exercise A individually. Then, have students exchange books to check each other's answers.
- Review the answers as a class. Write any common errors on the board (without calling out the students who made the errors) and review any pertinent parts of the grammar rules as necessary.

ACTIVE GRAMMAR Nonaction Verbs

Some verbs in English do not usually take the present continuous. They are called **nonaction verbs**. These verbs often refer to the senses, to feelings, or to beliefs, or they show possession.

agree	hate	love	seem
believe	have	need	smell
belong	hear	own	sound
cost	know	prefer	taste
feel	like	remember	think
forget	look	see	understand

Some verbs can show both action and nonaction.

I have a computer.	**I'm having** a good time.
	She's having a party.
I think he's a good teacher.	**I'm thinking** about my boyfriend.

More information in Appendix A.

A Complete the sentences. Use the present or the present continuous form of the verb in parentheses.

1. Which weather app (prefer) ___do___ you ___prefer___?
2. I (remember / not) ___don't remember___ my password for this site.
3. I (try) ___am trying___ to find a good recipe for banana bread. This one (sound) ___sounds___ good.
4. They (save) ___are saving___ money to buy a computer. Their children (need) ___need___ one for school.
5. Hannah (sit) ___is sitting___ at her computer. She (look) ___looks___ confused. She (know / not) ___doesn't know___ how to use this software.
6. My sister (belong) ___belongs___ to her high school basketball team.
7. We (think / not) ___don't think___ that our car gets good gas mileage. We (look / not) ___are not looking___ at SUVs or vans. We (think) ___are thinking___ about buying a hybrid.
8. Our neighbor (have) ___is having___ a party next week. (you / have) ___Do you have___ an invitation?
9. I (listen / not) ___am not listening___ to music. I (listen) ___am listening___ to a podcast.
10. That tablet (cost) ___costs___ too much!

72 Unit 5

MORE ACTION

Write a mix of correct and incorrect sentences with nonaction verbs on the board and have students decide if each sentence uses the verb correctly. If a sentence is incorrect, have students fix the sentence. For example:

I'm owning a car. (incorrect)

I own a car. (correct)

ACTIVE GRAMMAR Simple Present and Present Continuous

Time Expressions with Present Continuous	Time Expressions with Simple Present
now today at this moment at this time	once a day every day every morning all the time

Adverbs of Frequency
always usually sometimes never

A Circle the correct time expression.

1. Linda is checking her email **now** / **in the morning**.
2. She receives about twenty emails **right now** / **every day**.
3. Shanta is listening to a podcast **now** / **every day**. She listens to the podcast **now** / **every morning**.
4. The students are putting their cellphones in their backpacks **right now** / **all the time**.
5. Sarah just finished her report for science. She is using spell check **right now** / **in the evening**.
6. Stanley is taking a break **at this moment** / **twice a day**. He's playing a card game.
7. My wi-fi isn't working very well **every day** / **right now**.

B **LET'S TALK.** In a group, write three sentences about what you are doing in class now. Then, write three sentences on a separate sheet of paper about what you do in class every day.

C Ask and answer the questions with a partner.

1. Do you have a computer?
2. Are you using a computer now?
3. Do you have a phone with you?
4. Are you talking on your phone?
5. Are you carrying a wallet?
6. Do you have a credit card?
7. Are you working with a partner?
8. Do you often work with a partner?
9. Are you writing now?
10. Are you talking with the teacher?

Yes, I am. No, I'm not.	Yes, I do. No, I don't.

ACTIVE GRAMMAR: Simple Present and Present Continuous

A

- Check that students understand the meaning of the time expressions and adverbs in the charts at the top of the page.
- If necessary, explain the meaning of the time expressions by giving examples for each. For example: *Mario exercises once a day. He exercises at 10:00* a.m. *each day.*
- Ask students to complete Exercise A individually.
- Check the answers as a class.

B

- Give one example sentence for each category. Then, set a time limit for students to write their sentences.
- Invite volunteers to write their sentences on the board.
- Ask the other students to correct the sentences as necessary.

C

- Ask a volunteer to read the first question aloud.
- Answer using one of the four choices in the boxes.
- Have students complete the exercise with a partner. Explain that students should answer using the phrases in the boxes.

MORE ACTION

For homework, ask students to bring in a photograph of a person from a magazine. Have them write an imaginary description of what this person does every day and what he / she is doing right now (or at the moment the photo was taken). Remind students to use the present continuous. Then, have students share their pictures and sentences with the class.

THE BIG PICTURE: Technology

A

- Before students begin the exercise, ask volunteers to list the activities in the photos (going to the movies, taking a taxi, shopping, travel).
- Have students work in pairs to discuss how these activities are changing. Encourage them to take notes so they will be prepared to share with the class. Some ideas: technology provides more immersive experiences at the movies (like 3D experiences); technology can summon a ride on-demand; technology allows us to shop without leaving our homes; technology allows us to easily compare flight itineraries and prices.
- Have each pair share an idea or two.

B 25

Ask students to cover Exercise C. Play the audio one time.

C

- Have students read the exercise and answer the items that they can.
- Then, play the audio again so students can check their answers and answer any items they missed.

AT WORK

In addition to forcing some businesses to change their business model, for better or for worse, technology is also instigating changes in company culture. Companies have unique rules around cellphone use and use of company computer equipment, as well as social media policies of varying degrees of stringency. These vary widely from company to company. Most include policies against posting company secrets on social media; some may include social media bans on company equipment. Encourage students to familiarize themselves with the policies in place at their place of work to be sure they are compliant.

THE BIG PICTURE | Technology

A Technology is changing the way that people live and do business. Look at each photo. How do you think that the internet is changing each industry?

B **AT WORK** Listen to the ways that technology is changing businesses. 25

C Circle *True* or *False*.

1. Technology is hurting some businesses. **(True)** False
2. Most people make their airline reservations with a travel agent. True **(False)**
3. There aren't many video rental stores. **(True)** False
4. Many people watch movies at home. **(True)** False
5. People are using apps to request rides. **(True)** False
6. Taxi companies are hiring many new drivers. True **(False)**
7. Online shopping is becoming more popular. **(True)** False
8. It is difficult to compare prices online. True **(False)**

D CIVICS Explain how technology has changed the way people live. **Answers will vary.**

1. People called a travel agent to make airline reservations.
   People are making airline reservations online.
2. People rented videos at a video store.
3. People called taxis for a ride.
4. People bought books in bookstores.
5. People looked at maps for directions.
6. People read print newspapers.

E Complete the questions in the present continuous.

1. What *are you looking for*?
   I'm looking for a new vacuum cleaner.
2. Which site **are you using**?
   I'm using a home improvement website.
3. Which movie **is he ordering**?
   He's ordering the new superhero movie.
4. Who **is picking you up**?
   A taxi is picking me up.
5. How **is she getting** to the airport?
   She's getting to the airport by taxi.
6. Why **is the store closing**?
   The store is closing because too many people are shopping online.

F **LET'S TALK.** In small groups, talk about the apps you use.

1. How do you listen to music?
2. What are your favorite shopping sites?
3. When you need transportation, which app do you use?
4. Which app do you use to communicate with your friends?
5. Where do you watch movies online?
6. Which travel apps do you use?
7. What is your favorite app? Tell your group how it works.

D

- Give students a few moments to write their answers individually before comparing answers with a partner.
- Call the class together to share suggested answers, which may include:
  1. People stream/download movies online.
  2. People use apps like Uber and Lyft to request a ride.
  3. People buy books online, or download them as ebooks.
  4. People use their phones to get directions/use a GPS.
  5. People get their news online.

E

- Have pairs work together to write the questions. Then, call on pairs to read the questions and answers out loud.
- Listen for common mistakes and review any rules as necessary.

F

- Put students in groups of four or five to discuss the questions.
- Encourage them to take notes as they discuss, so they have something to refer to when they share with the class.
- Review the questions as a class. Try to call on at least two people from each group.

CIVICS

The internet is also changing the way people interact with many key institutions. In fact, it is often the expectation that the consumer will consult online resources before presenting themselves in person at any office. Examples include the DMV/RMV, where renewals can be filed online and paperwork for applications can be filled out in advance, and even urgent care medical offices, where tentative short-notice appointments can be booked and billing information can be submitted. Both of these cases result in better efficiency for the offices in question and shorter wait times (hopefully) for the consumer.

READING: Informational Text

A 26 (facing page)

- Discuss the questions with the class.
- Ask students what things they do on the computer and their phones. Make a list of activities on the board.
- Ask students what kinds of problems they think people might have because of technology addiction.
- Now, have students read the passage. Set a time limit for students to read the passage. After students finish reading, ask them to describe the topic of each paragraph, previewing Exercise C. (1: introduction to computer addiction; 2: characteristics of a computer addict; 3: how to defeat computer addiction)
- Encourage students to discuss the reading. Did they read anything that surprised them?
- You may choose to play the audio recording of this reading.

READING Informational Text

Technology Addiction

"Larry used to be an excellent student. Now, he's falling asleep in class. He's not completing his class work… He's always on the computer playing video games. Even at one and two o'clock in the morning, I can hear him playing video games in his room." —A mother's report

1. An addiction is an activity or a habit that people cannot control and that is harmful to them. Psychologists are talking about a new kind of addiction—technology addiction. People with a technology addiction can't stop using their electronic devices—checking email and social media, playing video games, chatting, browsing the internet.

2. Do you know any technology addicts? Hours, or even days, pass, and they are still sitting at the computer or looking at their devices. They get upset when someone interrupts them. They feel nervous or depressed when they aren't on the computer, playing a video game, or using the internet. When they finally use their electronic devices again, they feel relieved. They neglect their family and friends.

3. If you think you are becoming addicted to technology, there are steps that you can take to limit your time using electronic devices.

- Set an alarm for one or two hours. When the alarm goes off, do an offline activity, like reading a book or exercising.
- Choose a time to disconnect from your electronic devices at night. For example, turn off your computer at 11:00 every night.
- Do other activities that you enjoy. Go out to lunch with friends, take a class, or exercise.
- If these ideas don't help, you might need professional help. 26

Technology is now always at our fingertips.

76 Unit 5

TEACHING TIP

An alternative way to approach the reading is to assign each paragraph to a group of students and ask them to summarize the paragraph for the class.

MORE ACTION

Ask students about other obsessive technology behaviors, for example, taking selfies or updating social media. How do they interfere with people's lives? What is the danger in engaging in these activities too frequently? Do students ever find themselves distracted from their schoolwork by technology? As a class, make a chart with alternative ways for people to spend their time.

A Discuss these questions.

1. How many hours a day do you spend on the computer?
2. What are some examples of addictions?

B Circle the letter of each correct answer.

1. Eating too much ______ is **harmful** to your health.
   a. fruit — (b.) junk food
2. You **interrupt** someone who is reading when you ______.
   a. walk by quietly — (b.) start to talk to him or her
3. You feel **relieved** when your teacher tells you that ______.
   (a.) you passed the test — b. you failed the test
4. If you **neglect** your health, you ______.
   (a.) will get sick — b. will feel better
5. If you **limit** the time you watch TV, you watch ______.
   a. more TV — (b.) less TV

C ACADEMIC Write the number of the correct paragraph next to the topic of the paragraph.

__2__ The signs of technology addiction
__3__ Ways to control technology addiction
__1__ The definition of technology addiction

READING NOTE

Identifying the topic of a paragraph

The topic of a paragraph tells what the paragraph is about.

D ACADEMIC Answer the questions. Answers will vary.

1. Define technology addiction.
   Technology addiction is the habit of checking electronic devices that a person cannot control.
2. What is one sign of technology addiction?
   The person feels nervous and depressed when he or she is not using an electronic device.
3. What is one way to help a person limit the use of their devices?
   Set an alarm. / Choose a time to turn off electronic devices every night. Find other activities you enjoy.

MORE ACTION

For homework, ask students to write a paragraph about how they typically use computers, email, cellphones, text messaging, and other kinds of technology.

B

- Ask students to complete the exercise on their own.
- Remind students that the bold words in the exercise are the vocabulary words from the reading.
- Call on volunteers to answer each question. Ask students to read aloud the sentence in the passage that helped them find the answer.

C

- Have students complete the exercise individually. Then, check the answers as a class.
- Ask students to identify the place in the paragraph that helped them find the main topic.

D

- Ask students to try to answer the items about the reading from memory. Afterwards, they can look back at the passage to check their answers.
- Ask students if they know any technology addicts and how they would try to help them.

ACADEMIC

Point out to students the relationship between Exercises C and D. If they can correctly identify the topic of each paragraph in Exercise C, they will more easily be able to find the supporting information they need to answer the items in Exercise D, as there is one item per paragraph.

WRITING OUR STORIES: An email

A

- Discuss the differences between formal and informal emails. (Formal emails follow a standard structure, including a greeting, body, and closing, and are usually written for business or professional purposes, while informal emails are short and may not have proper grammar or spelling. Informal emails are usually written to friends and family.) Ask students how frequently they send formal and informal emails and to whom they typically send each.
- Invite students to comment on the layout and format of the email. Is it different from emails they usually send and receive? What features are different? Discuss the meaning of the icons at the top of the email.
- Have students read the email independently.

B

- Call on different students to read and then answer each question.
- Discuss the answers as a class.

ACADEMIC

Let students know that familiarity with common text formats, such as emails, and use of appropriate formal and informal register will be asked of them on common standardized tests.

WRITING OUR STORIES An email

A Read the email message.

To: dianagt@state*u.edu
Cc:
Subject: **My new computer**

Hi Diana,

I'm sitting in my dorm room with my new computer and I'm writing my first email to you.

Mom and Dad gave me this new laptop for my birthday. They also gave me a tablet.
I can draw and manipulate my photos on the tablet with special software. It's amazing!

I love college. I'm taking twelve credits this semester. I'm enjoying my art classes the most.

I'm taking a painting class and a graphic design class. I'm spending my life in the art studios!
I'm rooming with a girl from California. She's majoring in art, too.

How are you? Are you still going out with David? Are you enjoying State University?
Write back!

Ciao,
Lidia

B **ACADEMIC** Answer the questions.

1. Who wrote this email?
   Lidia
2. Who did she send the email to?
   To Diana
3. What is the recipient's email address?
   dianagt@state*u.edu
4. What does *.edu* mean?
   Education. It's the domain name often used for schools or universities.
5. What is Lidia majoring in?
   Art

TEACHING TIP

You may wish to take this opportunity to remind students that it is important to be polite in emails. Some basic rules include: always use a salutation and a closing, and don't write your message in all capital letters.

There are degrees of formality in emails. Write some examples of formal and informal language on the board. For example:

Dear sir or madam, best wishes, sincerely (formal)

Hey, what's up, how's it going (informal)

C Find and correct the mistakes with the simple present or present continuous.

1. She is ~~send~~ sending an email message.
2. She is learning how to use new software.
3. The school ~~have~~ has a computer lab.
4. She ~~sits~~ is sitting in the computer lab now.
5. ~~You~~ Are you writing an email to your friend?
6. How is everything with you?
7. What classes ~~she is~~ is she taking?
8. ~~I'm prefering~~ I prefer to use my tablet to a laptop.
9. She ~~meet~~ is meeting a lot of people.
10. ~~You~~ Are you still going out with David?

WRITING NOTE

Check for spelling errors

After you write, use your computer's spell check to find any spelling errors.

D Write an email message to a friend or a classmate.

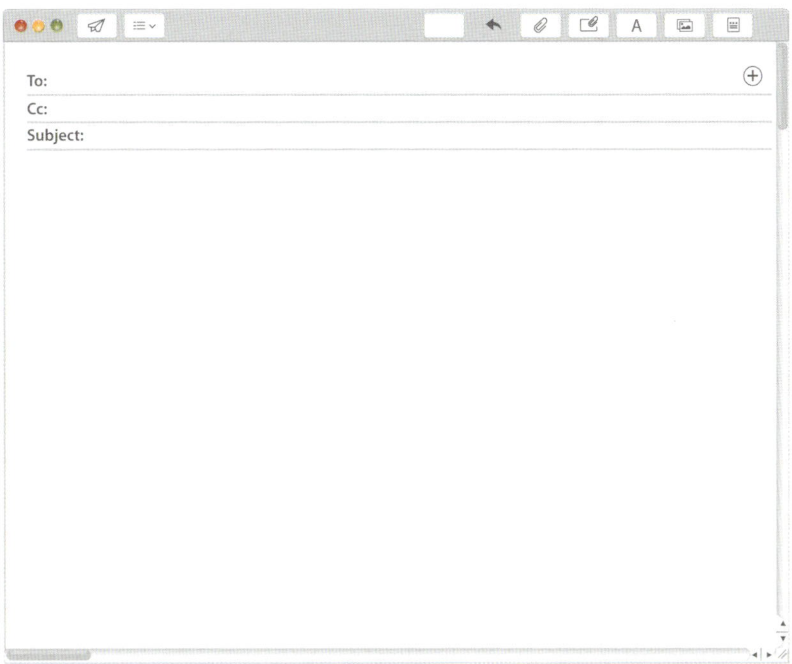

C

- Have students correct the mistakes independently.
- Write the sentences on the board and invite volunteers to come up and correct the sentences.
- Encourage students to identify the type of mistake in each sentence—for example, subject-verb agreement or word order.
- Ask students to explain why it is important to use correct spelling and grammar in emails.
- Read the Writing Note aloud to the class. Tell students that it is important for them to read their own writing for mistakes and not to rely on spell-checking software. Spell check only catches basic spelling and grammatical errors. It cannot catch nuanced mistakes in word use (for example, using *two* instead of *to* or *too*). Also discourage the use of online translators, which are notoriously unreliable.

D

Start this task in class and have students finish it for homework.

TEACHING TIP

Discuss alternative ways that students can check spelling and grammar in their emails or homework. Some tips might include using the spelling or grammar check in their email or word-processing program, using an online or electronic dictionary, or performing an internet search to look up words or grammatical structures. If you haven't mentioned it before (or even if you have; it bears repeating): stay away from online translators! Anything beyond a word level of length quickly becomes jibberish.

ENGLISH IN ACTION: Giving Clear Directions

A

- Ask students how many people use an alarm clock to wake up, and how many use their phone as an alarm, by a show of hands.
- Ask volunteers to read the directions out loud. Invite students to look at their own phones to compare the steps.
- See if anyone's phone matches the directions here. Does anyone have a very different system?

B

Give students a moment to read the options. Then, give them a few minutes to take notes on the process. Make sure they understand they only need to pick ONE process to explain.

C

- Pair students with different types of phones (Android and iPhone together) if possible.
- See if students can guide each other through the tasks they chose, using their notes.

D

Give students two minutes alone to complete the exercise. Then, call on volunteers to discuss the features they use the most often, or poll students with a show of hands. Which features stand out as the most important?

E

- Ask students to work in groups of three to compare their phone plans.
- Ask one representative from each group to report to the class. Which student in each group has the best cell phone plan?

ENGLISH IN ACTION Giving Clear Directions

A Read the directions for setting an alarm on a cellphone. How are these directions the same or different for your phone?

To set an alarm:

1. Tap the **clock** on the home screen.
2. Press the icon for **alarm**.
3. Touch **the plus sign**.
4. Enter the time you want the alarm to ring.
5. Select **a.m.** or **p.m.**
6. Press **Save** or **OK**.

B ACADEMIC Choose one of the features below or a favorite feature on your phone. In your notebook, give step-by-step directions on how to use the feature. Use words from the box to help you. Answers will vary.

choose	enter	press	select	tap	touch

a. how to take a photo and email it to a friend
b. how to write a text message and send it
c. how to enter a new contact into your phone
d. how to enter a new event on your calendar
e. how to record a voice memo
f. how to use a map app to get directions
g. how to listen to music or watch a video

C **LET'S TALK.** Give your phone to a classmate. Carefully explain your directions. Can your partner follow your directions?

D Complete the information about your cellphone. Then, talk about the features you use most often. Answers will vary.

1. I have a ____________ phone.
2. I talk on my phone about ____________ minutes a day.
3. My reception is **great / good / fair**.
4. My cellphone plan has these features. Check all that apply:

- ☐ It offers a family plan.
- ☐ It has unlimited talk.
- ☐ It has unlimited texting.
- ☐ It has unlimited data.
- ☐ I can lease a phone.
- ☐ There is no fee for early termination.

E **LET'S TALK.** In a group of three, make a chart to compare your cellphone plans. Include the company name, number of phones, data limits, signal quality, and cost. Answers will vary.

ACADEMIC

In both speaking and writing, encourage students to use signposts, such as *First*, *Second*, *After that*, and *Finally* as they explain a process. This strategy will help the relationship between the steps to be as clear as possible to the person listening/reading.

UNIT 6

A HEALTHY LIFESTYLE

ACADEMIC Make inferences; make predictions; take a survey; organize ideas

AT WORK Describe tasks associated with healthcare professionals

CIVICS Understand what to do during a 911 call

Swimming is a fun way to stay active.

CCRS Level A: R 1, 3, 4, 5; W 2; L 1, 4, 6; Level B: R 1, 3, 4, 5, 6; W 2, 4; L 1, 3, 4, 6; Level C: R 1, 3, 4; W 2, 4, 9; L 1, 3, 4, 6; Level D: R 1, 4; W 2, 4, 9; L 1, 3, 4, 6; Level E: R 1, 4; W 2, 4, 9; L4, 6

ELPS Level 1 Standards 1, 2, 3, 7, 8, 9, 10; Level 2 Standards 1, 2, 3, 7, 8, 9, 10; Level 3 Standards 1, 2, 3, 7, 8, 9, 10; Level 4 Standards 1, 2, 3, 7, 8, 9, 10; Level 5 Standards 1, 2, 3, 7, 8, 9, 10

CIVICS 7-7; 15-1; 15-2; 24-5; 27-4; 28-1; 28-4; 28-16; 28-17; 30-8; 52-4

CASAS 0.1.2; 0.1.5; 0.1.8; 0.2.1; 2.1.2; 3.1.4; 3.5.9; 3.6.3; 3.6.4; 3.6.5

IN THIS UNIT

In Unit 6, students will:

- Describe health problems, injuries, and the role of healthcare professionals
- Practice the future with *be going to*
- Take a survey
- Discuss what to do during an emergency

ABOUT THE PHOTO

Physical activity is a big element of a healthy lifestyle. Be it running, walking, playing sports, or practicing yoga, it has been proven that keeping our bodies in movement benefits our mental and physical health. This photo shows a woman bellyboarding, or bodyboarding, a water sport that involves riding waves on a small board. Swimming is another fun sport that offers great health benefits and can help tone our muscles while burning calories in a low-impact manner.

Ask students to discuss physical activities that they do as part of their routine and ask them to share how those activities help their health. Then, start a discussion about habits that negatively affect our health (not getting enough sleep, smoking, watching too much TV, eating too much salt or consuming too much sugar, excessive exposure to the sun, etc.). Preview the use of the future by asking students to identify changes they will make in their routine to avoid unhealthy habits. Guide them by modeling sentences like, *I don't walk enough during the week. I'm going to try to walk every day after lunch for 30 minutes.*, or *I spend too much time sitting in front of the computer before bed time. I will stop using my computer an hour before going to bed.*

A

- Have students read the words in the box and ask about any vocabulary they don't understand.
- Ask students to look at the photos and describe who the people are and what they are doing. Have students use the words from the box to describe what is happening.
- Ask questions about why it is important to have health examinations. For example: *Why is it important to check your blood pressure?* (Because high blood pressure is bad for your health.) *Why is it important to have a cavity filled?* (Because if a cavity is not filled, the rest of the tooth will decay.)
- Discuss what other things happen during a physical examination with the class. Make a list of additional vocabulary on the board.

AT WORK

Have students discuss healthcare professions other than the ones shown in the photos. Encourage them to share details about the professions by asking questions like *Where do they work? What do they do? What are some key responsibilities they have?*

Write any new vocabulary on the board.

A **AT WORK** Discuss the pictures. Where is each person? What is happening? What else happens during a physical examination at the doctor's office?

check his blood pressure	fill a cavity	give a vaccine	read an eye chart
check his cholesterol	floss her teeth	have a physical	take an X-ray
examine	get a vaccine	order a test	write a prescription

① 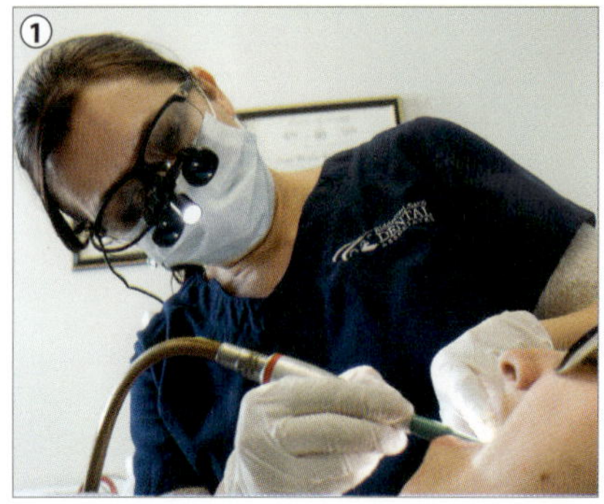

② 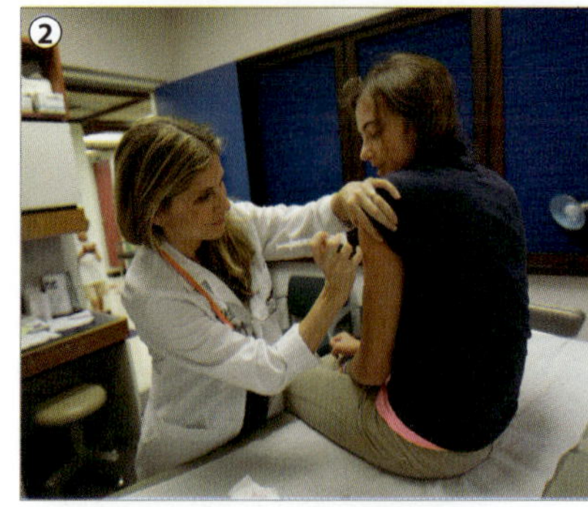

③ 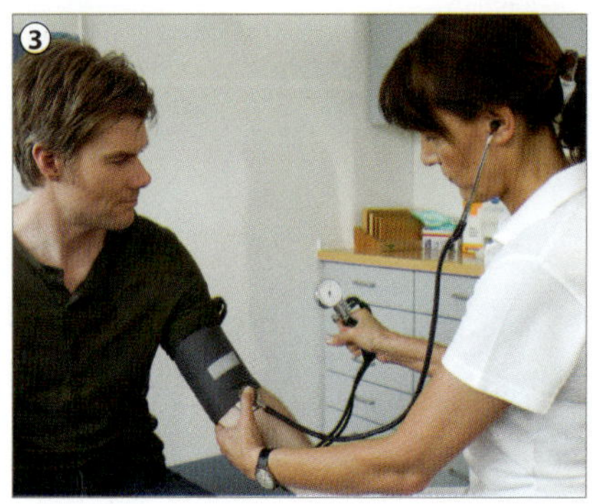

④ 

MORE ACTION

Give students a list of additional words related to common illnesses, health problems, and physical examinations. For example: *have blood drawn, have a fever, take someone's temperature, have the flu, lab work*, and so on.

ACTIVE GRAMMAR Future with *Be going to:* Statements

I	am	(not)	going to	**exercise**.
You	are			**make** an appointment.
He She	is			**call** the doctor.
We They	are			**take** medication.
It	is			**heal**.

A Read about Gloria. Underline each use of *be going to* plus verb.

Gloria is at the dentist. This is her first visit in two years. Gloria has four cavities. The doctor is filling two cavities today. He is going to fill two more cavities next week. Gloria is going to take better care of her teeth. She isn't going to drink soda with every meal. She isn't going to eat chocolate every day. She is going to floss her teeth every evening.

B Complete the sentences with the correct form of *be going to*.

1. I (go) ___am going to go___ to the dentist next week.
2. Many people (get) ___are going to get___ flu vaccines.
3. Jack fell and hurt his leg. The doctor (take) ___is going to take___ an X-ray.
4. The baby has an ear infection. The doctor (write) ___is going to write___ a prescription for an antibiotic.
5. My husband and I have high cholesterol. We (eat) ___are going to eat___ less fat. I (buy) ___am going to buy___ more fruits and vegetables.

C AT WORK **Pronunciation: Medical specialists** Listen. Mark the stressed syllable. Then, listen again and repeat. 27

súr·geon	ob·ste·trí·cian
car·di·ól·o·gist	der·ma·tól·o·gist
oph·thal·mól·o·gist	gy·ne·cól·o·gist
pe·di·a·trí·cian	ál·ler·gist
fám·i·ly dóc·tor	psy·chí·a·trist

CULTURE NOTE

If a person needs a specialist, his or her family doctor can suggest one. People can also find the name of a specialist by asking their friends or coworkers. What kind of doctor is in each picture on the previous page?

MORE ACTION

To review the meaning and pronunciation of these medical specialists, write each word on a note card and give one to each pair of students. One student will give a clue about the word, and the other student will guess the word and then spell it.

This exercise could also be organized as a competition by putting students in teams. Have each team stand in a row at the front of the class. Read a clue aloud to the team and have them guess the word. Then, the team has to correctly spell the word together, with each student contributing one letter. For example, for *allergist*, the first student in the row would say *a*, the second student would say *l*, and so on. Whichever team guesses and spells the most words correctly wins.

ACTIVE GRAMMAR: Future with *Be going to*: Statements

A

- Ask students to make sentences using the grammar chart.
- Have students complete Exercise A independently.
- Check the answers as a class.
- Ask the class some comprehension questions about the text.
  For example:
  T: *Is the dentist going to take out her tooth today?*
  S: *No, he's going to fill two cavities.*

B

- Have students work independently to complete the exercise.
- Check the answers as a class.

C 27

- Ask students to explain the medical specialists they are familiar with. Then, explain any specialists that students do not know.
- Play the first word and then pause the audio. Draw students' attention to the stressed syllable, indicated with the blue mark. Write it on the board as an example. Repeat with the second word.
- Play the rest of the audio all the way through without stopping. Have students mark the stress for each item.
- Play the audio again, pausing after each item so students can check their answers and repeat.

D

- Point at the photo and ask questions about Ayumi. Ask: *What's wrong with her? What is she going to do?*
- Review the words in the box and explain any unfamiliar words.
- Ask volunteers to make sentences about Ayumi using the words in the box.

E

- Model the first question with a volunteer. Make sure students understand to write two answers for each question. The first answer is their partner's answer, and the second answer is their own answer. Explain to students that, in the first item, the partner's name should precede *is going to*.
- Allow time for students to work in pairs and ask and answer the questions.
- Ask students to report on their partner's answers. For example: *Fadi's going to hang out with his friends this evening.*

ACADEMIC

Oral communication is a key component of learning a language. Exercises that require students to communicate verbally help them to practice the language, sharpen their listening skills, and build confidence in speaking the language in front of others as they become more fluent.

D ACADEMIC Talk about Ayumi's day. She has the flu. What is she going to do? What isn't she going to do? Answers may vary.

cook	stay in bed
drink a lot of fluids	take a hot shower
go shopping	take a walk
go to work	take aspirin
sleep most of the day	use a heating pad

She isn't going to go to work.
She's going to stay in bed.
She's going to take aspirin.
She isn't going to use a heating pad.

> She isn't going to go to work.

She's going to drink a lot of fluids.
She isn't going to take a hot shower.
She isn't going to take a walk.
She isn't going to go shopping.
She isn't going to cook.
She's going to sleep most of the day.

E **LET'S TALK.** Talk with a partner about your plans for today. Write your partner's response and your response to each question. Answers will vary.

1. What are you going to do after school?
   ______ is going to ______.
   (Your partner's name)
   I am going to ______.
2. What are you going to do this evening?
   ______.
   ______.
3. When are you going to do your homework?
   ______.
   ______.
4. What time are you going to go to bed?
   ______.
   ______.

MORE ACTION

Write some actions on the board and ask students to make sentences about when they are going to do them. For example, *go to the dentist or doctor, go to the library, go shopping, watch TV, cook dinner*, and so on.

S: *I'm going to go to the dentist next month. I'm not going to cook dinner tonight.*

ACTIVE GRAMMAR Future with *Be going to: Yes / No* Questions

Are	you	**going to**	**see** the doctor?	Yes, **I am**.	No, **I'm not**.
Is	he she		**stay** home from work?	Yes, he **is**. Yes, she **is**.	No, he **isn't**. No, she **isn't**.
Are	we they		**get** a flu vaccine?	Yes, we **are**. Yes, they **are**.	No, we **aren't**. No, they **aren't**.
Is	it		**get** better soon?	Yes, it **is**.	No, it **isn't**.

A Write the questions and answers. Use the words in parentheses.

1. Mary has a headache. (take some aspirin)
   Is she going to take some aspirin? Yes, she is.
2. Joseph has a toothache. (call the dentist)
   Is he going to call the dentist? Yes, he is.
3. Carol has the flu. (go to work)
   Is she going to go to work? No, she isn't.
4. I have a sore throat. (you / drink some tea)
   Are you going to drink some tea? Yes, I am.
5. My brother is in the hospital. (you / visit him)
   Are you going to visit him? Yes, I am.

B **LET'S TALK.** Ask your classmates the questions below. If a student answers "Yes," write the student's name in your notebook. If the student answers "No," ask another student the question. Try to find a student who answers "Yes" to each question. Answers will vary.

Are you going to join a gym?

No. (Ask another student!)

Are you going to join a gym?

Yes. (Write the student's name.)

1. join a gym?
2. have a physical examination?
3. get a flu shot?
4. change jobs?
5. move?
6. get a driver's license?
7. get married?
8. visit your native country?

ACTIVE GRAMMAR:
Future with *Be going to: Yes / No* Questions

A

- Ask students to read some of the questions and answers from the grammar chart aloud.
- Ask: *What type of word comes first in each question?* (a form of the verb *be*) *What comes second?* (the subject) *What comes third?* (*going to*) *What comes last?* (the verb) *What words are repeated in the answer?* (the subject and a form of the verb *be*).
- Read the first item in Exercise A aloud as an example.
- Have students complete the exercise individually.
- Invite volunteers to read their sentences aloud. Review the answers as a class.

B

- Model the exercise with two students.
- Set a time limit for students to complete the exercise.
- When students are finished, take a poll of how many students answered "Yes" to each question.

MORE ACTION

Hand out cards with sentences in the future form using *be going to*. For example, *I'm going to go to the dentist.* Have students get into pairs. One student should give a clue about the information on the card so that their partner can guess the sentence using the future form with *be going to*.
For example:
S1: *I have a toothache.*
S2: *Are you going to go to the dentist?*
S1: *Yes, I am.*

ACTIVE GRAMMAR:
Future with *Be going to*: *Wh-* Questions

A 28

- Ask students to read some of the questions from the grammar chart aloud.
- Write prompts for additional questions on the board. For example:
  T: *Why / see the doctor / he*
  S: *Why is he going to see the doctor?*
- Ask: *What type of word comes first?* (the question word) *What comes second?* (a form of the verb *be*) *What comes third?* (the subject) *What comes last?* (*going to* and the verb)
- Review and explain the vocabulary in the word box.
- Play the audio all the way through without stopping. Encourage students to take notes.
- Play the audio again and pause periodically to allow time for students to write their answers.
- Go over the answers as a class, playing the audio again as necessary.

B

- After students have completed the exercise individually, have them check their answers with a partner and practice asking and answering the questions.
- Then, have students cover the text and repeat the questions and answers using only the pictures as a guide.

ACTIVE GRAMMAR Future with *Be going to: Wh-* Questions

When How Why	**am**	I	**going to**	**lose weight?**
	are	you		
	is	he she		
	are	we they		
When	**is**	it	**going to**	**get better?**

A Discuss the new vocabulary. Then, listen to the conversation between Mr. West and the doctor. Answer the questions. 28

broken leg	cast	crutches	ice pack	painkiller	swelling	swollen

1. What's the matter with Jimmy?
   He has a broken leg.
2. Is the doctor looking at the X-rays?
   Yes, he is.
3. What is the nurse putting on Jimmy's leg? Why?
   She's putting ice packs on his leg because it's swollen.
4. How long is Jimmy going to stay in the hospital?
   He's going to stay in the hospital for two days.
5. When is the doctor going to put a cast on his leg?
   He's going to put the cast on in two days.
6. How long is Jimmy going to be in the cast?
   He's going to be in the cast for six to eight weeks.
7. What are they going to give him for pain?
   They are going to give him painkillers.

B Complete the questions about George. He sprained his ankle while playing basketball.

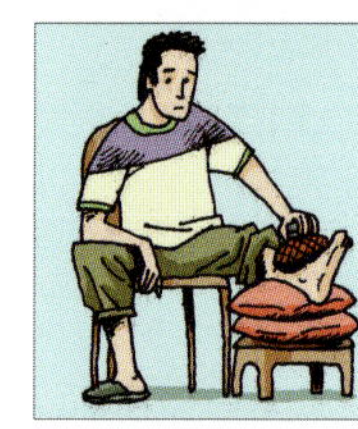

1. What *is George going to put on his ankle* ?
   He's going to put an ice pack on his ankle.
2. How long **is he going to use an ice pack** ?
   He's going to use an ice pack until the swelling goes down.
3. When **is he going to use a heating pad** ?
   He's going to use a heating pad in two or three days.
4. What **is he going to take for pain** ?
   He's going to take aspirin for pain.

5. Is he going to use crutches?

Yes, he's going to use crutches.

6. How long is he going to use crutches?

He's going to use crutches for a week.

7. What is he going to put on his ankle during the day?

He's going to put a bandage on his ankle during the day.

8. How long is he going to stay home from work?

He's going to stay home from work for two days.

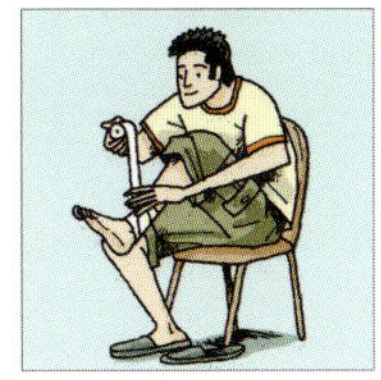

C STUDENT TO STUDENT

Student 1: Turn to Appendix C. Read the questions in Set A to Student 2. Student 2 will write the questions in the space below.

Student 2: Listen and write the questions. Then, turn to Appendix C. Read the questions in Set B to Student 1. Student 1 will listen and write the questions in the space below.

	Set A (Student 2 writes):	Set B (Student 1 writes):
1.	How are you feeling?	What's the problem?
2.	Are you going to need an operation?	When is the doctor going to talk to you?
3.	How long are you going to stay in the hospital?	When are they going to take X-rays?
4.	When are you going home?	When are you going to know the test results?
5.	What other tests are you going to need?	When are you going to return to school?

D LET'S TALK. In your notebook, write a conversation between a patient and a friend who is visiting him or her in the hospital. Use the questions in Exercise C. Then, act out your conversation for the class.

How are you feeling, Marie?

Well, I feel much better than yesterday.

How's your back? Are you going to need an operation?

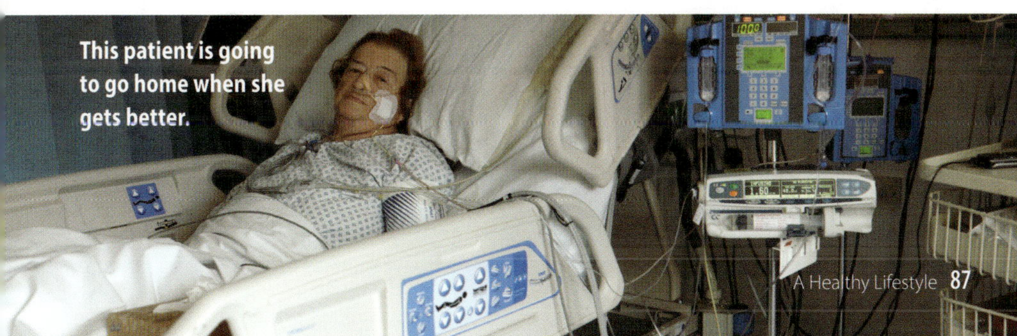

This patient is going to go home when she gets better.

C

- Model the first question in the exercise with two students.
- Students should check their answers together when they are finished.
- Encourage students to make up answers to the questions.

D

- Set a time limit for students to write their conversations.
- Ask volunteers to present their conversations to the class.

TEACHING TIP

Encourage peer feedback by having students exchange their written conversations from Exercise D with another pair of students. Pairs should read aloud each other's work so that they can listen for mistakes. Explain to students that reading their writing aloud is a valuable tool for catching mistakes, whether students read their writing aloud to themselves or listen to someone else read it to them. Students will often catch mistakes when they listen to their writing being read aloud that they would not catch if they read their work silently.

ACTIVE GRAMMAR: Future with *Will*

A 29

- Review the meaning of *will* and *won't* when talking about the future (they are auxiliaries used with the base form of the verb to express future time). Remind students there is no *to* after the auxiliary *will*.
- Read the example sentences in the grammar charts at the top of the page.
- Give some additional examples of offers and predictions and ask students to identify each.
  For example:
  I'll bring it to you. (offer)
  She'll do well on the test. (prediction)
- Play the audio and pause after each sentence so students can repeat.
- Have students take turns saying the sentences to a partner, helping each other with pronunciation.

B

- Point at the picture and ask what is happening. (The doctor is listening to Martin's heart.)
- Ask students what kind of lifestyle may cause chest pains. Then, read the recommendations in the word box and explain any unfamiliar words.
- Ask students to work in pairs to discuss Martin's lifestyle.

ACTIVE GRAMMAR Future with *Will*

I She They	**will** **won't**	**walk** every day. **join** a health club. **change** jobs.

Use *will* to express an offer to help. **I'll** drive you to school. Use *will* to make predictions. You**'ll** get the job. It**'ll** take a long time.

A **Pronunciation: *I'll*** Listen and repeat. 29

1. I'll help you.
2. I'll call her.
3. I'll drive you.
4. I'll make dinner.
5. I'll visit you.
6. I'll take you to the doctor.
7. I'll pick up your prescription.
8. I'll see you tomorrow.

B Read the doctor's advice. Martin went to the doctor with chest pain. Do you think Martin will follow his recommendations?

Change your diet.	Get a pet.	Lose weight.	Start to exercise.	Use less salt.
Cut down on sweets.	Get more sleep.	Lower your cholesterol.	Stop smoking.	Walk to work.

I agree. **I don't agree.**

Martin will change his diet.

I don't agree. Martin won't change his diet. He loves fried food.

C Offer to help your friend. She broke her leg and needs help for a few weeks. Use *it, them, him,* or *her* for the underlined words.

I can't drive the children to school.
I'll drive **them**.
I can't make dinner.
I'll make **it**.

1. I can't drive the children to school.
   I'll drive them.
2. I can't make dinner.
   I'll make it.
3. I can't do the laundry.
   I'll do it.
4. I can't carry the groceries.
   I'll carry them.
5. I can't answer the door.
   I'll answer it.
6. I can't make the beds.
   I'll make them.
7. I can't wash my hair.
   I'll wash it.
8. I can't return those library books.
   I'll return them.
9. I can't clean the kitchen.
   I'll clean it.
10. I can't walk the dog. [Note: Use *him* or *her* in the answer.]
    I'll walk him / her.
11. I can't change that light bulb.
    I'll change it.
12. I can't mail these letters.
    I'll mail them.

D ACADEMIC **LET'S TALK.** In groups, make predictions about your class and your school. Then, share your predictions with the class. **Answers will vary.**

The school will build a new cafeteria.

Our teacher won't give us any homework tonight.

All the students will get 100% on the next test.

MORE ACTION

Ask students to make predictions about other aspects of society or the community (for example, jobs, health care, education, and the environment). Do they think more jobs will be available in the next ten years? What kinds of new jobs will be created? Will any kinds of jobs be phased out? Ask students to write a paragraph about some of their predictions in their notebook for homework.

C

- Give example situations for when you might want to make an offer. For example:
  T: *I missed my train.*
  S1: *I'll give you a ride.*
  T: *I don't have money for the parking meter.*
  S2: *I'll lend you a quarter.*
- Do the first sentence for the class as an example. Then, have students work in pairs to complete the exercise.
- Review the answers as a class.

D

- Read the predictions in the speech bubbles. Ask students if they think these statements are true for your class or school.
- Have students work in groups and write at least ten predictions about your class or school.
- Then, ask a representative from each group to report their predictions to the class.
- Have the class vote on whether they think each group's predictions will come true or not.

THE BIG PICTURE:
The Accident

A

- Ask students to describe what is happening in the picture.
- Ask them to identify the words from the box that they can see in the picture. Explain any unfamiliar words.
- Encourage students to make sentences about the picture using the new words.

B

- Have students complete the sentences on their own.
- Then, check the answers as a class.

C 30

Play the audio all the way through. Tell students to take notes as they listen.

THE BIG PICTURE The Accident

A Discuss the new words. Which words do you see in the picture?

blanket	concussion	pale	stretcher
bleeding	confused	pressure bandage	windshield
blood pressure	intersection	stitches	witness

B Look at the picture again and complete each sentence with a word from Exercise A.

1. The man's arm is ____bleeding____ heavily, so the emergency worker is applying a ____pressure bandage____.
2. Another emergency worker is taking the man's ____blood pressure____.
3. The woman is lying on a ____stretcher____.
4. The ____windshield____ of the woman's car is broken.
5. A ____witness____ called 911.

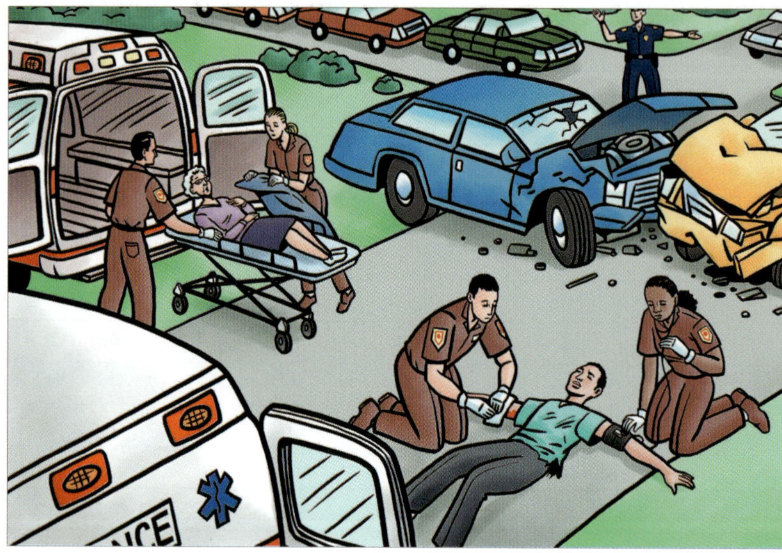

C Listen to the story about the accident. 30

90 Unit 6

TEACHING TIP

Tell students that if they witness a car accident, they should call for help by dialing 911. They should not try to pull anyone out of the car unless someone will be in danger if they stay in the car. Ask students if they have ever witnessed a car accident or been in one themselves. What happened? Was the accident serious? Did someone call 911?

D Answer the questions.

1. What are the man's injuries?
   His arm is cut badly.
2. What are the emergency workers doing? They are putting a pressure bandage on the man's arm and taking his blood pressure.
3. What treatment is the man going to receive at the hospital?
   He is going to need stitches.
4. What are the woman's injuries?
   She might have a concussion.
5. Whose injuries are more serious?
   Answers will vary.
6. What treatment is the woman going to receive at the hospital?
   Answers will vary.

WORD PARTNERSHIPS	
I was in / I had	an accident.
It was my fault.	

E Listen again and circle *True, False,* or *NI (Not enough information).* 30

1.	The man went past the stop sign.	True	(False)	NI
2.	The accident was the woman's fault.	(True)	False	NI
3.	The witness called 911 for emergency help.	(True)	False	NI
4.	The man has a broken arm.	True	False	(NI)
5.	The man is going to need stitches in his arm.	(True)	False	NI
6.	The woman is telling the workers her phone number.	True	(False)	NI
7.	The woman probably hit her head on her windshield.	(True)	False	NI
8.	The woman is going to stay in the hospital for a week.	True	False	(NI)

F Complete the sentences. Use the correct form of *be going to* or the present continuous.

1. The man (lie) ___is lying___ by the side of the road.
2. An emergency worker (apply) ___is applying___ a pressure bandage.
3. In a few minutes, the workers (take) ___are going to take___ him to the hospital.
4. The man (need) ___is going to need___ thirty stitches in his arm.
5. The workers (put) ___are going to put___ the woman in the ambulance.
6. At the hospital, the doctor (examine) ___is going to examine___ her carefully.
7. A police officer (direct) ___is directing___ traffic.
8. He (file) ___is going to file___ an accident report.

G Listen and write the sentences you hear. Refer to the words in the box for spelling. Your teacher will refer to Appendix D.

insurance	lawyer	overnight	report	stayed	sue

D

- Ask students to write their answers using their notes from Exercise C and to compare their answers with a partner.
- Then, ask volunteers to answer each question.

E 30

- Play the audio.
- Have students complete the exercise independently.
- Then, discuss the answers with the class.
- Invite students to agree or disagree with each other's answers and to explain their reasoning.

F

- Ask students to complete the sentences on their own.
- Check the answers with the class by calling on volunteers to read each statement.
- Ask students to explain their reason for using each verb form.

G

Read all the sentences in Appendix D without stopping. Then, read the sentences again, pausing after each sentence so students can write.

READING: Health Article

A 31 (facing page)

- Discuss the questions with the class. Ask additional questions, such as: *Does anyone in the class have asthma? What is an inhaler?*
- On the board, make a list of things students know about asthma.
- Then, make a list of questions about asthma that students would like to know the answers to. For example: *What causes asthma? Do adults get asthma? Is asthma genetic?*
- Set a time limit for students to read the passage. Remind them that the bold words in the passage are vocabulary words that they should write in their notebooks.
- Ask students if they found the answers to any of their questions in the reading. What was the most interesting or surprising fact about asthma that they learned from the reading? Ask students to point out where in the passage they found the answers to the questions that you wrote on the board.

READING Health Article

Asthma

Ricky Garcia is going to play outside with his friends. He is taking out his inhaler and taking two puffs. Five minutes later, he's in the park with his friends, running after a soccer ball. Ricky has asthma, but he knows how to control it.

Asthma is a lung disease. The airways of the lungs become **inflamed**—that is, red and swollen—making it difficult to breathe normally. A person with asthma may have wheezing, coughing, a tight feeling in the chest, or shortness of breath. Serious breathing problems are called **asthma attacks**. They can be mild or very serious, requiring immediate medical attention.

Asthma can begin at any age. Childhood asthma, often beginning when a child is younger than ten years old, is one of the most common childhood diseases. Doctors report that the number of young people with asthma is **increasing**. More than six million children in the US have the disease and the number is growing. It is the number-one cause of absence from school. Asthma is often **genetic**. If a parent has asthma, the children are more likely to develop the disease. Children with asthma need to be under a doctor's care. They and their parents can learn to understand this disease and to control it.

It is important to find out what **triggers** asthma. In other words, what causes the attack? The most common triggers are exercise, viral infections, stress, and **irritants** like dust, pollen, or animals. Big cities present added triggers for both children and adults because of air pollution, exhaust from buses and cars, cockroaches, and mold.

There are two kinds of asthma medications—control drugs and quick-relief drugs. Children take control drugs once or twice a day to help prevent asthma attacks. If a child begins to have an asthma attack, he or she needs immediate help, so a **quick-relief** drug is necessary. This medication is often taken through an inhaler. School-aged children usually carry their inhalers with them. This medication works quickly and children begin to breathe more easily in a few minutes. If a child has a serious asthma attack, he may need emergency care at a hospital or doctor's office.

About half of all children **outgrow** asthma, and their asthma attacks stop when they are teenagers. However, many people live with the disease into adulthood. 31

Air pollution can make asthma symptoms worse.

MORE ACTION

Ask students to highlight or underline the key ideas in each paragraph. Have volunteers write the main ideas from each paragraph on the board and see if the class agrees. Then, instruct students to use these key phrases or sentences to write a summary of the article (in class or for homework).

A Discuss these questions.

1. Where are your lungs? What do they do?
2. Does anyone in your family have asthma? What treatment is he or she receiving?

B Circle *True* or *False*.

1.	A child with asthma has breathing problems.	(True)	False
2.	Asthma can begin when a child is two or three years old.	(True)	False
3.	If a person has asthma, their children will have asthma.	True	(False)
4.	Air pollution does not trigger asthma.	True	(False)
5.	Every year, more children have asthma.	(True)	False
6.	An inhaler can help if a child is having an asthma attack.	(True)	False
7.	Parents must take the child to the hospital for every asthma attack.	True	(False)
8.	Many children with asthma need to take medication every day.	(True)	False

READING NOTE

Vocabulary in Context

When you are reading, you will see new words. The meaning, or definition, of a new word is often in the same sentence or in the sentence before or after.

1. The airways of the lungs become **inflamed**—that is, red and swollen.
   Inflamed means red and swollen.
2. Asthma is often **genetic**. If a parent has asthma, the children are more likely to develop the disease.
   Genetic means that a parent can pass a health problem to a child.

C Write the definitions of the words from the article. The definitions are in the same sentences as the words, or in the sentences before or after them.

1. asthma attack serious breathing problem
2. increasing growing
3. triggers causes
4. irritants dust, pollen, or animals
5. quick relief immediate help
6. outgrow stop when you are older

B

- Ask students to complete the exercise independently and then compare their answers with a partner.
- Encourage students to look back at the reading to find answers, if necessary.

C

- Review the Reading Note. Explain that there are often context clues in a sentence that can help you figure out the meaning of an unknown word. Sometimes the clue is right next to the word, and sometimes it is in a nearby sentence.
- Read the instructions for Exercise C and do the first question with the class. Point out the phrase *serious breathing problems* in the second paragraph on the previous page.
- Then, have students work individually to complete the exercise.
- Call on volunteers to answer each question. Go over each definition, asking students to point out the words or phrases in the reading that helped them define the unknown words.

TEACHING TIP

Explain to students that the definitions in a dictionary don't always match the intended meaning of a word in a specific text. Often times, terms in a dictionary have multiple meanings. Without reading how the word is used in the text, it is difficult to determine the correct definition. It's more helpful to try to work out the meaning first, based on context clues, and then check the definition in a dictionary.

WRITING OUR STORIES: Staying Healthy

A

- Ask students if they are health conscious. Do they eat well, exercise, and get plenty of rest? Do they have any habits that they would like to stop, such as smoking? What things do they do to stay healthy?
- Have students complete the survey individually.
- Then, discuss the results as a class. Talk about why these activities are healthy or unhealthy. Who is the healthiest person in the class?

B

- Ask one or two students to read the text aloud.
- Ask students to identify the main topic of each paragraph.
- Ask students what things from the text are true for them or what they would like to change in their own lives.
- Ask students to suggest three ways in which they could improve their own lifestyle.

ACADEMIC

Ask students to discuss in what other real-life scenarios they may need to take a survey, or in what situations the results of a survey might be helpful. You may want to encourage students to design a survey and share some of the questions that they would include in it with the class.

WRITING OUR STORIES | Staying Healthy

A ACADEMIC Take the survey. Answers will vary.

Health Questionnaire

1.	Do you smoke?	YES ☐	NO ☐
2.	Do you drive everywhere?	YES ☐	NO ☐
3.	Do you exercise three or more times a week?	YES ☐	NO ☐
4.	Do you eat fresh fruits and vegetables every day?	YES ☐	NO ☐
5.	Do you eat a lot of fried food?	YES ☐	NO ☐
6.	Do you always put salt on your food?	YES ☐	NO ☐
7.	Do you take vitamins?	YES ☐	NO ☐
8.	Do you drink a lot of caffeine?	YES ☐	NO ☐
9.	Do you drink a lot of soda?	YES ☐	NO ☐
10.	Do you eat a lot of sweets?	YES ☐	NO ☐
11.	Do you sleep at least seven hours a night?	YES ☐	NO ☐
12.	Do you drink six or more glasses of water a day?	YES ☐	NO ☐

B Read this text about a student's lifestyle.

In general, my lifestyle is healthy. However, there are a few things **I need to change**.

In the morning, I eat a good breakfast. I always have fruit and then I have cereal or yogurt. For lunch, I order soup or a salad in the small cafeteria at work. For dinner, I usually stir-fry some vegetables and meat and eat that with rice.

But my diet isn't perfect. First, **I love to put** salt on my food. I put soy sauce on everything I cook. I have a salt shaker on my kitchen table, and I add more salt to everything on my plate. From now on, I'm going to buy light soy sauce. Also, I will buy salt-free seasoning and try it. Second, I drink three or four cups of coffee every day. I need a cup of coffee in the morning, but I'm going to **try to drink** decaf in the afternoon and evening.

Unfortunately, I don't exercise enough. I work and go to school, so it's hard to find the time. I like to walk. There's a park near my house. I will try to walk there for thirty minutes on Saturday and Sunday. At school, my classroom is on the third floor. I usually take the elevator, but from now on **I plan to take** the stairs.

MORE ACTION

After they read the text in Exercise B, ask students to close their books and see how much they can remember. Prompt students by saying some of the key words, for example:

T: *salt*

S: *She loves to put salt on her food, but she wants to try salt-free seasoning instead.*

WRITING NOTE

Verb + infinitive

Many verbs take the infinitive form. Use an infinitive after *try, need, plan, like,* and *love.*

An infinitive is *to* + the base form of the verb.

There are a few things I need **to change**.

I love **to put** salt on my food.

C Complete each sentence with an infinitive after the verb.

1. I will (try / exercise) ___try to exercise___ more.
2. I (plan / walk) ___plan to walk___ to work.
3. I (love / eat) ___love to eat___ sweets, especially chocolate.
4. I (need / lose) ___need to lose___ twenty pounds.
5. I will (try / go) ___try to go___ to bed earlier.

D Complete the chart. This student organized her ideas before she wrote. She listed three things she wanted to change. Then, she made a plan for each thing.

Things to change	Plans for change
Salt	use light soy sauce, try salt-free seasonings
Coffee	one cup regular coffee, decaf in the afternoon and evening
Exercise	walk 30 minutes on weekends, take the stairs to class

E Make your own chart on a separate sheet of paper. Write two or three things you would like to change about your lifestyle. Then, make notes about your plans for change. You don't need to write complete sentences.

F Write a few paragraphs about your lifestyle. Then, write about the changes you want to make and your plans for change. Use your chart from Exercise E to guide you.

C

- Read the Writing Note and ask students to complete the exercise individually.
- Check the answers as a class.
- Ask students to make similar sentences that are true for them. Ask: *What do you want to try? What do you need to do? What do you plan to do this weekend?*

D

Have students complete the chart based on the text in Exercise B on the previous page. Then, have them check their answers with a partner.

E

- Explain to students that making a plan before they start writing will help them organize their ideas.
- Point out the chart from Exercise D and tell students to write their notes and ideas in a similar format.

F

Have students write their paragraphs in class or finish them for homework.

ENGLISH IN ACTION: Calling 911

A

- Invite volunteers to share any experiences they may have of calling 911.
- Ask students to suggest situations when you should and should not call 911.
- Discuss why you should not call 911 if it is not an emergency.
- Ask students what they would do to handle the situations that are not emergencies.

B 32

- Explain that a dispatcher is the person who answers the call when you dial 911. The dispatcher talks to you about the problem, tells you what to do, and sends an ambulance and other emergency services to your location.
- Read the Culture Note aloud. Emphasize that it is important to know your location and stay calm when you call 911.
- Read the directions for Exercise B aloud and ask students to predict what kind of questions the dispatcher will ask.
- Play the audio. Encourage students to take notes. Then, have students complete the exercise.
- Go over the answers as a class.

C

- Have students work in pairs. Allow them a few minutes to think about an emergency situation (a car accident, a house fire, someone is screaming for help, someone is robbing a store). Try to ensure that each pair has a different situation.
- Allow some time for pairs to write and practice their conversations.
- Move around the class to provide help as needed.
- Ask volunteers to present the conversations to the class.
- Give feedback. Ask the class which student was the best actor.

ENGLISH IN ACTION Calling 911

A CIVICS Discuss these questions.

1. Have you ever called 911? Describe the situation.
2. For what kinds of emergencies can you call 911?

CULTURE NOTE

Calling 911

1. Call 9-1-1 for emergencies.
2. Know your location.
3. Stay calm.
4. Answer the questions that the dispatcher asks.
5. Follow the dispatcher's directions.
6. Stay on the phone until the dispatcher tells you to hang up.

These are dispatchers. They contact the police and all emergency personnel directly when a person calls in an emergency.

B Listen to the conversation between a caller and a 911 dispatcher. Answer the questions. 32

1. What is the emergency?
   Her daughter ate some of her medication.
2. Who is calling?
   The mother
3. What did the dispatcher ask the caller? *What is the emergency? What is your location? How old is your daughter? Where is your daughter? Is she breathing? What kind of medicine did she take? How many did she take? Is your door unlocked?*
4. What directions did the dispatcher give?
   Stay calm. Repeat that address. Stay on the line. Unlock the door. Give the medics the bottle of medication.

C CIVICS **LET'S TALK.** Write a conversation between a caller and a 911 dispatcher. Then, act out your conversation for the class. You can use some of the sentences and questions from the box below.

What's the emergency?	Is your door unlocked?
Is anyone hurt / injured?	Is the person breathing?
How old is your daughter / father?	Stay on the line.
Where are you?	Stay calm. / Calm down.
What is your location?	The police are on the way.
Are you safe?	Unlock the door.
Are you in any danger?	

CIVICS

In the United States, people who are experiencing an emergency should call 911. This will connect them with a dispatcher who will contact the police, the fire department, or an ambulance for assistance.

When calling 911, the caller should speak clearly to the dispatcher and provide information about the emergency. The dispatcher will ask questions that will help them identify how to best address the emergency and contact the appropriate emergency personnel.

Some states, like Massachusetts, have a "Silent Code Procedure" that can be used if the caller is unable to speak when calling 911.

Understanding what to do and what to expect during an emergency call is very important. There are reliable sources online with information on what to do during an emergency. The website 911.gov provides details on using 911, what to expect during a 911 call, and what to do if you accidentally dial 911, among other relevant information.

CIVICS Analyze and compare information about cities and states in the United States

ACADEMIC Compare people and places; scan a text for information; give a presentation

AT WORK Use an online search engine

Landscape Arch in Arches National Park, Utah.

CCRS Level A: R 1, 5; W 7, 8; L 1, 2; Level B: R 1, 6; W 1, 4, 7, 8; L 1, 3, 6; Level C: R 1; W 1, 4, 7, 8, 9; L 1, 3; Level D: R 1; W 1, 4, 7, 8, 9; L 1, 3; Level E: R 1; W 1, 4, 7, 8, 9

ELPS Level 1 Standards 2, 3, 5, 9, 10; Level 2 Standards 1, 2, 3, 4, 5, 7, 10; Level 3 Standards 1, 2, 3, 4, 5, 7, 10; Level 4 Standards 1, 2, 3, 4, 5, 7, 10; Level 5 Standards 1, 2, 3, 4, 5, 7, 10

CIVICS 11-15; 23-3; 47-1; 47-3; 47-7; 47-11; 47-12

CASAS 0.1.2; 0.1.5; 0.2.1; 7.7.1; 7.7.2; 7.7.3; 7.7.5; 7.7.6

IN THIS UNIT

In Unit 7, students will:

- Compare data about cities and states in the US
- Scan a text for information
- Complete online research

ABOUT THE PHOTO

This photo shows a man jumping from one rock to another beneath an arch in Arches National Park, Utah. Today, Arches National Park is 119 square miles of protected land, but it started out as a cattle ranch in 1898. In the 1900s, it was established as a National Monument, and later became a National Park. The park was visited by over 1,500,000 people in 2016. Spanning 290 feet, the arch in the photo, Landscape Arch, is the fifth longest natural arch in the world.

Ask students what national parks in the US and in their state they are familiar with. Ask: *Do you know any national parks in the US? Are there any national parks in this state? Have you visited any national parks?* If they are familiar with US national parks, ask them to share details about the parks with the class. To preview how to form comparative adjectives, ask students to compare national parks or other important landmarks in their own country to US or world locations (for example, Angel Falls and Niagara Falls). Ask questions such as *Which place has more traffic? Which park receives more visitors? What park is more popular as a world tourist destination? What is the most popular time of year to visit that park? Which place is more populated?* Encourage students to draw comparisons using comparative adjectives (*more popular / older / larger / smaller / more interesting / sunnier than / taller*).

A

- Ask students to look at the photos and describe what they see.
- Ask students if they can identify any of the places.
- Have students label the photos on their own. Check the answers as a class.
- Ask if any students have visited these locations. Ask students which of these places they would like to visit and why.

B

- Ask volunteers to read each sentence aloud. Check if students understand the meaning of each sentence.
- Have students complete the exercise individually.
- Go over the answers as a class. For each sentence, ask volunteers to state the adjective and the word or phrase the adjective describes.
- Encourage students to talk about places they have visited in the US and why they went there.

CIVICS

Encourage students to become familiar with details about specific regions of the United States. Students who intend to take the citizenship test will find questions about the US territory and its history, so information about specific states may prove useful.

A Write the location under each picture.

One World Trade Center, New York	Atchafalaya Basin, Louisiana	Denali, Alaska
Niagara Falls, New York	~~Mt. Waialeale, Hawaii~~	Interstate 405, California

1. Mt. Waialeale, Hawaii

2. One World Trade Center, New York

3. Denali, Alaska

4. Niagara Falls, New York

5. Atchafalaya Basin, Louisiana

6. Interstate 405, California

B CIVICS Read the facts about the United States. Underline the adjectives.

1. Alaska is larger than Texas.
2. Florida receives more visitors than any other state in the United States.
3. The rainiest location in the United States is Mt. Waialeale in Hawaii.
4. Interstate 405 in Los Angeles, California, is the busiest highway in the United States.
5. One World Trade Center in New York City is the tallest building in the United States.
6. Denali is the highest mountain in the United States.
7. Louisiana has more alligators than any other state in the United States.
8. Niagara Falls in New York is one of the most popular tourist attractions in the United States.
9. Atchafalaya Basin in Louisiana is the largest swamp in the United States.

TEACHING TIP

Tell students that in English, adjectives usually go directly before the word or phrase they describe. Sometimes, however, the adjective follows a linking verb (such as *be*, *feel*, or *seem*). For example: *Alaska is larger than Texas*. Write a list of linking verbs on the board (*appear, be, become, feel, get, go, grow, look, prove, remain, seem, smell, sound, stay, taste, turn*) and have students practice using adjectives and linking verbs. Give students prompts. For example:

T: *Ted / be / tall*
S1: *Ted is tall.*
T: *flowers / look / pretty*
S2: *Those flowers look pretty.*

ACTIVE GRAMMAR Comparative Adjectives

Type of Adjective	Comparative Form		
One-syllable adjectives	old**er than**	larg**er than**	
Two-syllable adjectives ending in *-y*	bus**ier than**	sunn**ier than**	
Two-or-more-syllable adjectives not ending in *-y*	**more** populated **than**	**more** interesting **than**	
Irregular forms	good – **better than**	bad – **worse than**	far – **farther than**

More information in Appendix A.

A Write the adjectives in the correct column.

beautiful	famous	noisy
cold	friendly	safe
expensive	happy	tall

One-syllable adjectives	Two-syllable adjectives ending in *-y*	Two-or-more-syllable adjectives not ending in *-y*
long	busy	populated
tall	noisy	expensive
safe	friendly	beautiful
cold	happily	famous

B Write the comparative form of each adjective from Exercise A.

One-syllable adjectives	Two-syllable adjectives ending in *-y*	Two-or-more-syllable adjectives not ending in *-y*
longer than	busier than	more populated than
taller than	noisier than	more expensive than
safer than	friendlier than	more beautiful than
colder than	happier than	more famous than

C **Pronunciation: Comparative adjectives** Listen and repeat. 33

1. busier than
2. taller than
3. larger than
4. noisier than
5. friendlier than
6. farther than
7. rainier than
8. higher than
9. sunnier than

ACTIVE GRAMMAR: Comparative Adjectives

A

- Explain the rules for each category in the grammar chart at the top of the page. Point out that all comparative adjectives are immediately followed by *than.*
- Read the adjectives in the word box for Exercise A aloud and ask students to name synonyms or antonyms for each adjective. For example: *cold—freezing, tall—short.*
- Ask students to write the adjectives in the correct columns of the chart and check their work with a partner.
- Review the answers with the class.

B

- Point out the sample answers in the first row of the chart and review how the comparative form is made.
- Then, have students complete the chart individually or with a partner.
- Draw the chart on the board and call on volunteers to fill in the chart with their answers.
- Review the answers with the class.

C 33

Play the audio and pause after each word to allow time for students to repeat.

MORE ACTION

For additional practice with comparative forms, dictate a random list of adjectives on this page. Ask students to write the comparative form of these adjectives in their notebooks. To make the exercise more challenging, dictate a few adjectives that are not on the page (for example, *lucky, dangerous, clean, competitive*).

D

- Have students complete the task individually.
- Then, ask individual students to read their answers aloud.
- On the board, write the correct form of the adjective for each sentence so students can check their spelling.

E

- Ask students to complete the exercise individually. Then, ask them to work in groups and exchange information about their countries and / or cities.
- Ask volunteers to talk to the class about some of the differences between their own country or city and their partners' country or city.

F

- Model one or two example sentences with a student. For example: *I am taller than Marisa. My hair is shorter than Marisa's.*
- Set a time limit for students to come up with at least five comparisons.
- Ask volunteers to read two of their comparisons aloud.
- Ask the class if they agree with each student's sentences. Have students who disagree provide feedback.

D Complete the sentences. Use the comparative form of the adjectives.

1. Florida is (sunny) sunnier than Washington State.
2. New Jersey is (crowded) more crowded than any other state.
3. Chicago, Illinois, is (busy) busier than Columbus, Ohio.
4. Louisiana is (humid) more humid than Nevada.
5. Arizona is (dry) drier than Pennsylvania.
6. Santa Fe, New Mexico, is (old) older than Orlando, Florida.
7. For surfers, Hawaii is (popular) more popular than Maine.
8. New York City is (noisy) noisier than Dallas, Texas.

E Circle the adjective that compares your native country and/or city to the United States. Then, work in a group and talk about your answers. Answers will vary.

1. My country is **larger / smaller** than the United States.
2. My country is **more populated / less populated** than the United States.
3. The weather in my country is **hotter / colder** than the weather in this city.
4. The city where I was born is **rainier / drier** than this city.
5. The traffic in the city that I come from is **heavier / lighter** than the traffic in this city.
6. The city where I grew up has **more / less** crime than this city.
7. Houses in my country are **more expensive / less expensive** than houses in this city.
8. In my country, gasoline is **more expensive / less expensive** than in the United States.
9. The cost of living in the US is **higher / lower** than in my country.

F ACADEMIC **LET'S TALK.** Work with a partner. Compare yourselves, using the adjectives in the box. Then, tell the class two of your comparisons.

athletic	quiet
busy	short
hair / long	talkative
hair / short	tall
nervous	young

I am quieter than Sofia.

MORE ACTION

For homework, ask students to write a paragraph comparing their home city or country with the city or state where they live now. After students turn in their paragraphs, use them to make a list of anonymous comparative sentences for students to correct in class.

ACTIVE GRAMMAR *More / Less / Fewer* + Noun

New York Los Angeles	has	**more** **fewer**	universities jobs	**than**	Chicago. Dallas.
		more **less**	traffic noise		

Use *more* and *fewer* with count nouns.
Use *more* and *less* with noncount nouns.

A Describe the differences between a city and a town. Complete the sentences with *more*, *less*, or *fewer*.

1. A city has __more__ skyscrapers.
2. There is __less__ traffic in a town than a city.
3. Because of the traffic, there is __more__ noise in a city.
4. A city offers __more__ job opportunities.
5. There are __fewer__ stores and restaurants in a town.
6. There are __more__ tourists in a city than a small town.
7. A town has __less__ crime than a large city.
8. A town usually has __fewer__ people than a city.

B In your notebook, write two comparative sentences about each fact. **Answers may vary.**

1. Tourists to France: 84.5 million Tourists to Italy: 50.7 million
   France has more tourists than Italy.
   Italy has fewer tourists than France.
2. Cars in Japan: 60.8 million Cars in France: 32.3 million
   Japan has more cars than France. France has fewer cars than Japan.
3. Native speakers of Spanish: 389 million Native speakers of Mandarin: 1.39 billion
   There are fewer native speakers of Spanish than Mandarin. There are more native speakers of Mandarin than Spanish.
4. Saudi Arabia produces 13 percent of the world's oil. Iran produces 5 percent of the world's oil.
   Saudi Arabia produces more oil than Iran. Iran produces less oil than Saudi Arabia.
5. Cellphone users in China: 1.3 billion Cellphone users in India: 998 million
   China has more cellphone users than India. India has fewer cellphone users than China.
6. People in the US watch 5 hours of TV a day. People in Canada watch 4.5 hours of TV a day.
   People in the United States watch more TV than people in Canada. People in Canada watch less TV than people in the United States.

ACTIVE GRAMMAR: *More / Less / Fewer* + Noun

A

- Review the difference between count and noncount nouns. (Count nouns are items that can be counted individually. Noncount nouns are items that cannot be counted.)
- Ask for examples of count and noncount nouns that could be used to describe a city. Examples: *buildings, schools, museums, cars, parks* (count nouns); *pollution, traffic, crime, health care* (noncount nouns).
- Read the first sentence in Exercise A aloud as an example.
- Have students complete the exercise individually.
- Invite volunteers to read the sentences aloud. Ask whether the noun that goes with each answer is a count or a noncount noun. (count nouns: 1, 4-6, 8; noncount nouns: 2, 3, 7)

B

- Have students complete the exercise in pairs.
- Invite pairs to write their answers on the board. Review the answers as a class.

MORE ACTION

Have students research the statistics from Exercise B for their own countries and the United States (the number of tourists, cars, and so on). Have students write a set of comparative sentences about each fact and read them aloud to the class. Discuss any interesting facts or varying information that students present.

ACTIVE GRAMMAR: Superlative Adjectives

A

- Review the information in the grammar chart and explain the rules for each category. Point out that most superlative adjectives have the ending *-est* or *-iest* or use *most* before the adjective.
- Read through the adjectives in Exercise A and check that students understand their meanings by asking them to paraphrase the meanings. For example: *populated = a lot of people*.
- Ask students to write each adjective in the correct column and check their work with a partner.
- Review the answers with the class.

B

- Point out the sample answers in the first row of the chart and review how superlative adjectives are formed (*-est* / *-iest* or *most* + adjective).
- Then, have students complete the chart individually or with a partner.
- Draw a blank chart on the board and have volunteers fill in the chart with their answers.
- Review the answers with the class.

C 34

Play the audio and pause after each word to allow time for students to repeat.

ACTIVE GRAMMAR Superlative Adjectives

Type of Adjective	Superlative Form		
One-syllable adjectives	**the** old**est**	**the** larg**est**	
Two-syllable adjectives ending in *-y*	**the** bus**iest**	**the** sunn**iest**	
Two-or-more-syllable adjectives not ending in *-y*	**the most** populated	**the most** interesting	
Irregular forms	good – **the best**	bad – **the worst**	far – **the farthest**

A Write the adjectives in the correct column.

clean	healthy	noisy
fast	hot	popular
friendly	modern	populated

One-syllable adjectives	Two-syllable adjectives ending in *-y*	Two-or-more-syllable adjectives not ending in *-y*
high	rainy	expensive
fast	noisy	modern
clean	friendly	populated
hot	healthy	popular

B Write the superlative form of the adjectives in the correct column.

One-syllable adjectives	Two-syllable adjectives ending in *-y*	Two-or-more-syllable adjectives not ending in *-y*
the highest	the rainiest	the most expensive
the fastest	the noisiest	the most modern
the cleanest	the friendliest	the most populated
the hottest	the healthiest	the most popular

C **Pronunciation: Superlative adjectives** Listen and repeat. 34

1. the busiest
2. the tallest
3. the largest
4. the noisiest
5. the friendliest
6. the farthest
7. the rainiest
8. the highest
9. the sunniest

102 Unit 7

MORE ACTION

For further practice with superlative adjectives, dictate a random list of adjectives that are not on the page (for example, *careful, runny, neat, important*). Ask students to write them in their notebooks using the superlative form.

D Complete the sentences. Use the superlative form of the adjectives.

1. Alaska is (cold) the coldest state in the United States.
2. Florida is (popular) the most popular state for retired people.
3. (high) The highest city in the world is Wenchaun, China.
4. The Great Pyramid of Giza is one of (famous) the most famous structures in the world.
5. Oporto, Portugal, is one of (romantic) the most romantic cities in the world.
6. The Louvre in Paris is one of (interesting) the most interesting museums in the world.
7. Ojos del Salado, Chile, is (tall) the tallest volcano in the world.

E Match the place and the feature. Then, make a sentence about each place.

	Places	Features
c	**1.** Greenland	**a.** (large) desert
i	**2.** Everest	**b.** (cold) place
a	**3.** The Sahara	**c.** (large) island
j	**4.** Vatican City	**d.** (long) river
d	**5.** The Nile	**e.** (high) waterfall
b	**6.** Antarctica	**f.** (deep) ocean
f	**7.** The Pacific	**g.** (low) place
h	**8.** Asia	**h.** (large) continent
g	**9.** The Dead Sea	**i.** (tall) mountain
e	**10.** Angel Falls	**j.** (small) country

Greenland is the largest island in the world.

F In a small group, talk about students in your class. Use the words below.

athletic	funny	organized	serious	tall
friendly	(good) singer	quiet	talkative	young

We often use *one of the* ________ to talk about one of a group.

Zhen is one of the friendliest students in our class.

D

- Have students complete the task individually.
- Then, ask volunteers to read their answers aloud.
- Write the correct form of the adjectives for each sentence on the board so students can see how the answers are spelled.

E

- Ask students what information they can tell you about these places. Point out each location on the World Map in the back of the book.
- Set a time limit for students to work in pairs and find the answers.
- Check the answers as a class.
- Then, have pairs write sentences using the answers. Ask each pair to write one of their sentences on the board.

F

- Model one or two sentences with your class. For example: *Talia is one of the quietest students in our class.*
- Set a time limit for groups to write at least five sentences. Encourage them to use adjectives in addition to those in the word box.
- Ask volunteers to read their sentences aloud to the class and see if the class agrees with the sentences.

MORE ACTION

Encourage students to do more research online about different cities and countries in the world. Ask questions that students will have to research, for example: *Which country is the hottest? Which city is the largest?* Students can bring the answers to the next class and work in groups to create a quiz for other groups using this information.

ACTIVE GRAMMAR: *as ________ as, not as ________ as*

A

- Paraphrase the sentences in the first two grammar charts at the top of the page so students can better understand their meaning. For example: *China is as interesting as India. = China is interesting, and India is interesting, too.*
  Colombia isn't as populated as Brazil. = Brazil is more populated than Colombia.
- Give some additional examples by comparing students in the class and then asking questions. For example: *Ming is as tall as Alicia. Who is taller?* (They are the same height.)
- Turn to Appendix D. Read each sentence at natural speed. Then, repeat each sentence again more slowly so students have time to write.
- Students can check their answers by referring to Appendix D.

B

- Ask students to work in pairs to discuss and write sentences for each topic.
- After pairs write their sentences, ask volunteers to report to the class on their opinions. See if other students agree with their opinions.

ACTIVE GRAMMAR *as ______ as, not as ______ as*

China France	is	**as interesting as** **as beautiful as**	India. Italy.

Colombia Ecuador	isn't	**as populated as** **as large as**	Brazil. Mexico.

Use ***as*** ______ ***as*** to show that two people, places, or things are the same.
Use ***not as*** ______ ***as*** to show that two people, places, or things are not the same.
Florida is **not as large as** Texas. = Texas is **larger than** Florida.
Silver is **not as expensive as** gold. = Gold is **more expensive than** silver.

A Listen and write the sentences you hear. Your teacher will refer to Appendix D.

1. India is as interesting as China.
2. India isn't as large as China.
3. India is almost as populated as China.
4. India is as diverse as China.
5. Chinese food isn't as spicy as Indian food.

B **LET'S TALK.** Give your opinion. Use (*not*) *as* ______ *as* or a comparative adjective. Answers will vary.

1. art museums / history museums / interesting
2. Chinese food / Italian food / tasty
3. English / Mandarin Chinese / difficult
4. people in the city / people in the country / friendly
5. a week in New York City / a week in a national park / expensive

Art museums are not as interesting as history museums.

I think art museums are more interesting.

Beijing, China

Mumbai, India

MORE ACTION

Instead of dictating the sentences in Exercise A, write the sentences on strips of paper and give three strips to each student in a pair. Then, have students dictate the sentences to each other.

ACTIVE GRAMMAR Contrast: Comparative and Superlative Adjectives

A Complete the sentences. Use the correct form of each adjective.

1. New York is (large) ___the largest___ city in the United States, but Mexico City is (large) ___larger than___ New York City.
2. At this time, China is (populated) ___more populated than___ India. By 2025, India will probably be (populated) ___the most populated___ country in the world.
3. Shanghai has (long) ___the longest___ subway system in the world, but Beijing has (busy) ___the busiest___ subway system in the world.
4. Coffee is (popular) ___the most popular___ hot beverage in the United States. In many countries, tea is (popular) ___more popular than___ coffee.

B **LET'S TALK.** In a small group, complete the sentences about yourself. Then, compare yourself to other students. Answers will vary.

> Maria has two brothers and five sisters. She has the most brothers and sisters.

1. I have ______ brothers and sisters.
2. My house has ______ TVs.
3. I get up at ______ in the morning.
4. I live about ______ miles from school.
5. I can speak ______ languages.
6. I sleep ______ hours a night.

C Discuss these questions. Use adjectives in some of your answers.

1. What is the best soccer team in the world?
2. What is the busiest road in your area?
3. Who is the most famous leader in the world?
4. What is the best movie this year?
5. Which coffee is the tastiest?
6. What is the most interesting place to visit in your area?
7. What is the most difficult language to learn?

> Brazil has the best soccer team in the world.

> No way! Italy is better than Brazil.

> Spain has the strongest team this year.

ACTIVE GRAMMAR: Contrast: Comparative and Superlative Adjectives

A

- Review the difference between comparative and superlative adjectives. (Comparatives compare two things to each other. Superlatives compare one thing to a group of things.)
- Ask students to complete the task individually.
- Then, check the answers by asking students to dictate them to you as you write them on the board.

B

- Have students complete the sentences on their own.
- Then, have students work in groups to discuss their sentences.
- Ask volunteers from each group to read sentences from other students in their group.

C

- Appoint one student to lead the discussion.
- Encourage students to disagree with each other.

TEACHING TIP

While students are discussing the topics in Exercise C, make note of correct and incorrect sentences. At the end of the discussion, read the sentences aloud and ask students to say which are correct and which are incorrect. Write the incorrect sentences on the board and ask volunteers to correct them.

THE BIG PICTURE: Three Cities

A

Ask students to work in groups and discuss the questions about their own countries. Encourage them to ask each other questions and elaborate on their answers.

B 35

- Review the categories on the left-hand side of the chart. Explain any new words.
- Read the numbers in the column for Chicago. Ask volunteers to read the numbers in the column for Los Angeles so that students can practice pronouncing and listening to large numbers.
- Play the audio and have students take notes.
- Play the audio again so students can fill in the chart.
- Review all the information with the class. Ask which facts students find most surprising or interesting.
- Ask students to make sentences about the facts in the chart by using *more / less / fewer* and *as___as*. For example: *Los Angeles isn't as populated as New York. Chicago has fewer sunny days per year than New York.*

THE BIG PICTURE Three Cities

A Discuss these questions.

1. What is the largest city in your native country?
2. Are cities diverse in your country?
3. Is unemployment high or low in your country?
4. How do most people commute to work?

Los Angeles

B Listen and complete the chart with information you hear about New York City. 35

	Chicago	Los Angeles	New York
Population	2,704,958	3,976,322	8,537,673
Percentage of Hispanic origin	29.1%	48.2%	29%
Unemployment rate	5.2%	5.1%	4.6%
Median household income	$50,434	$51,538	$55,191
Median home price	$218,000	$605,000	$425,000
Average commute time	34.1 minutes	30.1 minutes	39.9 minutes
Percentage of people who drive to work	79.1%	72.3%	56.9%
Yearly rainfall	36.9 inches	12.9 inches	49.9 inches
Yearly snowfall	36.7 inches	None	25.1 inches
Sunny days per year	189	284	224

New York

TEACHING TIP

For extra listening practice, ask students to close their books. Write the categories from the left side and the top of the chart on the board and ask students to copy these in their notebooks. Dictate the numbers for each column and have students write them in the correct category. Then, students can open their books to check their answers.

C **CIVICS** Complete the sentences using the information from the chart in Exercise B.

1. The population of New York is (high) ___higher than___ the population of Chicago.
2. New York is (populated) ___the most populated___ city in the United States.
3. Los Angeles has (high) ___the highest___ percentage of Hispanics of the three cities.
4. A house in Los Angeles is (expensive) ___more expensive than___ a house in Chicago.
5. A house in Chicago is (expensive) ___less expensive than___ a house in New York.
6. New York has (high) ___the highest___ median household income.
7. Workers in New York have (long) ___the longest___ commute to work.
8. Chicago has (high) ___the highest___ unemployment rate of the three cities.

D **STUDENT TO STUDENT.** Listen and circle the correct city.

Student 1: Turn to Unit 7 in Appendix C. Read the questions in Set A to Student 2.

Student 2: Listen and circle the correct city. Then, turn to Appendix C. Read the questions in Set B to Student 1. See Appendix C for questions in sets A and B.

				Set A answers	Set B answers
1.	Chicago	Los Angeles	New York	1. New York	1. Chicago
2.	Chicago	Los Angeles	New York	2. Los Angeles	2. New York
3.	Chicago	Los Angeles	New York	3. New York	3. Los Angeles
4.	Chicago	Los Angeles	New York	4. Chicago	4. Los Angeles
5.	Chicago	Los Angeles	New York	5. New York	5. Chicago
6.	Chicago	Los Angeles	New York	6. New York	6. Los Angeles
7.	Chicago	Los Angeles	New York	7. Chicago	7. Chicago

Chicago

MORE ACTION

Ask students to form groups of three. Each group will choose three cities or places to compare. In groups, they should list the facts that they will compare. For example: population, average temperature, and so on. For homework, each person in the group will research as many facts about their chosen place as they can and bring the information to the next class. In groups, they will pool their information and make a report for the class.

C

- Ask students to complete the exercise individually.
- Check the answers as a class.
- Ask students to write five more sentences about these cities using comparative and superlative adjectives.
- Have volunteers read their sentences aloud to the class.

D

- Model the exercise with one pair of students.
- Then, ask students to complete the exercise in pairs.

CIVICS

The US Census is an official survey, mandated by the Constitution, that allows the US government to count the country's population. It is done every 10 years. The census gathers data on demographics, income, and housing in each state. Important governmental decisions are based on the results of the census, for example how many seats in the House of Representatives are allocated to each state and how federal funds are distributed.

In addition to the decennial national census, the Census Bureau issues many surveys every year to gather data.

The data used in Exercise B reflects census information available in 2016. These facts may change over time. The US government routinely updates and shares the latest data available through different official websites.

READING: Informational Text

A 36 (facing page)

- Ask where the nearest airport is and if anyone has used it. *What was the airport like? Was it busy? Were there many people on your flight?*
- Have students read the passage individually. Ask if they have any questions about vocabulary.
- Ask students if they have flown through any of the airports named in the article. If students have not flown through any of those airports, ask them to think of another airport they have used. *What were some of the features of the airport? What kind of jobs did you see airport employees doing?*
- Ask students to name different airport jobs and facilities. Write a list on the board.

READING Informational Text

The Busiest Airports

Three of the busiest airports in the world are in the United States. Los Angeles Airport (LAX) is located in Los Angeles, California. O'Hare Airport (ORD) is in Chicago, Illinois, and Hartsfield Atlanta International Airport (ATL) is in Atlanta, Georgia. These three are the busiest airports in the US because of the large number of passengers that pass through them every year. In addition, these airports move a great deal of cargo (packages, equipment, and so on).

LAX was established in 1928. It is now one of the busiest airports in the world, with 81 passenger and cargo airlines that use the airport. Each year, more than 59 million passengers travel through LAX. About 59,000 employees work at the airport. The employees work at a number of places throughout the airport, including airline counters, coffee shops, bakeries, and the 95 stores where passengers can shop. LAX is a pet-friendly airport with a small pet park where passengers can walk their dogs.

Each year, more than 77 million passengers use O'Hare, another one of the busiest airports in the world, with 70 airlines using its facilities. O'Hare was established in 1945. Today, many frequent fliers know O'Hare because flights often stop in Chicago on the way to other parts of the country or the world. Because so many passengers spend significant time in the airport, O'Hare offers a number of services, such as a hair salon, a children's museum, an athletic club, and a post office. About 52,000 employees operate the airport's 215 restaurants and stores.

Established in 1925, Hartsfield has become the busiest airport in the world. Over 104 million passengers pass through the airport each year. Forty-five passenger and cargo airlines use the airport. More than 63,000 employees work for the airlines and the 263 restaurants and shops. In fact, the airport is the largest employer in Georgia. To help people move from terminal to terminal, or from a terminal to one of the 30,000 parking spaces, the airport has an underground train, which connects all the airport terminals. 36

Three planes taxi at LAX.

108 Unit 7

CULTURE NOTE

Print out some information on frequent flier programs from the internet. If possible, bring in or print a picture of a frequent flier membership card. Explain to students that before they book a flight, they should sign up for that airline's frequent flier program so that they can start earning miles. Ask students if they are members of any frequent flier programs. What benefits do their programs offer?

TEACHING TIP

Lead a class discussion on the advantages and disadvantages of air travel. Do students like to fly? Do they think it is bad for the environment? Ask students what method of transportation they use the most. What is their preferred method of transportation for long trips? What are the advantages and disadvantages of that method?

A Discuss these questions.

1. What is the closest airport to your home?
2. What is the busiest airport in the country where you were born?
3. Do you know anyone who works at an airport? What is that person's job?

CULTURE NOTE

Many airlines offer frequent flier programs. A frequent flier is a person who often flies on a particular airline. Each time the passenger flies, the airline gives the passenger "miles." The passenger can use the miles to get free flights, upgrade to business or first class, or shop.

READING NOTE

Scanning for Information

When you scan an article, you do not need to read every word. You look through the article quickly to find the information you need.

B ACADEMIC Scan the reading and complete the chart.

Airport	Number of passengers	Year established	Number of airlines	Number of employees	Facilities offered
Los Angeles Airport (LAX)	more than 59 million	1928	81	59,000	pet park
O'Hare Airport (ORD)	more than 77 million	1945	70	52,000	hair salon, children's museum, athletic club, post office
Hartsfield Atlanta Airport (ATL)	over 104 million	1925	45	more than 63,000	train

C Correct the information. Write the name of the correct airport.

1. ~~LAX~~ ATL is the busiest airport in the world.
2. ~~ORD~~ ATL is the oldest airport of the three.
3. ~~ATL~~ ORD employs the fewest workers of the three airports.
4. ~~ORD~~ LAX is the most pet-friendly airport of the three.
5. ~~LAX~~ ATL handles the most passengers.
6. ~~LAX~~ ATL hires the most employees.

B

- Read the Reading Note about scanning. Explain that when you scan, you look quickly for specific words or information. Then, you read more carefully once you find what you are looking for.
- Set a time limit for students to scan the article and complete the chart.
- Review the answers as a class.

C

- Ask students to work individually. Then, have them compare answers with a partner.
- Go over the answers as a class.
- Ask students to make additional sentences about these airports using comparatives and superlatives.
- Ask volunteers to read their sentences aloud and see if the other students agree.

ACADEMIC

Emphasize that scanning allows students to quickly find information from a text. This strategy can be applied to any content area and is helpful when taking tests.

Around the World 109

WRITING OUR STORIES: An Invitation—Come to Machu Picchu

A

- Before reading, ask students what they know about Machu Picchu. *What country is Machu Picchu in?* (Peru) *What is Machu Picchu?* (an ancient Inca site) *Why is it famous?* (It is very high in the mountains with beautiful views.)
- Ask students to read the letter on their own.
- Then, ask some general comprehension questions. For example: *Who built Machu Picchu?* (the Incas) *What can you see there?* (the ruins of over 200 buildings) *When is the best time to visit Peru?* (from May to September)

B (facing page)

- Read the Writing Note and point out the position of the commas in the example sentences. Explain that, in a list of three of more items, commas should immediately follow each item, except the last item.
- Have students look at the letter in Exercise A. Point out how commas are used in the list in the first paragraph.
- Ask students to complete the exercise individually.
- Write the sentences on the board and invite volunteers to add commas to the sentences.

WRITING OUR STORIES | An Invitation—Come to Machu Picchu

A Read.

Dear Gabriel,

You should come to visit my country, Peru. It is one of the most interesting countries in South America. It has one of the most unusual places—Machu Picchu. Machu Picchu is one of the new Seven Wonders of the World. It is an ancient Inca site, located high in the Andes Mountains. It was the estate of the Inca emperor Pachacuti. You can visit the ruins of over 150 buildings, including houses, temples, and public buildings. One of the most famous places there is the Temple of the Sun. It has wonderful architecture. Don't miss the Temple of the Three Windows. It has a fantastic view of the Andes Mountains.

The best time to visit Peru is from May to September. That is the driest period. The busiest time is around our national holiday, July 28th, so it is better to travel before or after that date. If you come in the wintertime, you can experience one of our most exciting festivals, the Festival of the Sun.

See you in Peru,
Marco

Machu Picchu, Peru.

110 Unit 7

B Add commas to the sentences where necesssary.

1. Visit Machu Picchu early in the morning, late in the day, or during the rainy season if you want to avoid heavy crowds.
2. In Peru, the people speak Spanish and Quechua. (no comma added)
3. The Inca people did not use animals, iron tools, or wheels to build Machu Picchu.
4. Most tourists to Machu Picchu climb a mountain, take photos, and go back down to the city.
5. Hikers, tourists, and researchers say that Machu Picchu is a "magical" experience.

WRITING NOTE

Add commas (,) in a list of three or more people, places, or things:

The Amazon, the Nile, and the Yangtze are the three longest rivers in the world.

O'Hare, LAX, and Hartsfield are the three busiest airports in the United States.

O'Hare has many restaurants and stores. (No comma)

C Write a letter to a friend who is planning a vacation. Explain why your native country is a good place to visit. Use some superlatives. Here are some questions you can answer:

- Why should your friend visit your country?
- When is the best time to visit your country?
- What is one of the most popular places to visit? Describe it.
- What is one of the most historic places?
- What is one of the best beaches, lakes, or rivers? Why is it so good?
- What is the most interesting place? Why?
- What is the most fun activity to do in your country?

D Find and correct the adjective mistake in each sentence.

1. Russia is the ~~large~~ largest country in the world.
2. China is more populated ~~then~~ than Russia.
3. The Nile River is ~~more~~ longer than the Yangtze River.
4. The New York subway system is much ~~more~~ longer than the Boston subway system.
5. The Great Wall of China is one of the most popular attractions in the world.
6. The ~~most hot~~ hottest inhabited place in the world is Dallol, Ethiopia.
7. California is not as ~~larger~~ large as Alaska.

E ACADEMIC Give a short presentation to your classmates about an interesting destination in your native country. If possible, bring in a few pictures of the location.

One of the most interesting places in my country is...

C

- Review the questions with the class. Ask students to suggest additional questions that they can answer in their letter.
- Brainstorm a list of adjectives that students might want to use to describe their country, and write the list on the board. For example: *large, busy, diverse, sunny, happy, fun*, and so on.
- If necessary, have students finish the letter as homework and then exchange letters with a partner at the next class session.

D

- Have students complete the exercise individually or with a partner.
- Ask volunteers to write their corrected sentences on the board.

E

Encourage students to bring in books, brochures, or photographs to the next class to use during their presentations.

ACADEMIC

Have students refer to the English in Action feature in Unit 4 to review the criteria for giving a good presentation. It is important for students to practice their presentation at home and prepare detailed visuals of the destination they are presenting. They can draw pictures, print out maps, bring photos, or display images found online of their chosen destination.

ENGLISH IN ACTION: Using an Online Search Engine

A

- Ask students to name search engines (e.g., Google). Write a list on the board. Ask students which search engine they use the most and why.
- For question 5, have students explain why information on the internet may not be reliable. For example, a website may be an advertisement, someone's personal opinion, or contain facts that have not been checked for accuracy. Ask the class if some websites are more reliable than others.
- Suggest some ways to find out if information on the internet is reliable. For example, check the domain name of the website (is it a government or educational source?), who created the website, the date it was created, and the credentials or expertise of the creator of the website.

B

- Explain that students need to provide the search words they used, the website where they found the information, and the answer to the question. Encourage students to use a different website to answer each question.
- Review the answers as a class.

C

- Go over the answers as a class. For each question, write down the different websites that students used to find their answers. Which website was used the most?
- Ask if there are any websites on the list that are not reliable sources. Why should students avoid those websites? What websites should students use instead?

AT WORK

Computer literacy is essential in the workplace. As companies become more dependent on technology, employers seek employees who are proficient in the use of computers. For some careers, just a basic understanding of computer programs and applications can open the doors to potential employees. In other areas, in-depth knowledge and hands-on experience using specific computer software are required.

With the class, compare computer skills needed for different jobs. For example: an administrative assistant may only need a basic understanding of a computer program to write emails or schedule appointments; a web developer and a programmer need to know how to write code using specific software; teachers may only need to use online applications and email on a daily basis, but they may need to use specific software to record grades; a mechanic may need to know how to perform functionality tests using specific technology; a warehouse employee may need to use specific data software to track inventory or sales.

ENGLISH IN ACTION Using an Online Search Engine

A **AT WORK** Discuss these questions.

1. What online search engine do you use?
2. What kinds of information do you look up online?
3. What websites do you often use?
4. Is most information on the internet up to date?
5. How do you know if the information on the internet is true?

WORD PARTNERSHIPS

look up	a word information the meaning the definition the address

Online Search Tips: Keywords

1. Be specific. Put important words first.
   Example: Who won last year's World Series?
   Type: *World Series + date*.
2. Use three keywords or more:
   heart disease: too general
   heart disease causes: good—specific keywords
3. Put complete titles and phrases in quotes:
   "Blue Ridge Parkway"
4. Click on *Images*, *Maps*, or *Videos* to get a visual look at the information you want.

B In a group, go online and answer the questions. Write the answers in your notebook. Compare your answers.
Answers will vary.

URL = Universal Resource Locator, or internet address

1. What is the weather forecast for your city for tomorrow?
2. What is the population of Moscow, Russia?
3. How much is a ticket from the airport nearest you to Honolulu, Hawaii?
4. What are the hours of the Shedd Aquarium in Chicago? How much is an adult ticket?

C Compare your information as a class.

1. Does every group have the same information?
2. Did every group use the same website?
3. Are some websites more reliable than others?

UNIT 8 MOVING

Moving this historic home across the street, a block away from its original location, cost about $6,000,000.

ACADEMIC Read maps; understand pros and cons; design a timeline; use *so* to discuss cause-effect relationships

AT WORK Display work and schooling milestones in a timeline

CIVICS Report housing problems

CCRS Level A: R 3, 4, 5, 7, 8; W 3; L 1, 6; Level B: R 4, 5, 6, 7, 8; W 3, 4; L 1, 3, 6; Level C: R 1, 4, 5, 7, 8; W 4; L 1, 3, 6; Level D: R 4, 5, 7, 8; W 4; L 1, 3, 6; Level E: R 4, 5, 7, 8; W 4; L 6

ELPS Level 1 Standards 1, 2, 3, 6, 7, 8, 9, 10; Level 2 Standards 2, 3, 6, 7, 8, 9, 10; Level 3 Standards 2, 3, 6, 7, 8, 9, 10; Level 4 Standards 2, 3, 6, 7, 8, 9, 10; Level 5 Standards 2, 3, 6, 7, 8, 9, 10

CIVICS 04-01; 04-06

CASAS 0.1.2; 0.1.5; 0.1.8; 0.2.1; 0.2.4; 1.4.1; 1.4.7

IN THIS UNIT

In Unit 8, students will:

- Discuss housing conditions and moving
- Practice the simple past
- Learn about the tiny house movement
- Write about moving to the US

ABOUT THE PHOTO

Moving usually involves moving from one house to another, but as this photo shows, sometimes the house itself also moves. This photo shows the Harriet F. Rees house in Chicago, a 19th century building (1888) that was moved, at great cost to the city, from one block in Chicago to another to make room for new development.

Open the topic of moving to the class by taking a poll. Try to stay as much as possible in the simple past. Say: *Raise your hand if you moved only one time in your life. OK, what about two? Three?* Continue until you find the students who have moved the most (maybe stopping with *more than five times*). Tell students about some times you have moved and ask if anyone has moved for the same reason. Prompt them to raise their hand if they did something similar. For example: *I grew up in Philadelphia, but I moved to New York to go to school. (Anyone else?) Then, when I graduated, I got a job in DC, so I moved there. (Who else moved for a job?) But then I broke up with my boyfriend, so I moved back to Philadelphia. (Who else moved because of a relationship?)* Students may be willing to contribute some moving horror or success stories at this point; invite them to share.

A

- Read the statistic out loud. Do students think it is high or low? This statistic comes from fivethirtyeight, a well-known American website that specializes in statistics. The actual statistic they provide is that the average American moves 11.4 times.
- Ask questions about the picture, such as:
  Do you think these people are moving their own furniture, or is this a moving company? Is it expensive to rent a moving van? What about a storage space or pod? How much do you think it costs to use a moving company? What are the advantages or disadvantages of using a moving company? What alternatives are there?
- Ask students how many times they have moved. You can call out numbers of moves and have students raise their hands to show how many times they have changed homes. Ask students to give reasons why someone might move.
- Have students complete the exercise on their own.
- Invite volunteers to share their answers.

Some people use units like this one to store their belongings when they move.

A Read and complete. Answers will vary.

The average American moves eleven times during his or her life. What is your experience with moving?

1. In my native country, I ______________.

   a. never moved **b.** moved once **c.** moved ______________ times

2. I came to the United States in ______________.
3. I **had / didn't have** family in the United States.
4. Since I came to the United States, I have ______________.

   a. never moved **b.** moved once **c.** moved ______________ times

5. In the United States, I have lived in ______________ (city or state) and ______________ (city or state).
6. I moved because ______________.
7. Now I live in ______________ (city or state). In the future, I would like to live in ______________ (city or state).
8. In the future, I **will / won't** return to my native country to live.

MORE ACTION

Ask students the steps they would take to prepare for a move. For example: buy or find boxes, change their mailing address, rent a moving truck, ask a friend to help them move, sell any items they can't or don't want to take with them, and so on. For some steps, such as renting a moving truck, ask students to provide more detail. (For example: *You can rent a moving truck online with a credit card. You will need a driver's license.*) Write the ideas on the board, and then ask the class to create a chart advising people on how to move.

ACTIVE GRAMMAR Simple Past: Regular Verbs

I	**lived**	in Taiwan.
He	**moved**	to the United States.
They	**signed**	a lease.

1. Regular past verbs end in *-d* or *-ed*. (See Appendix B.)
2. The form is the same for singular and plural subjects.

A Read the story. Write the verbs in the simple past.

Miguel and Ana were unhappy in their last apartment. The apartment had only one bedroom and the kitchen was very small. They (want) _____wanted_____ (1) an apartment with two bedrooms and a large kitchen. They (look) _____looked_____ (2) online and (talk) _____talked_____ (3) to friends. Finally, they found an apartment they (like) _____liked_____ (4). They (sign) _____signed_____ (5) a lease and paid a security deposit. Miguel and Ana (prepare) _____prepared_____ (6) to move. They (pack) _____packed_____ (7) their clothes, books, and kitchen items into boxes. Miguel (rent) _____rented_____ (8) a small truck. On moving day, several of their friends (help) _____helped_____ (9) them move. They (carry) _____carried_____ (10) furniture and boxes out of the old apartment and into their new home.

This couple covered their fragile items with paper.

MORE ACTION

Have students close their books. Ask them to retell the story from Exercise A to a partner, using the answers on the board as prompts.

ACTIVE GRAMMAR: Simple Past: Regular Verbs

A

- Ask students what the people in the picture are doing. Do students know any other packing tips? Some might include marking boxes with a sticker (yellow for kitchen, blue for bedroom, etc.), or even labeling the box with the specific contents.
- Review the formation of verbs in the simple past.
- Give other examples of regular verbs and ask students to say the past forms. (For example: *talk—talked, want—wanted, park—parked*)
- Have students read the story and write the simple past forms.
- Ask them to compare their work with a partner.
- Check the answers by calling on volunteers to read their answers. Write the correct answers on the board.
- Then, ask students some comprehension questions about the paragraph. For example: *Why didn't Miguel and Ana like their old apartment?* (It was too small.) *How did they find their new apartment?* (They talked to friends and looked in the newspaper.) *Who helped them move?* (Their friends helped them move.)

B 37

- Say the first two verbs in the exercise (*changed, rented*), tapping on a hard surface to demonstrate one versus two syllables.
- Play the audio all the way through and have students write their answers.
- Play the audio again and pause after each word so students can repeat. After students have repeated each word, review the answers with the class.

C 38

- Contrast the difference in sound between the linked words in the exercise when pronounced separately (for example, *lived* and *in*) and the words when linked together.
- Then, play the audio and have students repeat the sentences.

D

Have students complete the exercise with a partner and compare their answers with another pair of students.

E

Remind students that they should write their sentences using the simple past. For example: *I asked my best friend to help me move.*

B **Pronunciation: Final *-ed*** Listen. Write the number of syllables you hear. Then, listen again and repeat. 37

> After most consonants, *-ed* is pronounced as /t/ or /d/.
> After /d/ and /t/, *-ed* is pronounced /əd/. This adds a syllable to the verb.

1. changed 1
2. rented 2
3. looked 1
4. needed 2
5. liked 1
6. wanted 2
7. helped 1
8. called 1
9. lived 1
10. painted 2
11. signed 1
12. waited 2

> The final *t* or *d* sound is often linked with the first vowel in the next word.

C **Pronunciation: Linking *-ed* + vowel sound** Listen and repeat. 38

1. He lived‿in a small apartment.
2. He looked‿at many apartments.
3. He filled‿out a rental application.
4. He signed‿a lease.
5. He packed‿all his things.
6. He borrowed‿a van.

D Talk about the things Miguel and Ana did when they moved into their new apartment.

> They registered their son in school.

1. register their son in school
   They registered their son in school.
2. introduce themselves to their neighbors
   They introduced themselves to their neighbors.
3. file a change of address form at the post office
   They filed a change of address form at the post office.
4. open a bank account
   They opened a bank account.
5. paint the kitchen
   They painted the kitchen.
6. wash the windows
   They washed the windows.
7. try a few restaurants in town
   They tried a few restaurants in town.
8. call the phone company
   They called the phone company.
9. change the address on their drivers' licenses
   They changed the address on their drivers' licenses.
10. apply for library cards
    They applied for library cards.

E Make a list of five things you did before or after you moved. Share your list with a partner.
Answers will vary.

MORE ACTION

For further practice with pronunciation and syllables, dictate a list of regular verbs in their base form, such as *like, want, jump, watch, call, open, answer, listen*, and so on. Then, ask students to write them in two columns: one-syllable words or two-syllable words, according to their simple past pronunciation.

ACTIVE GRAMMAR Simple Past: Irregular Verbs

A Listen and repeat. 39

Base Form	Past	Base Form	Past	Base Form	Past
be	was / were	fly	flew	run	ran
become	became	forget	forgot	say	said
begin	began	get	got	see	saw
bite	bit	give	gave	sell	sold
break	broke	go	went	send	sent
bring	brought	grow	grew	sit	sat
buy	bought	have	had	sleep	slept
come	came	hear	heard	speak	spoke
cost	cost	know	knew	spend	spent
do	did	leave	left	steal	stole
drink	drank	lose	lost	take	took
drive	drove	make	made	teach	taught
eat	ate	meet	met	tell	told
fall	fell	pay	paid	think	thought
feel	felt	put	put	wake	woke
fight	fought	read	read	wear	wore
find	found	ring	rang	write	wrote

B Ask and answer the questions. Use a verb from the list above. Answers will vary.

1. When did you come to the United States?
2. How did you come?
3. How much did you pay for your ticket?
4. What did you bring with you?
5. Who met you at the airport?
6. How did you feel?
7. Did you know anyone in the United States?
8. Where did you go when you left the airport?
9. What did you buy your first week in the United States?
10. When did you find your first job?
11. When did you begin to study English?

O'Hare International Airport, Chicago.

Moving 117

TEACHING TIP

Students will need several opportunities to learn the form of simple past verbs. Ask students to study the words in the chart in Exercise A at home. At the beginning or end of the next class, ask students to work with a partner or a small group and quiz each other on the simple past forms in Exercise A.

ACTIVE GRAMMAR: Simple Past: Irregular Verbs

A 39

- Play the audio and have students repeat the verbs.
- Ask students if there are any words they don't understand.
- Pick a few of the verbs and make example sentences using the present and simple past forms. For example:
  She goes to college there.
  She went to college there.
  He sleeps until noon.
  He slept until noon.

B

- Invite students to comment on the people in the photo. Ask: *Where do you think they are going? What do you think they have with them?*
- Have students take turns asking and answering the questions with a partner.
- As students work, move around the room, checking students' pronunciation and offering help as needed.

ABOUT THE PHOTO

Chicago's O'Hare International Airport is one of two major international airports serving Chicago and is one of the busiest airports in the the world (#6 in 2018, according to *Business Insider*). This photo shows the connecting tunnel between concourses B and C in Terminal 1; the kinetic neon light sculpture, by Michael Hayden, is called "The Sky's the Limit."

ACTIVE GRAMMAR: Past Time Expressions

A

- Review the words in the grammar chart and check comprehension by giving a time or date that can be rephrased using a time expression from the chart. For example:
  T: *Wednesday night.* (To be said on a Thursday.)
  S1: *Last night.*
  T: *In 2019.* (To be said in 2024.)
  S2: *Five years ago.*
- Explain that past time expressions like *yesterday* or *last* _____ are sometimes used at the start of a sentence when someone is beginning a story. For example: *Last night, I was walking my dog when…*
- Have students complete Exercise A individually.
- Go over the answers as a class and write the answers on the board.

B

- Remind students to use the past time expressions from the chart at the top of the page.
- Have students discuss their answers with a partner and then share some of their responses with the class.

ACTIVE GRAMMAR Past Time Expressions

Yesterday	Last	Ago
yesterday morning	last night	a few minutes ago
yesterday afternoon	last week	an hour ago
yesterday evening	last weekend	a week ago
	last Saturday	two years ago
	last month	
	last year	

Use a time expression at the beginning or the end of a sentence.

A Complete the sentences. Use *yesterday*, *last*, or *ago*.

1. We moved ____last____ year.
2. My brother visited us ____last____ month.
3. I graduated from high school six years ____ago____.
4. My sister broke her arm ____last____ Tuesday.
5. He got his driver's license ____last____ August.
6. The teacher left the classroom a few minutes ____ago____.
7. I went to the dentist ____yesterday____ morning.
8. We got married five years ____ago____.
9. I paid my rent ____yesterday____ afternoon.
10. I came to the United States a year ____ago____.

B Talk about the last time you did the things listed below. Answers will vary.

1. buy new sneakers
2. take a vacation
3. come to class late
4. see a movie
5. eat out
6. give someone a present
7. go to a party
8. lose something
9. wake up late
10. get a traffic ticket
11. go to the hospital
12. have a bad cold
13. text a friend
14. drive out of state
15. take a test

I bought a new cellphone last year.

I got a new pair of sunglasses last summer.

MORE ACTION

Have students make a list of three important events in their life, such as getting married, getting a job, or moving to the United States. Then, have them write sentences about these events using the simple past and past time expressions. Have them trade their sentences with a partner and correct each other's sentences.

ACTIVE GRAMMAR Simple Past: Negatives

I	**didn't live**	in the city.
You	**didn't watch**	the movie.
We	**didn't have**	her car.
She	**didn't lock**	the car.
They	**didn't take**	the bus to school.

Use *didn't* and the base form of the verb to form the negative.

A Complete the sentences about the place where you grew up. Answers will vary.

1. I (live) ______lived______ in the city.
2. I (live) ______didn't live______ in a small town.
3. I (grow up) ____________ on a farm.
4. When I was a child, I (walk) ____________ to school.
5. I (have) ____________ my own bedroom.
6. We (know) ____________ our neighbors.
7. My friends and I (play) ____________ outside in our neighborhood.
8. We (lock) ____________ our doors.

B **LET'S TALK.** Compare your life now with your life in the country where you grew up.

> In my country, I watched TV two or three hours a day. Now, I'm too busy. I only watch TV on the weekends.

1. watch TV
2. wear a warm coat
3. study English
4. have a cellphone
5. drive
6. eat ________ food
7. go to the market every day
8. work
9. know my neighbors
10. eat at fast-food restaurants

C **ACADEMIC** In your notebook, make a chart. Write three differences between your life now and your life in the country that you come from. Answers will vary.

Then	Now
I didn't eat at fast-food restaurants.	I eat at fast-food restaurants once a week.

ACTIVE GRAMMAR: Simple Past: Negatives

A

- Read the example sentences in the grammar chart and ask students to explain the difference between the affirmative and negative forms of the simple past. (The negative uses *did* + *not* and the base form of the verb.)
- Tell students that they do not have to change the base form of the verb when using the negative form of the simple past. They only have to add *didn't* before the verb.
- Have students complete Exercise A independently.
- Ask volunteers to read their sentences to the class. If other students have the same answer for a question, tell them to raise their hands. Then, ask students who had a different answer to raise their hands. Invite students to discuss all the answers as a class.

B

Ask students to use the topics in the exercise to talk with their partners.

C

- Have students use their answers from Exercise B to create a chart in their notebooks.
- Ask volunteers to write one difference from their chart on the board.

MORE ACTION

For homework, ask students to write a paragraph in their journal based on their notes in the chart in Exercise C.

ACADEMIC

As students work through exercises B and C, you may want to introduce them to the concept of a Venn Diagram. Two overlapping circles—one for here and one for their home country—show things that are the same in the overlapping space, and things that are different in each place in the spaces that do not overlap.

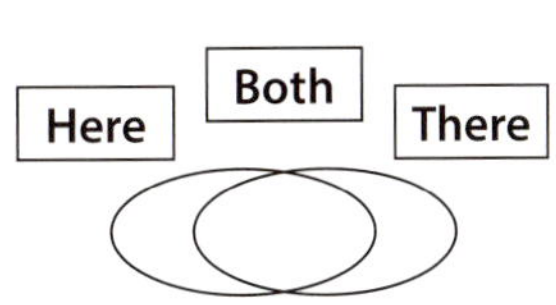

D

- Have two students role-play the conversation in the speech bubbles.
- Then, ask partners to compare their first-year experiences.
- Review some of the answers by choosing items in the list and asking different students to share their responses.
- Continue the discussion by including some items unique to your city or region that might be fun for the class to share: experiences with weather; visits to landmarks; first time trying a particular dish; first time hearing a particular regional expression; first time with a specific holiday.

E 40

- Point out the timeline and explain to students how to complete it. (Dates go on the horizontal line in the middle, and events go in the boxes above and below the year in which they occurred.)
- Play the audio once all the way through and have students take notes.
- Play the audio again and pause after each fact so students have time to fill in the timeline.
- Draw the timeline on the board and have volunteers fill it in.

F

- Tell students that before they make their timeline, they should write a list of the dates and events they want to include. Remind students to add events in chronological order.
- If necessary, have students finish their timeline for homework. Then, display the timelines on the wall of the classroom.

D Talk about your first year in the United States.

> I arrived at JFK Airport.

> I didn't fly here. I drove across the border at Tijuana.

1. arrive at an airport
2. live with a relative
3. begin to study English
4. like the weather
5. like the food
6. miss my family
7. visit relatives
8. come to the United States with my family
9. find a job
10. call my family a lot
11. meet new friends
12. get a driver's license
13. travel
14. go to high school here

E Listen and complete the timeline about Jarek's life. 40

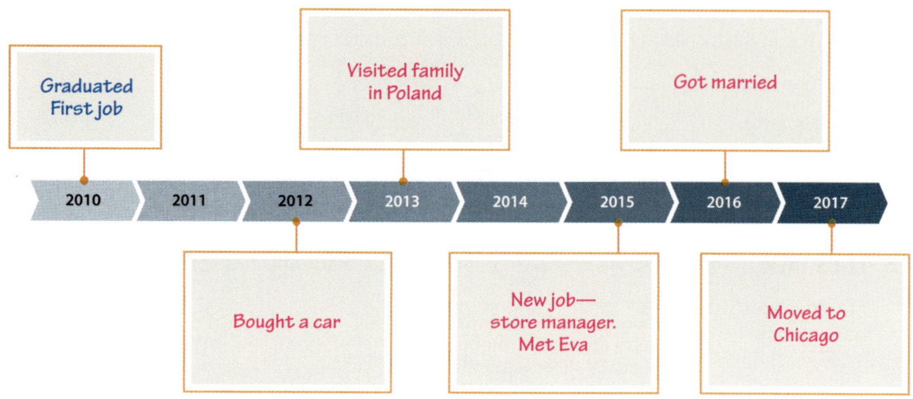

F AT WORK **LET'S TALK.** Below, draw a timeline with at least seven important dates in your life. Make sure to include work and study activities in the US. Share your timeline with another student. What events did you both include on your timeline? What events are different?

AT WORK

Students will be asked to present some format of timeline as they apply for jobs, be it on a resume or an application. Encourage them to have important dates like when they arrived in the US and when they started and ended different jobs clear in their minds when they present themselves for interviews.

TEACHING TIP

Print out other styles of timelines or take students to the library to research other timeline designs. Encourage them to use a design different from the one on this page, and to decorate their timelines with color, drawings, and photos.

ACTIVE GRAMMAR Past of *Be*

Be	
Present	**Past**
I **am** busy.	I **was** busy.
You **are** lonely.	You **were** lonely.
He **is** friendly.	He **was** friendly.
It **is** safe.	It **was** safe.
We **are** homesick.	We **were** homesick.
They **are** noisy.	They **were** noisy.

1. ***Was*** and ***were*** are the past of ***be***.
2. The negative forms are ***wasn't*** and ***weren't***.
   I ***wasn't*** busy.
   You ***weren't*** lonely.

A Explain the reasons why Boris didn't like his old apartment.

The neighbors were unfriendly.

1. neighbors / unfriendly
   The neighbors were unfriendly.
2. apartment / small
   The apartment was small.
3. appliances / old
   The appliances were old.
4. neighbors / noisy
   The neighbors were noisy.
5. elevator / usually broken
   The elevator was usually broken.
6. neighborhood / (negative) safe
   The neighborhood wasn't safe.
7. apartment / dark
   The apartment was dark.
8. rent / high
   The rent was high.
9. landlord / (negative) helpful
   The landlord wasn't helpful.
10. apartment / (negative) near public transportation
    The apartment wasn't near public transportation.
11. apartment / too far from work
    The apartment was too far from work.
12. basement / often wet
    The basement was often wet.

B **LET'S TALK.** Complete the conversation with your own ideas. Then, practice it with a partner. Finally, act out your conversation for the class. Answers will vary.

A: Why did you move?

B: I didn't like my old apartment!

A: Why not? What was the problem?

B: ______________________________

A: How about your neighbors?

B: ______________________________

A: How much was the rent?

B: ______________________________

A: How do you like your new apartment?

B: I love it! It's ______________ and ______________.

Moving 121

MORE ACTION

Ask students to form groups of three or four. One student in each group will tell the others about problems in his / her house or apartment. The other students will try to suggest different solutions. Each person in the group should take a turn role-playing a conversation with the student about the problems in his / her house or apartment. Finally, groups can report back to the class on the best solution for each student's problem.

ACTIVE GRAMMAR: Past of *Be*

A

- Use the grammar charts to introduce the simple past forms of *be*.
- Read the simple past sentences aloud and ask students to say the comparable simple present forms. (*was* = *am* or *is; were* = *are, wasn't* = *am not* or *isn't, weren't* = *aren't*)
- Read the direction line to Exercise A out loud. Call on a student to read the example in the speech bubble.
- Have students work in pairs to write their sentences. Then, call on volunteers to read their answers.
- Invite students to discuss reasons they have not liked apartments or homes they've lived in.

B

- Model the exercise for the class with a student.
- Have students complete the conversation individually and then compare their answers with a partner. Have partners pick one conversation to practice (or they can combine their answers to make a new conversation).
- Then, ask volunteers to present their conversations to the class.

CIVICS

Encourage your students to be familiar with their rights as tenants and to look into resources in the community that can support them if they encounter issues. After students work through Exercise A, pause for a moment to discuss which issues with Boris's apartment might be covered in a lease. Leases and rental laws vary significantly from state to state, but generally require a baseline level of maintenance and quality (the elevator should be working, for example) and responsiveness from the landlord.

THE BIG PICTURE:
Moving

A

- Present the exercise as a class discussion.
- Read aloud the first two examples in the list.
- Ask one volunteer to write the list of ideas on the board.

B 41

- Direct students to look at the map. Do they know what state this is? (Florida) See if they can also identify the neighboring states: from left to right, Mississippi (not actually touching Florida), Alabama, and Georgia.
- Play the audio all the way through and have students take notes as they listen. Remind them to write key words and phrases, not complete sentences, as they take notes.

THE BIG PICTURE Moving

A Why do people move? Add five more reasons to the list. **Answers will vary.**

1. They get a new job.
2. They want better schools for their children.
3. They want to be near their family.
4. They buy a house.
5. They find a better apartment.
6. They get married.
7. They need a bigger apartment.

B ACADEMIC Listen to the conversation and follow the dialogue on the map. 41

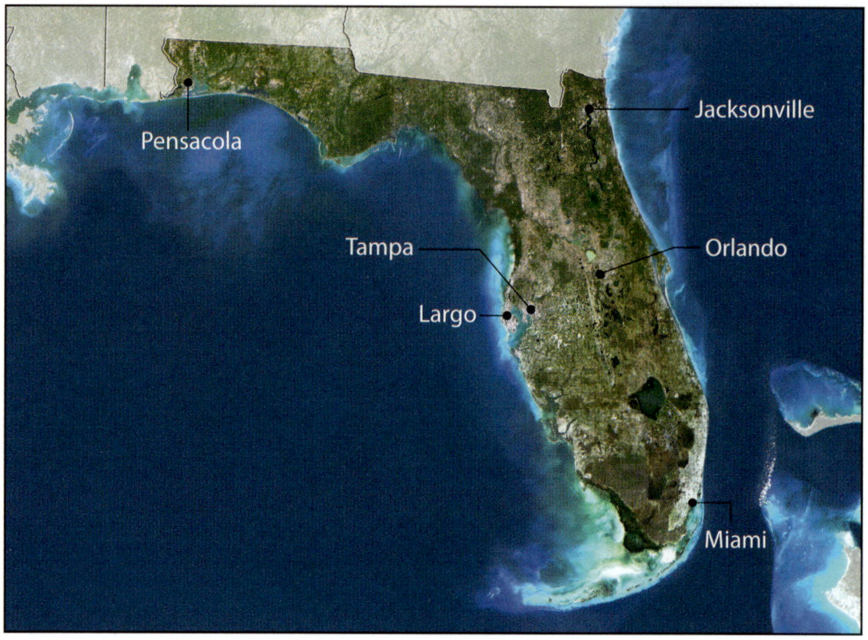

C Listen to the dialogue again. Write the reason for each move in the chart. 41

Move	Reason for move
Puerto Rico to Tampa	Her father had a job offer in Florida.
Tampa to Tampa	She got married.
Tampa to Largo	Their apartment had a lot of problems.
Largo to Tampa	They had a baby.
Undecided	Diego got a promotion.

D Complete the sentences in the simple past. You will use one verb twice. Some of the sentences are negative.

be	fix	have	~~live~~	meet	move	rent

1. We ___lived___ in the same house for twenty-two years.
2. I ___met___ Diego a year after we ___moved___ to Florida.
3. We ___rented___ a one-bedroom apartment near my family.
4. The apartment building ___had___ a lot of problems.
5. The landlord ___didn't fix___ things.
6. One time, we ___didn't have___ air conditioning for a week.
7. In Largo, we ___were___ only a few blocks from the beach.

E Listen and write the sentences you hear. Your teacher will refer to Appendix D.

1. Yolanda's father had a job offer in Florida.
2. He moved his family to Tampa.
3. Yolanda and Diego liked Largo.
4. They lived there for two years.
5. After Yolanda had a baby, they moved back to Tampa.
6. Yolanda needed to go back to work.
7. Diego's job just offered him a promotion.

F **LET'S TALK.** In a small group, talk about where you live and your future plans.

1. Where do you live?
2. When did you move there?
3. What do you like about your home or area? What don't you like?
4. Do you live near your family?
5. Are you thinking about moving? Where would you move? Why?

Moving 123

MORE ACTION

For further listening practice, tell your students about a situation where you or someone you know decided to move. Explain what happened. Encourage students to ask you questions. Then, ask volunteers to share their stories with the class as well.

C 41

- Play the audio again. Have students complete the exercise individually. If they took notes in Exercise B, have them refer to those for help.
- Then, check the answers as a class.

D

- Students should be able to complete this task without the audio. Give them a few minutes to complete the items individually. Then, call on students to read each sentence.
- As students give their answers, reinforce correct pronunciation of the final *-ed*. Have the whole class repeat any words that need additional practice.

E

- Read the sentences in the appendix (or printed here in the answer key) at a regular speed. Read the sentences a second time, if necessary.
- Have students check their answers in the appendix, or display the answers with the Classroom Presentation Tool.

F

- Give groups 5–10 minutes to complete the exercise. Ask each group to take notes as they discuss the questions.
- Ask one student from each group to relay the information they learned about a classmate. Make an effort to call on students who may not normally volunteer.
- If you have more time for discussion, explore the superlative categories for the first few questions. For example (1) who lives closest/farthest from school; (2) who has lived where they live the longest. This will naturally provide opportunities for students to continue to practice the simple past.

VIDEO AND READING: Informational Text

A 42 (facing page)

- Ask students to look at the picture and describe the house. What are the advantages and disadvantages of living in this type of home?
- Ask if any students have ever lived in, or if they know anyone who lives in, a tiny home (or even just a very small apartment).
- Have students read the passage individually.
- Ask what the main idea of the passage is (the pros and cons of living in a tiny home). On the board, draw two columns, one labeled "Pros" and the other labeled "Cons." Ask students for suggestions for each column. Are there more advantages or disadvantages?
- Read the questions in Exercise A aloud to the class. Ask two or three students to answer each question.

ABOUT THE PHOTO

Greg (top) and Renee (right) Cantori live in this tiny home with their 19-year-old daughter, Andrea (center). The Cantoris chose to downsize to a tiny house so they can travel—the house can be hitched to a truck and towed.

VIDEO AND READING Informational Text

Tiny Living

How much space do you need? If you think that you can live in a small, **efficient** space, maybe a tiny home is right for you. Tiny homes are **affordable** alternatives to normal-sized homes. There are tiny house communities from California to Texas to Georgia. The American Tiny House Association can give you more information. There are also TV shows about building tiny homes.

Tiny homes come in many styles. Owners can buy and use construction plans or they can customize their tiny homes. Some homes look very modern, but others look like most other homes—just smaller. One thing that tiny homes have in common is that they are very small, but they have the **essentials**: a place to sleep, a kitchen, a refrigerator, a bathroom, a compact washer/dryer, and an open living space. Others have outdoor space or a balcony. If a person chooses to live in a tiny home, storage space is very important. There is storage everywhere.

There are pros and cons to owning a tiny home. One of the main advantages is the cost. It is cheap to own a tiny home, and the utility bills are lower, especially if the home has solar power. Tiny homes are convenient if an owner decides to move. That is why some tiny homes are on wheels. However, if your home is on wheels, you need a pickup truck to move it. Another advantage is that it takes less time to clean, but you must be organized. A tiny home can be uncomfortable if it is **messy**. Finally, another pro is that a couple will spend more time together. A con is that you will lose some of your privacy.

In Detroit, Michigan, a program is offering tiny homes to low-income single residents. This program helps individuals who have had hard times because of homelessness, prison, or low income. Any person with a **steady** job, even at minimum wage, can apply for a new tiny home. Each home has a kitchen, a bathroom, a living room, a backyard, and a washer-dryer. Some homes have separate bedrooms too. The homes cost between $40,000 and $50,000. The residents pay $1 per square foot, so a home of 250 square feet will cost $250 a month. Similar tiny home communities for low-income residents are available in other states. 42

This family owns a 238-square-foot tiny home in Pasadena, Maryland.

CULTURE NOTE

Tiny houses have become a trend in the US in reaction to a number of factors. The movement to "Go Tiny" encourages people to find their happiness in experiences, not possessions, and promotes fiscal responsibility (and freedom) by providing a path to home ownership without hundreds of thousands of dollars of debt. The movement appeals to people of all ages, though the path to homeownership may be particularly appealing to millenials. It is not without its perils, though—cook an onion in a tiny home and your entire house will smell like onion, not just the kitchen.

TEACHING TIP

An alternative way to discuss the reading is to ask students to create questions about the passage. Each group can work together to create several questions. Then, have each group read their questions to the rest of the class. The only rule is that no question can be asked more than once.

A After reading, discuss these questions. Answers will vary.

1. Do you live in a house? If so, how many bedrooms and baths does it have?
2. Do you think you need more space or less space? Why?
3. Do you like tiny homes?

B Read the statements. Are they *true* or *false*?

1. All of the tiny houses are in California. false
2. There are many types of tiny houses. true
3. Tiny houses do not have outside space. false
4. Tiny houses need good storage spaces. true
5. Electricity bills are lower. true
6. There is less privacy in a tiny home. true

C Match each word with its definition.

d 1. affordable
e 2. efficient
b 3. essentials
a 4. messy
c 5. steady

a. not neat; not in order
b. very important things
c. regular; constant
d. a cost that is not too high
e. works with little waste; well organized

READING NOTE

Understanding two sides of an issue

Articles often show two different sides of the same issue or idea. These are called the advantages and disadvantages, the pros and cons, or the positives and the negatives.

D ACADEMIC Read the article again. List two more pros and cons of tiny homes.

Pros	Cons
1. lower cost	1. need a pickup truck to move
2. takes less time to clean	2. uncomfortable if messy
3. Couples will spend more time together.	3. You will lose some privacy.

E ▶ WATCH Watch the video and discuss these questions.

1. What are some of the problems with the current housing we have?
2. How do tiny houses help solve those problems?

TEACHING TIP

Encourage students to practice using the dictionary to look up words they don't understand. Divide the class into small groups and give each group a dictionary. Have them look up the vocabulary words in Exercise C in the dictionary and decide which definition best fits the context. Ask each group to report back to the class. Students should read the definition first and then explain the meaning of the term in the context of the reading.

ACADEMIC

When presenting an argument or making a decision, it is important to consider all sides of the issue. This process is called making an informed decision. The opposite—only considering the information you want to hear—is called cherry-picking information.

B

- Give students a moment to do the exercise on their own. As they go, suggest that they underline or make note of the parts of the passage that support each answer.
- Then, ask volunteers to read each item out loud. Which lines from the reading helped them answer each item?

C

- Give students a minute or two to complete the exercise, then have them compare answers in pairs.
- Ask volunteers to make up sentences using each word in context.

D

- Read the Reading Note aloud. Point out the three different ways of describing the two sides of an issue (advantages / disadvantages; pros / cons; positives / negatives).
- Ask students to complete the chart for Exercise D. Then, have them compare their answers with a partner.
- Emphasize that answers should be in note form (key words or phrases), not full sentences copied from the passage.
- Draw the chart on the board and ask students to dictate the answers to you.

E ▶ WATCH

Play the video and give students a few minutes to discuss the questions. Then, ask if they have any new ideas on tiny houses. If students would not live in a tiny house, would they considering staying in one for a vacation?

WRITING OUR STORIES: Moving to a New Country

A

- Ask students to read the story and underline any words or phrases they don't understand. Some new phrases you may want to point out are *family affair, sponsor us,* and *on the first try.*
- Write the unknown words and phrases on the board and discuss them with the class.
- Read the Writing Note aloud to the class. Point out that *so* acts as a conjunction that connects two sentences. Explain that the second half of the sentence is the result of something that happened in the first half of the sentence.
- Review the Writing Note and explain the cause-effect relationship between the two parts of each sentence. Reverse the clauses using *because* if you think this is helpful. For example, the sentences in the box could also be expressed as *I couldn't find a job because I didn't speak English* and *We moved to Arizona because we didn't like the cold weather*. Likewise, sentence 1 in Exercise B on the following page can be written as: *I didn't like my job, so I quit* or *I quit my job because I didn't like it*. Explain that the person quit their job after they realized they didn't like it.

WRITING OUR STORIES Moving to a New Country

A Read.

My First Year in the United States

My arrival in the United States was a family affair. My mother and father, four brothers, and I came to the United States from Peru together. My two older brothers met us at the airport. They had been here for many years and they were finally able to sponsor us.

We arrived in October, not able to speak any English. By January, I was studying English at the local adult school.

One of my brothers helped me find a job in a nail polish factory. I didn't like it at all because the salary was very low, and new workers came and went every few weeks. After a year, I was able to attend beauty school and get a manicurist license. When I finished, I got a job at a nail salon. Many of my customers were American, so I was able to become more confident speaking English.

The first summer we were here, my brother taught me how to drive. I passed my driving test on my first try! At first, I only drove near my house, but now I can go a little farther.

I think the first year in a new country is difficult and a little scary, but it's also exciting. It really helps if your family is together and you can help each other.

WRITING NOTE

Using *so*

Use *so* to show the result of an action or a situation.

I didn't speak English, **so** I couldn't find a good job.
We didn't like the cold weather, **so** we moved to Arizona.

B Match the two parts of each sentence.

b 1.	I didn't like my job,	a.	so I came to live with him.
a 2.	My brother already lived here,	b.	so I quit.
c 3.	I couldn't speak English,	c.	so I registered for an English class.
e 4.	English was very difficult,	d.	so I rented one with a friend.
d 5.	Apartments were very expensive,	e.	so I studied very hard.

C Complete the sentences. Answers will vary.

1. I didn't have a car, so ________________.
2. My neighborhood wasn't safe, so ________________.

D Check the information that is true about your first year in the United States. Complete the sentences. Answers will vary.

☐ 1. I came to the United States alone.
☐ 2. I came to the United States with my family.
☐ 3. I found a job at ________________.
☐ 4. I didn't find a job.
☐ 5. I began to study English.
☐ 6. I got my driver's license.
☐ 7. I moved from ________ to ________.
☐ 8. I traveled to ________________.
☐ 9. I bought a ________________.

E ACADEMIC Write about your first year in the United States. Write more details about the information you checked in Exercise D. Include one or two sentences with *so*.

F Find and correct the mistakes.

1. I came to ^the United States in 2015.
2. I ~~not~~ didn't have any family in this country.
3. I ~~live~~ lived with some friends for a month.
4. I found a job, but I ~~no~~ didn't like it.
5. In my country, I ~~have~~ had a better job.
6. At first, I ~~am~~ was very lonely.
7. I ~~miss~~ missed my family a lot, so I called them every week.
8. My first year was difficult because I ~~don't~~ didn't speak English.
9. I ~~begin~~ began to study English at an adult school.

MORE ACTION

Have students correct each other's essays from Exercise E. Encourage students to rewrite their essays based on their partner's corrections.

B

Ask students to complete the exercise independently and then check their answers with a partner.

C

- Ask students to complete the sentences. Then, call on different students to read their answers.
- Choose some of the sentences that contain new and useful language and write them on the board.

D

Encourage students to take notes while completing the exercise in preparation for writing an essay in Exercise E.

E

- Have students brainstorm ideas for their essay using their checklist from Exercise D and their timeline. If necessary, have students complete the essay as homework.
- Then, have volunteers read their essay aloud to the class. Discuss any interesting information or similar experiences that other students had.

F

Write the sentences on the board and ask volunteers to correct the sentences.

ACADEMIC

Using connectors like *so* helps show the connection between ideas and improves the clarity of writing. Encourage the use of connectors, including *so*, *because*, *but*, and others, to help improve students' writing.

ENGLISH IN ACTION: Reporting a Housing Problem

A

- Discuss the pictures with the class and ask students if they can describe the problems without looking at the word box.
- Ask what students would do if any of these problems occurred in their home or apartment. Would they call someone to help, or would they try to fix the problem themselves?

B 43

- Play the audio once all the way through and have students listen only.
- Then, play the audio a second time so that students can write their answers.
- Check the answers as a class.
- Discuss whether any students would have handled the situation differently.

C

- Invite volunteers to role-play their conversations for the class.
- Encourage other students to suggest how they would have handled the situation.

ENGLISH IN ACTION Reporting a Housing Problem

A Write the letter of the housing problem under the correct picture.

a. The faucet is leaking.	**d.** The paint is peeling.
b. The lock is broken.	**e.** The air conditioner isn't working.
c. There are cockroaches.	**f.** We don't have any heat.

1. f

2. b

3. e

4. c

5. a

6. d

B Listen to the conversations. Write the problem and the apartment owner's response. 43

Conversation 1

Problem: The air conditioning isn't working.

Response: The owner will fix it tomorrow around 10:00.

Conversation 2

Problem: The freezer isn't working.

Response: She will check the freezer today at 9:00.

CULTURE NOTE

If you have an apartment, keep a record of your calls with the landlord. Write the date, the time, and the name of the person you spoke to. Keep a copy of any notes you send. If possible, take a photograph of the problem.

C **LET'S TALK.** With a partner, write a phone conversation between a tenant and a landlord. Then, act out your conversation for the class.

128 Unit 8

TEACHING TIP

Tell students that if they rent a house or apartment, their landlord is legally obligated to keep the property safe and liveable. This means that the landlord is responsible for addressing any safety or housing quality issues that arise, such as repairs and animal infestations. If students are having difficulty getting their landlord to fix problems, there are a number of steps they should take. First, they should review their lease and see if the landlord has violated any conditions in the lease. Then, they should document the dates and times of incidents, with pictures if possible, and follow up with a formal letter to the landlord. (Students should keep a copy of all correspondence they send to and receive from their landlord; see the Culture Note on this page.) If students still have difficulty with their landlord, they can search online for organizations that provide free or low-cost legal assistance to renters, such as tenant unions, the county clerk's office, and Legal Aid societies.

UNIT 9

NATURAL DISASTERS

A man in a coastal city looks through his window during a flood.

ACADEMIC Read and understand maps; write a report; infer information

AT WORK Understand emergency procedures in the workplace

CIVICS Understand how to prepare for an emergency or a weather event

CCRS Level A: R 1, 2, 5; W 2, 7, 8; L 1, 5, 6; Level B: R 1, 2, 6; W 2, 7, 8; L 1, 5, 6; Level C: R 1, 2, 7; W 2, 7, 8, 9; L 1, 5, 6; Level D: R 1, 2, 7; W 2, 7, 8, 9; L 6: Level E: R 1, 2, 7; W 2, 7, 8, 9; L 6

ELPS Level 1 Standards 1, 2, 3, 5, 7, 8, 9, 10; Level 2 Standards 1, 2, 5, 7, 8, 9, 10; Level 3 Standards 1, 2, 3, 5, 7, 8, 9, 10; Level 4 Standards 1, 2, 3, 5, 7, 8, 9, 10; Level 5 Standards 1, 2, 3, 5, 7, 8, 9, 10

CIVICS 16-1; 16-2; 16-3; 16-7

CASAS 0.1.2; 0.1.5; 2.3.3; 3.4.8

IN THIS UNIT

In Unit 9, students will:

- Write a report
- Discuss emergency preparedness
- Understand what to do during an emergency

ABOUT THE PHOTO

Extreme weather is becoming more and more common around the world. Faced with the effects of climate change, some countries are exploring and developing solutions to cope. For example, Vanuatu, a country in the Pacific island region, has implemented climate adaptation measures like breeding pigs that are more tolerant to the heat and cultivating crops that better adapt to climate change. Rotterdam, a city in the Netherlands, has built parking lots, parks, and plazas that can become emergency reservoirs and retain floodwaters. The city also counts on the Maeslantkering, a sea gate of massive proportions built with the most extreme climate change models in mind to prevent the city from flooding.

This photo shows a man looking out the window of his home in Dordrecht, the Netherlands during a storm. Heavy rain and winds up to 70 miles per hour caused severe flooding in his neighborhood. Dikes, which are long walls built to prevent flooding, and moveable barriers kept flooding to a minimum in this city.

Ask students if they know what a natural disaster is and if they can give any examples. Share with the class a news article or report on a recent natural disaster in the US (for example, a forest fire). Preview the use of the past by asking questions such as *Did you hear about this natural event? How did you learn about this? When did this happen? Where did it happen? Did anyone get hurt?*

A 44

- Ask students to explain what is happening in each photo.
  Ask: *Where in the US do these events occur? Which ones occur in our state?*
- Play the audio and have students complete the exercise individually.
- Review the answers and ask students to explain each word or phrase in their own words.
- Discuss the photos with students. Invite them to ask questions and comment on the pictures. Include as many students as possible in the discussion. For example:

  S1: *What do you call the red stuff in photo B?*

  T: *That's lava. When a volcano erupts, lava comes out. Has anyone ever seen a volcano?*

  S2: *I saw volcanoes with lava when I went to Hawaii.*
- Write any key words that come up during the discussion on the board. For example: *lava, funnel cloud, shake, blow*, etc.
- Encourage students to start a new page in their vocabulary notebooks on the topic of natural disasters.

A Listen and repeat the words in the box. Then, write the correct natural disaster or event under each picture. 44

drought	forest fire	snowstorm / blizzard
earthquake	heat wave	tornado
flood	hurricane	volcanic eruption

a. forest fire

b. volcanic eruption

c. flood

d. tornado

e. drought

f. earthquake

g. snowstorm/blizzard

h. hurricane

i. heat wave

130 Unit 9

MORE ACTION

In pairs or small groups, have students pick a natural disaster and write safety tips for surviving that type of disaster. Make sure that each group chooses a different natural disaster. Students should think about tips for what to do before, during, and after the disaster occurs. For example, to prepare for a hurricane, people should buy canned goods and bottled water and board up their house. Ask each group to present their tips to the class. Have the class give suggestions for other ideas that groups can add to their lists.

B Write the letter of the event from Exercise A next to its description.

__d__ **1.** We saw a large black cloud in the sky and we ran into the basement.

__h__ **2.** The rain was very heavy and the wind was terrible. It knocked down thousands of trees in our area. We lost part of our roof.

__a__ **3.** We could see the flames and the smoke for fifty miles.

__f__ **4.** The house shook. I quickly got under the table. Some of our pictures fell off the walls.

__c__ **5.** The water in the river kept rising and rising. We had to evacuate our house.

__b__ **6.** For days before, the mountain made loud noises and smoke came out of the top. Then, there was a terrible explosion and rocks shot up in the air. The lava started to flow down the mountain.

__i__ **7.** It was very hot for weeks. The city issued a warning that people should not exercise outdoors. We had our air conditioner on all day.

__g__ **8.** It snowed for two days. We had three feet of snow. School closed for three days. It took us two days to shovel our driveway.

__e__ **9.** There was no rain all summer. The city declared water restrictions. We couldn't water the lawn or wash our cars.

C ACADEMIC Discuss these questions.

1. What is a "natural" disaster? Can you think of any other natural disasters?
2. Have any of these natural disasters ever occurred in your state?
3. Look at a map of the United States. What areas of the United States are more likely to have hurricanes? Snowstorms? Earthquakes? Tornadoes?
4. Which of these events or disasters sometimes occur in your native country?
5. Have you ever experienced a natural disaster? Tell the class about the event.

New plants grow in a forest after a fire.

Natural Disasters 131

B

- Ask students to complete the exercise on their own.
- Check the answers as a class.
- Ask which words in each sentence helped students identify the correct disaster.
- Write any new words on the board and ask students to write them in their vocabulary notebooks, identifying each one as a noun, verb, or adjective.

C

- Ask students what natural disasters occur in their own countries. Have they or anyone they know ever experienced a natural disaster? Have volunteers provide some details about the event.
- Ask students to identify what natural disasters occur in the United States. Using the map at the end of the book, point at different areas in the United States and ask what natural disasters occur in each region.
- Discuss these questions in small groups or as a class.

ABOUT THE PHOTO

This photo was taken in an area near Eklutna Lake, in Chugach State Park, Alaska, some time after a massive wildfire spread over more than 1,000 acres of land.

An average of up to 5 million acres of land are destroyed by wildfires each year in the US. Although wildfires can occur all over the world, they are most common on the west coast of the US, where the combination of drought, high temperatures, and lightning and thunderstorms present the necessary conditions for a wildfire to occur. States like California, Oregon, and Colorado have experienced some of the worst damage caused by wildfires.

Although wildfires can cause destruction, and sometimes even put animal and human life at risk, wildfires can also have a positive effect on nature by eliminating harmful insects or clearing underbrush.

TEACHING TIP

Disasters may be a sensitive topic for some students, especially if they or their family have experienced one. Make sure not to press volunteers too hard for information if they appear uncomfortable talking about the subject. If you prefer, you can write a list of recent disasters on the board and include the date and location where each disaster occurred.

ACTIVE GRAMMAR: Past of *Be*: Questions

A 45

- Review the grammar charts with the class. Point out that the answers to the *be* questions are singular or plural depending on the subject of the question.
- To practice *be* questions and *yes / no* answers, write some pronouns on the board, point to a pronoun, and say a prompt word. Have one student ask the question and another student answer affirmatively or negatively. For example:
  T: (points to *he*) *Hungry.*
  S1: *Was he hungry?*
  S2: *Yes, he was hungry.*
- To practice *wh-* questions, write the question words on the board. Choose one natural disaster and ask students to make up questions about it using *who, what, where, when, why,* and *how*. Have other students answer the questions.
- Have students complete Exercise A individually.
- Then, play the audio so students can check their answers.
- Write the correct answers on the board. If students have difficulty understanding why an answer is correct, underline the subject of the sentence and point out whether it is singular or plural.

ACTIVE GRAMMAR Past of *Be*: Questions

Were you home?	Yes, I **was**.	No, I **wasn't**.
Was he cold?	Yes, he **was**.	No, he **wasn't**.
Was it windy?	Yes, it **was**.	No, it **wasn't**.
Were they scared?	Yes, they **were**.	No, they **weren't**.

Where were you?	I **was** at home.
Why was she scared?	Because the fire **was** near her house.
Where was the forest fire?	It **was** in California.

A Complete the questions and answers. Then, listen and check your work. 45

1.	How deep __was__ the water?	It __was__ six feet deep.
2.	How strong __was__ the wind?	It __was__ a hundred miles per hour.
3.	__Were__ you in Texas during the drought?	Yes, I __was__.
4.	How long __was__ the drought?	It __was__ five months long.
5.	__Was__ there any rain?	No, there __wasn't__.
6.	Where __were__ the tornadoes?	They __were__ in Nebraska.
7.	__Were__ you at home?	No, I __wasn't__. I __was__ in my car.
8.	How many tornadoes __were__ there?	There __were__ four.
9.	When __was__ the earthquake?	It __was__ last year.
10.	How strong __was__ the earthquake?	Thankfully, it __wasn't__ strong.
11.	__Were__ the children in school?	Yes, they __were__.
12.	__Were__ any children hurt?	No, they __weren't__.
13.	Where __was__ the forest fire?	It __was__ in the hills near my town.
14.	__Was__ there a lot of snow during the blizzard?	Yes, there __was__.
15.	__Were__ schools closed for a long time?	No, they __weren't__. Schools opened the day after the storm.

MORE ACTION

For further practice with *wh-* questions, ask students to work in pairs and choose one natural disaster each, but not to tell it to their partner. Their partner will ask questions using the past with *be* to try to guess what the disaster is. For example: *Where was the disaster? Was it hot? Was there a lot of water?* When the first student guesses correctly, students should switch roles.

ACTIVE GRAMMAR Simple Past: *Yes / No* Questions

Did	you	**evacuate**?	Yes, I **did**.	No, I **didn't**.
	he	**go** to work?	Yes, he **did**.	No, he **didn't**.
	it	**rain** all week?	Yes, it **did**.	No, it **didn't**.
	they	**lose** power?	Yes, they **did**.	No, they **didn't**.

In conversation, *Did you* sounds like */Diju/* or */Didja/*.

A **Pronunciation: *Did you*** Listen and repeat. 46

1. Did you see the tornado?
2. Did you watch the storm on TV?
3. Did you evacuate?
4. Did you have any damage?
5. Did you feel the earthquake?
6. Did you lose power?

B Ask and answer questions about a heat wave. Use the words and pictures below.

Did people exercise outside?

No, they didn't. They exercised at the gym.

1. people / exercise outside
Did people exercise outside? No, they didn't. They exercised at the gym.

2. people / drink a lot of water
Did people drink a lot of water? Yes, they did.

3. the power / go out
Did the power go out? No, it didn't.

4. you / take long, cool showers
Did you take long, cool showers? Yes, I did.

5. you / keep your air conditioner on all day
Did you keep your air conditioner on all day? Yes, I did.

6. you / turn off your air conditioner at night
Did you turn off your air conditioner at night? No, I didn't. The air conditioner was on all night.

C In your notebook, write five more questions about the heat wave.

ACTIVE GRAMMAR: Simple Past: *Yes / No* Questions

A 46

- Review the questions in the grammar chart and the note next to the chart. Point out that *did* is repeated for both singular and plural subjects in the affirmative and negative responses. Explain that the base form of the verb is used after *did*.
- Say the first sentence of Exercise A at slow speed and then again at normal speed. Ask students if they can hear the difference in how *did you* is pronounced in each sentence.
- Play the audio, pausing after each sentence, and have students repeat each sentence.

B

- Read the instructions and model the first question with a student.
- Then, ask students to complete the exercise in pairs.
- Ask volunteers to present their questions and answers to the class.

C

- Have students write their questions individually.
- Then, have students take turns asking a partner their questions.

ACTIVE GRAMMAR:
Simple Past: *Wh-* Questions

A

- Ask students to identify the order of the words in the grammar chart at the top of the page. (*Wh-* word + *did* + subject + verb)
- Have students complete Exercise A individually.
- Then, check the answers by asking volunteers to write their sentences on the board.

B

- Have students practice their conversations. Encourage students to use a mix of *wh-* and *yes / no* questions.
- Ask volunteers to practice their conversations in front of the class.
- Correct pronunciation and grammar as necessary.

ACTIVE GRAMMAR Simple Past: *Wh-* Questions

When	**did**	the storm	**begin?**
Where	**did**	you	**stay?**
How many days	**did**	it	**rain?**
How much damage	**did**	you	**have?**

A Write the words in the correct order to make questions.

1. flood / when / the / did / happen / ?
   When did the flood happen?
2. rain / days / how many / it / did / ?
   How many days did it rain?
3. did / evacuate / how many / the city / people / ?
   How many people did the city evacuate?
4. your home / did / have to / leave / you / ?
   Did you have to leave your home?
5. did / how / your family / get / to a safe place / ?
   How did your family get to a safe place?
6. did / in a shelter / you / how long / stay / ?
   How long did you stay in a shelter?
7. have / your home / did / any damage / ?
   Did your home have any damage?

B **LET'S TALK.** Use the questions in Exercise A. In pairs, practice a conversation about a flood. Act out your conversation for the class.

When did the flood happen?

It happened in June.

In August 2017, it rained in Houston, Texas, for four days. Hurricane Harvey brought more than four feet of rain and flooded much of the city.

TEACHING TIP

While students are practicing their conversations, move around the room and take notes of any common errors. Make a list of these sentences and write them on the board. Ask students to correct them.

C ACADEMIC Read the article. Then, complete the questions and answers. Answers may vary.

A forest fire that burned 15,000 acres was finally brought under control on Wednesday morning. The fire began Sunday in Black Bear Park.

On Monday, the mayor ordered all residents to leave their homes. The police evacuated more than 500 residents. The fire destroyed twenty homes in the area and caused heavy damage to forty others. There were no injuries. Officials estimated the damage to homes and cars at twenty million dollars. The governor declared the town a disaster area.

The fire spread quickly in the hot, dry conditions. It was difficult to fight the fire because of the strong winds.

Police closed Route 40 to traffic on Tuesday because of heavy smoke conditions. Thousands of travelers had to drive an hour north to Route 28 to pass the fire area.

Some residents did not follow the evacuation order. Paul Grayson sent his wife and two children to safety, but he stayed to hose down his roof with water. As flames came near his house, he started thinking, "Am I crazy? Did I stay here too long, just for a house?"

1. How many acres did the forest fire burn?
   It burned 15,000 acres.
2. When did it start?
   It started on Sunday.
3. Where did the forest fire begin?
   It began in Black Bear Park.
4. How many residents did the police evacuate?
   The police evacuated more than 500 residents.
5. How many homes did the fire destroy?
   The fire destroyed twenty homes.
6. How much damage was there?
   There was about twenty million dollars in damage.
7. Why was it difficult to fight the fire?
   It was difficult to fight the fire because of the strong winds.
8. Which road did the police close?
   The police closed Route 40.

A forest glows in the dark during a wildfire.

C

- Have students read the article silently.
- Then, ask some general questions about the main points of the story. For example: *Where was the fire? What did the mayor do? Was there a lot of smoke?*
- Ask students to complete the questions in the exercise. Have students underline the part of the passage that helped them answer each question.
- Ask volunteers to read their answers aloud to the class and explain where they found the information.

MORE ACTION

For homework, ask students to research a disaster in your state. They can use the internet to research facts and details. Then, they can present the information and ask each other questions in the next class.

D

- Point at the photo and ask students to describe what they see.
- Have students work in groups to brainstorm questions about the snowstorm. Each student should write down all the final questions from the group in their notebooks. Suggest that students pose some of their questions to the man in the picture (for example: *Did you lose power? How long did it take you to clear the sidewalk of snow?*) Encourage students to be creative when writing their questions.
- Then, have each student ask one of their group's questions to another group in the class.

E

- Discuss some ways in which people usually get information about the weather (weather apps, TV or radio forecasts, news or weather websites).
- Ask students if they usually check the weather, how often, and with what purpose.
- Ask students to complete the exercise individually. Then, ask them to share their suggestions in small groups.
- Ask a member of each group to share with the class the group's suggestions.
- On the board, make a list of the most popular suggestions from students.

CIVICS

In the US, it is very common to use the weather as a topic to make small talk. Simple statements like *What a beautiful day!* or *It is so rainy today* can easily, and safely, be used as conversation starters with English speakers.

D **LET'S TALK.** Work with a group. Write six questions about the snowstorm. Then, join another group. Ask and answer your questions. Answers will vary.

A man clears the sidewalk in front of his home after a snowstorm in Boston, Massachusetts.

1. How many inches of snow did Boston get?
2. ____________
3. ____________
4. ____________
5. ____________
6. ____________

E CIVICS **LET'S TALK.** Your friends have recently moved to a cold climate. The weather forecast is for three feet of snow! How should they prepare? Write three suggestions. Answers will vary.

1. ____________
2. ____________
3. ____________

136 Unit 9

MORE ACTION

Bring in photos of other types of natural disasters. Attach each photo to the top of a large piece of paper, leaving space underneath the photo for students to write. Have students work in pairs and give one photo to each pair of students. Have pairs write one question about their photo and then pass it along to another pair. Have each pair add a question until each photo has ten questions written underneath it. Finally, have students role-play a conversation about one of the disasters using the questions under the photo. As students write, walk around the classroom and correct their questions as necessary. Make sure that students do not repeat questions that have already been written and that they do not write the same question for every photo.

ACTIVE GRAMMAR Simple Past: *Who* Questions

Who helped a neighbor after the flood?	Jack **did**.
Who saw the tornado?	Ivan and Raisa **did**.
Who was at home when the earthquake hit?	Ursula **was**.

In these questions, *Who* is the subject.

A Read.

Kim and Don live in southern California. There was a large forest fire near their home.

Carla lives in Kansas. Last week, she saw a tornado coming toward her house.

Brian lives in Buffalo, New York. During the last snowstorm, Buffalo got three feet of snow.

Marisa and Marco live in Florida. They listened to the reports of the hurricane coming toward their city.

B Ask and answer questions about what you read with *Who*.

Who shoveled the driveway?

Brian did.

1. shovel the driveway Who shoveled the driveway? Brian did.
2. run down to the basement Who ran down to the basement? Carla did.
3. evacuate Who evacuated? Kim and Don did. / Marisa and Marco did.
4. have an accident in the snow Who had an accident in the snow? Brian did.
5. listen to the weather channel Who listened to the weather channel? Marisa and Marco did.
6. see the fire in the distance Who saw the fire in the distance? Kim and Don did.
7. hear the tornado warning Who heard the tornado warning? Carla did.
8. pack the car and leave Who packed the car and left? Kim and Don did. / Marisa and Marco did.

C In a group of five or six students, ask and answer the questions. Answers will vary.

1. Who watched the news last night?
2. Who had a big breakfast today?
3. Who listened to the news today?
4. Who listened to the weather report this morning?
5. Who called a family member last night?
6. Who got up late this morning?
7. Who took the bus to school?
8. Who went to bed after midnight last night?

No one did.
I did.
Two of us did.
A couple of us did.
A few of us did.
All of us did.

TEACHING TIP

When students are working in groups, it is sometimes useful to assign roles to some of the students to make sure that all students participate equally. For example, one student can be the group leader whose responsibility is to ensure that everyone speaks. Another can be the group secretary, who takes notes of the answers. A third student can take notes of any grammar or vocabulary questions that come up.

ACTIVE GRAMMAR: Simple Past: *Who* Questions

A

- Read the questions in the grammar chart and review the formation of *who* questions that ask about the subject.
- Contrast the difference between *who* questions about a subject and *who* questions about an object.
- Ask volunteers to read the information in the word box aloud for the class.
- Model the example in the speech bubbles with a student.

B

- Ask students to work in pairs to complete the exercise.
- Have each pair ask and answer one of the questions. Write any incorrect questions and answers on the board and correct them as a class.

C

- Review the answers to *who* questions in the blue box next to the exercise. Explain that most of these responses are given by a group of people. Ask which pronoun in the answers demonstrates this (*us*).
- Have students get into groups. Ask each group to select a volunteer to write down the group's answers to the questions.
- Then, have groups take turns asking and answering the questions.

THE BIG PICTURE: The Hurricane

A

- Ask students to comment on what they see in the picture.
- Ask: *What is the woman carrying? What is the man doing? What is in the box on top of the car? What does it look like outside?*

B 47

- Play the audio and have students take notes as they listen.
- Have students complete the exercise individually, then compare answers in pairs.
- Check the answers as a class.

CIVICS

FEMA, the Federal Emergency Management Agency, is an organization in the US that helps states and communities before, during, and after an emergency or a disaster. Another organization that also provides emergency assistance in the US is the American Red Cross. This organization not only participates in disaster relief efforts but also offers programs to educate the public on how to respond to an emergency. Both of these organizations share information on how to prepare for an emergency. Some basic tips are:

- Have a first aid kit readily available.
- Keep flashlights and extra batteries handy.
- Always keep your cellphone charged.
- Have cellphone chargers handy.
- Keep a fire extinguisher in your home.

THE BIG PICTURE The Hurricane

A CIVICS This family is preparing for a hurricane. Explain what they are doing and why.
Answers will vary.

B Listen to the conversation. Then, answer the questions. 47

1. Where does the couple live?
   North Carolina
2. How much warning did they have before the hurricane?
   a week
3. What did they put in the garage? Why? They put the yard furniture, barbecue grill, and garbage cans in the garage so they wouldn't fly through a window.
4. What did they buy at the store?
   food, batteries, water, a power saw
5. Why did they need a power saw?
   to cut up trees that might fall
6. Why do you think they filled the bathtub with water?
   for washing, for the toilet
7. How strong was the wind?
   80–100 miles per hour
8. How long was the power out?
   two days
9. What damage did their neighbor have?
   a tree came down on his roof
10. Where did the woman stay during the hurricane?
    in the bathroom

TEACHING TIP

Ask students some *yes / no* questions about the audio from Exercise B that are false. Ask students to correct you. For example:

T: *Was the power out for three days?*

S: *No, the power was out for two days.*

C Complete the questions with *Did* or *Was*. Then, write the answers.

1. Did they listen to the weather forecast? Yes, they did.
2. Was there enough warning? Yes, there was.
3. Did they buy water? Yes, they did.
4. Was the wind strong? Yes, it was.
5. Did they evacuate their home? No, they didn't.
6. Was the woman scared? Yes, she was.
7. Did she stay in the bathroom? Yes, she did.
8. Was her husband relaxed? Yes, he was.
9. Was the rain heavy? Yes, it was.
10. Did a tree fall on their house? No, it didn't.

D Complete the conversation.

1. **A:** How much warning did you have?
   B: We had warnings for about a week.
2. **A:** Where did you put everything?
   B: We put everything in the garage.
3. **A:** What did you buy?
   B: We bought extra food, batteries, and a power saw.
4. **A:** Did you evacuate?
   B: No, we didn't evacuate. We stayed in the house.
5. **A:** How strong was the wind?
   B: It was 80 miles per hour.
6. **A:** Did you lose electricity?
   B: Yes, we lost electricity for two days.
7. **A:** Did you have any damage?
   B: No, we had very little damage.
8. **A:** Were you scared?
   B: I was so scared! I stayed in the bathroom most of the time.

C

- Read the first example sentence. Remind students that *did* is an auxiliary verb that requires a main verb. In the first sentence, the main verb is *listen*. In the second sentence, there is not a main verb, so the answer is *was*.
- Ask students to complete the exercise on their own.
- Review the correct answers by having one student read a question and then having him or her call on another student to answer.

D

- Have pairs of students complete the conversation together.
- Then, call on different pairs to read some of their sentences to the class.
- As a follow-up, have one student in each pair close their book and try to answer the questions from memory while their partner asks the questions. Then, have students switch roles.

MORE ACTION

For homework, ask students to find an article about a natural disaster and bring it to the next class. In pairs or groups, students can role-play interviewing a person who experienced this disaster by using the information in the article. Have students in the group assign themselves parts: one student will be the person affected by the disaster, and other students will be interviewers who write and ask the questions. Have students switch roles so every student has the chance to ask and answer questions.

VIDEO AND READING: Descriptive Text

A 48 (facing page)

- Point to the picture and ask students to comment on what they see. Ask: *What do you think the funnel cloud is made of? How tall do you think the funnel cloud is? How fast do you think it's moving?*
- Ask a student to read the eight statements aloud.
- Then, have students circle the answers.
- Have students read the passage silently. Then, if necessary, they should correct their answers.
- Ask general comprehension questions about the passage. For example: *When does a tornado form? What are the warning signs of a tornado? What damage is a tornado capable of doing?*
- Go back to the *true / false* statements and discuss the answers again. Which items did students answer correctly before reading the passage? If students changed their answers after reading the passage, have them point out the part of the passage that directed them to the new answer.

VIDEO AND READING Descriptive Text

Tornadoes

A tornado, also called a twister, is a **violent**, spinning cloud that reaches from the **ground** up to storm clouds in the sky. Most tornadoes are weak, lasting only a few minutes, and have winds of less than 110 mph. But the strongest tornadoes can last more than an hour and have wind speeds of 200 mph or more. They can destroy houses in seconds, turn over cars, and pull people, trees, and furniture into the air.

The United States has more tornadoes than any other country in the world. In a typical year, there are 800 to 1,000 tornadoes in the United States. Most **occur** in the middle of the country. Tornadoes **form** when warm and cool air meet. In the Midwest, the warm air from the Gulf of Mexico often meets the cold air from Canada.

Tornadoes can occur at any time of year, but the usual tornado season is from March through May. Tornadoes form most often in the afternoon and early evening. There is often little **warning** of a tornado. People who live in the Midwest know the signs of tornado activity. The sky becomes a dark, often greenish color. Dark clouds appear in the sky and there is often large hail. Suddenly, there is a loud sound, like a train or a jet plane. Sometimes, tornadoes occur in groups. Two, three, five, ten, or more tornadoes can form over a large area.

One of the strongest tornadoes in history hit Joplin, Missouri, on May 22, 2011. Twenty minutes before the tornado, sirens rang, warning of the tornado. Some people heard the warnings, but others did not. The tornado was one mile wide and destroyed everything it touched, including homes, businesses, churches, the hospital, and the high school. The tornado killed 158 people and injured 1,150 others. One family ran down into their basement. Twenty minutes later, when they came up from the basement, nothing was left of their house. At the local Home Depot, the tornado **lifted** off the roof. According to local reports, between twenty-eight and thirty people in the back of the store **survived**, but the eight people in the front of the store were killed.

The safest place to be during a tornado is in a safety shelter, a small underground room that some people build to protect their families. Other safe places are basements or a first-floor bathroom, which is often the most solid room in the house. 48

This tornado with winds between 166 and 175 mph struck a neighborhood in Katie, Oklahoma.

140 Unit 9

TEACHING TIP

For additional reading practice, write some facts from the reading on the board and ask students to write the question for each fact. For example:
110 mph (How fast are most tornadoes?)
800–1,000 (How many tornadoes are there every year in the US?)

READING NOTE

Analyzing *True / False* statements

In a *True / False* statement, take note of words like *all, every, always*, and *never*. These statements are often false. Sentences with words like *many, some, sometimes*, and *often* are usually more accurate.

Look at the difference:

All tornadoes cause damage. False *Many* tornadoes cause damage. True

A Circle *True* or *False*.

1.	All tornadoes can destroy homes.	True	(False)
2.	Some tornadoes cause millions of dollars of damage.	(True)	False
3.	Tornadoes always occur in the afternoon or early evening.	True	(False)
4.	Tornadoes never occur at night.	True	(False)
5.	More tornadoes occur in the United States than in any other country.	(True)	False
6.	All families in the Midwest have safety shelters.	True	(False)
7.	People always know when a tornado is going to occur.	True	(False)
8.	Tornadoes can come in groups of two, three, or more.	(True)	False

B ACADEMIC The first word in each line is from the reading. Circle the word with a similar meaning.

1.	violent:	(strong)	dark
2.	ground:	(earth)	storm
3.	occur:	(happen)	area
4.	form:	active	(develop)
5.	warning:	typical	(sign)
6.	lifted:	(picked up)	destroyed
7.	survived:	died	(lived)

C Complete each sentence with one of the numbered words from Exercise B.

1. A ___violent___ tornado can cause loss of life and property.
2. The tornado destroyed our house, but we all ___survived___.
3. Weather forecasters can predict a hurricane a week or two in advance, but there is often no ___warning___ of a tornado.
4. Tornadoes can ___occur / form___ at any time of year.
5. The tornado was so strong that it ___lifted___ the car off the ground.

D ▶ WATCH Watch the video. Discuss these questions.

1. What are some ways people stay informed during a natural disaster?
2. What important information does the reporter share with the public about this event?

B

- Ask students to complete the exercise individually and then look back at the passage to check their answers.
- Review the answers as a class. Ask students to explain how they worked out their answers.
- Have students write any new vocabulary in their notebooks.

C

- Have students complete the exercise using the main vocabulary words from Exercise B.
- Go over the answers as a class.

D ▶ WATCH

- Play the video. Have students take notes on what they see.
- Play the video again. Discuss the questions as a class.
- For further practice, use the video worksheet at the back of this book.

TEACHING TIP

As a follow-up to the reading passage, ask pairs or groups of students to write additional *True / False* sentences about the passage and exchange them with another pair or group of students. Remind them to include some sentences using *many, some, sometimes*, and *often*.

WRITING OUR STORIES:
A Short Report

A

- Ask students to comment on the photograph at the bottom of the page and any facts they know about Hurricane Katrina. Ask: *What does the photo show?* (Flooding from Hurricane Katrina.) *What city did Hurricane Katrina hit?* (New Orleans) *What happened to the city?* (The city was flooded and the majority of it was destroyed.)
- Ask students to review the notes on Hurricane Katrina. Explain that when taking notes about a subject, it is helpful to write down as much information as possible so that you have plenty of information to draw from when writing the final report. It is better to have too much information that you can narrow down later than not enough information.
- Ask students if there are any facts that surprised them. What facts did they find most interesting?
- Then, have students read the report on their own.
- Ask students if there are any notes that were not used in the reading that they think would have been helpful information to include.

WRITING OUR STORIES A Short Report

A Look at the notes about Hurricane Katrina. Then, read the report.

Notes:
Formed late August 2005, near the Bahamas
Moved across Florida into the Gulf of Mexico
Became stronger – category 5
Hit Louisiana and Mississippi on August 29th as a category 3
Heavy wind and rain – 8 to 12 inches
New Orleans – very low, below sea level
Strong walls called levees protect the city.
The water went over the levees and flooded the city.
80 percent of city – under water. Destroyed most of city
More than 1,500 people died.
Damage – over $125 billion
More than 150,000 people did not evacuate.
Thousands rescued by boat, helicopter
50 percent of the population left for other cities.
Today – New Orleans – still rebuilding

Damage caused by Hurricane Katrina in New Orleans, Louisiana.

Hurricane Katrina was one of the worst hurricanes in the history of the United States. On August 29, 2005, Katrina hit the city of New Orleans as a category 3 hurricane. New Orleans is located below sea level. Strong walls, called levees, protect the city from water. The water broke the levees and flooded the city. The water flooded 80% of the city. Boats and helicopters rescued thousands of people, but more than 1,500 died. After the storm, more than 50% of the population left the city for other areas. Today, New Orleans is still rebuilding.

A wave reaches Miyako City, Japan, during the 2011 tsunami.

B ACADEMIC Write a report about the tsunami that hit Japan in March 2011. Use the notes below. Choose the facts you would like to include. Answers will vary.

Notes:

March 11, 2011
Strong earthquake in the Pacific Ocean
This earthquake caused a tsunami.
Tsunami – a giant wave, wall of water
Japan had tsunami warnings.
The tsunami hit northeast Japan.
Waves in Japan: up to 130 feet high
Waves in Hawaii: 11–12 feet high
Waves in California and Oregon: 9 feet high
More than 20,000 people died.
Fires destroyed thousands of homes and businesses.
The Fukushima Daiichi Nuclear plant lost power.
The lost power caused an increase in radioactive material.
The government evacuated residents within 12.5 miles of the plant.
Several countries sent help and financial support to Japan.

C Find and correct the mistakes.

1. There ~~were~~ was a lot of rain.
2. There ~~was~~ were several tornadoes in Nebraska.
3. Before the hurricane, we ~~listen~~ listened to the radio.
4. Many people ~~evacuate~~ evacuated the city.
5. More than 100,000 people ~~die~~ died.
6. The nuclear power plant ~~lose~~ lost power because of the flooding.
7. The damage to the cities ~~were~~ was about 199 billion dollars.

WRITING NOTE

Taking notes for a report

When you are preparing to write a report, look at several sources of information: the internet, books, and newspapers. Take notes on the information you read, but do not copy sentences. In a report, it is important to use your own words. It is not necessary to use all your notes in your report.

B

- Point at the photo and ask students to explain what they think is happening.
- Ask students what they already know about the tsunami in Japan.
- Have students read the notes. Ask them if there is any additional information they would like to add or research.
- Read the Writing Note to the class.
- Have students mark the notes they want to include in their report with an asterisk (*).
- After students write their reports, have them trade papers with a partner. Have students check their partner's report against the notes in the book and correct any errors. Also, have students correct any mistakes in grammar or punctuation. Then, students should return the reports to their partner and rewrite any sentences with mistakes.

C

- Using their reports from Exercise B, have students write any sentences with mistakes in grammar or punctuation on the board. Then, ask volunteers to correct the sentences. This will allow students to check the accuracy of their own corrections.
- Write the sentences from the exercise on the board and invite volunteers to come up and correct the sentences.

ACADEMIC

In some cultures, it is acceptable to copy material from outside sources in class assignments. Explain to students that copying material from sources and presenting it as one's own work—without properly giving credit to the original source—is called *plagiarism*.

In the US, and in many other countries, plagiarism is not an acceptable practice and will carry serious academic consequences. Emphasize to students that they must either paraphrase or quote third-party material that they use for reports in their classes. Paraphrasing is restating material in your own words, while quoting is copying material word for word. Bring in information from a book, magazine, or online article and write sentences demonstrating how students can paraphrase or directly quote information. Remind them that if they copy information directly, they must use quotation marks around those parts and attribute them to the original author. For example:

The news network CNN reported that the earthquake that caused the tsunami was "the largest earthquake ever to hit Japan."

ENGLISH IN ACTION: Preparing for an Emergency

A

- Have students work in groups.
- Draw the chart on the board and ask volunteers from each group to fill in the columns.

B

- Have students get into groups and read the emergency directions.
- Explain any unfamiliar vocabulary.
- Ask students to think of other suggestions for each emergency.
- Go over the answers as a class. Ask groups to share additional suggestions.

C

- Ask students to think about the items that are most important to them. For example, they may want to take photos and other personal items, but they should also consider items that they need, such as medication.
- Ask a member of each group to read their list aloud and explain their choices. As a class, determine the top ten items that students would pack.

D

- Model how to answer the first question by telling students what you would do if there was an emergency in the classroom.
- Ask volunteers to share their answers with the class. Ask them to describe in as much detail as possible how emergencies are handled in their workplace.
- If students do not know about a specific emergency plan at work, ask them if they have developed a plan for emergencies at home and to describe it for the class.

ENGLISH IN ACTION Preparing for an Emergency

A How much warning do people usually have for these disasters? In a small group, write each disaster in the correct column. Compare your answers with another group's. **Answers may vary.**

earthquake	hurricane	tsunami
flood	snowstorm	volcanic eruption
forest fire	tornado	

WORD PARTNERSHIPS

issue	a flood warning
	a tornado warning
	an evacuation order

Several Days' Warning	Short Warning	Little or No Warning
snowstorm	volcanic eruption	tornado
hurricane	forest fire	earthquake
	flood	tsunami

B **CIVICS** Read the emergency directions. Which disaster in Exercise A do they refer to?

1. Secure your home. Move essential items to an upper floor. Turn off utilities. Disconnect electrical appliances. Do not touch electrical equipment if you are wet or standing in water. ___flood___
2. Evacuate. If there is time, connect garden hoses. Fill any pools, hot tubs, garbage cans, tubs, or other large containers with water. ___forest fire___
3. Go to a safe area, such as a basement, or to the lowest building level. If there is no basement, go to the center of an interior room on the lowest level (closet, interior hallway) away from corners, windows, doors, and outside walls. Do not open windows. ___tornado___
4. Drop to the ground, take cover by getting under a strong table or other piece of furniture, and hold on until the shaking stops. Stay away from glass, windows, outside doors and walls, and anything that could fall, such as lighting fixtures or furniture. ___earthquake___

C **LET'S TALK.** Work in a small group. There is a forest fire near your home. You have thirty minutes to evacuate. You are not sure your home will be standing when you return. Decide on ten items to pack.

D **AT WORK** Discuss these questions. **Answers will vary.**

1. Do you know what to do in the event of an emergency in your workplace?
2. How are people notified when there is an emergency?
3. Is there an evacuation plan?
4. Have you ever participated in an evacuation drill?

144 Unit 9

CIVICS

It is useful to have an emergency plan in case of a disaster. An emergency plan usually includes knowing local evacuation routes, planning how to get in touch with relatives, shutting off utilities, bringing important documents, and planning for family members with special needs. Students should write an emergency plan and share it with their family. For help, students can research disaster preparedness organizations online, such as the Federal Emergency Management Agency (FEMA).

AT WORK

Employers need to establish and practice safety protocols to ensure employees' safety in the workplace. Those protocols vary depending on the business, but should include:

- Procedures to report an emergency
- Evacuation procedure
- Maintenance and testing of fire alarms

UNIT 10

WEDDING PLANS

Friends and family lift the bride and groom while dancing the Hora, a tradition in Jewish weddings.

ACADEMIC Discuss obligations; classify words with similar meanings; write a story

AT WORK Discuss job requirements; describe the application process for a job

CIVICS Identify requirements for a civil marriage; understand etiquette and social rules

CCRS Level A: R 1, 5; W 3, 5; L 1; Level B: R 1, 4, 5, 6; W 2, 4, 5; L 1, 3; Level C: R 1, 4; W 2, 4, 5, 9; L 1, 3, 6; Level D: R 1, 4; W 2, 4, 5, 9; L 1, 3; Level E: R 1, 4; W 2, 4, 5, 9

ELPS Level 1 Standards 2, 3, 9, 10; Level 2 Standards 1, 2, 3, 9, 10; Level 3 Standards 1, 2, 3, 7, 9, 10; Level 4 Standards 1, 3, 7, 9, 10; Level 5 Standards 1, 2, 3, 7, 9, 10

CIVICS 11-2; 11-5; 11-9; 33-1

CASAS 0.1.2; 0.1.5; 0.2.1; 4.1.8; 4.4.4; 4.4.6

IN THIS UNIT

In Unit 10, students will:

- Discuss wedding customs, traditions, and etiquette
- Express obligation and advice with modals *have to* and *should*
- Read about American customs and etiquette

ABOUT THE PHOTO

This photo shows a Modern Orthodox Jewish wedding reception in Florida. Jewish weddings are unique for their many beautiful traditions. Jewish couples are traditionally married under a canopy called a chuppah, which symbolizes the home the pair will build together. After traditional readings, words from the rabbi, and an exchange of rings, the ceremony is closed by stomping on a glass (wrapped in a napkin). Then, the bride and groom spend some time alone together before joining their guests at the reception. This photo shows wedding guests dancing the Hora, a circle dance that brings the two families together as one. The bride and groom are lifted up on chairs in the middle of the circle in celebration.

Students are going to talk about weddings in this unit. Use the photo as a springboard to elicit the basic vocabulary they will need. Ask students who the people in the photo are and what is happening. Ask: *What kind of event is this?* (A wedding) *Who is the woman?* (The bride) *Who is the man?* (The groom) *Is this the ceremony or the reception?* Clarify if necessary: *The ceremony is a formal part. The reception is a party.* (The reception) *Who are the other people in the photo?* (The guests) *What do you call the person who performs the ceremony?* (A priest, judge, officiant—in this case, a rabbi)

If students start to volunteer stories about their own weddings, let them know that there will be a lot of opportunities to share in the unit, and control the discussion as appropriate so as to prevent redundancy later on.

A

- Call on a volunteer to read the invitation out loud. Help with any unfamiliar symbols or abbreviations, such as the ampersand (&) and RSVP (request for a response, abbreviated from the French *répondez s'il vous plaît*).
- Before completing Exercise A, make sure students understand the terms *bride* and *groom*. Give students a moment to work alone to answer the questions. Then bring them together in pairs to compare answers.
- Point out the naming convention on the invitation. Both the first and middle names of the bride and groom are given, not the last names (it can be inferred the last names match the parents—Acosta and Davis—but without knowing the people in question, it is not possible to know which last name belongs to the bride and which to the groom).
- Point out to students that we can tell a lot about the wedding from the format of the invitation. Ask: *Who is paying for the wedding? The bride and groom, the groom's family, or both families?* (It looks like both families; the custom is for the people paying to be the ones making the "request.") *Is the wedding in a church?* (No; it looks like the wedding and the reception are at the same place. Otherwise, the change of location would be noted.)
- Tell students it would be very rude not to RSVP to a wedding, or to RSVP with extra people (the invitation should make it clear if a date or children are invited). They may enjoy learning or sharing other social no-nos.
- Ask if any students have attended a wedding in the US. What was it like? What did they find interesting or unusual about it? What kind of food, clothing, and other customs did they notice?

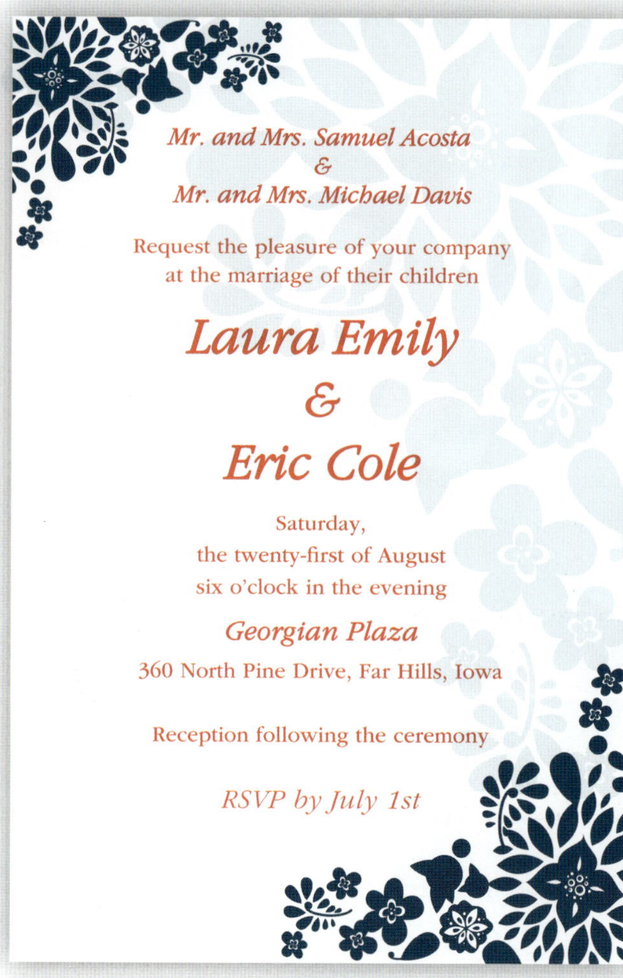

A Answer the questions about the wedding invitation.

1. What is the name of the bride? Laura Emily
2. What is the name of the groom? Eric Cole
3. What is the date of the wedding? August 21
4. What time is the wedding? 6:00 p.m.
5. Where is the wedding? Georgian Plaza, 360 North Pine Drive, Far Hills, Iowa

MORE ACTION

Invite students to bring in pictures taken at their own wedding or at a friend or family member's wedding. Ask each student to present their picture and describe the wedding to the class. After all the students have presented their pictures, discuss the similarities and differences between the weddings as a class. Are any of the wedding customs different? How long did each wedding last? What foods did the guests eat? How old were the bride and groom? What did they wear?

B Work with a group of students—from different countries if possible. Answer the questions about wedding customs in the country where you were born. Answers will vary.

1. How old is the average man at marriage? How old is the average woman?
2. How do most couples meet?
3. Do you know any couples who met online?
4. Are marriages ever arranged?
5. Where do most people get married?
6. What do brides wear?
7. What do grooms wear?
8. Who pays for the wedding?
9. How many people usually come to a wedding?
10. What kinds of gifts do people give?
11. Do couples go on a honeymoon after they get married?
12. Does the bride keep her own name, or does she take her husband's name?

WORD PARTNERSHIPS	
get	divorced engaged married

C Listen to a couple talk about an upcoming wedding. Circle the correct answer. 49

1. Jack **has to** / **doesn't have to** make airline reservations.
2. Travelers **have to** / **don't have to** buy an airline ticket for a child who is two or older.
3. They **have to** / **don't have to** make hotel reservations.
4. Jack **has to** / **doesn't have to** rent a car.
5. Jack **has to** / **doesn't have to** rent a car seat.
6. Cindy **has to** / **doesn't have to** find a dress for the wedding.
7. Jack **has to** / **doesn't have to** buy a pair of black shoes.
8. They **have to** / **don't have to** remember Calli's favorite blanket.

Skyline of downtown Austin, Texas

MORE ACTION

For homework, have students write a description of a wedding in their native country. Students can answer the questions in greater detail or compare a wedding in their native country to a wedding in the US. Have students trade their descriptions with a partner and correct their partner's description.

B

- Ask students to work in groups and interview each other about a typical wedding in their native country.
- Select a few of the questions from Exercise B and ask each group those questions. Discuss the differences between the weddings as a class. Are there many similarities between the weddings?
- Have groups work with other groups to compare their answers to the rest of the questions.

C 49

- Play the audio once all the way through and have students take notes. Then, have students complete the exercise independently.
- Play the audio a second time so students can check their answers. Go over the answers as a class.

ABOUT THE PHOTO

Austin is the capital of Texas. It is home to about a million people and is famous for TexMex and barbecue food, as well as a lively music scene. Another one of its attractions is the South Congress Bridge, seen here crossing the Colorado River in the lower right. The bridge is famous for the large population of bats that live under it; every evening between March and November, tourists and locals gather at dusk to watch the natural show the bats put on when they emerge for the evening. The bats control the bug population in the city and are but one example of why the city maintains an unusual slogan: Keep Austin Weird.

ACTIVE GRAMMAR: *Have to / Has to*

A

- Review the meaning of *have to* and *has to*. Point out that *have to* and *has to* are always followed by the base form of a verb. For example: *I have to study*.
- Ask for examples of things students have to do at school. For example: *You have to be on time. You have to bring a pencil*.
- Have students complete the exercise independently. Then, ask volunteers to read their answers to the class.

B 🎧50

- Point out that in everyday conversation, *have to* is often pronounced as */hafta/* and *has to* sounds like */hasta/*. Have students repeat these pronunciations.
- Play the audio and have students repeat each item. Then, play the audio again and have students circle their answers.
- Review the answers as a class.

C 🎧51

Play the audio and pause after each sentence so students can repeat.

D

After students discuss their answers in pairs, discuss the questions as a class.

ACADEMIC

Understanding and following the rules of a classroom is good practice for following the rules and requirements at work. Skills like punctuality, being organized, working in a group, disconnecting from technology, and taking turns speaking (not interrupting) will serve students well in both settings.

ACTIVE GRAMMAR *Have to / Has to*

I You We They	**have to**	**go** through security. **bring** photo ID.
He She	**has to**	

Have to and *has to* are modals.
They show necessity or obligation.
The base form of a verb is used after the modal.

A Complete the sentences about Jack and Cindy's airport departure. Use *have to* or *has to* and the verb in parentheses.

1. Jack (check in) ___has to check in___ online.
2. Jack and Cindy (bring) ___have to bring___ their driver's licenses.
3. They (arrive) ___have to arrive___ at the airport two hours early.
4. They (check) ___have to check___ their large bags.
5. They (wait) ___have to wait___ in the security line.
6. Jack (take off) ___has to take off___ his belt.
7. Cindy (take) ___has to take___ her laptop out of her bag.

B **Pronunciation: *Have to / has to*** Listen and circle the correct modal. 🎧50

1. (a.) have to b. has to
2. a. have to (b.) has to
3. (a.) have to b. has to
4. (a.) have to b. has to
5. a. have to (b.) has to
6. a. have to (b.) has to

C Listen and repeat. 🎧51

1. I have to go to the laundromat.
2. She has to work overtime tomorrow.
3. They have to do their homework.
4. I have to pay my phone bill.
5. He has to get gas on the way home.
6. She has to make a doctor's appointment.

D ACADEMIC Discuss with a partner.

1. Name something you have to do before you come to class.
2. Name something teenagers have to do before they can get a driver's license.
3. Name something you have to take with you when you go on vacation.
4. Name something your teacher has to do every day in class.
5. Name something you have to do when you get to work.

I have to do my homework.

TEACHING TIP

Distinguish the meaning between the modal *have* and the main verb *have*, meaning possession. For example:

I have to leave. (modal)

I have a car. (possession)

In the first sentence, *have* is followed by the base form of the verb. In the second sentence, *have* is followed by a noun.

ACTIVE GRAMMAR *Don't have to / Doesn't have to*

I You We They	**don't**	**have to**	**order** the invitations. **work** today.
He She	**doesn't**		

Don't have to and *doesn't have to* are modals.
They show that an action is not necessary.

A Listen to Hannah's conversation with a coworker. Who does each chore in her family now? Write *D* for *Dad*, *M* for *Mom*, or *H* for *Hannah*. 52

M **1.** clean the house
H **2.** clean her room
D **3.** cook
M **4.** wash the dishes
M **5.** do the food shopping
D, M **6.** pay the bills
H **7.** pay the cellphone bill
M **8.** do the laundry

B With a partner, talk about the things Hannah has to do and doesn't have to do at home.
Answers may vary.

> Hannah doesn't have to cook dinner. Her father cooks dinner.

C With a partner, talk about your family. What chores do you have to do? What are some chores you do not have to do? How does each person help? Answers may vary.

D With a partner, talk about the things that you have to do or don't have to do in your English class.
Answers may vary.

1. arrive on time
2. buy books
3. bring a dictionary to class
4. attend school in the summer
5. work in groups
6. pay tuition
7. take tests
8. do a lot of homework
9. raise our hands to speak
10. stand up when we speak
11. turn off our cellphones before class
12. write our compositions on a computer

> We have to speak English in class.

> We don't have to study in the library.

MORE ACTION

Have a contest to see which pair of students can think of the most *have to / don't have to* statements in three minutes. You can pick a theme for the sentences, such as school, the workplace, or home. At the end of the exercise, find out which pair has the most ideas and ask them to read their statements to the class. Then, invite other pairs to read some of their own sentences.

ACTIVE GRAMMAR: *Don't have to / Doesn't have to*

A 52

- Review the sentences in the grammar chart and check that students understand their meaning.
- Read the items in Exercise A. Ask students what chores they have to do at home.
- Play the audio and have students write their answers.
- Play the audio again so students can check their answers.

B

Circulate the class and monitor the conversations. Ask questions to jumpstart the conversations. You can also occasionally ask about information that is not mentioned in the audio to see how well they remember. Ask: *Does Hannah have to take out the trash?* (Not mentioned)

C

- Ask students to compare their responsibilities in their home country with their responsibilities now. How are they different?
- Ask pairs to share their findings with the class.

D

- Read the list of responsibilities. Ask students to name any additional activities they have to do in class.
- Have students practice saying the sentences with a partner. Then, ask volunteers to read their sentences to the class.

ACTIVE GRAMMAR: *Have to / Has to: Yes / No* Questions

A

- Review the formation of *yes / no* questions and ask a few questions about rules at your school. For example: *Do you have to come to class on time? Do you have to speak in English?*
- Have students take turns asking each other the questions from Exercise A.
- Explain any new vocabulary and list it on the board as it comes up.
- Give students a few minutes to write two questions of their own to ask each other. Then have them ask and answer the questions in pairs.

B

- Have students read the statements on their own and then write a *yes / no* question about each.
- While students are writing, move around the class and check their work. Remind them to form their questions like those in the grammar chart at the top of the page.
- Invite volunteers to write their questions on the board.

CIVICS

Explain the customs covered in Exercise B and answer any questions.

(1) In most states, the legal age for marriage is 18 (some states allow younger with parental consent; this is rare). (2) Legal photo ID includes a driver's license, passport, and green card. (3) A witness is usually a friend (the best man/maid of honor) and also requires ID. (4) Fees for both the ceremony and license vary by venue/officiant and town, so let students know they can shop around. In Massachusetts, for example, some towns charge up to $100 for a license, and others as little as $5. (5) Both parties can legally change their name at the time of a marriage, though no one is obliged to.

ACTIVE GRAMMAR *Have to / Has to: Yes / No* Questions

Do	I you we they	**have to**	**work** overtime? **send** a gift?
Does	he she		

Yes, I **do**. Yes, you **do**. Yes, we **do**. Yes, they **do**.	No, I **don't**. No, you **don't**. No, we **don't**. No, they **don't**.
Yes, he **does**. Yes, she **does**.	No, he **doesn't**. No, she **doesn't**.

A **AT WORK** With a partner, discuss the requirements for your job. **Answers will vary.**

1. What time do you have to check in at work?
2. Do you have to show a photo ID?
3. Do you have to wear a uniform?
4. Do you have to wear any protective gear, or equipment, on your hands, head, or eyes?
5. Do you have to work overtime?
6. Do you have to attend many meetings?
7. Do you have to join a union?
8. Do you have to have special training for your job?
9. Do you have to operate any special equipment?
10. What other requirements are there at your workplace?

B **CIVICS** Read the list of requirements for civil marriage ceremonies in San Francisco, California. Then, write a *Yes / No* question about weddings in other countries.

1. Both people have to be 18 years old.
   Do both people have to be 18 years old?
2. The bride and groom have to have legal photo identification.
   Do the bride and groom have to have legal photo identification?
3. The couple has to have at least one witness.
   Does the couple have to have at least one witness?
4. The couple has to pay for the marriage license and the ceremony.
   Does the couple have to pay for the marriage license and the ceremony?
5. Both people can change their last names.
   Do both people have to change their names?

MORE ACTION

Have students make questions and answers about weddings in different countries based on the topics in Exercise B. Write a list of students' native countries on the board and have students ask and answer questions about different wedding topics. For example: *In China, does the bride wear blue?* (No, she doesn't.) It may help to write a list of additional topics on the board, such as *length of ceremony, people in the wedding party,* and so on.

ACTIVE GRAMMAR *Had to / Didn't have to*

I You He She We They	**had to** **didn't have to**	**work.** **drive.**

Had to is the past of *have to* and *has to*. *Didn't have to* is the past of *don't have to* and *doesn't have to*.

A Complete the sentences about life in the country you come from. Use *had to* or *didn't have to*.
Answers will vary.

1. I ________________ speak English.
2. I ________________ work full time.
3. When I lived in my country, I ________________ wear winter clothes.
4. I ________________ take public transportation.
5. When I was in high school, we ________________ do many hours of homework.
6. Students ________________ pay for their books.

B Check the things you had to do in your country and the things you have to do now. With a partner, compare your lists. Answers will vary.

	Now	Before
Buy car insurance		
Work full time		
Go to the grocery store every day		
Have a credit card		
Be on time for appointments		
Wear winter clothes		
Get a driver's license		
Lock my doors at night		

In my country, I didn't have to buy car insurance. But here, I have to buy car insurance. It's very expensive!

ACTIVE GRAMMAR: *Had to / Didn't have to*

A

- Review the sentences in the grammar chart.
- Read the note box to the right of the grammar chart aloud. Tell students that people often use the phrase *You didn't have to* as an expression of thanks when they receive an unexpected gift.
- Ask students to tell you about rules in their previous school or about rules at their school when they were children. For example: *We didn't have to wear a uniform. We had to do a lot of homework.*
- Ask students to complete the sentences in Exercise A on their own.
- Review the answers as a class.
- Encourage students to give reasons for their answers. For example: *I didn't have to wear winter clothes. The weather is always warm in my country.*

B

- Set a time limit for students to complete the exercise.
- Ask for volunteers to read their answers as complete sentences. For example, *Julio didn't have to wear winter clothes.*

ABOUT THE PHOTO

Explain to students some of the basic services city hall (or town hall) provides. You can get copies of birth, death, and marriage certificates at city hall; pay or dispute a parking ticket; register to vote; pay property taxes. Services may vary somewhat by city.

Wedding Plans 151

ACTIVE GRAMMAR: *Should / Shouldn't*

A

- Discuss the difference in meaning between *should* (advice or opinion) and *have to* (obligation).
- Point out that *should* is followed by the base form of a verb.
- Ask students to complete the sentences in Exercise A individually.
- Ask volunteers to read their sentences.

B

- Have students get in groups of five or six. Ask them to discuss the statements and their reasons for agreeing or disagreeing with each statement.
- Have a secretary for each group tally the answers and write them down.
- Then, ask each group to elaborate on some of the reasons why they agreed or disagreed for each question.

C

- Students can complete this exercise in the same groups as Exercise B.
- When students have finished making their list, invite volunteers from each group to come to the board and write their ideas in a list.
- Discuss the list as a class. Which ideas are the most common? Which ideas does the class think are the most important?

ACTIVE GRAMMAR *Should / Shouldn't*

I You He She We They	**should** **shouldn't**	**get married** in the summer. **send** a gift.

Should is a modal.
Should gives advice or an opinion.

A Complete the sentences. Use *should* or *shouldn't* and the verb in parentheses.

1. Luis and Marta don't have a lot of money. They (have) ___should have___ a small wedding. They (take) ___shouldn't take___ out a loan to pay for the wedding.
2. I don't think my sister (get) ___should get___ married in the park. What will she do if it rains?
3. If you don't have a lot of money, you (hire) ___shouldn't hire___ a band. You (hire) ___should hire___ a DJ.
4. Yolanda and Jim are going to get married in a church. They (choose) ___should choose___ a reception location near the church.

B LET'S TALK. With a group of five or six students, discuss each statement. Then, write the number of students who agree with the statement and the number of students who disagree with the statement. Answers will vary.

Statement	Agree	Disagree
1. People should wait until the age of 21 to get married.		
2. A bride should take her husband's name.		
3. The bride's family should pay for the wedding.		
4. The bride should always wear white.		
5. Money is the best gift to give for a wedding.		

C LET'S TALK. In a small group, talk about how to have a long, happy marriage. Make a list of your five best ideas. Answers will vary.

1. *You should go out together once a week.*
2. ______
3. ______
4. ______
5. ______
6. ______

D Complete each sentence with a word or phrase from the box. Words or phrases may be used more than once.

~~didn't have to~~	don't have to	has to	should
doesn't have to	had to	have to	shouldn't

Mrs. Sullivan is 40 years old. Three years ago, her husband died, leaving her to raise her two sons alone. Now, her sons are seventeen and fifteen. Before her husband died, she (work) ___didn't have to work___ (1) outside the home. She stayed home and took care of her home and family. Mrs. Sullivan (make) ___had to make___ (2) many lifestyle changes after her husband died. Now, she (work) ___has to work___ (3) full time in order to support her family. Her company offers good medical benefits, so she (worry) ___doesn't have to worry___ (4) about doctors' bills. Twice a year, Mrs. Sullivan goes away on business, so she (find) ___has to find___ (5) someone to watch her children. Mrs. Sullivan is busy, but she is lonely.

Last year, Mrs. Sullivan started to date a very nice widower in her town. He is 10 years older than she is. He has asked her to marry him. Her sister thinks she (wait) ___should wait___ (6) to get married until her boys are older. Her brother thinks she (look) ___should look___ (7) for a younger man. But her mother has given her the best advice. "You (listen) ___shouldn't / don't have to listen___ (8) to anyone else. You (follow) ___should / have to follow___ (9) your own heart."

E With a partner, read the questions to a wedding planner. Give each person advice. Use *should, shouldn't, have to,* or *don't have to.*

1. My fiancée and I want to have a small wedding with our families and closest friends. We can't afford a big wedding. Do we have to invite our bosses?

2. I'm getting married in six months. My mother wants me to wear the same wedding dress that she wore, but I don't want to wear it. I want to choose my own dress, but I don't want to hurt her feelings.

3. In four months, I'm going to get married for the second time. My first wife and I are divorced, but we are still friends. She's a good mother to our two children. Should I invite her to the wedding?

4. I'm the oldest daughter in an Indian family. My parents expect to have three days of celebration and about 300 guests. They would like my fiancé's family to pay half the expenses. My fiancé is an American from a small family. They can't afford to have such a big wedding. I don't want them to feel uncomfortable. What should I do?

D

- Allow time for students to read the text carefully and decide on the answers. Point out that they will use some of the words and phrases in the box more than once.
- Have students complete the exercise individually. Then, check the answers as a class.

E

- Ask students to form pairs and read each note together.
- Have students focus on one note at a time. Have them write a reply note for each question using *should, shouldn't, have to,* and *don't have to.*
- Move around the room offering help as necessary.
- Ask pairs to share some of their suggestions with the class.

MORE ACTION

Make up additional issues about the themes of weddings and marriage. Write each problem on a piece of paper. Distribute one piece of paper to each pair or group of students and ask them to write one piece of advice in response. Then, have them pass the paper on to another pair or group of students. After each group has written advice for every problem, have groups read out loud all the advice for their original problem and take a class vote on the best piece of advice for each problem.

CULTURE NOTE

Traditionally, the bride's family was expected to pay for the wedding, while the groom's family would host a rehearsal dinner. This was very common several decades ago, when it was common to get married in your early 20s and women often did not work outside the home. However, as more people are getting married later (late 20s and beyond) and women are more integrated into the workforce, it is more common now for the couple to pay for part or most of the wedding themselves, with gifts and support from the family.

THE BIG PICTURE: Wedding Travel

A

Ask students to look at the picture. What do they think is happening? Who are the people?

B

- Encourage students to use their dictionaries (including on their phones) to look up the terms.
- Ask pairs to write a sentence with each word to show its meaning. Ask volunteers to share their sentences.

C 53

- Play the audio and ask students to listen only.
- Then, have students review the questions and complete as many answers as they can before listening to the audio a second time.
- Play the audio again so students can finish filling in their answers and check the answers they have already completed.
- Review the answers as a class.

AT WORK

Military service can provide many benefits for veterans and active members, including a path to citizenship, healthcare, financing for education, and preference on applications for certain jobs.

THE BIG PICTURE Wedding Travel

CULTURAL NOTE

Some couples have their wedding at a location away from their home. Popular choices for these *destination weddings* are tropical resorts, cruise ships, and other countries. Guests can drive or fly to those locations. Some people join the couple for a weekend, and others stay a few more days—even a week.

A Describe the picture and discuss these questions.
Answers will vary.

1. What is the agent doing?
2. What is your experience going through airport security lines?
3. Have you ever traveled to attend a wedding? Where was the wedding? How did you travel?

B Discuss the meaning of these words with a partner. Look up the words you don't know. Answers will vary.

veteran	background check	drug screening	metal detector

C AT WORK Listen to the security agent describe his job. Then, answer the questions. 53

1. When did he become a citizen?
   He became a citizen after he completed his __military__ service.
2. How old was he when he got the job?
   He was __30__ years old.
3. What kind of examination did he have to pass?
   He had to pass a __medical__ examination.
4. How long did he wait to get the job?
   He waited for __4 months__.

CULTURE NOTE

Weddings can be an expensive affair, even for guests. A destination wedding obviously includes expenses like airfare and hotel, but even local weddings can add up, especially for people in the wedding party (who will have to buy/rent specific clothing, plan and pay for showers/bachelorette parties). Encourage students to consider all the expenses before committing to be in or attend a wedding.

D Listen again and circle *True* or *False*. 53

1.	The TSA is a government agency.	(True)	False
2.	He served in the US military.	(True)	False
3.	He was born in the United States.	True	(False)
4.	He became an agent six years ago.	True	(False)
5.	He operates special equipment.	(True)	False
6.	When he sees something dangerous, he has to tell another agent.	(True)	False
7.	He sometimes opens passengers' bags.	(True)	False

E Read the chart about requirements to become a TSA agent. Complete the sentences with *has to / have to / doesn't have to / don't have to* and the verb in parentheses.

Required	Not required
US citizen / US naturalized citizen	Be a veteran
18 years of age	Have previous experience
Pass a background check	Do the same thing every day
Pass a drug screening test	Get a bachelor's degree
Wear a uniform	Like animals

1. Agents (be) ___have to be___ citizens.
2. An agent (be) ___doesn't have to be___ a veteran.
3. All applicants (pass) ___have to pass___ background checks.
4. An applicant (have) ___doesn't have to have___ previous experience.
5. Agents (do) ___don't have to do___ the same thing every day.
6. Agents (wear) ___have to wear___ uniforms.
7. Agents (get) ___don't have to get___ bachelor's degrees.
8. Agents (like) ___don't have to like___ animals.
9. An agent (pass) ___has to pass___ a drug screening test.

F **AT WORK** The security agent had a long application process. With a partner, discuss your screening for your current job. **Answers will vary.**

1. What forms did you have to complete for your current job?
2. Did you have to have a medical examination for your job?
3. What kinds of screenings did you have to pass?
4. How old did you have to be?
5. Did you have to have any special licenses or training?
6. How long did you have to wait between your job application and your job offer?

D 53

- Have students read the sentences independently.
- Play the audio and have students circle their answers.
- Review the answers as a class.

E

- Have two volunteers read each column out loud, checking to make sure students understand each of the terms.
- Give students a few minutes to complete the items on their own. Then invite volunteers to read each item out loud.

F

- Let students know that they will be sharing their partner's answers, so they should take notes as they talk.
- If students are not currently working, they can talk about the process at a previous job.
- Give students a few minutes to discuss in pairs. Then, call the class together to discuss the hiring process.

AT WORK

Go over common requirements in a hiring process, which include: contact information and SSN; past employers and contact information; police records. Employers are not allowed to ask about age, marital status, and, in some states, pay history. Requirements like citizenship are generally limited to government positions.

READING: Etiquette Guide

A 54 (facing page)

- Point to the photo and invite students to comment. Ask: *What are these people doing? Where are they? Are they wearing special clothes?*
- Have students read the text silently. Ask volunteers to explain new vocabulary, such as *response card*, *black tie*, and *wedding registry*. Have students write these terms in their vocabulary notebooks.
- Read the Reading Note on the next page aloud and ask students to compare a piece of information in the reading with their own experience. Students could discuss clothing, invitations, and types of wedding gifts.
- Ask volunteers to answer the discussion questions.
- Encourage students to add information to their answers. For example: *We arrived the day before the wedding because it was so far away. The wedding took place in India.*

READING Etiquette Guide

It is common for the bride and groom to have photos taken after the ceremony.

Attending a Wedding

You get a wedding invitation from a friend, and you are excited because this is the first American wedding you will attend. Weddings are different from culture to culture. What are the rules of **etiquette** for American wedding guests?

First of all, **respond** to the invitation as soon as possible. The bride and groom have to pay for each guest, so it is important to **notify** them that you will attend. Most wedding invitations include a response card. If you cannot attend, it is **polite** to call the couple if you are close friends.

Read the invitation's envelope carefully. Can you take a guest? Maybe your invitation says, "Marianna Lopez and Guest." That means that you can bring only one guest.

What should you wear to the wedding? Check the invitation for details. For a "black tie" wedding, women wear elegant dresses—called evening gowns—and men wear tuxedos. "Semiformal attire" is usually a dress for women and a suit for men. Remember, female guests should not wear white. The guests should be looking at the bride—not at the other guests.

What rules should you follow at the wedding ceremony? The most important rule is to be on time. You should arrive about fifteen minutes before the wedding begins. If you're late, you should enter quietly and find a seat. If something happens during the ceremony that you do not understand, wait until after the ceremony and ask someone to explain.

Please respond by May 30

M ____________

______ We'd be delighted!

______ We regretfully decline.

What kind of gift should you buy? Most guests at American weddings do not have to worry about choosing a gift. Many American couples use a wedding gift **registry**. The couple goes to a store or online to register for their gifts. They decide what they need and share their registry information with their guests. The guests look at the registry at the store or online, find out which items are still available, and buy their gift for the couple. Then, the store delivers the gift. You don't have to bring the gift to the ceremony. In fact, it is more convenient if you mail the gift.

Couples also **appreciate** gifts of money. In fact, money is the most popular wedding gift. Place cash or a check in a card that is specially made for money or in a regular greeting card, and put it in an envelope.

Have fun at the wedding! 54

TEACHING TIP

Have students write key words and facts from the reading in their notebooks and research these points for a culture other than their own. To give students inspiration, bring in some pictures of weddings from other cultures and explain a little bit about the picture. (For example, in Poland, members of the bridal party and other guests pin money onto the bride and groom during a special ceremony.) Other topics that students could research are what people typically wear to a wedding and what kinds of gifts are given. Have students present a report on their research and include pictures if possible.

A After reading, discuss these questions with a partner. Answers will vary.

1. Describe the last wedding you attended.
2. How early did you arrive for the ceremony?
3. Did you bring a gift? What was it?
4. What did you wear to the wedding?

etiquette = rules of social behavior

READING NOTE

Comparing the text to your own experiences

As you read, compare the information in the reading to your own experiences.

Example: *First of all, respond to the invitation. There is a response card inside the invitation to fill out and return.*

Compare to your experiences:

In my country, we don't respond with cards. We call the family.

I was invited to a wedding last year. I had to ask a friend how to fill out the card.

B Circle the correct words.

1. Guests **have to** / **don't have to** respond to the wedding invitation.
2. Guests **have to** / **don't have to** call the couple about the invitation.
3. Guests **should** / **shouldn't** take as many friends as they want.
4. Female guests **should** / **shouldn't** wear white.
5. Guests **have to** / **don't have to** arrive on time.
6. A guest **should** / **shouldn't** find out if the couple registered for gifts.
7. A guest **has to** / **doesn't have to** give money as a gift.

C Match each word to its definition.

b	**1.** respond	**a.**	a list of gifts
d	**2.** polite	**b.**	to answer
e	**3.** notify	**c.**	to like
a	**4.** registry	**d.**	nice; well-mannered
c	**5.** appreciate	**e.**	to tell

D Discuss the questions with a partner. Answers will vary.

1. What are common wedding gifts in the country where you were born?
2. What gifts do most wedding couples in your country appreciate the most?
3. Have you ever attended an American wedding? Compare your experience to the information in the reading.

E **LET'S TALK.** Bring in photos of your wedding or that of a family member. Tell the class about the preparations and the wedding day.

B

- Ask students to complete the exercise individually and then look back at the passage to check their answers.
- Review the answers as a class.

C

- Have students cover the right column of definitions with a piece of paper. Then, ask students to try to write their own definition for each term in their notebooks.
- Have students uncover the definitions and complete the exercise. Have them see how closely their definitions match.
- Go over the answers as a class.

D

- Have students discuss the questions with a partner and compare their own experiences with some of the topics from the reading, such as wedding attire, gifts, and etiquette. How do students' experiences differ from those described in the reading?
- Have volunteers share their responses with the class.

E

This exercise could be done as a formal presentation or as an informal question-and-answer activity.

WRITING OUR STORIES: My Wedding

A

- Ask students to comment on what they see in the photograph. Ask: *What do you know about Indian weddings? And this custom in particular?*
- Ask students to read the passage. Then, ask comprehension questions, such as: *What is an arranged marriage?* (An arranged marriage is a marriage where parents pick a spouse for their child. The marriage is negotiated between the families of the two people who will marry each other.) *How long did the wedding activities take?* (about a week) Encourage students to discuss any information from the passage that they found interesting.

WRITING OUR STORIES My Wedding

A Read.

An Indian bride displays beautiful henna body art on her hands.

I am from India, and my family arranged my marriage. I was living in the United States when my uncle found a husband for me. My uncle told my father about a man named Justin, who would be a good husband for me. My family and I went back to India for a meeting with Justin and his family. We stayed for about a month. At the end of the visit, I decided to marry Justin. We got married a year and a half later.

The pre-wedding activities, the ceremony, and the reception lasted about a week. On the first day, my family and Justin's family exchanged gifts. During the week, we had to participate in separate religious services. Some services were at my home, and others were at Justin's home. According to custom, the services were only for our families.

The day before the wedding ceremony, my family had to put up a large tent in our yard. About 100 guests attended our wedding. The guests gave us many gifts, including gifts of gold jewelry. We ate sweets and took many photos with our family and guests. The guests also gave Justin and me gifts of money, which his sister attached to his clothes.

On the day of the wedding, a priest married us. The ceremony and the reception lasted about seven hours. After the reception, Justin and I left in a car that his family had decorated with flowers.

Nisha

B ACADEMIC In your notebook, write a story about your wedding or a wedding that you attended. Include the following information: Answers will vary.

- Date
- Names of bride and groom
- How the couple met
- Your relationship to the couple
- Country of the wedding
- Location of the ceremony
- Number of people in the wedding party
- Bride and groom's clothing
- Your clothes for the wedding
- Size of the wedding
- Number of guests
- Location of the reception
- Music
- Food

C Read your partner's story. Ask about any details that are missing.

WRITING NOTE

Giving Reasons and Results: *so* and *because*

Because gives a reason:

1. The couple had a small wedding **because** they wanted to keep costs down.
2. The groom didn't have to rent a tuxedo **because** he decided to wear his best suit.

So gives a result:

3. The couple wanted to keep costs down, **so** they had a small wedding.
4. The groom decided to wear his best suit, **so** he didn't have to rent a tuxedo.

D Complete with *because* or *so*.

1. The bride's sister works at a bakery, ___so___ they don't have to buy a cake.
2. The groom doesn't own a suit, ___so___ he is going to rent one.
3. The bride and groom are taking dance classes ___because___ they aren't good dancers.
4. The bride and groom are saving money ___because___ they want to go to Europe on their honeymoon.
5. The bride can't find a dress that she likes, ___so___ she's going to go to a dressmaker for something special.
6. The bride and groom are going to two florists today ___because___ they want to choose the flowers for the reception.

MORE ACTION

Divide the class into groups and have each group write five sentences with blanks that should be completed with *because* or *so*. Have each group exchange papers with another group and complete each other's sentences. Then, have students return the papers to the original group for corrections. Walk around the room and take note of any incorrect sentences. Write them on the board and correct them together as a class.

B

- Suggest that students model their writing on Nisha's story if they have never attended a wedding.
- When writing their stories, students can follow the sequence of questions listed. Less fluent writers may wish to copy some of the sentence patterns Nisha used and simply change the facts to fit their own lives. More fluent writers will be able to depart further from the format given in the reading passage.

C

As students read each other's work, remind them to keep an eye out for common errors, like correct capitalization and subject/verb agreement.

D

- Review the Writing Note. Point out that a comma is used only before *so*, and not before *because*.
- Have students complete the sentences individually and then check their answers with a partner.

ACADEMIC

Remind students that using an outline to plan their writing is a useful skill that will transfer to other academic classes. It's also a good idea to go through an editing stage. Adding an extra set of eyes (a classmate's, for example) can reveal errors students might not see themselves.

ENGLISH IN ACTION: Understanding Customs

A

- Point at the pictures and ask students to describe what is happening in each one. Ask: *Who are these people? What are they doing? What are their ages? What is the situation in each picture?*
- Ask students to describe or explain the custom in their own countries for each of the situations. Do they feel uncomfortable following any customs in the United States?
- Discuss general customs in the US for greetings, saying goodbye, and talking informally. Ask if students have found any other differences between customs in the US and their own countries.

B

- Have students work in groups to compare customs in their countries. Try to put students from different countries in each group.
- When students have finished discussing, have groups come to the front of the class and act out the different versions of the custom in their countries.

CIVICS

Explain to students that it is important for them to learn the customs of the country they are living in so that they do not inadvertently offend someone. Violating customs can make it difficult to find a job or make friends. Ask students to discuss what they would do if they accidentally offended someone through verbal or nonverbal communication. Have students brainstorm ways for learning the customs in a country.

ENGLISH IN ACTION | Understanding Customs

A **CIVICS** Discuss these customs in the United States. Is each custom the same or different in the country where you were born?

1.

Women sometimes hug or kiss a friend once on the cheek when they meet.

2.

Men often shake hands or give a friend a pat on the back when they meet.

3.

People stand a comfortable distance apart when they speak.

4.

People stand in line at buses, stores, and ticket counters. It is not polite to push or cut in line.

B In a group, talk about customs in your country and in the United States.

1. When you enter a house, do you remove your shoes?
2. What time do people arrive for meetings and appointments?
3. If you are invited to dinner, do you bring a gift for the host?
4. If you are invited to a party that begins at 9:00, what time do you arrive?
5. What US custom do you find very different from your country?

UNIT 11 AT WORK

A fisherman carries his catch of lobsters.

AT WORK Match a job with its required skills; describe a job; read and understand signs in the workplace; discuss workplace policies and regulations; describe a work style; prepare for a job interview

ACADEMIC Make a polite request; make predictions; edit a piece of writing

CIVICS Discuss general regulations; understand classroom rules

CCRS Level A: R 1, 3, 4, 5; W 3, 5; L 1, 6; Level B: R 1, 3, 4, 5, 6; W 3, 4, 5; L 1, 3, 6; Level C: R 1, 3, 4; W 4, 5, 9; L 1, 3, 6; Level D: R 1, 3, 4; W 4, 5, 9; L 1, 3, 6; Level E: R 1, 3, 4; W 4, 5, 8; L 6

ELPS Level 1 Standards 1, 2, 3, 7, 8, 9, 10; Level 2 Standards 1, 2, 3, 7, 8, 10; Level 3 Standards 1, 2, 3, 7, 8, 10; Level 4 Standards 1, 2, 3, 7, 8, 10; Level 5 Standards 1, 2, 3, 7, 8, 10

CIVICS 33-8; 33-10; 36-1; 37-10; 51-6

CASAS 0.1.2; 0.1.5; 4.1.5; 4.1.8; 4.3.1; 4.3.2; 4.4.2; 4.8.1; 4.8.3

IN THIS UNIT

In Unit 11, students will:

- Practice making polite requests
- Discuss job skills and qualifications
- Provide advice on what is and is not acceptable behavior in the workplace
- Role-play a job interview

ABOUT THE PHOTO

This is a fisherman carrying his catch of crabs and lobsters in Cromer Beach, Norfolk, UK. Fishing is a key element of the economy in coastal communities all over the world. A very quick glance at commercial fishing in North America shows a wide variety of options for seafood consumers: scallops in Nova Scotia, crabs in Oregon and California, oysters in Rhode Island and Florida, salmon in British Columbia and Alaska, lobsters in Maine, white bass in Ohio, and shrimp in Alabama, just to name a few. The fishing industry, including lobster and crab fisheries, generates billions of dollars in the US. The state of Maine alone is the nation's largest lobster producer, with 75% to 80% of all US lobster production, which provides as much as a billion dollars in revenue to the state in a single year.

Ask students to think about the fisherman in the photo and what tasks might be involved in his daily work. Ask questions to preview the use of modals and to practice vocabulary related to jobs: *What are some tasks this man may need to do every day at work? What other product may he catch on a work day? What expertise or knowledge do you think this man may need to do his job?*

Ask students to think about a job they would like to have, or their own job. Ask them to draw comparisons between their job and the job in the photo. Some possible elements they can compare: schedule; safety gear or equipment; time sitting at a desk or physical activity required.

A

Ask students to describe each picture. Ask: *What is each person's job? What skills does each person need in his or her job?*

B

- Read the blue note box to the right of the exercise aloud. Explain that *can* means the same as *be able to*.
- Have students complete the task individually. If necessary, define any new vocabulary, such as *tune-up* (repairs to improve the performance of a car).
- Ask volunteers to read their answers aloud.

C

- Write the names of different jobs on scraps of paper and hand them out to students. If a student is not sure what a job is, describe the job or give the student a different one. Some examples of jobs are teacher, waiter, construction worker, chauffeur, and security guard. Give students time to think about their descriptions and write them in their notebooks.
- Have students describe the job in front of the class.

AT WORK

A job description provides information about the general tasks and duties involved in a particular job. Discuss the importance of reviewing and understanding a job description when applying for work.

A Look at the photos and write the jobs.

1. a chef / cook

2. a nurse

3. a journalist

B Match each occupation with the job skill.

Can is a modal. It shows ability.

c	1. hairdresser	a.	I can plan roads, bridges, and tunnels.
d	2. optometrist	b.	I can help you file your income taxes.
a	3. civil engineer	c.	I can cut and color hair.
e	4. health aide	d.	I can check your eyes and prescribe glasses or contacts.
b	5. accountant	e.	I can take a pulse and blood pressure.
f	6. mechanic	f.	I can give a car a tune-up.
h	7. florist	g.	I can help you with car, house, and life insurance.
g	8. insurance agent	h.	I can arrange flowers for weddings.

C **AT WORK** Describe a job. Use *can*. Your classmates will guess what the job is.

I can make furniture.

Are you a carpenter?

Yes, I am.

162 Unit 11

A carpenter builds furniture in his shop.

MORE ACTION

Make a list of the jobs from Exercise C on the board. Ask students to name additional duties for each job and write them on the board. Then, ask students to decide which of these jobs is the most interesting, difficult, dangerous, boring, exciting, challenging, and fun.

ACTIVE GRAMMAR *Could you / Would you*

Could you please	call Mr. Henderson?
Would you please	copy this report?

Could and *would* are modals.
Use *could you* and *would you* to make polite requests.
Could you please copy this report?

A ACADEMIC Restate each sentence as a polite request. Answers may vary.

1. Fill out this form.
Could you please fill out this form?
2. Take this call.
Would you please take this call?
3. Send an email to the employees.
Could you please send an email to the employees?
4. Clean the workroom.
Could you please clean the workroom?
5. Fill this order.
Would you please fill this order?
6. Take Ms. Miller's temperature.
Would you please take Ms. Miller's temperature?
7. Bring me some change.
Could you please bring me some change?
8. Open the door for me.
Would you please open the door for me?
9. Help the next customer.
Could you please help the next customer?
10. Unpack those boxes.
Would you please unpack those boxes?

B Listen. Then, write the request for each item. 55

1. 
Could you please answer the phone?

2. 
Would you please bring this to the mail department?

3. 

Would you please make five copies of this form?

4. 
Could you please repair the printer?

C **Pronunciation: *Would you* and *Could you*** Listen again. Repeat each request in Exercise B. 55

D In your notebook, write three more requests. Answers will vary.

Student-to-student requests: Could I please use your dictionary?

Teacher-to-student requests: Would you please hand in your papers?

MORE ACTION

For further practice, ask students how they could reply to the requests in Exercise B. Positive replies might include: *Sure! Of course! No problem!* Negative replies might include: *I'm sorry, I'm busy right now. I'd like to help you, but* (give a reason or an excuse).

ACTIVE GRAMMAR: *Could you / Would you*

A

- Read the sentences in the grammar chart and the grammar note aloud. Explain that *could you* and *would you* are used almost interchangeably for polite requests.
- Contrast formal polite requests with more informal requests, for example: *Could you please call Mr. Henderson?* (formal) *Can you call Mr. Henderson?* (informal)
- Show the first item in Exercise A as an example.
- Ask volunteers to say their answers aloud to the class.

B 55

- Play the audio and pause after each request to allow time for students to write their answers.
- Ask volunteers to read their answers aloud.

C 55

- Point out that when we say *could you* and *would you*, the two words run together (*/Cudju/* and */Wudju/*).
- Play the audio and pause after each question so students can repeat each request.

D

Give students time to write their requests in their notebooks. Then, have volunteers read their requests aloud.

ACTIVE GRAMMAR:
Must / Must not / Can't

A

- Review the meaning of *must, must not,* and *can't*.
- Give examples of rules in your school using *must, must not,* and *can't*. For example: *You must have a student ID. You must not smoke. You can't come to class late.*
- Contrast *must not* with *don't have to*. For example:
  You must not smoke here. (You are not allowed to smoke here.)
  You don't have to wear goggles. (You are not required to wear goggles.)
- Explain the first sign in Exercise A as an example.
- Allow time for students to complete the task individually. Then, have students compare answers in pairs.
- Ask volunteers to read their sentences aloud.

AT WORK

According to the Occupational Safety and Health Administration (OSHA), employers are required to communicate and provide training to employees on hazards in the workplace and how to prevent them.

Safety signs help warn employees of potential risks and hazards. It's important to understand and respond to signage to avoid work-related injuries. OSHA classifies signs in three categories:

- **Danger signs** warn of an immediate hazard that will cause serious injury or death, if not avoided.
- **Warning signs** are used to warn of hazardous situations that could result in serious injury or death.
- **Caution signs** indicate that a hazard could cause a minor or moderate injury.

ACTIVE GRAMMAR *Must / Must not / Can't*

I You He	**must**	**wear** a name tag. **sign** in. **file** a report.

I You He	**must not** **can't**	**make** personal calls. **argue** with a customer. **use** a cellphone.

Must, must not, and *can't* are modals.
Must states rules, policies, and regulations.
Can't and *must not* show that an action is not allowed or not permitted.

A AT WORK Explain what each work sign means. Use *must, must not,* or *can't.* Answers may vary.

1. 

You must wear a hard hat.

2. 

You must wear eye protection.

3. 

You can't eat or drink in this room.

4. 

You can't park here unless you have a handicapped parking permit.

5. 

You must not open this door unless there's a fire.

6. 

You must not touch.

7. 

You must wear goggles and rubber gloves.

8. 

You must not put your hands near the belt.

9. 

You must not use your cellphone.

10. 

You can't smoke here.

11. 

You must wash your hands.

12. 

You can't take photos or video.

MORE ACTION

On the board, list other places where there are rules. For example, a swimming pool, a gym, a movie theater, a shopping mall, or a museum. Have students get into groups, choose one place, and make a list of rules. Groups should then read their rules aloud to the class and have the other groups evaluate their rules for accuracy. You could also do this exercise as a competition to see which group can come up with the most rules for their location.

B **LET'S TALK.** Work in a small group. Write four of your school or class rules. Answers will vary.

Students must not copy from other students during an exam.

You must turn off your phone during class.

______

______

______

______

C **AT WORK** Talk about these company policies and regulations. Use *must*, *must not*, or *can't*.

1. Work hours: 8:00–4:00.
2. Punch in and out.
3. If you are late, call your supervisor.
4. Wear your ID tag at all times.
5. No jeans or athletic clothing.
6. No smoking.
7. No cellphones.
8. Do not bring your children to work.
9. Report unsafe working conditions.
10. No offensive pictures on office walls.
11. Report any accidents immediately.
12. Use the internet for business only.

Workers must report to work by 8:00.

WORD PARTNERSHIPS	
clock sign punch	in out
swipe my card	

D **CIVICS** With a partner, discuss these questions.

1. What are some rules at your workplace?
2. What are some regulations at an airport?
3. What are some laws about children in cars?
4. What are some laws about texting and using cellphones while driving?
5. What are some laws about pets?
6. What are some common apartment regulations?

This welder must wear a welding mask to protect his face.

B

- Set a time limit and see which group can come up with the most rules.
- Ask a representative from each group to write their sentences on the board. Ask the other students if the rules are accurate.

C

- Give students time to read through the list and ask any questions about vocabulary.
- Have students complete the exercise with a partner. Then, go over the answers as a class.
- Discuss what types of jobs and workplaces have these kinds of rules.

D

- Set a time limit for pairs to discuss the questions and come up with lists of rules, laws, and regulations for each question.
- You could also conduct the exercise by giving a different question to each pair of students and then having them read their answers to the class.

AT WORK

Depending on the industry or the focus of a specific job, workplace rules and regulations can vary. For example, some companies have strict work hours or regulate how much overtime employees can work. In some places, use of company-owned equipment is restricted to work-related tasks. Encourage students who work to become familiar with their workplace rules and regulations.

MORE ACTION

For homework, have students research laws about behavior in the community. For example: laws about parking, littering, or walking pets in your community. Have the class brainstorm laws together. Then, have each student pick a law to research in greater detail. Have each student report their findings to the class using *must*, *must not*, and *can't*.

CIVICS

The ability to follow rules and regulations is fundamental when integrating into a community. For newcomers, some rules may not be immediately obvious, especially in social scenarios. Encourage students to compare and contrast rules, regulations, or social norms in the US and their home countries. Prompt volunteers to share if adapting to different rules in the US has been easy or difficult, and why.

ACTIVE GRAMMAR:
May and *Might*

A

- Review the formation of sentences with *may* and *might*. (Both are followed by a verb without *to*.)
- Explain that *may* and *might* are used interchangeably to show possibility. Give some examples of things that you may or might do tomorrow or this weekend.
- Give students time to write their answers.
- Ask volunteers to read their answers aloud.

B

- Ask two students to read the speech bubble for the first item aloud.
- Have students discuss the pictures and write their sentences with a partner. Encourage students to write more than two sentences for each picture if they can.
- Ask different pairs to read their sentences aloud to the class.

ACADEMIC

Inferring activates students' critical thinking skills, both a life skill and an academic skill required for standardized testing. Whether they are asked to infer information from visuals or from text, students must think carefully, read or observe attentively, and, in some cases, draw from their personal experience to make their inferences. In the process, English learners can also develop or expand their vocabulary.

When students are working on Exercise B, ask them to explain their inferences by asking questions like *Why do you think she might slip on the floor?* Then, encourage them to make additional inferences beyond what the illustrations show. For example, ask: *What might happen after she falls?* (Possible answers: *She might hurt her leg. Her papers might get wet.*)

ACTIVE GRAMMAR *May* and *Might*

I He They	**may (not)** **might (not)**	**change** jobs. **get** a promotion. **take** a sick day.

May and *might* are modals.
May and *might* show possibility.

A Complete the sentences. Write what may or might happen. **Answers will vary.**

1. Yolanda got to work late today, so the boss ___might give her a warning___.
2. You need a job. A new clothing store is opening in your area, so you ___may / might apply for a job___.
3. Nelson has a bad cold. He ___may / might not go___ to work.
4. The boss is very happy with Mia's work. He ___may / might promote her___.
5. The economy is bad and our company is not doing very well. The boss ___may / might lay off some workers___.
6. The economy is very good and our company is doing very well. The boss ___may / might hire some new workers___.
7. Shelly works full time. She wants to begin college in the fall. She ___may / might quit___ her job in the fall.

B **ACADEMIC** Talk about the pictures with a partner. Then, in your notebook, write two sentences about what may or might happen in each.

She might slip on the floor.

1.

2.

3.

4.

5.

6.

166 Unit 11

ACTIVE GRAMMAR *May* and *Might* vs. Future

I **might go** to nursing school. **Maybe** I **will go** to nursing school. I'**m going to go** to nursing school. I **will go** to nursing school.	*May* and *might* are modals. They show possibility. *Maybe* also shows possibility. *Maybe* is the first word in a sentence. *Will* and *(be) going to* show that you are sure or certain.

A Rewrite the sentences. Use *may* or *might*. **Answers will vary.**

1. Maybe I will quit my job. I may / might quit my job.
2. Maybe the boss is going to fire him. The boss may / might fire him.
3. Maybe she will get the job. She may / might get the job.
4. Maybe we are going to have a test. We may / might have a test.

B In a small group, talk about your future plans. Use *may*, *might*, *maybe*, or the future.

I might change jobs.

Maybe I will change jobs.

I don't like my job. I will change jobs soon.

1. change jobs
2. get a dog
3. visit my home country
4. open a small business
5. continue to study English
6. take a computer class
7. take out a loan
8. go on a cruise
9. buy a new TV
10. move
11. paint my bedroom
12. visit friends

C With a partner, ask and answer the questions. Use *may*, *might*, or the future.

1. What are you going to have for dinner tonight?
2. What are you going to do this weekend?
3. Where are you going to go on your next vacation?
4. When are you going to have a party?
5. When are you going to go to the dentist?

ACTIVE GRAMMAR: *May* and *Might* vs. Future

A

- Review the sentences in the grammar chart. Contrast *may, might,* and *will / be going to*.
- Ask students which terms are more definite (*will, be going to)*.
- Ask students to give additional examples using *might, maybe, be going to,* and *will*.
- Read the first item in Exercise A aloud. Explain the use of *may / might* in that example (possibility, not certainty).
- Have students complete the exercise individually and then read their answers aloud to the class.

B

- Have students say their sentences aloud and then write them down in their notebooks.
- Walk around the room as groups are working and provide help as needed.
- Ask volunteers to read their sentences aloud to the class. Write any incorrect sentences on the board for the class to correct.

C

As students complete the exercise, take note of sentences with errors. Write them on the board and ask students to correct them.

MORE ACTION

Ask students to read aloud one sentence from Exercise C about their future plans. When they have finished, call on individual students to try to remember what the student said.

ACTIVE GRAMMAR: Modal Contrast

A

- Review the meanings of the modals in the grammar chart.
- Have students cover the second and third column in the chart. Then, quiz students about the meaning of each modal.
- Ask students for additional example sentences for each modal.
- Ask students to complete Exercise A individually.
- Discuss the context of each sentence. For example: *Who is saying this? Why? What is a situation in which someone would say this?*

ACTIVE GRAMMAR Modal Contrast

Modal	Meaning	Example
have to	obligation necessity	I **have to do** my homework.
(not) have to	no obligation no necessity	I **don't have to get up** early on Sunday.
should	advice opinion	You **should apply** for the job. You **should wear** a suit.
must	necessity a rule or policy	I **must pay** taxes.
must not can't	something is not permitted	I **must not park** here. I **can't wear** jeans to work.
can	ability	I **can fix** a flat tire.
could would	polite request	**Could** you **answer** the phone? **Would** you **file** these papers?
may might	possibility	I **may get** the job. I **might lose** my job.

NOTE: Modals change the meaning of a verb. After a modal, use the base form of the verb. Do not use *-s*, *-ed*, or *-ing*.

A Circle the correct modal.

1. Tony has a job interview. He **should** / **doesn't have to** arrive on time.
2. At our company, all employees **must** / **might** wear name tags.
3. A nurse **has to** / **must not** wash her hands after caring for each patient.
4. Work begins at 7:30. You **must not** / **don't have to** arrive late.
5. **Could you** / **Should you** please repair the copy machine?
6. You are very good at math. I think you **should** / **have to** study accounting.
7. Friday is casual dress day. We **have to** / **don't have to** wear suits.
8. I received a good evaluation, so I **have to** / **might** get a raise.
9. Employees **must not** / **don't have to** take home company products.
10. You aren't happy at your job. You **should** / **have to** look for another opportunity.
11. We **don't have to** / **can't** make personal phone calls at work.

168 Unit 11

MORE ACTION

Give each student a strip of paper with a work-related situation written on it. For example:
You want to find a better job.
You want to get promoted.
You want to ask for a raise.
You need to take a few days off.
You don't have a job and need to find one.
Then, have students practice asking and giving advice for these situations with a partner, using as many different modals as they can.

B Listen. Circle the letter of the sentence with the same meaning as the sentence you hear. 56

1. **a.** I should take a break. (**b.**) I might take a break.
2. (**a.**) Could you please look up the number? **b.** You should look up the number.
3. **a.** You don't have to smoke. (**b.**) You must not smoke.
4. **a.** You might get a haircut. (**b.**) You should get a haircut.
5. (**a.**) You must renew your license. **b.** You might renew your license.
6. (**a.**) We don't have to work. **b.** We must not work.

C AT WORK Complete the conversations. Stephan is asking questions about his new workplace. Use a modal and the verb in parentheses. Answers may vary.

1. **A:** What time does work begin?

   B: All employees (sign in) have to / must sign in by 8:00.

2. **A:** Which office will I work in?

   B: We're not sure yet. You (be) might / may be in Room 245. Or you (be) might / may be in Room 246. We're going to decide later today.

3. **A:** What papers do I need to fill out?

   B: You (complete) have to / must complete your tax withholding form and an employee data form.

4. **A:** What is the dress code here?

   B: It's pretty casual—nice pants and a sweater are fine. You (wear) don't have to wear a suit. But don't dress too casually. You (wear) shouldn't wear jeans and a T-shirt.

D CIVICS Talk about your classroom rules. Use modals.

We don't have to stand up when we speak.

1. stand up when we speak
2. do our homework
3. speak English in class
4. bring coffee into our classroom
5. pay for our books
6. have a fire drill this month
7. turn off our cellphones
8. call our teacher by their first name
9. wear jeans to class
10. have a test next week

E **LET'S TALK.** With a partner, write three sentences about your class. Use modals. Then, read your sentences to the class. Your classmates will decide if the sentences are true or false.

B 56

- Explain that students should select the sentence that has the same meaning as the one they hear on the audio. (The sentences they will hear are different from the ones printed in their books.) Do the first item together as an example.
- Play the audio and pause after each sentence so students can choose their answers.
- Play the audio again so students can check their answers. Ask students to explain their choices.

C

Explain that for some questions, more than one modal may be correct.

D

Have students work with a partner and make sentences using modals. Encourage them to vary the modals they use.

E

- Have students write three sentences about the class using topics other than those in Exercise D.
- Ask pairs to come to the front of the class and read their sentences.
- Then, take a vote of which sentences students think are true. If the entire class does not agree about whether a sentence is correct, have the pair rewrite the sentence until the class agrees that it is correct.

AT WORK

Have students interview each other about rules at their jobs, in their apartment buildings, or in their homes. Students should answer the questions using the modals in the chart on the previous page.

THE BIG PICTURE: A Confident Employee

A

- Discuss the questions with the class and ask students to share any experiences they have of visiting or working in a diagnostic medical lab.
- Write a list of any useful vocabulary on the board, such as *blood work, lab test,* and *lab technicican*.

B 57

- Ask students to look at the pictures and describe what is happening in each one.
- Play the audio and have students take notes.
- Play the audio again and have students write their sentences.
- Invite volunteers to write their answers on the board.

THE BIG PICTURE A Confident Employee

A Discuss these questions.

1. What kinds of tests does a diagnostic medical lab perform?
2. Who are some of the employees at a diagnostic lab?
3. What kind of paperwork does a medical lab keep?

A diagnostic medical lab performs medical tests ordered by a doctor.

B Listen and look at the pictures. Sharon Taylor is an administrative assistant in a diagnostic lab. Write six of her responsibilities. 57 Answers may vary.

1. She schedules employees.
2. She works with patients.
3. She orders supplies.
4. She schedules patients.
5. She files insurance forms / claims.
6. She supervises the office.

C Complete the sentences. Use the correct modal and the verb in parentheses. In some sentences, more than one answer is correct. **Answers may vary.**

1. (work) ___Could you please work___ an extra hour today? Carla needs to leave early.
2. If you want a copy of your lab results, you (call) ___have to / must call___ this number.
3. The lab sends the test results to the doctor. The patient (bring) ___doesn't have to bring___ the results to the doctor.
4. (add) ___Could you / Would you please add___ two boxes of latex gloves to our order?
5. For a fasting blood test, a patient (eat or drink) ___can't / must not eat or drink___ anything for twelve hours.
6. (make) ___Could you / Would you please make___ a copy of this insurance card?
7. If a patient has insurance, he (bring) ___must / has to bring___ his insurance card.
8. If a patient has insurance, she (pay) ___doesn't have to pay___ the full amount.
9. If a patient doesn't have insurance, he (pay) ___has to / must pay___ for the test.

D AT WORK Discuss the qualities of a good employee in the box. Then, complete the sentences.

confident
good with details
patient
team player
well-organized
~~works well under pressure~~

1. The office is always busy, but Sharon ___works well under pressure___.
2. Sharon sometimes needs to repeat information, but she is always ___patient___.
3. Everyone knows the responsibilities and schedule, so it is a ___well-organized___ office.
4. Sharon knows how to run the office. She feels ___confident___ in her abilities.
5. Sharon manages all the supplies and orders. She's ___good with details___.
6. Sharon works well with others. She is a good ___team player___.

E Think about your work style. Circle *Yes* or *No* for each statement. Then, talk about your answers in a group. **Answers will vary.**

1.	I'm always patient with customers or clients.	Yes	No
2.	I am a good team player.	Yes	No
3.	I work well under pressure.	Yes	No
4.	I am organized and good with details.	Yes	No
5.	I feel confident at my job.	Yes	No

TEACHING TIP

To extend Exercise E, ask students to make a list and prioritize which qualities are most important in their jobs. Have them add other qualities not mentioned in Exercise E. For students who don't work, ask them to think about the qualities needed to be a good homemaker, parent, or student.

C

- Have students read through the sentences on their own and write their answers. Define any vocabulary that students do not know.
- Then, have students compare their answers in pairs.
- Call on individual students to read their sentences aloud.
- Discuss any differences with other students' answers. For many of the questions, more than one answer is possible.

D

- Ask students to define the terms in the box and explain why these characteristics might be important in the workplace.
- Have students complete the exercise on their own.
- Then, check the answers as a class.

E

- Have students circle their answers individually.
- Then, have students work in groups to discuss their answers.
- Review the answers as a class.

AT WORK

Strong communication skills, dependability, critical-thinking skills, ability to adjust well to change, good attendance, and a strong work ethic are some of the factors that make a good employee.

Discuss other aptitudes, as well as technical and soft skills that contribute to a candidate's employability (for example, planning and organizing, positive disposition, work experience, teamwork, giving and accepting feedback, good time management, leadership, problem solving). Prompt students to give real-life examples of those traits applied to specific jobs. For example, a teacher must have excellent communication skills.

READING: A Humorous Article

A 58 (facing page)

- Ask students to look at the photo and describe what is happening.
- Discuss the answers to the questions in Exercise A, encouraging students to use modal verbs.
- Read the Reading Note aloud to the class and explain that this article provides examples of things people should *not* do at work if they want to keep their jobs. Ask students to read the passage silently.
- Then, ask students to summarize the main idea and purpose of the article. (It's a humorous way of telling you how to succeed at keeping your job.)
- Ask students which points they found most humorous or not humorous at all.
- Ask students for additional ideas of things people can do to "help" them lose their jobs.

AT WORK

Understanding what is acceptable behavior in the workplace is as important as understanding social norms. The reading on this page highlights practices that would not be acceptable, but some of them could be discussed, addressed, and corrected without grave consequences. There are behaviors, however, that are entirely unacceptable in the workplace and should never be taken lightly as they carry more severe consequences, such as termination of employment or even legal action. For example, discrimination (because of color, religion, sex, race, or national origin) and any kind of harassment are unacceptable practices at work.

READING A Humorous Article

READING NOTE

A Humorous Article

Sometimes an article is not serious. It looks at a situation from a comical or funny point of view. For example, this article explains what you should *never* do at work.

How to Lose Your Job in Five Easy Steps

1. Don't worry about time policies.

If you have a half hour for lunch, no one is going to say anything if you take an extra ten minutes. If work begins at 8:30, arrive at 8:45. You can always **blame** the heavy traffic. No one is counting how many breaks you take. If you have two breaks, no one will **notice** if you take three.

2. Blame your coworkers if you miss a deadline or do a poor job on a project.

Be sure that nothing is your **fault**. If the boss complains about your work, explain to him that "Randy gave me the wrong directions." Or say, "I did my part. Tom didn't do his part."

3. Don't worry about the office dress code.

You should wear what you like to work. Be comfortable. You don't need to wear the **traditional** dress style of the older employees. Shorts, sweatpants, and T-shirts are always appropriate.

4. Post your feelings about work online.

You can **trust** all your friends. No one will share your posts. Your boss and your company don't follow what is happening online. They will never see posts like these:

"My boss always **complains** about everyone. But no one ever sees *him* working."

"I lied to my boss today. I told her I had a big exam and needed the day off. Hah! She believes anything!"

5. Call other employees by nicknames.

Give each employee a funny name based on their personality or their habits. If a coworker eats candy all the time, call him *Jelly Beans*. He'll think it's funny. 58

A chair race at the office.

172 Unit 11

MORE ACTION

Have students exchange stories about people who got into trouble at work. Students can work with a partner and present their stories as a role play or as an interview. Students can work together to develop a set of rules and advice for how to keep a job.

A **AT WORK** After reading, discuss these questions.

1. What time does your work begin? What is the policy about arriving late?
2. What is the dress code at your work place?
3. Who speaks to an employee who does not follow a policy?

B Discuss the meaning of the words in the box. Then, write the letter of the correct answer.

blame	complain	fault	notice	traditional	trust

1. Jorge often complains about __a__.
   a. his schedule **b.** the internet
2. The accident was his fault. He __b__ at the red light.
   a. stopped **b.** didn't stop
3. The boss noticed that one of the employees __b__.
   a. was wearing a uniform **b.** was leaving early
4. The boss blamed the secretary for __a__ the copy machine.
   a. breaking **b.** fixing
5. The boss trusted the team to __a__.
   a. complete the project **b.** make a mistake
6. Employees should wear traditional clothes, such as __b__.
   a. jeans and a T-shirt **b.** nice pants and a button-down shirt

C Change the suggestions. How can you *keep* your job? Answers will vary.

1. If work begins at 8:30, arrive at 8:45.
   If work begins at 8:30, arrive at 8:20.
2. Blame your coworkers if you do a poor job on a project.
   Take responsibility for all the work that you do. Explain that you learned from your mistakes.
3. Wear shorts, sweatpants, and T-shirts to work.
   Wear clothes that follow the dress code.
4. Post your feelings about work online.
   Do not post your feelings about work online.
5. Take an extra break.
   Only take the approved number of breaks.
6. It's fine to give nicknames to other employees.
   Call coworkers by their names.

B

- Have students complete the exercise individually.
- Call on students to give their answers and explain why they chose them.
- Ask students to make additional example sentences for each word in the word box. If possible, the sentences should be true about themselves or their workplace.

C

- Ask students to work in pairs and write their suggestions.
- Invite volunteers to read their suggestions aloud.
- Take a class vote on the best suggestions and write them on the board.
- Discuss what rules have been broken in each sentence. Discuss what kinds of rules are often written, in an employee handbook or elsewhere (for example, concerning punctuality, dress code, and sexual harassment), and what rules are normally understood.

MORE ACTION

It may be helpful to bring in (or ask students to bring in) some examples of rules from a company's employee handbook. Students may find it useful to discuss some of the more common rules, such as those about a dress code or absences / tardiness. Have students discuss whether they think the rules at their workplace are fair or not.

CIVICS

Our cultural background defines our boundaries for acceptable social behavior. When a person visits or moves to a different country, those social rules may be different, and what's acceptable in one place may not be well received in another place.

Understanding those cultural differences can make the process of adjusting to life in a new country more manageable.

Some basic social "rules" in the US are:

- Keep your distance when speaking to others. People appreciate their personal space.
- Do not touch other people, especially if you are not close with them. Some people are not comfortable being touched or hugged by people they just met. (Among close friends, hugging may be an acceptable greeting.)
- Be punctual. If you are invited for a dinner party at 6, show up on time. Never show up before the time you were invited, and never more than 10–15 minutes late.
- Do not ask personal questions (e.g., salary) as small talk.

WRITING OUR STORIES: My Job

A

- Ask students to tell the class about their job and what things they do and do not like about their job.
- Ask students to comment on the photograph. Encourage them to imagine what skills might be needed in this job and what makes this job interesting or difficult.
- Ask students to read the passage. Ask what topics are described and what details are given about each topic. For example, the writer discusses that the work is done in teams and then describes why (there is a lot of equipment to carry into the house).
- Read the Writing Note on the facing page aloud. Ask students to provide some examples of details used in the passage. For example: the specific steps in cleaning a carpet and the writer's work benefits.

WRITING OUR STORIES My Job

A AT WORK Discuss these questions. Then, read Tony's story.

1. Where do you work?
2. What do you do there?
3. What do you like about your job? What don't you like?

A carpet specialist.

I work for A1 Carpet Cleaning in Amesville. My company cleans rugs and carpets, and strips and waxes floors. I'm a carpet specialist. On most days, I clean carpets in four different homes. We work in teams—there are always two people together because there is a lot of equipment to carry into the house. First, we put small floor protectors under all furniture legs. Next, we remove any stains in the carpet. Then, we lightly shampoo the carpet and remove the water, both with the same machine.

I work the day shift, from 8:00 to 4:00. We have to wear company uniforms. Everyone must wear an ID at all times. When I arrive at work, my boss gives me the names, addresses, and phone numbers of the homes I have to visit that day. I drive a small company truck and I have to be very careful. If I have an accident, I might lose my job. When I arrive at a home, I have to call the office. When I finish the job, I have to call the office again.

I like my boss because she is organized and helpful. I also like my hours. I'm home by 5:00, and I don't have to work on the weekends. I get two weeks' paid vacation every year. There is one major problem with my job, though. I don't have any health benefits.

MORE ACTION

Have students role-play an interview with the carpet specialist above about his job using the information in the article. Ask for students' opinions about what they would and would not like about his job. Try to reach a consensus on the most important characteristics of a good job.

WRITING NOTE

Adding Details

Details make a story more interesting. Give specific information and examples when you write.

B Read the text below. The writer did not give many details. What questions can you answer?

> I work for a carpet cleaning company. I'm a carpet specialist. I clean carpets in homes.
>
> I work the day shift. We have to wear a white company shirt. When I arrive at work, my boss tells me the houses I have to visit that day.
>
> I like my boss. I also like my hours. I get two weeks' paid vacation every year. I don't have any health benefits.
>
> Martin

1. What is the company's name? What town is it in? We don't know.
2. Does Martin work alone? We don't know.
3. What does he do when he gets to a house? We don't know.
4. What are his hours? The day shift, but we don't know the hours.
5. What does he wear? A white company shirt.
6. What are some of the company policies and procedures? We don't know.
7. Why does he like the boss? We don't know.
8. Does this composition have many details? No, it doesn't.
9. Which composition is more interesting, the one on the previous page or this one? The one on the previous page.

C Write a few notes about your job or a job you would like to have. Then, write a few paragraphs about the job. Include a lot of details. Answers will vary.

Company and location	
Job title	
Job responsibilities	
Hours	
Uniform or dress code	
Policies	
Things I like	
Things I don't like	

D In a small group, read your stories to one another. Ask questions about the jobs.

E ACADEMIC Revise your work. Add the information that your classmates asked about.

TEACHING TIP

An alternative approach to Exercise D is to ask students to read their stories aloud without mentioning the name of the job. Students in the class can then try to guess what the job is.

B

- Ask a student to read the text aloud.
- Ask other students to identify the differences between this text and the one on the previous page. What information is missing? Ask students to identify the missing information without looking at the questions under the text. (If students have difficulty thinking of the missing information, read the first question: *What is the company's name?*)
- Then, have students compare their lists of missing information with the questions in Exercise B.
- Review the answers as a class.

C

- Draw the chart on the board. With help from students, fill in the chart with details from the carpet specialist's story on the previous page.
- Have students use the chart on the board as a model for their own charts.

D

Ask students to share some interesting information they learned about another student's job.

E

Students can revise their compositions as homework.

ACADEMIC

Remind students that revising is an important stage of the writing process. During this step, students should look at the text and rewrite it based on what they have in their drafts. While revising, they should focus on the message they are trying to convey, not on stylistic details. Following the proper writing process is helpful in any content area.

ENGLISH IN ACTION: Preparing for a Job Interview

A

- Call on students to read the interview tips aloud and paraphrase each in their own words.
- Ask for opinions and comments about each tip.
- Invite students to share their own experiences with job interviews. What kind of questions were they asked? How did they prepare for the interview? What additional advice would they give to someone preparing for a job interview?

B

- Have students role-play an interview and practice asking and answering the questions.
- Every student should role-play the interview so that their group can give them feedback.

C

- Have students review the interview tips on this page before conducting their interviews.
- Ask each interviewer to make note of which tips their partner followed well during the interview.
- Walk around the class as students conduct their interviews. Ask students who perform well to role-play their interview for the class.
- Have each student give their partner feedback on how they can improve their interview skills.

D

Have students name one thing that each person in the picture should and should not do to improve their chances of getting a job. Ask volunteers to share their ideas with the class.

ENGLISH IN ACTION | Preparing for a Job Interview

A Read the interview tips.

Interview Tips

1. Research the company.
2. Practice the interview several times.
3. Dress appropriately.
4. Arrive a few minutes early for the interview. Turn off your cellphone!
5. Shake hands with the interviewer.
6. Look at the interviewer. Make eye contact. Smile from time to time.
7. Explain your strengths. Talk about your skills.
8. Answer questions clearly. Give a few details in each answer.
9. Thank the interviewer and shake hands again.
10. Send a thank-you note two or three days after the interview.

B AT WORK In a group, ask and answer the interview questions about a job you would like.

1. What are your job responsibilities now?
2. What skills do you have?
3. Why do you want to work for us?
4. What are your strengths?
5. Why should we hire you?
6. What questions do you have for us?

C **LET'S TALK.** With a partner, practice an interview for a manager position. Then, two or three pairs will role-play their interviews for the class. Look at the interview tips. What did the job applicant do well? How can the applicant improve his or her interview skills?

D Look at the picture. The people are waiting for job interviews. How can they improve their chances of getting a job? Use *should* or *shouldn't*.

176 Unit 11

AT WORK

There are many useful online sources with tips and advice on how to prepare for a job interview. There are also videos of good and bad interview techniques. These can easily be found by searching using the keywords *job interview tips and mistakes*. Ask students to research some of these sources and share any additional tips and advice they found with the class.

UNIT 12

WORKING PARENTS

ACADEMIC Understand a sequence of events; match phrasal verbs and their meanings

AT WORK Read about working parents

CIVICS Write a note to a teacher; read a report card; learn about before- and after-school care

A member of the European Parliament with her daughter during a work session.

CCRS Level A: R 1, 2, 5, 7, 8; W 5; L 1, 6; Level B: R 1, 2, 5, 6, 7, 8; W 4, 5; L 1, 3, 6; Level C: R 1, 2, 7, 8; W 4, 9; L 1, 3, 6; Level D: R 1, 2, 7, 8; W 4, 5, 9; L 1, 3, 6; Level E: R 1, 2, 7, 8; W 4, 9; L 1, 6

ELPS Level 1 Standards 1, 2, 3, 7, 8, 9, 10; Level 2 Standards 1, 2, 3, 7, 8, 10; Level 3 Standards 1, 2, 3, 7, 8, 10; Level 4 Standards 1, 2, 3, 7, 8, 10; Level 5 Standards 1, 2, 3, 7, 8, 10

CIVICS 11-13, 13-3

CASAS 0.1.2; 0.1.5; 0.2.1; 2.5.8; 2.5.9; 2.8.6; 2.8.8

IN THIS UNIT

In Unit 12, students will:

- Discuss schedules with phrasal verbs and time clauses
- Learn about childcare resources in the US
- Write a letter to a child's teacher
- Read and interpret a report card

ABOUT THE PHOTO

The woman in the photo is Licia Ronzulli. She is a member of the European Parliament, representing Italy, and she is on the commission for work and social affairs, and women's rights. Licia gained some international fame in 2010 when she began sometimes bringing her then-6-week-old daughter, Vittoria, to work with her because Vittoria was still nursing. The photo is somewhat controversial, with people on both sides of the argument about bringing a child to work, but it highlights the many competing pressures working parents have. In fact, although Licia has worked on issues of employment rights for years, she has stated that only when she brought her daughter to work was attention given to the matter.

Students will be learning time clauses in this unit. Use the photo to model some of the language, and encourage students to imagine what Licia's day is like. Ask: *What is the baby doing while the mother is working?* (She seems to be drawing.) *What else do you think the baby does? Does she sleep while her mother works? How does Licia prepare? What does she do before she goes to work?* (Packs toys, snacks, etc.)

Let students discuss if they agree with Licia bringing her baby to work. Students may note that it is distracting or not the best thing for the baby, that the baby should be in daycare; on the other side, they may note the cost of daycare, the convenience for nursing, and the importance of bringing awareness to employment and childcare issues for working parents.

A 🎧59

- Ask students to describe each picture.
- Encourage them to predict what Henry's work, home, family, and daily routine are like. If they have trouble, remind them to look for clues like clocks and signs. They should be able to tell things like how many children he has and that he works as a loan officer in a bank before you play the recording.
- Play the audio and compare students' predictions with what they hear. Which things were the same and which were different?
- Ask students to paraphrase Henry's daily schedule.

B 🎧60

- Ask students to read the sentences silently.
- Play the audio for the first item and repeat it together as a class.
- Play the other sentences and ask students to repeat them together.

A Look at the pictures and listen to Henry's schedule. 🎧59

1.

2.

3.

4.

5.

6.

B **Pronunciation: Pauses** Listen and repeat. Pay attention to the pause at the comma. 🎧60

1. After he drops off the children, Henry stops at a coffee shop.
2. As soon as the children get home from school, they call their father.
3. After they eat dinner, Henry helps the children with their homework.
4. When they finish their homework, they can play video games.
5. Before he goes to sleep, Henry watches TV.

TEACHING TIP

In addition to noting the pauses in the sentences in Exercise B, it may be helpful to point out proper intonation. Write the sentences on the board and draw arrows above them to indicate rising and falling intonation. For example:

After he drops off the children, Henry stops at a coffee shop.

Point out that the rise in intonation tends to occur on the word just before the comma. As students are asked to read longer pieces aloud, you may periodically want to remind them that they should use punctuation to their advantage. Students can always pause at punctuation—a comma, a period, a dash; this will help make reading longer pieces aloud more manageable, as they can focus on smaller chunks of text, pausing briefly as they move on from each one.

ACTIVE GRAMMAR Present Time Clauses

He watches TV **before** he goes to bed. (main clause) (time clause) **Before** he goes to bed, he watches TV. (time clause) (main clause)

1. A time clause explains when an action happens. It begins with a word such as *after, before, when, as soon as, until*, or *if*. A time clause has a subject and a verb.
2. If the time clause is at the beginning of the sentence, use a comma after the time clause. If the time clause is at the end of the sentence, don't use a comma.

As soon as Henry gets home, he asks the children about school.
The children play games **until** their father comes home.

A ACADEMIC Circle *True* or *False*.

1.	After Henry gets to work, he drops off the children at school.	True	(False)
2.	Before he drops off the children, Henry gets a cup of coffee.	True	(False)
3.	As soon as the children get home, they call their father.	(True)	False
4.	As soon as the children get home, Henry leaves work.	True	(False)
5.	The children eat dinner before Henry gets home from work.	True	(False)
6.	After the children do their homework, they can play video games.	(True)	False
7.	Henry watches TV after the children go to bed.	(True)	False

B Listen to Henry's conversation with his coworker, Mark. Then, practice it with a partner. 61

Mark: You get a call every day at 3:15, don't you?

Henry: Yes, that's my son. He's 11. My daughter is 10. They walk home together after school. My son has to call me as soon as they walk in the door.

Mark: Oh, I see. My boys are still little. They stay at daycare until I pick them up at 4:30.

Henry: Big kids, little kids. . . Childcare is a challenge when you're working.

A father takes his baby to daycare on his way to work.

Working Parents 179

MORE ACTION

Have students look back at the pictures on the previous page and make sentences about each picture using time clauses. They can write the sentences and then check the answers against the audio from Exercise B.

ACTIVE GRAMMAR: Present Time Clauses

A

- Read the information in the grammar chart aloud.
- Explain the difference between a main clause and a time clause. (A time clause is introduced by a time word [a conjunction]. A time clause cannot stand alone as a complete sentence.)
- For each example in the chart, ask which event happens first and which happens second.
- Point out the conjunctions in the grammar chart: *after, before, when, as soon as, until,* and *if.*
- Have students complete Exercise A individually.
- Ask volunteers to read their answers. For answers that are false, ask students to explain how they came to that conclusion.
- If students have difficulty with this exercise, it may be helpful to draw a timeline of Henry's day on the board.

B 61

Play the audio. Then, ask students to practice the conversation in pairs.

ACADEMIC

Standardized tests may require students to derive a timeline for a sequence of events presented out of order. For this reason, listening carefully for time clauses can help clarify the chronological sequence. Use an item from the grammar chart or from Exercise A to illustrate. For example: *Which sentence means the same as this one?*
Target sentence: *Before he goes to bed, he watches TV.*
Henry watches TV in bed.
Henry watches TV. Then he goes to bed. (correct)
Henry goes to bed. After, he watches TV.

C

- Read the sentences aloud.
- Have students circle the time words in each sentence in addition to underlining the time clause.
  Answers:
  1. until
  2. As soon as
  3. After
  4. before
  5. While
- Ask volunteers to read their answers to the class.

D 62

- Explain that students should write single words or short phrases, not complete sentences, for their answers. Point out the example answer. You might give them a hint to look back at Exercise C and think about the kinds of activities Tammy will mention (like *bottle* and *bed*).
- Play the audio and have students listen only.
- Then, play the audio again and have students take notes.
- Have students complete the exercise independently. Then, review the answers as a class.

E

- Ask students to complete as many of the sentences as they can without looking at the sentences in Exercise C. Explain that more than one time word is correct for some sentences.
- Ask volunteers to read their sentences to the class.

C Underline the time clauses.

1. Tammy stays in bed until she hears Emma wake up.
2. As soon as Emma wakes up, she wants her bottle.
3. After Emma has her bottle, Tammy feeds her breakfast.
4. Emma has breakfast before Tammy gets her dressed.
5. While Emma plays in her crib, Tammy takes a shower and gets dressed.

D Listen to Tammy talk about Emma's day. Take notes. 62 Answers may vary.

7:00	bottle, breakfast	4:00	shopping or library
9:00	clean, laundry	5:00	home, make dinner
10:30	park	6:00	husband comes home
12:00	lunch, bottle	7:00	dinner
1:00	nap	8:00	bed

E Complete the sentences. Use *before, after, when, as soon as,* or *until.*

1. Tammy is going to stay home ___until___ Emma is two years old.
2. ___As soon as / After / When___ Emma wakes up, she has a bottle.
3. ___After___ she has her bottle, she eats breakfast.
4. Tammy cleans the house ___before___ she takes Emma to the park.
5. They stay at the park ___until___ it is time for lunch.
6. Emma takes a nap ___after___ she eats lunch.
7. ___When___ Tammy takes Emma to the library, she checks out five or six books.
8. Emma plays with her father ___until___ they eat dinner.
9. Her father reads her a story ___before / when___ she goes to bed.

180 Unit 12

MORE ACTION

Have students write five sentences about their day using the time words *before, after, when, as soon as,* and *until.* After students have written their sentences, have them practice reading them to a partner. As students work, move around the room and correct grammatical and pronunciation errors.

F Combine the sentences using the time words. First, write the sentence with the time clause at the beginning of the sentence. Then, write the sentence with the time clause at the end.

1. I turn on my computer. I check my email. (after)
   After I turn on my computer, I check my email.
   I check my email after I turn on my computer.
2. He gets up. He has a cup of coffee. (as soon as)
   As soon as he gets up, he has a cup of coffee.
   He has a cup of coffee as soon as he gets up.
3. I leave for school. I make my bed. (before)
   Before I leave for school, I make my bed.
   I make my bed before I leave for school.
4. She gets to school. She talks with her friends. (when)
   When she gets to school, she talks with her friends.
   She talks with her friends when she gets to school.
5. I am busy every moment. I go to sleep at night. (until)
   Until I go to sleep at night, I am busy every moment.
   I am busy every moment until I go to sleep at night.

G **LET'S TALK.** Write your daily schedule in the chart. Then, tell a partner about your day. Give more details as you talk. Use *before*, *after*, *as soon as*, and *when* in your description. **Answers will vary.**

Time	Activity
	turn off the alarm
	go to sleep

As soon as I get to school, I buy a cup of coffee in the cafeteria.

F

- Go over the example answer with the class. Explain that if students vary their sentence structure, their writing will be less repetitive and more interesting.
- Make sure students understand to use commas after time clauses when they come first in a sentence.
- Allow time for students to complete the exercise individually.
- Move around the room and check students' work as they are writing.
- Ask volunteers to read their sentences aloud. Correct intonation as needed.

G

- Give some examples of daily activities. For example: *wake up, take a shower, eat breakfast, drop off kids, exercise, buy a cup of coffee, check email, read the newspaper, go to work, pick up kids, make dinner,* and *go grocery shopping.*
- Have students complete the chart individually.
- Then, have students work in pairs to tell each other about their day, using time clauses.
- Move around the class, taking note of good example sentences and sentences with mistakes.
- Use your notes to give feedback to the class.

MORE ACTION

Ask students to write a paragraph describing their day. They should use time clauses whenever possible. After students have written their paragraphs, use the paragraphs to write a list of example sentences with blanks for the time words on the board. Students can fill in the blanks and also guess who wrote the sentences.

Another variation of this exercise would be to have students write about the typical day of a famous person, a fictional character, or even of another classmate, in the first person (still using time clauses, of course). They can then read their paragraphs aloud for the class to guess their identity. For example:

After I wake up, I put on my glasses and my robe and gather my things. I meet my friends in the Gryffindor common room before I go to breakfast. While we eat breakfast, we read the paper and talk about the news. Then, we go to class and... (Harry Potter)

ACTIVE GRAMMAR: Phrasal Verbs

A

- Review the information in the grammar chart. Point out that the example sentences *I put my coat on* and *I put on my coat* have the same meaning.
- Students likely don't know the difference between different types of multiword verbs (phrasal, prepositional)—nor do they need to. Let students know that one aspect of phrasal verbs is that the meaning changes completely based on the combination. For example *get up = wake up and exit the bed*, but *get off = exit a train, bus, etc. at a designated stop*. The meaning of the verb cannot be derived from the word *get* alone (which, on its own, is nearly meaningless).
- Ask volunteers to tell you which verbs in the word box they know the meaning of and to give an example sentence for each. Explain that the verbs followed by an (S) are separable verbs that can be separated by the object of the sentence.
- Have students cover the verbs in the word box. Quiz students about which verbs are separable and which ones are not.
- Have students complete Exercise A individually.
- Then, go over the answers as a class.

B

- Read the example answer.
- Have students complete the exercise individually. Have them write an *S* next to the sentences that use a separable verb.
- Go over the answers as a class.
- Then, have students rewrite the sentences that use separable verbs. For example, *Can you drop the children off at school?* can be rewritten as *Can you drop off the children at school?*
- Ask volunteers to write their rewritten sentences on the board. Have the class correct them as necessary.

ACTIVE GRAMMAR Phrasal Verbs

Some verbs in English are made up of two words. They are called *phrasal verbs*.

Some phrasal verbs can have other words between the two parts of the verb. These are called separable (S) verbs.

I **put on** my coat. I **put** my coat **on**.

Some phrasal verbs can't be separated.

I **get on** the bus at 7:30 every morning.

NOT ~~I **get** the bus **on** at 7:30 every morning.~~

drop off (S)	get out of	put on (S)
eat out	get up	take off (S)
get in	hang up (S)	turn off (S)
get off	look at	turn on (S)
get on	pick up (S)	wake up (S)

WORD PARTNERSHIPS

put on	makeup a seat belt pajamas

A ACADEMIC Match each phrasal verb with its meaning.

f	**1.** hang up	**a.** to leave a car or taxi
a	**2.** get out of	**b.** to remove a hat, coat, or other clothing
d	**3.** turn off	**c.** to leave a bus, train, or plane
c	**4.** get off	**d.** to stop a device or electronic equipment
g	**5.** eat out	**e.** to leave a person at a place
e	**6.** drop off	**f.** to put clothing on a hanger or a hook
i	**7.** get in	**g.** to eat at a restaurant
h	**8.** turn on	**h.** to start a device or electronic equipment
j	**9.** pick up	**i.** to enter a car or taxi
b	**10.** take off	**j.** to go somewhere and get someone

B Complete the sentences. Use phrasal verbs.

1. It's raining hard this morning. Can you ___drop___ the children ___off___ at school?
2. It's cold outside. ___Put on___ your hat and gloves before you go out.
3. Don't leave your coat on the floor. ___Hang___ it ___up___ in the closet.
4. If you are hot, ___take off___ your sweater.
5. When you ___get on___ the bus, you have to pay the exact fare.
6. I wake up my son at 6:30, but he doesn't ___get up___ until 7:00.
7. I can't see very well. Please ___turn on___ the light.
8. I always ___pick up___ my children after school.
9. I'm too tired to cook tonight. Let's ___eat out___.

MORE ACTION

Have students make additional example sentences using the verbs at the top of the page. If they use a separable verb in the sentence, have them write it in two different ways. Have students check their sentences with a partner. Then, have them rewrite their sentences using a blank for the verbs. Students can give their sentences to a new partner and take each other's quizzes.

C **LET'S TALK.** Read each pair of actions. Explain the order in which you usually do the two actions. Use *before* or *after*. Answers will vary.

> I put on my seat belt **after** I start the car.

> Not me. I put on my seat belt **before** I start the car.

- put on my seat belt / start the car
- wash the dishes / eat dinner
- turn off the lights / leave my house
- get dressed / eat breakfast
- return to my car / the parking meter time expires
- eat dinner / do my homework
- turn on the computer / check my email
- put on my pajamas / go to bed
- sharpen my pencil / come to class
- turn off the light / get into bed

D Listen to your teacher and complete the sentences. Your teacher will refer to Appendix D in the back of the book.

Mimi has a difficult time falling asleep at night. She gets in bed and puts her head on the pillow. But ___as soon as she closes her eyes___(1), she begins to worry—about her job, her health, and her family. So, she now has a routine to relax herself ___before she goes to sleep___(2). ___Before she goes into her bedroom___(3), she drinks a cup of hot herbal tea. Then, she brushes her teeth. ___After she brushes her teeth___(4), she washes her face and puts on her favorite face cream. ___When she gets into bed___(5), she picks up a magazine and reads for a few minutes. Then, she listens to some quiet music. ___When she finally turns off her light___(6), she falls asleep more easily.

Drinking tea before bed can help you sleep.

Working Parents 183

C

- Ask two students to read the text in the speech bubbles.
- Then, have students work in pairs to complete the exercise.
- Ask volunteers to read the actions in order for the class.

D

- Have students read the paragraph and try to predict the missing information before you dictate.
- Then, turn to Appendix D and read the dictation while students listen only.
- Read the dictation again, pausing so that students have time to write their answers.
- Check the answers by having volunteers supply the missing information as you read the dictation aloud again.

MORE ACTION

You can extend Exercise C by having students come up with three additional pairs of activities and then get together with a partner to discuss. You can encourage them to be playful by providing a couple of models:

kiss the dog
kiss my husband/wife
do my homework
check my social media

THE BIG PICTURE: Working Parents

A

- Ask different students to explain or pantomime each word in the box.
- Then, have other students make up sentences using each word.
  For example:
  S1: *I don't like to wake up early.*
  S2: *I wake up at 7:00 every morning.*

B 63

- Ask students to describe what is happening in the pictures.
- Play the audio and ask students to say what they heard using the words from the word box in Exercise A.
- Ask if any students in the class are parents or responsible for caring for young children. Is their morning routine similar to Matt and Ava's?

A Discuss the words and phrases.

buckle	drop off	jump out of	put on
climb into	get dressed	look at	wake up

B Look at the pictures and listen to Matt and Ava's morning routine. 63

1. 
2. 
3. 
4. 
5. 
6. 
7. 
8. 

9. 

TEACHING TIP

Another way to approach Exercise B is to write the key events of the story on strips of paper with one sentence on each strip. Distribute the strips of paper to groups of students. Have the groups work together to put the sentences in the order they think they will occur in the story. Then, play the audio so that students can check their predictions.

184 Unit 12

C Complete each sentence with the correct form of one of the verbs from the box.

buckle
climb into
drop off
get dressed
~~get up~~
jump out of
put on
wake up

1. Matt ___gets up___ at 5:45 in the morning.
2. He ___jumps out of___ bed when the alarm clock rings.
3. He ___wakes up___ Ava after he takes a shower.
4. Matt ___puts on___ a movie for the boys.
5. Ava ___gets dressed___ after she eats breakfast.
6. The boys ___climb into___ their car seats.
7. Ava ___buckles___ the boys into their car seats.
8. She ___drops off___ the boys at the daycare center.

D **ACADEMIC** Complete the sentences. Use *before, after, when,* or *as soon as*. For some sentences, more than one answer is possible. **Answers will vary.**

1. ___After / As soon as / When___ the alarm rings, Matt gets up.
2. Matt takes a shower ___before___ Ava gets up.
3. ___After / As soon as / When___ Matt gets out of the shower, he wakes Ava up.
4. ___After / As soon as / When___ the boys wake up, they watch a movie.
5. Matt says goodbye to everyone ___before / when___ he leaves for work.
6. ___When / As soon as___ everyone is ready, they leave.
7. The kids always climb into their car seats ___as soon as / when___ they get into the car.
8. Ava's customers don't get angry ___when___ she's late for work.

E Answer the questions with a partner. **Answers may vary.**

1. Who gets up first? *Matt does.*
2. What time does Matt get up?
   He gets up at 5:45.
3. When does he wake Ava up?
   After he takes a shower
4. What does Ava do after she wakes up?
   She wakes up the children.
5. When does Ava eat breakfast with the boys?
   After Matt leaves
6. When does Ava get dressed?
   After breakfast
7. What does Ava do before she starts the car?
   She buckles the boys into their car seats.
8. Where does Ava take the kids before she goes to work?
   To the daycare center
9. Why aren't Ava's customers annoyed when she is a little late?
   Because they are parents, too.

C

- Have students complete the exercise individually.
- Then, go over the answers as a class.

D

- Read the sentences aloud.
- Ask volunteers to give answers. When more than one answer is correct, be sure to elicit all answers from the class.

E

- Play the audio from Exercise B, Track 63.
- Have students work with a partner to complete the exercise.
- Then, have pairs check their answers with another pair of students.

MORE ACTION

Ask volunteers to describe their morning routine for the class.

READING: Article about Community Resources

A 64 (facing page)

- Read the questions in Exercise A on the next page. Ask parents in the classroom where their children currently are (who takes care of them while the parent is in class). What about when the parent is at work? See if students can volunteer information on childcare from their own lives: costs, location, activities. How much is their extended family able to help with childcare?
- Ask students to look at the photo. Where are the children? What time of day do they think it is?
- Call on students to read each paragraph out loud, pausing to answer any questions they may have, especially regarding the words in bold.

READING Article about Community Resources

Before- and After-School Care

Childcare is one of the biggest concerns and biggest expenses for working families today. Most single parents work. In 61% of families with two parents, both parents work. About half of school-age children in the United States need care before and/or after school. There is after-school care for many children, but many others go home to empty houses.

In many families with working parents, grandparents and other family members are the ones who take children to school and pick them up after classes end. This type of care works for families because children are comfortable with their relatives and have time to play, talk, and do homework. This care is often free. In some families, one person with a small child may stay home and watch the children of other family members. In these families, the parents often pay something for the childcare. For other families, neighbors and friends help with after-school care.

About 25% of children attend after-school programs. The **majority** of these programs are at public schools. The others are at YMCAs, Boys and Girls Clubs, local recreation centers, and religious organizations. For programs at other locations, a van or bus is needed to pick up the children and bring them to the site. When programs do not offer this service, children of working parents do not have the transportation they need.

As of 2018, more than ten million children attend after-school programs, but there are not enough programs. Over nineteen million more children would **participate** if there were programs in their area.

The cost of an after-school program varies depending on the neighborhood where the program is located and what kinds of activities are provided. Average costs can range between $50 and $100 per week, for one child. Many families **qualify** for government help to pay for these programs. Also, these programs offer tax **advantages** for many families when they file their income taxes.

It's not always easy to find information about after-school programs. Parents can ask the child's school about programs in the area, or call their local recreation department because many offer their own programs. Another great resource is the YMCA or Boys and Girls Clubs, which often have activities for middle school and high school students. Parents can also go online to see if any local faith organizations provide care. One of the best sources of information is other parents. Talking to coworkers, neighbors, and the parents of your children's friends can be very helpful.

Good after-school care can help parents relax at work. Most parents are happy with the after-school programs their children attend. These programs offer snacks, physical activities, help with homework, and STEM (science, technology, engineering, and math) activities. Studies show that children who attend good after-school programs have better school attendance, better **behavior**, and better grades. 64

Children play in the Lions Park Playscape, in Alabama.

186 Unit 12

TEACHING TIP

Divide the class into five groups and have each group look up and discuss a different word in bold from the reading. Each group should write a sample sentence for their word. Then, have a representative from each group read the definition and the group's sample sentence. Have all the students write down the definitions and sample sentences from the other groups in their notebooks.

A Discuss these questions. Then, read the article on the previous page.

1. Do you know any working families with children? How old are the children?
2. Who cares for the children before and after school?

B Match. Then, complete the sentences.

d	**1.** majority	**a.**	to take part in an activity
a	**2.** participate	**b.**	to meet the requirements for; to be eligible for
b	**3.** qualify	**c.**	a way someone acts
e	**4.** advantages	**d.**	more than half of a group
c	**5.** behavior	**e.**	good things about something; benefits

1. Some children participate in sports after school.
2. My son's teacher is happy because he has good behavior at school.
3. The majority of working parents need after-school care for their children.
4. Many families qualify for tax benefits related to after-school care.
5. After-school programs offer many advantages for working parents.

READING NOTE

Identifying Supporting Ideas and Reasons

Informational texts have one or more main ideas. The text gives reasons or details to support each main idea.

C In your notebook, write reasons or details that support each of these main ideas from the article about community resources on the previous page. Answers will vary.

1. Family care is a good choice for many children. Children are comfortable with their relatives.
2. Many children can't participate in after-school programs.
3. After-school programs offer many advantages for working families.

D AT WORK Check the true statement(s) based on information from the article.

1. In 61% of families with two parents, both parents work.
   - ☐ **a.** In most families with two parents, only one parent works.
   - ☑ **b.** In most families with two parents, both parents work.
2. About 25% of children attend after-school programs.
   - ☐ **a.** Most children attend after-school programs.
   - ☑ **b.** Most children do not attend after-school programs.

B

- Have students complete the matching section first. Go over the answers as a class.
- Then, have students complete the sentences.
- Have volunteers read their answers to the class.

C

- Draw students' attention to the Reading Note. Give them a moment to read and answer the questions. You may want to ask them to underline relevant parts of the article that support their answer.
- Go through the answers as a class, pointing out details in the text that support the answers.

D

- Have students complete the exercise individually and then compare their answers with a partner.
- Review the answers as a class.

AT WORK

Childcare can be a huge expense for families, especially before students enter the public school system, so much so that it is often a factor in whether or not both parents choose to return to work. A parent will sometimes stay home only because childcare costs would be the equivalent of their salary! However, there are resources available to help support working parents. One resource students should be aware of is an FSA (flexible spending account), which allows people to put away up to $5000 a year for childcare with pre-tax dollars.

WRITING OUR STORIES:
A Note to the Teacher

A

- Brainstorm a list of situations in which a parent might have to write a note to their child's teacher (for example, when a child fails a test, when a family member has died, or to thank a teacher at the end of the school year).
- Discuss why it is important to meet your child's teacher and have a good relationship with him or her.
- Encourage students to exchange experiences of meeting their child's teacher or writing them a note or an email.

B

- Allow some time for students to read the notes silently.
- Ask students to summarize the main idea of each note. What is the tone of each note?
- Have students discuss each note. Is the point of each note clear? Would it be better for the parent to schedule a meeting with the teacher rather than write a note?

WRITING OUR STORIES | A Note to the Teacher

A Discuss these questions.

1. Do you ever write short notes or emails? If so, who do you write to?
2. Do you have any children in school? Do you have to write a note or an email when they are absent from school?

B Read the notes to a teacher.

February 10

Dear Ms. Toma,

Please excuse Melissa's absence from class last week. She had the flu. Melissa missed a lot of classwork and homework. Please give her the assignments so she can complete the work at home.

Thank you,

Paula Romero

From: Kadeen Assad
To: Carla Miller
Cc:
Subject: Ride Home for Omar Assad

Dear Ms. Miller,

My son Omar usually takes the bus home from school. Today, I have to work overtime, so my brother Taariq will pick up Omar. He will come to the school at 3:00 and take him home. If you need to reach me, my number at work is 555-8989.

Sincerely,
Kadeen Assad

October 10

Dear Mr. Evans,

When my daughter came home yesterday, she was crying. When she was playing outside at recess, a girl pushed her. Another girl pulled her hair. My daughter does not know the names of the girls. She said they are older and in another class. Can you please talk to my daughter and to the older girls? My daughter is very upset. Thank you.

Julie Lin

MORE ACTION

You may want to use the notes in Exercise B to role-play parent–teacher conversations about each problem. On the board, make a list of useful language to use in such a conversation, such as *absences, homework, needs help with, has trouble with,* and so on. Suggest that pairs of students choose one problem from Exercise B and practice their conversation before presenting it to the class.

C Write the reason for each note in Exercise B. Answers may vary.

1. Her child was absent from school. The child needs the homework assignments.
2. Omar's uncle will pick him up from school.
3. Some older girls pushed her daughter and pulled her hair.

WRITING NOTE

Writing a Note to a Teacher

Notes to teachers should be short and specific.

- Do not include unnecessary information.
- Include the date.
- Spell the teacher's name correctly. Use *Mr.* for a *man* and *Ms.* for a *woman.*
- Sign your full name.

D Edit the note. Add any missing information. Cross out any unnecessary sentences.

March 3

Dear Ms. Yang,

My son Victor has an appointment at the doctor on Wednesday at 9:00. I will bring him to school immediately after the appointment. ~~This was the only time available.~~ I am sorry that he will be late tomorrow. ~~You are a very good teacher, and Victor is very happy in your class.~~

Thank you.

Tamara Lapinsky

E CIVICS Write a note to a teacher. You have a parent-teacher conference on Monday night at 7:00, but you work at night. Suggest a different day and time for the conference.

F In a small group, read your notes. Which note does the group like best? Why?

CIVICS

Communication between schools and parents is carefully structured to promote both the safety of the students and the ability of the school and parent to work as a team. Written notice is usually required of the parent for absences, tardiness, and changes to the pick up routine (for younger children). In return, parents should expect a call from the school by mid-morning if their child does not show up on a given day (whether or not a note is submitted in advance). The goal of these policies is to deter disciplinary issues (skipping school) and ensure that the child is picked up by an authorized adult. Encourage students to become familiar with their school's parent-school communication policies. Let them know they should also expect polite and timely communication back from both the teacher and the administration if they reach out. Parents should be made to feel welcome, as communication with parents is part of the teachers' and administrators' jobs, not an interruption or inconvenience.

C

- Have students read the notes on the previous page again and then complete the exercise on their own.
- Then, have volunteers read their answers to the class.
- You may want to bring up the word "bullying" in connection with the third note. Discuss what forms bullying can take and possible ways to deal with it. For example, physical bullying can involve pushing or hitting, while other forms of bullying may be spoken or written in a note. Some ways of dealing with bullying are to report it to a teacher or guidance counselor or to directly confront the bully.

D

- Read the Writing Note aloud.
- Ask students to identify the mistakes in the note in Exercise D.
- Have students make the corrections in their books.

E

Have students write the note on their own and use the information in the Writing Note as a guide.

F

Have each student read their note from Exercise E aloud to their group. Ask the other group members to list some things that are good about the note and some things that could be improved. Have the group edit each note together and then present the note that they think is the best.

ENGLISH IN ACTION: Reading a Report Card

A

Encourage students to describe their experiences with report cards in their native country and in the US.

B

- Have students work in pairs to read the report card and answer the questions.
- Check the answers as a class.
- Make sure that students understand the teacher's comments for each subject and the division of grades by quarter.
- Ask them why grades are important and what they would do if their child had failing grades in any subject.
- Read the teacher's comments. Put (+) next to a positive teacher comment. Put (–) next to a negative teacher comment.

C

- Give students a few minutes to write their suggestions for Claudia.
- Go over their suggestions as a class. Do they have any suggestions for the teacher as to how to help Claudia? What about her parents?

CIVICS

Make sure students understand the A-F grading system in the US. Tell them that F is a failing grade and can result in students being held back (not being moved forward to the next grade). Explain that the school usually requires a signature to prove that the parent has seen the report card, and should also invite parents to discuss progress (at least twice a year). Ask students about report cards in their native countries. What was the grading system? What did students do if they received a bad grade? Discuss the questions as a class.

ENGLISH IN ACTION Reading a Report Card

A Discuss these questions.

1. When you were a child, how often did you receive a report card?
2. How often do children receive report cards today? Do parents have to sign them?

B **CIVICS** Look at the report card and answer the questions.

WASHINGTON MIDDLE SCHOOL
Student Progress Report

Student: Claudia Figueroa **Student ID:** 123-12-123 **Grade:** 8

Attendance	Q1	Q2	Q3	Q4
Absent	5	3		
Tardy	4	6		

Subject	Q1	Q2	Q3	Q4	Teacher's Comment
English	B	C			Always cooperative; often late for class; fails to complete assignments; needs extra help
Spanish 2	A	B			Follows directions well; good class participation
Geography	D	C			Improved skills; disorganized work; rarely asks for help; good class participation
Social Studies	C	D			Always cooperative; more study required; disorganized work; rarely asks for help
Algebra 1	C	D			Performs poorly on tests; rarely asks for help; needs extra help; conference needed
Physical Education	B	B			
Computer Science	B	B			Always cooperative; excellent effort; very good work
Art	A	A			Very good work

A = Excellent B = Good C = Fair D = Having Difficulty F = Failing

1. What grade is Claudia in? *Eighth grade*
2. What does *tardy* mean? *Late*
3. How many times was Claudia absent in the second quarter? *Three*
4. What is Claudia's best subject? *Art*
5. What subjects are difficult for Claudia? *Social Studies and Algebra 1*
6. In which subject is Claudia improving? *Geography*

C Look at the teacher's comments on Claudia's report card. In your notebook, write Claudia's problems. Then, write a suggestion to help Claudia solve each problem. *Answers will vary.*

A pickpocket steals this woman's wallet while she tries to get a taxi.

UNIT 13 CRIME

ACADEMIC Understand a sequence of events; recall and retell information

AT WORK Discuss the role of authorities in a criminal investigation

CIVICS Learn about jury duty

CCRS Level A: R 1, 5; W 3; L 1, 6; Level B: R 1, 3, 5, 6; W 3, 4; L 1, 2, 3, 6; Level C: R 1, 3; W 4, 9; L 1, 2, 3, 6; Level D: R 1, 3; W 4, 9; L 1, 3, 6; Level E: R 1, 3; W 4, 9; L 1, 6

ELPS Level 1 Standards 1, 2, 3, 7, 8, 9, 10; Level 2 Standards 1, 2, 3, 7, 8, 9, 10; Level 3 Standards 1, 2, 3, 7, 8, 9, 10; Level 4 Standards 1, 2, 3, 7, 8, 9, 10; Level 5 Standards 1, 2, 3, 7, 8, 9, 10

CIVICS 7-10; 19-4; 24-1; 24-9; 45-4

CASAS 0.1.2; 0.1.5; 0.2.1; 0.2.4; 2.3.1; 5.3.7; 5.3.8; 5.6.3

IN THIS UNIT

In Unit 13, students will:

- Understand a sequence of events
- Organize ideas before writing a composition
- Use the past continuous
- Discuss serving on a jury

ABOUT THE PHOTO

In this photo, we see a woman focused on getting a taxi while someone steals her wallet. Compared with people from other countries, Americans tend to be very trusting. In many places, mail and even packages are delivered in the open, without any security; men carry their wallets in their back pockets; or women carry their purses unzipped. In small towns, people sometimes leave their front doors unlocked. However, not every place offers that sense of security, and for people from big cities or other countries, those actions may be surprising. Regardless of the location, it's a good idea to take simple precautions and use common sense to avoid unpleasant incidents. When you park, roll up the windows and lock your car. Keep your wallet in a zipped purse, or in a front pocket. Be aware of your surroundings. Avoid walking alone in poorly lit areas at night.

In this unit, students will learn the past continuous and contrast it with the simple past. To preview the target grammar and some of the vocabulary in this unit, ask students to look at the photo and describe what they see. *What is this woman doing?* (She's trying to get a taxi / bus.) *What else is happening in this photo?* (She is being pickpocketed. / Someone is stealing her wallet.) Ask: *Has any of you ever lost your wallet? Or, have you ever been robbed?* Ask volunteers to describe the incidents using past time clauses with words like *before*, *when*, *after*, or *as soon as*. On the board, write some of the details students provide on a timeline to show how different past actions relate in time.

A

- Have students describe each photo. Ask: *Where are these people? What is happening?*
- Ask students to make sentences using the words underneath each photo. For example: *The shoplifter is stealing a shirt.* Correct students' pronunciation or grammar as needed.
- Discuss what you can do to avoid or prevent these crimes and what you should do if you see or experience a crime like one of these.
- Write a list of new vocabulary on the board. You may want to add words for other types of crimes such as *pick pocketing*, *fraud*, *identity theft*, or *vandalism*.

B

Ask volunteers to share their experiences with the class.

A Discuss each kind of crime.

1. Crime: shoplifting
   Person: shoplifter
   Action: shoplift, steal

2. Crime: mugging
   Person: mugger
   Action: mug, steal

3. Crime: robbery, burglary
   Person: robber, burglar
   Action: steal (a thing),
   rob (a place, person)

4. Crime: car theft
   Person: car thief
   Action: steal

B Discuss these questions with a partner.

1. Have you ever been the victim of a crime? What happened?
2. Was the person who committed the crime found?

TEACHING TIP

This topic may be sensitive for students who have been victims of a crime. Invite volunteers to tell as much information as they want to share. Do not ask too many questions, as this may make students uncomfortable.

ACTIVE GRAMMAR Past Time Clauses

A Listen to Jonathan make a statement to a police officer about a robbery at his apartment. Write the things the thief stole. 65

1. table
2. TV
3. video game system
4. video games
5. leftover Chinese food

B Complete the sentences. Use verbs from the box. One of the verbs is negative. Some of the verbs can be used more than once.

be	find	go	leave	lock	open	realize	thank	try	walk

1. When Jonathan left his apartment, it was 8:30.
2. Jonathan locked his door when he left his apartment this morning.
3. Before Jonathan went to bed last night, he opened the windows.
4. Jonathan thinks that he locked the windows before he went to work.
5. Jonathan realized that something was wrong as soon as he tried to put his keys on the table.
6. When Jonathan walked into the living room, there was a big empty space where his TV used to be.
7. When Jonathan opened the refrigerator, he didn't find his leftover Chinese food.
8. Jonathan thanked the police officer before she left.

ACTIVE GRAMMAR: Past Time Clauses

A 65

- Ask students to look at the picture and describe what they see. Point out specific items, such as the broken mirror, the messy kitchen, and the papers scattered on the floor. Ask students to guess what items might have been stolen from Jonathan's apartment.
- Play the audio and have students write their answers.
- Review the answers with the class.

B

- Read the first example.
- Have students complete the exercise individually.
- Check the answers as a class.

MORE ACTION

Have students make questions about Jonathan's story. For example: *What did Jonathan do before he discovered the burglary? What did he do after the police left?*

C 66

- Review the information in the grammar box.
- Remind students that in Unit 12, they learned about time clauses and practiced pronouncing pauses. Now, students are going to practice pronouncing word stress with time clauses.
- Play the audio for the first item and then pause. Ask students to repeat the sentence.
- Point out that the bold words are the stressed words. They convey the important information in each sentence.
- Continue playing the audio and have students repeat each sentence.

D 67

- Read the questions and encourage students to predict the answers.
- Play the audio and review the answers as a class.

E

- Have students work in pairs to write their conversations. Encourage them to write about what happened before, during, and after the robbery.
- Have pairs act out their conversations for the class.

I locked my door **before** I went to work.	**Before** I went to work, I locked my door.
(main clause) (time clause)	(time clause) (main clause)

1. A past time clause explains when an action happened. It usually begins with a time word such as *when, before, after,* or *as soon as.* A time clause has a subject and a verb.
2. A time clause can come at the beginning or the end of a sentence. If the time clause is at the beginning of a sentence, use a comma (,) after the time clause.

C **Pronunciation: Word stress** Listen and repeat. Pay attention to the words in **bold**. 66

1. Before I **left** my **house**, I **locked** the **door**.
2. When we **went** on **vacation**, we **stopped** the **mail**.
3. She **turned on** the **alarm** before she **left** her **apartment**.
4. They **closed** all the **windows** before they **left**.
5. I **called** the **police** as soon as I **saw** the **broken door**.
6. I **dialed 911** when I **heard** a **noise downstairs**.
7. After **someone robbed** their **house**, they **bought** a **dog**.

WORD PARTNERSHIPS	
break into	a house an apartment a car

D Listen and complete the conversation. 67

A: You don't look very happy. What's the matter?

B: When I was at work, someone broke into my house.

A: Really? How did they get in?

B: I forgot to lock the windows before I went to work.

A: Oh. What did they take?

B: They took my computer, the TV, and my camera.

A: Did you call the police?

B: I called the police as soon as I walked in the door.

E **LET'S TALK.** With a partner, write a conversation about a robbery. Then, act out your conversation.

MORE ACTION

Have students practice making a 911 call about a robbery. Students can use different scenarios such as catching a robber in their house / apartment, coming home to find that their house / apartment has been robbed, or witnessing a robbery occur. Have students role-play their 911 call for the class.

F Combine the sentences. Yesterday, John and Sue visited their friends. They did not know that a thief was watching their car.

1. John and Sue found a parking space. They parked their car. (when)
   When John and Sue found a parking space, they parked their car.
2. They locked their car. They walked away. (before)
   They locked their car before they walked away.
3. The thief looked around carefully. The couple left. (after)
   The thief looked around carefully after the couple left.
4. He didn't see anyone. He walked to the car. (when)
   When he didn't see anyone, he walked to the car.
5. He touched the car. A large dog jumped up and began to bark. (as soon as)
   As soon as he touched the car, a large dog jumped up and began to bark.
6. The thief ran away. He saw the dog. (when)
   The thief ran away when he saw the dog.

G **LET'S TALK.** Choose eight of the phrases. Tell a partner about events in your life. Use *before*, *after*, or *when*.

> After I saved enough money, I bought a house.

> Before I got my driver's license, I went to a driving school.

became a citizen	found a job	got my driver's license
bought a house	found an apartment	got robbed
came to this country	got a visa	graduated from college
enrolled in English classes	got divorced	graduated from high school
fell in love	got married	had a baby

F

- Have students describe what is happening in each picture.
- Then, have students work individually to combine the sentences using the words in parentheses. For some items, more than one answer is possible.
- Ask volunteers to read their answers aloud to the class.

G

- Review the list of phrases and explain any new vocabulary.
- Give examples from your own life, such as after you graduated from college or when you became a teacher.
- Have students work in pairs to tell each other about their lives.
- Then, have students write sentences using the phrases in their notebooks.
- Have several students read a sentence about their partner for the class.

MORE ACTION

Make a list of important events in your life and write them on the board in random order (for example, graduating from college, getting married, becoming a teacher, and so on). Then, tell students a story about yourself using these events and ask them to put the events in the correct order in their notebooks. Afterwards, ask them to retell your story to a partner using the phrases from Exercise G and sentences with *before*, *after*, and *when*.

ACTIVE GRAMMAR:
Past Continuous

A

- Review the information in the grammar charts. Explain that the past continuous is often used with time words when telling a story. For example, *I was working when...*
- Write three or four different times (noon, 4:00, and so on) on the board and ask students to tell you what they were doing at each of those times yesterday, using the past continuous.
- Have students complete Exercise A individually.
- Then, ask volunteers to read their answers aloud.

B

- Ask three students to model the first question.
- Have groups complete the exercise and then report their findings to the class. You can also quiz students by asking them what specific group members did at a certain time.

ACTIVE GRAMMAR Past Continuous

I	**was**	sleep**ing**.
He		
She		
It		work**ing.**

You	**were**	work**ing**.
We		
They		

The past continuous describes an action that was in progress at a specific time in the past.

A Complete the sentences. Use the past continuous form of the verbs. What was happening at 4:00 yesterday afternoon?

1. Yesterday at 4:00 p.m., I (drive) was driving home from work.
2. I (listen) **was listening** to the radio.
3. My wife (shop) **was shopping** at the supermarket.
4. My children (study) **were studying** at the library.
5. You (sleep) **were sleeping**.
6. My neighbors (watch) **were watching** TV.
7. Three police officers (investigate) **were investigating** a bank robbery.
8. A thief (climb) **was climbing** through my window!

B **LET'S TALK.** In groups of three, ask and answer the questions about your activities last weekend. Take notes. **Answers will vary.**

	Student 1	Student 2
Where were you on Friday night?		
What were you doing?		
Where were you on Saturday morning?		
What were you doing?		
Where were you on Saturday afternoon?		
What were you doing?		
Where were you on Saturday evening?		
What were you doing?		
Where were you on Sunday afternoon?		
What were you doing?		

MORE ACTION

Ask students to work in pairs. Have each student write down three or four different times of the day. Then, their partner has to guess what they were doing at each of those times yesterday.

ACTIVE GRAMMAR Past Continuous with *While*

While I **was driving** to school, I **was listening** to the radio.	Use *while* with the past continuous to show that two actions were happening at the same time.
I **was listening** to the radio **while** I **was driving** to school.	
While the professor **was talking**, the students **were taking** notes.	
The students **were taking** notes **while** the professor **was talking**.	

A Complete the sentences. Use your own ideas. **Answers will vary.**

1. While I was walking to school today, I was talking on my cellphone.
2. While the teacher was returning the tests, the students ________.
3. While the class was listening to the teacher, I ________.
4. The boss ________ while the employees ________.
5. While I was taking the bus to school, I ________.
6. While Mr. Green was vacuuming the living room, Mrs. Green ________.
7. I ________ while I was studying.
8. My friend ________ while I was watching TV.

B With a partner, take turns making sentences with *while* and the past continuous. **Answers may vary.**

1. I / cook dinner — I / listen to some music
While I was cooking dinner, I was listening to some music. / I was cooking dinner while I was listening to some music.
2. neighbors / have a party — I / try to sleep
While the neighbors were having a party, I was trying to sleep. / The neighbors were having a party while I was trying to sleep.
3. He / watch TV — he / cook dinner
While he was watching TV, he was cooking dinner. / He was watching TV while he was cooking dinner.
4. She / walk in the park — she / talk to her friend
While she was walking in the park, she was talking to her friend. / She was walking in the park while she was talking to her friend.
5. I / do my homework — the baby / cry
While I was doing my homework, the baby was crying. / I was doing my homework while the baby was crying.
6. He / talk on his phone — he / drive
While he was talking on his phone, he was driving. / He was talking on his phone while he was driving.
7. you / watch TV — I / take a nap
While you were watching TV, I was taking a nap. / You were watching TV while I was taking a nap.
8. I / cook dinner — my daughter / set the table
While I was cooking dinner, my daughter was setting the table. / I was cooking dinner while my daughter was setting the table.
9. You / work — I / apply for a job
While you were working, I was applying for a job. / You were working while I was applying for a job.
10. I / enter the building — many students / leave
While I was entering the building, many students were leaving. / I was entering the building while many students were leaving.

While I was cooking dinner, I was listening to music.

TEACHING TIP

Point out the difference between *while* and *when* to students. Explain that *while* is used to describe two activities that were going on at the same time. For example, *Spike robbed the store while Tina waited in the car outside. When* is used to describe an activity that interrupts another activity. For example, *I was walking to the bus station when I saw a robbery.*

ACTIVE GRAMMAR: Past Continuous with *While*

A

- Review the formation of the past continuous and the meaning of *while*. Ask questions about the sentences in the grammar chart: *When did these events happen?* (in the past) *Which event happened first?* (They were happening at the same time.)
- Ask what differences students notice between the first, second, and third sentences, and the fourth, seventh, and eighth sentences. (reversed order of clauses and no comma)
- Have students complete Exercise A individually.
- Invite volunteers to read their answers aloud or write them on the board. Ask students to correct any mistakes.
- After reviewing the sentences as a class, ask students to rewrite sentences 4, 7, and 8 so that the *while* clause comes first.

B

- Encourage students to vary the order of the clauses in their sentences.
- Ask volunteers to read some of their sentences aloud to the class.

ACTIVE GRAMMAR: The Past Continuous and the Simple Past

A

- Review the sentences in the grammar box. Ask: *When did these events happen?* (in the past) *Which event started first?* (sleeping and shopping)
- Ask: *Which verb form follows* while *in these sentences?* (past continuous) *Which verb form follows* when? (simple past)
- Have students complete Exercise A individually.
- Check the answers as a class.

B

- Ask students to describe what is going on in each photo.
- Have students complete the exercise on their own.
- Then, ask students to exchange notebooks with a partner and check each other's work.

ACTIVE GRAMMAR The Past Continuous and the Simple Past

The past continuous can describe an action that was interrupted. One action was going on when another action happened.

While I **was sleeping**, I **heard** someone in my living room.

I **was shopping** in the mall when a thief **stole** my car.

A Complete the sentences. Use the verbs in parentheses.

1. I (watch) __was watching__ TV when a man (look) __looked__ in my window.
2. We (sit) __were sitting__ in class when the fire alarm (ring) __rang__.
3. A shoplifter (steal) __was stealing__ a tablet when the security guard (see) __saw__ her.
4. While the security guard (take) __was taking__ a break, two men (rob) __robbed__ the jewelry store.
5. Someone (steal) __stole__ my car while I (work) __was working__.
6. While I (drive) __was driving__ to work, I (see) __saw__ an accident.

B In your notebook, write two sentences about each photo. Use *when* or *while*.

While I was on vacation, someone broke into my apartment.

I was on vacation when someone broke into my apartment.

1.

I was on vacation.
Someone broke into my apartment.

2.

Natalie was walking to work.
A man stole her purse.

3.

Thieves were taking the TV.
Tyler called the police.

4.

The driver was speeding.
A police officer pulled him over.

MORE ACTION

Ask students to take turns pantomiming situations in which an action is interrupted by an event. Call on another student to make up a sentence about the situation using the past continuous. For example, one student could pantomime sleeping and then suddenly waking up and putting a telephone to her ear. The other student would say: *You were sleeping when the telephone rang*, or *While you were sleeping, the telephone rang*.

C ACADEMIC Read the timeline of the bank robbery. Then, complete the sentences.

2:55	Several customers were in the bank.
2:58	The security guard went on break.
3:00	A robber entered the building. He told everyone to lie down.
3:01	A teller pressed the alarm.
3:02	The robber took $10,000.
3:03	The robber ran out the door. He jumped in his car and drove away.
3:05	The police arrived at the bank. They questioned everyone.

1. Marco was using the ATM machine when *the robber entered the bank.*
2. When the robber entered the bank, the security guard *was taking a break.*
3. As soon as the robber entered the bank, *he told everyone to lie down.*
4. A teller pressed the alarm when *she saw the robber.*
5. Before the robber left the bank, *he took $ 10,000.*
6. The robber ran out before *the police arrived.*
7. While the police were rushing to the bank, *the robber jumped in his car.*
8. After the police arrived at the bank, *they questioned everyone.*

Crime **199**

C

- Encourage students to ask and answer questions about the picture. Have them identify the people in the bank (customers, teller, loan officer, security guard, robber).
- Explain the meaning of any new words and write them on the board.
- Have students read the timeline and answer questions about what each person was doing when the robbery happened. *What was Marco doing?* (He was withdrawing money from an ATM.) *What were Jenny, Soo, and Sofie doing?* (They were standing in line.) *What was Hassan doing?* (He was signing some papers.) *What was Olga doing?* (She was helping a customer.)
- Continue with similar questions about the timeline. *What happened when the robber entered the bank?* (He told everyone to lie down.) *What did the teller do when she saw the robber?* (She pressed the alarm.) *What did the police do when they arrived at the bank?* (They questioned everyone.)

ACADEMIC

As students work on the exercise on this page, emphasize that understanding a sequence of events plays a crucial role in reading comprehension and the writing process. This skill can be applied across content areas. Encourage students to discuss what tools can be used to sequence events. Outlines can be used to organize ideas for a piece of writing or to understand the structure of a text; timelines can be used to organize events (personal, historic, or from narrative texts); lists can be used to organize the steps of a process.

THE BIG PICTURE:
A Burglary at the Jewelry Store

A 68

- Ask students to make predictions about the story based on the pictures. For example, *Is the robbery successful?* (no)
- Play the audio all the way through and encourage students to take notes as they listen.
- Have students ask questions about the story.

B

- Read the words in the word box. Ask volunteers to define each word or phrase.
- Ask students to match each vocabulary item with the proper picture in Exercise B and use the vocabulary word in a sentence. For example:
  S: Chase *matches picture 12.*
  T: *What's happening in picture 12?*
  S: *The police are chasing a man.*

C

Have students work with a partner to retell the story without their notes. After they have said as much as they can remember, have students use their notes for additional details.

ACADEMIC

In Exercise C, students are asked to retell information from Exercise A. Looking at the illustrations can help students recall some details, but taking notes while listening may help students better remember and retell the story to their partners.

While students take notes, remind them to focus on key information, and write short phrases instead of full sentences. Reinforce that good note-taking skills are key for test preparation and can be applied to any content area.

THE BIG PICTURE A Burglary at the Jewelry Store

A Last night, Spike and Tina tried to rob a jewelry store. Look at the pictures and listen to the story. 68

B Match each word with the correct picture from the story. Write the number of the picture. Some words match more than one picture. Answers may vary.

1,15,16 arrest	13 block	4 fist	14 take off
2, 14 mask	4 break into	3,10, 12 get out of	5 climb into
2 put on	11,12 chase	15, 16 handcuff	8 pick up

C ACADEMIC Look at the pictures. Tell a partner what you remember about each picture.

200 Unit 13

MORE ACTION

Another way to approach Exercise A is to assign one picture to each pair of students and have them write a sentence about it on a scrap of paper. Then, collect the scraps of paper and shuffle them. Have pairs work together to put the sentences in the correct order.

D Complete the sentences. Use *before, after, when, while,* or *as soon as*.

1. Spike put on gloves ___before___ he went into the store.
2. Spike looked around ___before___ he entered the store.
3. Spike took some jewelry ___after / as soon as / when___ he got into the store.
4. ___While___ Spike was robbing the store, Tina was sitting in the car.
5. The alarm rang ___as soon as___ Spike dropped his bag.
6. Tina started the car ___when / as soon as___ she heard the alarm.
7. The police officers handcuffed Spike and Tina ___before___ they put them into the police car.

E Circle *True* or *False*.

1.	Spike put on gloves after he broke the window.	True	**(False)**
2.	Spike climbed into the store after he broke the window.	**(True)**	False
3.	While Spike was looking around the store, the police arrived.	True	**(False)**
4.	When Spike saw the pizza, the alarm rang.	True	**(False)**
5.	Before Spike left the store, he took some jewelry.	**(True)**	False
6.	As soon as Spike saw the police car, he tried to run away.	**(True)**	False
7.	Spike took off his mask and hat while he was running away.	**(True)**	False

F Answer the questions. Answers may vary.

1. What did Spike put on while he was going to the store? He put on a hat, gloves, and a mask.
2. How did Spike break the window? He broke the window with his fist and a towel.
3. What was Tina doing while Spike was in the store? She was waiting in the car and watching for the police.
4. What did Spike do as soon as he got into the store? He looked around at the jewelry.
5. What did Spike steal? He stole some watches, necklaces, and rings.
6. When did Spike see the pizza? He saw the pizza when he was ready to leave.
7. What happened when he picked up a slice of pizza? He dropped the bag of jewelry.
8. When did the alarm ring? As soon as the bag fell on the floor, the alarm rang.
9. When did the police officer get out of the car? He got out of the car as soon as he saw Spike.
10. What did the police officers do after they arrested Spike and Tina? They handcuffed them and put them in the police car.

D

- Have students complete the exercise individually.
- Call on volunteers to read their answers aloud.
- Discuss any alternative answers. Write all the answers on the board.

E

- One way to conduct this exercise is as a class poll. Have students raise their hands to say if the sentence is true or false.
- Write the class results for each sentence on the board without saying the correct answer.
- Then, play the audio from Exercise A again to verify the correct answers.

F

- Have students work in pairs to ask and answer the questions.
- Review the answers as a class.

MORE ACTION

Have students work in groups of three to role-play a police officer interviewing Spike and Tina about the robbery. Make sure students use *before, after, when, while,* and *as soon as*.

READING: Article about Civic Duty

A 🎧69 (facing page)

- Discuss the topic of a jury with the class. Ask: *What is a jury?* (a group of people selected to give a verdict in court)
- Have students go over the discussion questions. Encourage students to exchange experiences of being called for jury duty or having been part of a jury. What was the process like? How did they feel? What were they asked to do? Were there rules they had to follow? How long did they have to serve for?
- Allow time for students to read the article about serving on a jury.
- Discuss any new concepts or vocabulary that students may not be familiar with.

CIVICS

The use of a jury has been part of the American judicial system since colonial times, back in the 17th century. Failure to serve as a juror when asked to do so was punished under Colonial law as early as 1647. The right to a trial by jury has been recorded in the United States Constitution since the early 1870s.

Some students may come from countries where citizen participation in the judicial system is not customary. These students may need some background information. Before students read the article on this page, be sure to provide some context as you go over the discussion questions in Exercise A. You may want to share information about:

- jury service as a civic responsibility
- how a person is summoned for jury duty (by written communication via snail mail—never by email or phone)
- possible reasons why someone may not be able or required to serve: being 70 years old or older; having a disqualifying mental or physical condition; citing service as a cause of hardship; having reported for jury duty in the previous 2 years

Once students are familiar with the concept of a jury and a citizen's responsibilities regarding jury duty, you may want to take the conversation further by asking, *What may be some advantages and disadvantages of using a jury?*

READING Article about Civic Duty

Serving on a Jury

One of the responsibilities of a US citizen is to serve on a jury. A jury is a group of ten to twelve citizens who decide if an **accused** criminal is **guilty** or not guilty of a crime. The jury members listen to **evidence** and make a decision. Someone accused of a crime has the right to a jury **trial**. This right is written in the United States Constitution, a document of the laws and government of the United States of America.

How does a district select people for jury duty? First, the district sends a **summons**, or written letter to a citizen in the mail. The district court makes a random selection of registered voters, licensed drivers, and tax payers. The citizen must reply to the summons. If the citizen doesn't reply, that person will have to pay a fine.

What are the requirements to serve on a jury? First, the person must be a US citizen and a resident of the district. The person must be at least 18 years old and be physically and mentally able to serve on the jury. The person must not have any criminal **convictions**, but can still serve if they have traffic violations.

Some people do not want to serve on a jury, but the court will only excuse people for certain reasons, such as if the person is a high school student, the person has to take care of someone who cannot take care of him/herself, or if the person does not understand enough English to follow the trial.

If the court selects you for a jury, there are rules that you must follow:

- Do not discuss the case until you hear all of the evidence.
- Do not investigate the case yourself.
- Do not discuss the case with family members or anyone else.
- Listen to the judge's instructions.

If you are selected to sit on a jury, the average trial is one to three days, but trials may be longer. Also, it is possible that you will report for jury duty, but you will not be part of the jury. The district court calls many people, and only a small number can serve on a jury. If, after one or two days, the court does not call you to trial, your service is complete for at least one year. 🎧69

Members of the jury have to take an oath before serving. They have to swear that they will be fair and that they will give a true verdict.

202 Unit 13

A CIVICS After reading, discuss these questions.

1. Do you know anyone who has served on a jury?
2. Have you ever received a jury summons? Did you serve?

B Read and circle the correct answer.

1. A person who is accused of a crime has a right to…
   - a. receive a summons.
   - (c.) have a jury trial.
   - b. serve on a jury.
   - d. decide if a person is guilty or not guilty.
2. The United States Constitution is a…
   - a. building in Washington, D.C.
   - c. type of trial jury.
   - (b.) document of the laws and government of the US.
   - d. list of jury responsibilities.
3. What is the first step in selecting a jury?
   - a. Decide if the accused is guilty or not guilty.
   - c. Listen to the evidence in court.
   - (b.) Send summonses to citizens of the district.
   - d. Pay the fine for jury duty.
4. Which of the following is **not** a requirement for jury service?
   - a. You must be at least 18 years old.
   - (c.) You must have a driver's license.
   - b. You must be a US citizen.
   - d. You must understand English well.
5. Which *two* of the following statements are **false**?
   - (a.) You can talk to your friends about the trial.
   - (c.) Everyone with a summons serves on a jury.
   - b. You must reply to the jury summons.
   - d. People can be excused from jury duty.

C Complete the sentences with the words from the box.

accused	convictions	evidence	guilty	~~summons~~	trial

1. Last summer, I received a jury ___summons___ in the mail.
2. A juror only has to serve on one ___trial___ a year.
3. There was no strong ___evidence___, so the jury said, "Not guilty."
4. The ___accused___ person had a history of past crimes.
5. A jury decides if a person is ___guilty___ or not guilty.
6. I am able to serve on a jury because I have no ___convictions___ for any crimes.

B

- After students read the article, allow them time to choose their answers.
- Ask volunteers to read their answers aloud.
- Discuss any items that students might have answered incorrectly, by reviewing the article.

C

- Ask students to find the words from the box in the reading and see if they can figure out each word's meaning from the context.
- Ask students to paraphrase the meaning of the words in the box in their own words.
- Then, have students complete the exercise individually.
- Review the answers as a class.

TEACHING TIP

Encourage students to add new vocabulary from this unit to their notebooks. Or, you can create a quiz exercise using vocabulary cards.

WRITING OUR STORIES: A Moving Van

A

Discuss the answers to the questions. Encourage students to ask questions of other students who share their experiences.

B

- Ask students to read the story on their own.
- Check comprehension by asking questions such as: *Who did Martin's grandfather see?* (He saw two men putting Maria and Pablo's belongings into a truck.) *What did the robbers take?* (They took a sofa, two armchairs, a coffee table, two TVs, a bed, and a dresser.) *What did Martin's grandfather do?* (He chased the thieves in his car.) *Did Maria and Pablo thank Martin's grandfather?* (No—they said they were glad he didn't catch the thieves because their insurance would pay for the stolen items.)
- Discuss the organization of ideas in the story (the first paragraph sets the scene, the events are presented in chronological order, and the last sentence conveys a concluding message to the story).
- Read the Writing Note on the facing page aloud. Point out that using quotes from people is a way of giving a story more detail and making it more interesting.

WRITING OUR STORIES A Moving Van

A Discuss these questions.

1. Have you or anyone you know ever been robbed?
2. Where did the robbery happen? What did the thief take? Was anyone hurt?

B Read Martin's story about a robbery in his neighborhood.

In July 2017, my grandparents and a neighbor were talking in the living room. It was a Saturday night at about 9:00. My grandfather was looking out the window when he saw a large green truck on the street. Ten minutes later, he saw two men. They were wearing brown uniforms. The men were putting a sofa, two armchairs, and a coffee table in the truck. Then, he saw them putting two TVs, a bed, and a dresser into the truck. He asked my grandmother and the neighbor, "Are Maria and Pablo moving?"

As soon as the neighbor saw the men, he said, "They're thieves!" My grandmother called 911. My grandfather ran out of the house and got into his car with the neighbor. My grandfather and the neighbor drove after the thieves, but the thieves' truck was faster than my grandfather's car, so they couldn't catch them. The police were no help because they arrived ten minutes later.

When the owners of the house, Maria and Pablo, came back from the beach, my grandfather said, "I'm sorry. I saw what happened, but I couldn't stop them. My car is too slow."

Maria and Pablo said, "I'm glad you didn't catch the thieves. Don't worry. Our furniture was very old. The insurance will pay for new furniture."

My grandfather was surprised. He said, "I will never risk my life again for problems that aren't mine."

204 Unit 13

MORE ACTION

Discuss what Martin's grandfather did. Was it a good idea or a bad idea? Ask students what they would do in such a situation. As a class, write an alternative ending to the story where Martin's grandfather calls 911.

WRITING NOTE

Using Quotes

To show the exact words of a speaker, use quotation marks ("). Start the quote with a capital letter. Put quotation marks at the beginning and end of the quote.

The neighbor said, **"**They're thieves!**"**

My grandfather said, **"**I'm sorry. I saw what happened, but I couldn't stop them.**"**

C Rewrite each sentence with the proper punctuation and capitalization. Answers may vary.

1. The robber said give me your wallet
   The robber said, "Give me your wallet."
2. The police officer asked did you lock your door this morning
   The police officer asked, "Did you lock your door this morning?"
3. I answered yes. I always lock the door in the morning
   I answered, "Yes, I always lock the door in the morning."
4. A woman on the street shouted help
   A woman on the street shouted, "Help!"
5. The store owner said I'm going to call the police
   The store owner said, "I'm going to call the police."

D ACADEMIC You are going to write about a crime that happened to you or that you heard or read about. Plan your writing so that it includes these important facts: Answers will vary.

1. Who did the crime happen to? ______
2. Who committed the crime? ______
3. What was the crime? ______
4. When did the crime happen? ______
5. Where did it happen? ______

E In your notebook, write about the crime. Use the information in Exercise D. Include one or two quotations in your story.

F Read your story to a partner. Your partner will ask you more questions about the crime.

G AT WORK Discuss these questions with your partner.

1. Did any authorities investigate the crime you wrote about?
2. What did the officer(s) do during the investigation?
3. Did the authorities solve the case? How?

MORE ACTION

For additional practice with punctuation, dictate some sentences for which students will have to fill in quotation marks. For example:

The teacher said, "Bring your stories to class tomorrow."

Mary called out, "Dial 911!"

You could also write these sentences on strips of paper for students to dictate to each other.

AT WORK

As students answer the questions in Exercise G, encourage them to also discuss the roles, responsibilities, and tasks of the different people involved in a criminal investigation. For example, law enforcement agencies (investigate the crime, make arrests, issue citations, gather physical evidence, interrogate witnesses); fire investigators (determine the cause of a fire and if any human was involved, carry out inspections, gather physical evidence from the scene of a fire); or first responders or medical personnel (examine or attend to a victim) may be asked to testify in a trial.

C

- Ask students to complete this exercise individually. Remind them that they will need to use proper capitalization and punctuation.
- Write the sentences from the book on the board and invite volunteers to come up and edit the sentences.
- Ask other students to fix any details that were missed or marked incorrectly.

D

- Read the instructions. Bring in newspaper clippings about different crimes for students who don't have anything to write about.
- Remind students that they are only taking notes. They will use these notes to write a story about the crime in Exercise E.

E

Have students write a short story about the crime using their notes. Remind them to include details to make their story interesting.

F

- Have students read each other's essays and give feedback. Ask partners to edit sentences for proper punctuation and capitalization.
- Have students rewrite their essays using their partner's suggestions.

G

- Ask students to work in pairs and discuss the questions.
- Circulate the classroom and provide corrective feedback as needed.

ENGLISH IN ACTION: Looking at a Jury Trial

A

- Ask students to look at the picture and explain what each person in the courtroom does. This is a good opportunity for students to add vocabulary to their notebooks.
- Have students complete the exercise individually and then check their answers with a partner.
- Check the answers as a class.

CULTURE NOTE

- Read the Culture Note aloud and make sure that students understand their rights. Explain to students that they have these rights whether they are US citizens or not.
- Have students get into groups and research the statements presented in the Culture Note. For example, *You have the right to remain silent* means that individuals who are arrested do not have to answer any questions that police officers ask them.
- Have groups present their findings to the class.

ENGLISH IN ACTION Looking at a Jury Trial

A CIVICS Complete each definition with a word or phrase from the photo.

1. The ___judge___ is the person in charge of the court.
2. The ___defendant___ is the person charged with a crime.
3. The ___defense lawyer___ is the lawyer for the defendant. He / She tries to show that the defendant is innocent—that is, not guilty.
4. The ___plaintiff___ is the person who files a legal complaint against another person.
5. The ___prosecutor___ is the lawyer for the plaintiff. He / She tries to prove that the defendant is guilty.
6. A ___witness___ is a person who brings information to the court about a crime.
7. The ___jury___ is the group of people who sits in court and decides if a person is guilty.

CULTURE NOTE

When the police arrest a person, they must read the person his or her rights: "You have the right to remain silent. Anything you say can and will be used against you in a court of law. You have the right to speak to an attorney and have an attorney present during any questioning. If you cannot afford a lawyer, one will be provided for you at government expense."

206 Unit 13

MORE ACTION

There are many websites about crime prevention. Suggest that students research the following topics: *home safety, home security, crime prevention*, or *preventing burglary*. Ask students to report to the class one idea about how to stop crime.

UNIT 14 CAREERS

An engineer stands at the top of a wind turbine. His "office" sits at 220 feet in the air.

CCRS Level A: R 5, 7; W 2, 5, 6, 7, 8; L 1, 5; Level B: R 5, 6, 7; W 2, 4, 5, 6, 7, 8; L 1, 3, 5; Level C: R 7; W 2, 4, 5, 6, 7, 8; L 1, 3, 6; Level D: R 7; W 2, 4, 5, 6, 7, 8; L 1, 3; Level E: R 7; W 2, 4, 5, 6, 7, 8; L 1

ELPS Level 1 Standards 2, 5, 9, 10; Level 2 Standards 2, 3, 5, 7, 9, 10; Level 3 Standards 2, 3, 5, 7, 9, 10; Level 4 Standards 2, 3, 5, 7, 9, 10; Level 5 Standards 2, 3, 5, 7, 9, 10

CIVICS 14-3; 33-7; 33-10; 33-16; 49-3; 52-8

CASAS 0.1.2; 0.1.5; 0.2.1; 4.1.3; 4.1.8; 4.1.9; 4.4.5; 7.1.1; 7.1.2; 7.7.1; 7.7.2; 7.7.3; 7.7.5; 7.7.6

IN THIS UNIT

In Unit 14, students will:

- Scan a text for information
- Write a resume
- Describe educational and skill requirements for various career profiles

ABOUT THE PHOTO

In this photo, an engineer works on one of the wind turbines at the Nine Canyon Wind Project in Richland, Washington. The US Department of Energy recently found that 6.4 million Americans work in the energy industry. Three hundred thousand jobs were added in 2017, many of them in renewable energy. The wind industry in America employs over 102,000 workers. Wind turbine technician is the fastest growing occupation in America. The Bureau of Labor Statistics predicts that employment in the wind energy sector will grow by 108% by 2024. Other renewable energy positions include solar panel installer, clean car engineer, and sustainable builder.

Ask students if they know anyone who has a job like the one in the photo. To preview helpful job-related vocabulary, ask: *What skills do you think this person must have to do this job? Do you think this person needs specialized training? What are some challenges this person may face to do his job?* Preview the target grammar by asking students to think about tasks associated with this job. For example, put on safety gear, climb a ladder, look for the problems with the turbines, fix the problems. On the board, write a statement about two consecutive actions using future time clauses: *Before he climbs the stairs, he will put on his safety gear. He will find out what the problem is after he climbs the stairs.*

A

- Ask volunteers to identify each job in the photos.
- Encourage them to add as much detail as they can about each job. For example, for the photo of the nurse:
  T: *What can you tell the class about nurses?*
  S: *Nurses usually work in hospitals. They wear uniforms.*
  T: *That's right. What else?*
  S: *They often work very long hours, sometimes at night.*

B

- Ask students to work in pairs to discuss the questions.
- Then, call on different students to answer each question.
- Invite volunteers to ask additional questions about jobs students would like to have.

AT WORK

Ask students to describe their own jobs. For example, do they work inside or outside? What are the hours? Did they need any special training or education? Do they supervise anyone?

A Write the name of the job under each picture.

1. teacher

2. hairstylist

3. nurse

4. police officer

5. Answers will vary.

6. scientist; lab worker

B **AT WORK** Discuss these questions.

1. Would you like to have one of the jobs in the photos? If so, which one?
2. Where would you like to work—in an office or outside?
3. Would you like to supervise other people?
4. What kind of job did you have before coming to this country?
5. What job would you like to have in the future?
6. What kind of education do you need?

208 Unit 14

C **AT WORK** Write each occupation under the education it requires. Some occupations fit in more than one category. Answers will vary.

Occupations	Education Required
carpenter	**Professional Degree**
chef	1. ______
computer engineer	2. ______
dental hygienist	3. ______
dentist	**Bachelor's Degree (Four-year college)**
electrician	1. ______
emergency medical technician (EMT)	2. ______
hairstylist	3. ______
home health aide	4. ______
lawyer	**Associate's Degree (Two-year college)**
licensed practical nurse (LPN)	1. ______
machine operator	2. ______
manicurist	3. ______
physical therapist	**Vocational Training**
physician	1. ______
plumber	2. ______
registered nurse (RN)	3. ______
respiratory therapist	4. ______
secondary school teacher	**Learn on the job / Short-term training**
social worker	1. ______
	2. ______
	3. ______
	4. ______
	5. ______
	6. ______

WORD PARTNERSHIPS

college associate's bachelor's master's professional	degree

C

- Discuss the words in the Word Partnerships box. Ask how many years each degree usually takes. (Associate's degree—2 years; Bachelor's degree—4 years; Master's degree—2–3 years; Professional degree—3 or more years) Explain that people usually need to have a bachelor's degree before they are able to pursue a professional degree.
- Go through the list of occupations in Exercise C and make sure students understand each one. Ask if any students have the jobs listed.
- Have students complete the exercise in small groups.
- Write the degree categories on the board and ask volunteers from each group to list the jobs under each category.
- Discuss any different answers that students provide. Ask students which jobs and degrees they are interested in learning more about.
- Ask students to give a list of jobs other than those listed in Exercise C and guess what kinds of degrees or training those jobs require.

MORE ACTION

For homework, ask students to choose one job that they are interested in and research what kind of training and qualifications are needed for it. They can share the information with the class in the next lesson.

ACTIVE GRAMMAR: Future Time Clauses: Statements

A

- Review the information in the grammar chart.
- Ask students to explain which part of each sentence happens first and which happens second. For example, in the first sentence, *She graduates from high school* happens first. *She will go to college* happens second. Which word shows that this event happens second? (*after*)
- Ask students to identify the verb forms in each example sentence in the grammar chart (future with *will* and present) and the meaning of each form (both refer to the future).
- Read the items in Exercise A and clarify any new vocabulary.
- Allow time for students to match the items on their own.
- Ask volunteers to read their sentences aloud.
- Review the answers as a class.

B

- Ask students to read the sentences and predict the verb form that should be used in the blanks.
- Read the sentences in Appendix D and have students fill in their answers.
- Ask volunteers to read the sentences aloud.

ACTIVE GRAMMAR Future Time Clauses: Statements

She **will go** to college after she **graduates** from high school.
(main clause) (time clause)

After she **graduates** from high school, she **will go** to college.
(time clause) (main clause)

Notes:

1. A time clause begins with words such as *if, before, after, as soon as,* and *when*. A time clause has a subject and a verb.
2. The verb in the main clause is in the future (with *will* or *be going to*). The verb in the time clause is in the present.
3. A time clause can be at the beginning or at the end of a sentence.

A Match.

b 1. If I do well in my English course,
e 2. After Julia completes her engineering degree,
g 3. When Frank becomes a nurse,
a 4. Before Rick applies to the police department,
f 5. If I receive a good evaluation,
c 6. After Laura finishes high school,
d 7. Before I go to the job interview,

a. he will need to take a physical exam.
b. I will become an interpreter.
c. she'll enter a community college.
d. I will research the company.
e. she'll design cars.
f. I will get a promotion.
g. he will have to give medication.

B Listen to your teacher and complete the sentences. Your teacher will refer to Appendix D in the back of the book.

1. Maria ___is going to look___ for a job before she ___graduates___.
2. Before she ___looks___ for a job, she ___will write___ her resume.
3. She ___will send___ out her resume when she ___sees___ a good job posting.
4. If she ___hears___ of a job opening, she ___will call___ the company.
5. When she ___goes___ on an interview, she ___is going to wear___ a suit.
6. If she ___makes___ a good impression, the company ___will hire___ her.

C Complete the sentences about Bernato. He would like to open his own restaurant someday.
Answers will vary, but should include the forms will and be going to.

1. After Bernato (graduate) __graduates__ from high school, he (go) __will go__ to culinary school.
2. When he (go) __goes__ to culinary school, he (work) __will work__ in a restaurant part time.
3. Bernato (take) __is going to take__ a few business classes after he (graduate) __graduates__ from culinary school.
4. Bernato (work) __will work__ in a restaurant for several years after he (finish) __finishes__ his education.
5. When he (decide) __decides__ to open a restaurant, he (discuss) __is going to discuss__ his plans with his family.
6. If he (have – negative) __doesn't have__ enough money, he (apply) __will apply__ for a bank loan.
7. He (look) __will look__ for a good location when he (be) __is__ ready to open a restaurant.

D **AT WORK** Use the words below to write sentences about Miguel.
Answers will vary, but should include the forms will and be going to.

1. When / Miguel's company / close he / apply for / unemployment benefits
   When Miguel's company closes, he will apply for unemployment benefits.
2. After / he / get laid off he / register for night classes
   After he gets laid off, he is going to register for night classes.
3. When / his friend / have / extra work Miguel / help him
   When his friend has extra work, Miguel will help him.
4. Miguel's wife / work / full time when / Miguel / get laid off
   Miguel's wife will work full time when Miguel gets laid off.
5. When / his wife / be / at work Miguel / take care of / the children
   When his wife is at work, Miguel is going to take care of the children.

C

- Read the instructions and discuss what kind of preparations Bernato might have to make to open his own restaurant one day.
- Read the first item. Explain that they'll need to use the future (with *will* or *be going to*) and the present to complete the remaining sentences.
- Set a time limit for students to complete the exercise.
- Review the answers by asking individual students to read their sentences aloud.

D

- Ask students to look at the pictures. Discuss what Miguel might do after his company closes. For example, he might apply for unemployment benefits, take some college classes, get a new job, or stay at home to spend more time with his family.
- Have students complete the exercise individually.
- Then, ask volunteers to read their sentences aloud.

AT WORK

Ask students to describe a resume—what it's used for, what information it contains, and so on. Then, have students research tips for writing a resume. Ask each student to bring in one or two tips and present them to the class. Remind students that colleges often have a career services office that will help students write and edit their resumes. Students will have the opportunity to write and edit their own resumes later in the unit.

MORE ACTION

Ask students to write five sentences about themselves using the verbs in Exercise C as a model. Have them pick a goal and then write their sentences based on what they are going to do in order to reach that goal.

E

- Discuss what kind of work a bookkeeper does and what qualifications and skills are needed for this job. (A bookkeeper keeps track of a business's financial records. They need to have math and accounting skills, and some jobs require an associate's degree.)
- Allow time for students to read the job profile and ask questions about vocabulary.
- Ask students their opinions about this job. Is it interesting or boring? Does it pay well or not? Is it hard work? Is it a job they want to learn more about?

F

- Have students complete the exercise individually. Point out that more than one verb form is correct for some of the answers.
- Call on individual students to read their sentences aloud.
- Review the answers as a class.

E Read about this career.

Bookkeeping, Accounting, and Auditing Clerks

What They Do

Bookkeeping, accounting, and auditing clerks are financial record keepers. They record financial transactions, update statements, and check financial records.

How to Become a Bookkeeping, Accounting, and Auditing Clerk

Most bookkeeping, accounting, and auditing clerks have some college education, especially courses in accounting. Experience with spreadsheets and bookkeeping software is required. Also, new clerks often receive on-the-job training from experienced employees.

Pay

In 2016 the median annual salary of bookkeeping, accounting, and auditing clerks was $38,390.

Job Outlook

There will be little change in the number of bookkeepers, accountants, and auditors needed by companies from 2016 to 2026.

F AT WORK Complete with the correct form of the verbs in parentheses.

Lian wants to be a bookkeeper. At this time, Lian (work) ___works___ (1) in the shipping department of a company. At night, she (study) ___studies___ (2) English. When she (complete) ___completes___ (3) her English classes, Lian (apply) ___will apply___ (4) to the community college near her home. She (take) ___is going to take___ (5) courses in accounting. She (continue) ___will continue___ (6) to work full time while she (study) ___studies___ (7) accounting. After she (take) ___takes___ (8) a few classes, she (look) ___will look___ (9) for an entry-level job in accounting. She (earn) ___will earn___ (10) her associate's degree in accounting in three years. After she (complete) ___completes___ (11) her degree, she (apply) ___will apply___ (12) for a promotion at work.

Accounting clerks need to be detailed oriented, very organized, and excellent problem solvers.

212 Unit 14

MORE ACTION

Have students interview a partner about their career plans. Then, have each student write a paragraph about their partner and read it to the class.

G Read about this career.

Physical Therapy Assistants

What They Do

Physical therapy assistants work under the supervision of physical therapists. They help people who are recovering from injuries and illnesses improve their movement. Most physical therapy assistants work in physical therapy offices or hospitals.

How to Become a Physical Therapy Assistant

Physical therapy assistants need an associate's degree from an accredited program. They must have a license or a certificate.

Pay

In 2016, the median annual salary for physical therapy assistants was $56,610.

Job Outlook

Experts think the employment for physical therapy assistants will grow by 30 percent from 2016 to 2026, much faster than many other occupations.

H AT WORK Listen to Jessica's career plans. Take notes. Then, answer the questions. 70

Answers may vary.

1. Where does Jessica live?
   At home.
2. What is she studying now?
   English, math, and biology.
3. What program is she going to begin when she completes these classes?
   Physical Therapy.
4. Is she going to work while she attends the program?
   No.
5. What is she going to do before she begins the program? She is going to apply for financial aid.
6. How many years is the program?
   Two years.
7. Who is going to help Jessica with expenses?
   Her parents.
8. What kind of experience is Jessica going to get before she graduates? She is going to work in a physical therapy practice two afternoons a week.
9. When will she apply for a job?
   Before she graduates.
10. How much money will she earn after she graduates?
    About $56,000 a year.

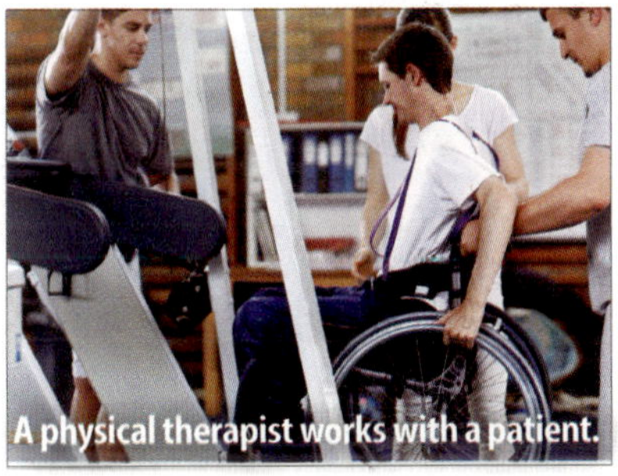

A physical therapist works with a patient.

G

- Discuss what kind of work a physical therapy assistant does, and what qualifications and skills are needed for this job. (A physical therapy assistant helps treat injured or disabled people. Most jobs require an associate's degree and sometimes a special license.)
- Allow time for students to read the job profile and ask questions about vocabulary.
- Ask students their opinions of this job. Ask: *Is it interesting or boring? Does it pay well? Is it hard work? Is it a job you want to learn more about?*

H 70

- Have students read the questions before playing the audio.
- Play the audio and have students take notes.
- Then, have students compare their notes with a partner. Have students complete the exercise independently.
- Ask students to make sentences about Jessica using time clauses.

AT WORK

Explain to students the difference between *a job* (an occupation) and *a career* (work a person dedicates to for a considerable amount of time).

Career planning is a very important step for a person's professional development. A career plan allows us to see what our long-term goals are, where we currently are in our career path, and what we need to do in order to reach our goals. A career plan can make the difference between professional satisfaction and an unfulfilling professional life.

ACTIVE GRAMMAR: Future Time Clauses: Questions

A 71

- Ask students to identify the main clauses and the time clauses in the grammar chart. Ask: *How can you identify a time clause?* (It is introduced by a word such as *when* or *after*.) *When do you need to use a comma?* (after a time clause if it comes first in the sentence)
- Ask students to identify the verb forms in each question in the grammar chart (future with *be going to* and the present) and the meaning of each form (both refer to the future).
- Play the audio and ask students to follow along in the book. Point out how the speaker's voice rises and falls in each sentence.
- Play the audio again, pausing after each sentence so students can repeat.
- Have students take turns reading the sentences to each other.
- Encourage them to correct each other's intonation patterns if necessary.

B

- Have students complete the exercise with a partner.
- Ask volunteers to read and answer the questions for the class.

ACTIVE GRAMMAR Future Time Clauses: Questions

What **are** you **going to do** after you **graduate**? Where **is** he **going to live** if his company **transfers** him? When he **starts** school, **is** he **going to work** full time?	In a question with a future time clause, use the future question form in the main clause.

A **Pronunciation: Question Intonation** Listen and repeat. 71

1. What are you going to do if you win the lottery?
2. What will you do after you finish this class?
3. If she gets a promotion, what is she going to buy?
4. When he finishes college, where will he work?

B Answer the questions. Answers may vary.

1. What are they going to do if they win the lottery?
   She is going to go on a vacation.
   He is going to buy a car.

2. What is she going to do if she gets laid off?
   She is going to register for college classes.

3. What are they going to do if it starts to rain?
   They are going to go inside.

4. What is he going to buy if he gets a promotion?
   He is going to buy a car.

C Ask and answer the questions with a partner. **Answers will vary.**

1. What are you going to do today when you finish this class?
2. What are you going to do if you go back to the country where you were born?
3. What career will you study when you finish your English classes?
4. When you finish your classes, where will you work?
5. What will you do when your friends come to visit?
6. What are you going to do if you win the lottery?

D Listen to the conversation. Then, practice it with a partner. 72

A: What are your plans for next year?
B: I'm going to finish my English classes.
A: What are you going to do when you finish your classes?
B: When I finish my English classes, I'm going to enter nursing school.
A: Where are you going to work after you graduate?
B: I'm going to work in the emergency room of a hospital.

E Write down your plans for the future. **Answers will vary.**

My Plans

F **LET'S TALK.** Tell a partner about your future plans. Then, write a conversation about your plans. Act out your conversation for the class.

C

- Have students ask the questions with a partner and report their partner's answers to the class.
- Encourage students to ask their partner additional questions about things they will do in the future.

D 72

- Play the audio, pausing after each sentence so students can repeat.
- Have students practice the conversation in pairs. Then, students can substitute their own information and make a new conversation to practice.

E

- Discuss the importance of setting goals. Give some examples of goals, such as getting a college degree or getting in shape.
- Have students write down their plans.
- Ask volunteers to share some of their plans with the class.

F

Have students role-play a conversation based on their answers in Exercise E. Students should write a conversation like the one in Exercise D.

MORE ACTION

Ask each student to write one goal on a piece of paper. Have students trade their piece of paper with a partner and then ask their partner five questions about what they are doing to achieve their goal.

THE BIG PICTURE: Medical Careers

A 73

- Read the instructions. Discuss the careers in the chart. Ask students if they know what is involved in the careers listed. *Do you know what a phlebotomist does?* (A phlebotomist collects blood samples from patients.) *What is an occupational therapy assistant?* (An occupational therapy assistant provides therapy to help patients maintain or recover skills that they need to function in their daily lives.) *What is a surgical technician?* (A surgical technician works at a hospital and is in charge of preparing operating rooms, arranging surgical instruments and equipment, and assisting medical staff during surgeries. They are also called surgical technologists.)
- Play the audio and have students complete the exercise.
- Check the answers as a class.

THE BIG PICTURE Medical Careers

A AT WORK The chart presents three medical careers. Listen and complete the information. 73

Career	Phlebotomist	Occupational Therapy Assistant	Surgical Technician
Training/Education	Most need a professional certificate, or on-the-job training	An associate's degree; 16 weeks of hands-on experience; courses in: biology, psychology, and health education	Community college or vocational school program
Salary (2016)	$32, 710	$ 59,010	$ 45,160
Job Outlook	25 %	28 %	12 %
Job Responsibilities	Draw blood; make patient feel comfortable; enter information into a computer	Teach patients how to use equipment; work closely with the therapist	Prepare the operating room for surgery; sterilize equipment; prepare patients for surgery

An occupational therapist practices an exercise with a patient.

216 Unit 14

B Listen again. Circle the correct answer. 73

1. Ronaldo doesn't want to…
   a. work with people. b. work in a hospital. (c.) study for a long time.
2. Ronaldo wants a job that…
   (a.) will keep him busy. b. will allow him to work part time. c. will be easy.
3. Ronaldo would be a good phlebotomist because he…
   a. doesn't need any training. (b.) is good with people. c. wants an easy job.
4. If Ronaldo studies to become an occupational therapist, he may not have to…
   a. take any other courses. (b.) take biology or psychology. c. take health education.
5. Ronaldo has a ________________ who is a surgical technician.
   a. neighbor b. friend (c.) relative

C Listen and circle the job(s) that fits each description. 74

1. a. Phlebotomist (b. Occupational therapy assistant) c. Surgical technician
2. a. Phlebotomist (b. Occupational therapy assistant) c. Surgical technician
3. (a. Phlebotomist) b. Occupational therapy assistant c. Surgical technician
4. a. Phlebotomist (b. Occupational therapy assistant) (c. Surgical technician)
5. (a. Phlebotomist) b. Occupational therapy assistant c. Surgical technician
6. a. Phlebotomist (b. Occupational therapy assistant) c. Surgical technician
7. (a. Phlebotomist) (b. Occupational therapy assistant) (c. Surgical technician)

D Discuss these questions. **Answers will vary.**

1. Which career do you think Ronaldo should choose? Why?
2. Which career do you think you would like best? Why?

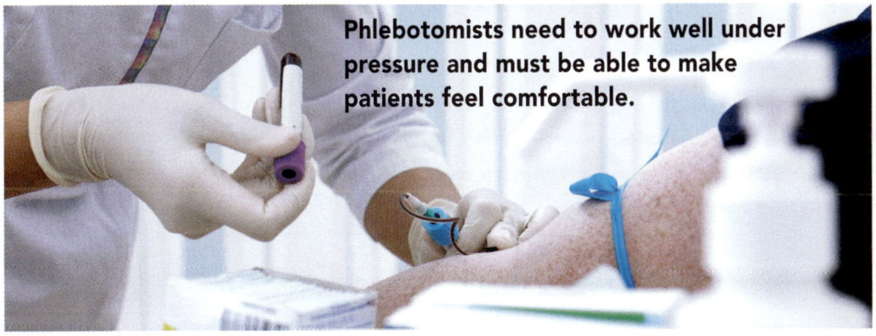

MORE ACTION

If time permits, follow up the discussion in Exercise D by dividing the class into three groups. Assign one of the jobs to each group. Have each group write a story about what happens to Ronaldo if he takes the job. Then, have volunteers read their group's story to the other groups.

B 73

- Play the audio once and ask students to listen carefully. Encourage them to focus solely on the audio. Tell them they will listen to the audio again.
- Play the audio again and ask students to circle their answers.
- Review the answers as a class.

C 74

- Play the audio and pause after each item so students can circle their answers.
- Play the audio again if necessary.
- Review the answers as a class.

D

Have students discuss the questions in pairs. Then, ask volunteers to share their answers with the class.

READING: Occupational Outlook Handbook

A 75 (facing page)

- Read the information in the blue box and ask students to name professions they are interested in learning more about.
- Read the Reading Note aloud. Help students practice their scanning skills by asking students additional questions about the Quick Facts at the top of the page. For example: *How many automotive service technicians and mechanics were there in 2016?* (749,900) *What was the hourly median pay in 2017?* ($19.02 per hour)
- Have students scan the article to find the answers to the questions.
- Ask volunteers to read their answers. Discuss any differences in answers.

ACADEMIC

Remind students that when they scan a text, they should read the text quickly and identify specific information, without reading every word.

You may want to contrast scanning with skimming (reading quickly to understand the general idea of a text).

Scanning and skimming are both key reading strategies that students can apply to any content area, and that may be very helpful when taking tests.

READING Occupational Outlook Handbook

Automotive Service Technicians and Mechanics

What Automotive Service Technicians and Mechanics Do

Automotive service technicians and mechanics, often called *service technicians* or *service techs*, inspect, maintain, and repair cars and light trucks. Basic repairs include changing oil, checking fluid levels and rotating tires. Service technicians identify problems, often by using computerized equipment. In large shops, automotive technicians specialize in different types of repairs, such as brakes or air conditioning.

Work Environment

Almost 60% of technicians work for automobile dealers or in repair shops. Another 13% are self-employed. Most dealers and shops are well-ventilated and well-lit. Technicians commonly work with greasy parts and tools, sometimes in uncomfortable positions. Workplace injuries, such as small cuts, sprains, and bruises are common.

How to Become an Automotive Service Technician or Mechanic

High school courses in automotive repair provide a good background, but employees prefer that automotive service technicians and mechanics complete an automotive technology program at a postsecondary institution. Industry certification is usually required once the person is employed.

Pay

The median annual wage for automotive service technicians and mechanics was $39,550 in May 2017. Technicians at automotive dealers usually earn more than technicians at repair shops.

Job Outlook

Employment of automotive service technicians and mechanics is projected to grow 6% from 2016 to 2026, about as fast as the average for all occupations. There should be many job opportunities for qualified technicians. 75

Source: Bureau of Labor Statistics, U.S. Department of Labor, *Occupational Outlook Handbook*, Automotive Service Technicians and Mechanics, on the Internet at https://www.bls.gov/ooh/installation-maintenance-and-repair/automotive-service-technicians-and-mechanics.htm (*November 06, 2017*).

Two mechanics inspect parts of a car.

218 Unit 14

Quick Facts	
2017 Median Pay	$39,550 per year $19.02 per hour
Typical Entry-Level Education	Postsecondary nondegree award
Work Experience in a Related Occupation	None
On-the-job Training	Short-term
Number of Jobs, 2016	749,900
Job Outlook, 2016-26	6% (As fast as average)
Employment Change, 2016-26	45,900

The *Occupational Outlook Handbook* is an online career guide published by the United States Department of Labor. You can find current information on hundreds of careers:

- Explanations of exactly what people do at each job
- Descriptions of work environments
- The training and education needed for each career
- Pay information
- The job outlook, or number of jobs in the future, for each career

A ACADEMIC Scan the Quick Facts box and the article about automotive service technicians. Underline the correct answers to these questions.

1. What was the median pay for automotive technicians in 2017?
   $39,550 per year / $19.02 per hour
2. How many more automotive workers will be needed by 2026?
   45,900 more
3. Where do most service technicians work?
   automobile dealers or repair shops
4. What is one negative of this work?
   Workplace injuries are common.
5. What education do most automotive dealers and shops prefer?
   Completion of an automotive technology program at a postsecondary institution.
6. What is the job outlook for the future?
   6%

READING NOTE

Scanning for Information

Sometimes it is not necessary to read every word. You can scan the text, looking at the text quickly to find specific information you need.

B AT WORK Go online and research a career that interests you. Take notes about the career you choose.

1. Career: ______________________
2. Job Description: ______________________
3. Education Required: ______________________
4. Job Outlook: ______________________
5. Pay: ______________________

C Listen to other students describe the careers they researched to the class. Write two careers that interest you.

B

- Ask students to complete the exercise independently.
- Ask volunteers to read some of their notes for the class.

C

- Have students discuss the careers they researched for the class.
- Ask students to listen attentively and choose two of the careers they hear about.
- You may want to list on the board the careers students researched, and take a poll to see what careers were the most popular with students.

AT WORK

The Occupational Outlook Handbook also includes career videos that give brief occupational overviews and describe the educational requirements and tasks associated with hundreds of jobs.

MORE ACTION

If possible, bring in or copy some information from *the Occupational Outlook Handbook* and discuss other careers that students are interested in. Have students form groups according to the career they are most interested in. Ask groups to read the information in the *Occupational Outlook Handbook* about the career they are interested in and summarize it for the class. Write the following heads in a chart on the board: *Nature of the Work, Education, Employment, Job Outlook,* and *Earnings*. Ask students to write the information about their jobs under these heads. Then, compare the jobs as a class. Which job has the best pay? Which requires the most training? Which has the best prospects?

WRITING OUR STORIES: A Resume

- Ask students questions about the resume. For example: *What is Diego's last name?* (Medina) *What is his address?* (937 Franklin Lane, Red Bank, NJ 07701) *What is his career objective?* (To pursue a career as a paralegal.) *Where did he go to school?* (Essex County College) *What skills does he have?* (He has experience with legal software, is fluent in Spanish, and speaks advanced Portuguese.)
- Point out the organization of the resume and the layout. Ask questions about the layout. For example: *What is at the beginning of the resume?* (Diego's name, address, telephone number, and email address) *What is at the end?* (Diego's skills) *What is on the first line of each entry under Employment History?* (the name of an employer) *Which job comes first, his most recent job or his first job?* (his most recent job)
- Ask students to name the verbs used to describe the job responsibilities (*maintained, obtained, conduct, organize*). Point out that the verbs for the first job entry under Employment History are in the present because that is the job Diego currently holds.
- Ask students to suggest other verbs they could use to describe job duties and responsibilities. For example: *monitored, managed, implemented, supervised, developed, created, designed,* and so on. Make a list of the verbs on the board.

WRITING OUR STORIES | A Resume

Diego Medina
937 Franklin Lane
Red Bank, NJ 07701
732-555-6347
dmedina@call*me.com

Put your name, address, telephone number, and email address at the top of the resume.

Career Objective:

To pursue a career as a paralegal in the public or private sector; to use my experience conducting case research, and collecting and analyzing evidence for attorney use.

Explain the kind of job you are looking for.

Education:

Essex County College, Newark, NJ
A.A.S. in Paralegal Studies, GPA 3.6, May 2017

Write the names of the schools you attended and the date you graduated.

Employment History:

- Lord and Robbins, P.C. Personal and Injury Law, 2015 to present
  Conduct case research, organize and track files
- Paner and Elliot, LLC, Criminal Law Intern, summer 2016
  Maintained reference files for ongoing cases
- County Court, Intake Intern, 2015
  Obtained intake information on juveniles

List the jobs you have had and your responsibilities. Write your resume in reverse chronological order, from the present to the past.

Activities:

Paralegal Club, Essex County College,
Paralegal Association of New Jersey

Name activities and organizations you belong to.

Skills:

Computer experience with legal software
Languages: fluent Spanish, advanced Portuguese

List your computer skills, languages you can speak, and other skills you have.

220 Unit 14

AT WORK

Encourage students to ask questions about what should and shouldn't be included on a resume (age, gender, marital status, and so on).

Ask students to look online for different resume types and formats in English, and to note the differences in the information included for different careers. For example, an actor's resume must include the height, weight, and age of the candidate, as well as a photo. A resume for an administrative position in an office should not include that information.

A Prepare to write your resume. Complete the information. Answers will vary.

Career Objective:

___

___

___

Education: (Note: Start with the name of your current school.)

___

___

___

Employment History: (Note: Start with your current job.)

___

___

___

Activities:

___

___

___

Skills:

___

___

___

B Use your notes and write your resume. Follow the form on the previous page.

WRITING NOTE

Editing a Resume

1. Type your resume.
2. Ask a teacher or counselor to proofread your resume.
3. Review all the dates on your resume.

A

- Have students complete the exercise by writing notes for each category.
- Walk around the room and assist as needed.
- Identify some of the main problems that students are having with their notes. For example, it may be difficult for them to write their career objective or find the appropriate language to describe their previous job duties.
- Write these problems on the board and ask the class to offer solutions.

B

- Read the Writing Note aloud.
- Have students write their resume and then have a partner edit it. Then, have students revise their resume for homework based on their partner's suggestions.

TEACHING TIP

There are many ways of formatting a resume. Bring in some examples of other resume layouts (from word processing programs, the internet, and so on). Ask students to read the different resumes and critique them. What features do they like about each resume? What features do they dislike? Talk to students about the physical appearance of a resume.

Remind them that a resume needs to look professional and be easy to read. The information for each section should be short and concise. Also, point out to students that resumes are usually printed on white paper or provided in electronic format. When creating their resumes, they should not use unusual fonts or colors, or include pictures of themselves.

ENGLISH IN ACTION: Researching a Career

A

- Read through the list and explain any unfamiliar vocabulary.
- Allow time for students to discuss their lists in pairs and then complete the chart.
- Ask volunteers to choose one skill or interest from the chart and describe an experience they've had with that skill or interest. For example: *I am artistic. I designed a business card for my friend's restaurant.* Ask them whether their partner shares that same skill or interest.

B

- After students have completed the sentences, ask volunteers to read theirs aloud to the class.
- Correct grammar and vocabulary as needed.

C

- Have students complete this exercise individually.
- Ask volunteers to read their steps to the class.
- Have other students suggest additional steps for each volunteer.

CIVICS

Read through the list of career resources in the Culture Note and ask students if they have any other suggestions to add to the list.

You may want to bring in information about local job fairs or opportunities for volunteer work.

ENGLISH IN ACTION Researching a Career

CULTURE NOTE

CIVICS In the United States, students use many resources to think about their careers. Some of these resources are:

1. Career counselors at high schools and colleges
2. Career books and online career resources
3. Volunteer jobs and part-time work
4. Job fairs – Events at schools or other locations where professionals give information and advice about their careers.
5. Talking to people in the kind of work you are interested in

A LET'S TALK. Talk about your skills and interests with a partner. Check your skills and your partner's skills.

Skills	You	Your Partner
1. I am artistic. I like to draw and design things.		
2. I am good at math. I like to work with numbers.		
3. I like to teach people how to do things.		
4. I like to operate and drive vehicles.		
5. I like science and solving problems.		
6. I like to read and write and work with information.		
7. I like to work with computers and software programs.		
8. I like to repair and maintain machines.		
9. I like to entertain people. I can sing, dance, or play an instrument.		
10. I like to help people who are sick.		

B Complete.

1. I like to ______________________________.
2. Two possible careers for me are ______________ and ______________.
3. My partner likes to ______________________________.
4. Two possible careers for him / her are ______________ and ______________.

C In your notebook, write the steps you need to take to find a job in the career you researched.

MORE ACTION

If possible, take your students to the library to explore the resources available there for researching careers. Ask your students to research good websites where they can find information about careers. As a class, make a list of the ten most useful websites.

APPENDIX A Grammar Summary

UNIT 1

Simple Present

STATEMENTS		
Subject	**Verb**	
I	work	every day.
You	work	at night.
We	work	in the morning.
They	work	in a restaurant.
He	work**s**	at a hospital.
She	work**s**	downtown.
It	work**s**	each time.

Notes:

1. The simple present tells about a repeated or routine action.
2. The simple present tells about facts that are true all the time.

   I live in the city. *I drive to school.*
3. The verb ends in -*s* for affirmative statements with *he*, *she*, and *it*.

There is / There are

AFFIRMATIVE STATEMENTS
There is a book on the desk.
There are four books on the desk.
There are some books on the desk.

NEGATIVE STATEMENTS
There isn't a book on the desk.
There aren't any books on the desk.

YES / NO QUESTIONS
Is there a map in your classroom?
Are there any maps in your classroom?

SHORT ANSWERS	
Yes, **there is**.	No, **there isn't**.
Yes, **there are**.	No, **there aren't**.

Notes:

1. A sentence beginning with *There is* often shows location.

   ***There is** a book on the desk.*
2. A sentence beginning with *There are* often tells how many.

   ***There are** twenty students in our class.*
3. Use *some* in a plural statement in the affirmative. Use *any* in a plural statement in the negative. Use *any* in a plural question.
4. Use *there* the first time you talk about a thing. Use *it* or *they* the second time.

   ***There** is a book on the desk.* ***It** is a dictionary.*

   ***There** are many students in our class.* ***They** are from different countries.*

QUANTIFIERS		
None One	of us of the students	is married. walks to school.
None A couple Some A few Most All	of us of the students of the children	are married. live in New York.

Note:

None is used with both the singular and the plural form of a verb.

***None** of us **is** married.*
***None** of us **are** married.*

UNIT 2

Simple Present

AFFIRMATIVE STATEMENTS	
Subject	**Verb**
I You We They	work.
He She It	works.

NEGATIVE STATEMENTS		
Subject	***Do not / Does not***	**Verb**
I You We They	do not / don't	work.
He She It	does not / doesn't	

PRESENT TIME EXPRESSIONS			
every morning **every** day **every** night	**once** a week **twice** a month **three times** a year	**on** the weekend **on** Sundays	**in** the summer **in** the winter

ADVERBS OF FREQUENCY
I **always** wear my seat belt. I **usually** eat breakfast. I **frequently** eat out. I **often** eat out. I **sometimes** work overtime. I **hardly ever** get up late. I **rarely** get up late. I **never** take a taxi.

Notes:

1. Time expressions usually appear at the end of a sentence.
2. Put adverbs of frequency after the verb *be.*

   *I am **never** late for work.*

   *She is **rarely** sick.*
3. Put adverbs of frequency before other verbs.

   *I **often** walk in the park.*

   *He **never** takes a taxi.*

UNIT 3

Simple Present

YES / NO QUESTIONS			
Do / Does	**Subject**	**Verb**	
Do	I you we they	bank have pay	online? a car loan? rent?
Does	he she		
	it	cost	a lot?

SHORT ANSWERS	
Affirmative	**Negative**
Yes, you **do**. Yes, I **do**. Yes, we **do**. Yes, they **do**.	No, you **don't**. No, I **don't**. No, we **don't**. No, they **don't**.
Yes, he **does**. Yes, she **does**. Yes, it **does**.	No, he **doesn't**. No, she **doesn't**. No, it **doesn't**.

***WH*- QUESTIONS**			
Wh- word	*Do / Does*	Subject	Verb
When	do	I	work?
Where	do	you	study?
What	do	we	need?
When	do	they	eat?
How much	does	he	save?
How	does	she	get to work?

ANSWERS		
Subject	Verb	
You	work	at 2:00.
I	study	at the adult school.
We	need	a computer.
They	eat	at 7:00.
He	save**s**	$100 a week.
She	take**s**	the bus.

Who Questions

WHO AS A SUBJECT

Who works at City Bank?
Laura does.

Who saves money every month?
Henry and **Ivan** do.

Note:
When *Who* is the subject of a sentence, it is always singular.

WHO AS AN OBJECT

Who does he drive to work?
He drives **his brother** to work.

Who do they send money to?
They send money **to their parents**.

Note:
When *Who* is the object of a sentence, it can be singular or plural.

UNIT 4

Count Nouns

SINGULAR	**PLURAL**
a state	states
every state	all the states
each of the states	many of the states

Notes:

1. Count nouns are people, places, or things that we can count individually (one by one). Count nouns can be singular or plural.
2. Expressions with *one of the*, *every*, and *each* are singular.

   ***Every** state **has** a capitol building.*
3. Expressions with *a few of the*, *some of the*, *many of the*, *all of the*, etc., are plural.

   ***All of the** states **have** capitol buildings.*

QUANTIFIERS WITH COUNT NOUNS				
There	is isn't	a	seaport desert	on the coast. in the North. in the South. in the East. in the West. in the central part of the country.
	are	a few several many a lot of	seaports mountains rivers forests farms	
	aren't	any		

COUNT AND NONCOUNT NOUNS	
Count Nouns	Noncount Nouns
a river	rain
mountains	pollution
tourists	tourism

Notes:

1. *Aren't* can also be used with *many* and *a lot of.*
2. Noncount nouns cannot be counted. They are always singular.
   - Liquids or gases: *water, oil, oxygen, rain*
   - Items that are too small or too numerous to count: *sand, corn, rice*
   - General categories: *traffic, scenery, music, tourism*
   - Ideas: *information, beauty, work*
   - Some words can be both count and noncount: *crime—crimes, industry—industries*

QUANTIFIERS WITH NONCOUNT NOUNS				
There	is	no a little a lot of	traffic rain crime industry	in this city. in my country. in the United States.
	isn't	any much		

HOW MUCH / HOW MANY				
How much	snow traffic	is	there	in your city? in your country?
How many	museums parks	are		

Note:

A lot of can be used with *isn't.*

There **isn't a lot of** rain in the desert.

TOO MUCH / TOO MANY / NOT ENOUGH			
There	is	too much	rain.
		not enough	industry.
	are	too many	fast-food restaurants.
		not enough	parks.

Note:

We often use *not enough* and *too many / too much* to talk about problems or to complain.

too many, too much = more than you want or need

There are ***too many*** *cars on the road. There is* ***too much*** *traffic.*

not enough = less than you want or need

*There are****n't enough*** *farms in that country. There is****n't enough*** *food.*

UNIT 5

Present Continuous

STATEMENTS			
Subject	*Be*	(not)	*-ing* Form
I	**am**		send**ing** an email.
You	**are**		order**ing** a movie.
He	**is**		mak**ing** reservations.
She	**is**	(**not**)	typ**ing** an essay.
It	**is**		work**ing**.
We	**are**		text**ing**.
They	**are**		play**ing** a video game.

Notes:

1. The present continuous talks about an action that is happening now.

   *He **is using** his computer.*

2. The present continuous talks about an action that is temporary.

   *He **is living** with his brother.* (He expects to move soon.)

3. The present continuous can talk about specific future plans.

   *I'**m leaving** at 2:00.*

YES / NO QUESTIONS		
Be	Subject	*-ing* Form
Am	I	tak**ing** a picture?
Are	you	send**ing** an email?
Is	she	listen**ing** to music?
Is	it	work**ing**?
Are	they	mak**ing** reservations?

SHORT ANSWERS	
Affirmative	Negative
Yes, you **are**.	No, you **aren't**. / No, you'**re not**.
Yes, I **am**.	No, I'**m not**.
Yes, she **is**.	No, she **isn't**. / No, she'**s not**.
Yes, it **is**.	No, it **isn't**. / No, it'**s not**.
Yes, they **are**.	No, they **aren't**. / No, they'**re not**.

WH- QUESTIONS			
Wh- word	*Be*	Subject	*-ing* Form
What	**am**	I	do**ing**?
Which movie	**are**	you	order**ing**?
How	**is**	it	work**ing**?
Where	**are**	they	go**ing**?

ANSWERS
Subject + Verb
You're check**ing** prices.
I'm order**ing** *Space Age*.
It's work**ing** well.
They're go**ing** to the lab.

WHO QUESTIONS		
Who	Verb	
Who	is buying	a camera?
Who	is fixing	the computer?

Notes:

1. When *Who* is the subject of a sentence, it is always singular.

   Who is buying *a camera?* — *Laura **is**.*

   Who is working *today?* — *Sarah and Ali **are**.*

2. When *Who* is the object of a sentence, it can be singular or plural.

   Who is *Max calling?* — *He **is calling** his sister.*

   Who are *they speaking with?* — *They **are speaking** with the customers.*

NONACTION VERBS			
hate	feel	agree	belong
like	hear	believe	cost
love	look	forget	have
prefer	see	know	need
	seem	remember	own
	smell	think	
	sound	understand	
	taste		

Notes:

1. Some verbs in English are not used with the present continuous. They are called nonaction verbs. These verbs often show feelings, senses, beliefs, and possession.

2. Some verbs can show both nonaction and action.

   *I **have** a computer.* — *I'**m having** a good time.*

   *She'**s having** a party.*

   *I **think** he's a good teacher.* — *I'**m thinking** about my vacation.*

UNIT 6

Future with *Be going to*

STATEMENTS				
Subject	*Be*	*(not)*	*Going to*	Verb
I You He They	am are is are	(not)	going to	**exercise**. **make** an appointment. **call** the doctor. **take** medication.

YES / NO QUESTIONS			
Be	Subject	*Going to*	Verb
Are Is Are	you she they	going to	**see** the doctor? **stay** home from work? **get** a flu shot?

ANSWERS	
Affirmative	Negative
Yes, I **am**. Yes, she **is**. Yes, they **are**.	No, **I'm not**. No, she **isn't**. No, they **aren't**.

WH- QUESTIONS				
Wh- word	*Be*	Subject	*Going to*	Verb
When Where Why	am are is are	I you he they	going to	exercise?

Future with *Will*

STATEMENTS		
Subject	*Will / Won't*	Verb
I You He She We They	will won't	**walk** every day. **join** a health club. **change** jobs.

Notes:

1. Use *will* to express an offer to help.
   *I'**ll drive** you to school.*
2. Use *will* to make predictions.
   *You'**ll get** the job.*

UNIT 7

COMPARATIVE ADJECTIVES

New York is **larger than** Atlanta.
Chicago is **busier than** Denver.
Houston is **more populated than** Boston.

Notes:

1. Comparative adjectives compare two people, places, or things.
2. For one-syllable adjectives, add *-er* + *than*.
   tall – taller than *long – longer than*
3. For one-syllable adjectives ending in a consonant followed by *-y*, change the *-y* to *-i*, and add *-er* + *than*.
   dry – drier than
4. For two-syllable adjectives ending in *y*, change the *y* to *i*, and add *-er* + *than*.
   busy – busier than *happy – happier than*
5. For other adjectives with two or more syllables, use *more* + adjective + *than*.
   beautiful – more beautiful than *populated – more populated than*
6. These comparative adjectives are irregular.
   good – better than *bad – worse than* *far – farther than*

MORE / *LESS* / *FEWER* + NOUN

New York Los Angeles	has	more fewer	universities jobs	than	Los Angeles. New York.
		more less	traffic noise		

Notes:

1. Use *more* and *less* with noncount nouns.
2. Use *more* and *fewer* with count nouns.

SUPERLATIVE ADJECTIVES

Russia is **the largest** country in the world.
Atlanta Airport is **the busiest** airport in the world.
New York is **the most populated** city in the United States.

Notes:

1. Superlative adjectives compare three or more people, places, or things.
2. For one-syllable adjectives, add *the* + *-est*.
   tall – the tallest *long – the longest*
3. For two-syllable adjectives ending in *y*, change the *y* to *i*, and add *the* + *est*.
   busy – the busiest *happy – the happiest*
4. For other adjectives with two or more syllables, use *the most* + adjective.
   beautiful – the most beautiful *populated – the most populated*
5. These superlative adjectives are irregular.
   good – the best *bad – the worst* *far – the farthest*

AS... AS			
China France	is	as interesting as as beautiful as	India. Italy.

NOT AS... AS			
Colombia Ecuador	isn't	as populated as as large as	Brazil. Mexico.

Notes:

1. Use *as . . . as* to show that two people, places, or things are the same.
2. Use *not as . . . as* to show that two people, places, or things are not the same.

   *Florida is **not as large as** Texas. = Texas is **larger than** Florida.*

   *Silver is **not as expensive as** gold. = Gold is **more expensive than** silver.*

UNIT 8

Simple Past

REGULAR VERBS
I **lived** in Taiwan. He **moved** to the United States. They **signed** a lease.

Notes:

1. Regular simple past verbs end in *-d* or *-ed* (See Appendix B).
2. The simple past form is the same for singular and plural subjects.
3. **Irregular** past verbs do not follow the same rules.

PAST TIME EXPRESSIONS		
Yesterday	Last	Ago
yesterday morning	last night	a few minutes ago
yesterday afternoon	last week	an hour ago
yesterday evening	last weekend	a week ago
	last Saturday	two years ago
	last month	
	last year	

Note:

Use a past time expression at the beginning or the end of a sentence.

NEGATIVES
I **didn't paint** the bedroom. We **didn't live** in an apartment. He **didn't study** English. She **didn't take** the test. They **didn't go** to the park. It **didn't work**.

Note:

Use *didn't* and the base form of the verb to form the negative past form.

BE	
Present	Past
I **am** busy.	I **was** busy.
You **are** lonely.	You **were** lonely.
He **is** friendly.	He **was** friendly.
It **is** safe.	It **was** safe.
We **are** homesick.	We **were** homesick.
They **are** noisy.	They **were** noisy.

Notes:

1. *Was* and *were* are past forms of *be*.
2. The negative form of *was* is *was not / wasn't*. The negative form of *were* is *were not / weren't*.

   *I **wasn't** busy.*

   *You **weren't** lonely.*

UNIT 9

Note:
The past *forms* of the verb *be* are *was* and *were*.

BE		
Present	Past	
I **am** home.	I **was** home.	I **wasn't** at home.
You **are** at work.	You **were** at work.	You **weren't** at work.
We **are** scared.	We **were** scared.	We **weren't** scared.
They **are** at school.	They **were** at school.	They **weren't** at school.
He **is** cold.	He **was** cold.	He **wasn't** cold.
She **is** upset.	She **was** upset.	She **wasn't** upset.
It **is** windy.	It **was** windy.	It **wasn't** windy.

Simple Past

***YES / NO* QUESTIONS**		
Did	Subject	Verb
Did	you	**evacuate**?
	he	**go** to work?
	it	**rain** all week?
	they	**lose** power?

SHORT ANSWERS	
Affirmative	Negative
Yes, I **did**.	No, I **didn't**.
Yes, he **did**.	No, he **didn't**.
Yes, it **did**.	No, it **didn't**.
Yes, they **did**.	No, they **didn't**.

***WH-* QUESTIONS**			
Wh- word	*Did*	Subject	Verb
When	**did**	the storm	**begin**?
Where	**did**	you	**stay**?
How many days	**did**	it	**rain**?
How much damage	**did**	you	**have**?

***WHO* QUESTIONS**		
Who	Verb	
Who	**helped**	their neighbors after the storm?
Who	**saw**	the tornado?

Note:
In these questions, *Who* is the subject.

UNIT 10

HAVE TO / HAS TO		
I You We They	**have to**	**go** through security. **bring** photo ID.
He She	**has to**	

Note:
Have to and *has to* are modals. They show necessity or obligation.

DON'T HAVE TO / DOESN'T HAVE TO			
I You We They	**don't**	**have to**	**order** the invitations. **work** today.
He She	**doesn't**		

Note:

Don't have to and *doesn't have to* are modals. They show that an action is not necessary.

Have to / Has to

YES / NO QUESTIONS			
Do	I you we they	have to	work overtime? send a gift?
Does	he she		

ANSWERS	
Yes, you **do**. Yes, I **do**. Yes, we **do**. Yes, they **do**.	No, you **don't**. No, I **don't**. No, we **don't**. No, they **don't**.
Yes, he **does**. Yes, she **does**.	No, he **doesn't**. No, she **doesn't**.

HAD TO / DIDN'T HAVE TO		
I You He They	**had to** **didn't have to**	**work**. **send** a gift.

Notes:

1. *Had to* and *didn't have to* are modals.
2. *Had to* is the past of *have to* and *has to*.
3. *Didn't have to* is the past of *don't have to* and *doesn't have to*.

SHOULD / SHOULDN'T
You **should wear** your blue dress. She **shouldn't get** married now. She **should finish** college first.

Notes:

1. *Should* is a modal. *Should* gives advice or an opinion.
2. *Should* has the same form for all persons.

UNIT 11

CAN
I **can install** internet service in your home. He **can change** the lights in your home.

Notes:

1. *Can* is a modal. It shows ability.
2. *Can* has the same form for all persons.

COULD YOU / WOULD YOU
Could you please call Mr. Smith? **Would you** please help this customer?

Notes:

1. *Could you* and *Would you* are modals. Use these expressions to make polite requests.
2. *Could you* and *Would you* have the same form for all persons.

MUST / MUST NOT / CAN'T
I **must** wear a name tag. We **must** sign in. You **must not** make personal calls at work. You **can't** use your cellphone.

Notes:

1. *Must, must not,* and *can't* are modals. They explain rules, policies, and regulations.
2. *Must* and *have to* are similar in meaning.

   *I **must wear** a uniform.* *I **have to wear** a uniform.*
3. *Must not* and *can't* show that an action is not allowed or permitted.
4. Be careful! *Must not* and *(not) have to* do not have the same meaning.

   *I **must not bring** my children to work.* ≠ *I **don't have to** bring my children to work.*

   Must not refers to an action that is not allowed. *Don't have to* refers to something that is not necessary.
5. *Must, must not,* and *can't* have the same form for all persons.

MAY **AND** ***MIGHT***
I **may** quit my job. The company **might** close.

Notes:

1. *May* and *might* are modals. They show possibility.
2. *May* and *might* have the same form for all persons.

UNIT 12

PRESENT TIME CLAUSES	
He watches TV <u>before he goes to bed</u>. (main clause) (time clause)	<u>Before he goes to bed</u>, he watches TV. (time clause) (main clause)

Notes:

1. A time clause explains when an action happens. A time clause begins with a word such as *after, before, when, as soon as, until,* or *if.* A time clause has a subject and a verb.
2. If the time clause is at the beginning of the sentence, use a comma after the time clause. If the time clause is at the end of the sentence, don't use a comma.

   ***When** Henry gets home, he makes dinner.*

   *The children watch TV **until** their father comes home.*

PHRASAL VERBS

Some verbs in English are made up of two words. They are called *phrasal verbs.*

*Anna likes to **get up** early on Sundays.*

Some phrasal verbs can have other words between the two parts of the verb. These are called separable (S) verbs.

*I **put on** my coat.* *I **put** my coat **on**.*

Some phrasal verbs can't have other words between the two parts of the verb.

*I **get on** the bus at 7:30 every morning.* NOT ~~*I **get** the bus **on** at 7:30 every morning.*~~

UNIT 13

PAST TIME CLAUSES	
I locked my door **before** I went to work. (main clause) (time clause)	**Before** I went to work, I locked my door. (time clause) (main clause)

PAST CONTINUOUS		
I	**was**	read**ing**.
You	**were**	work**ing**.
He	**was**	sleep**ing**.
She	**was**	play**ing**.
It	**was**	mak**ing** noise.
We	**were**	watch**ing** TV.
They	**were**	driv**ing**.

Note:
The past continuous describes an action that was in progress at a specific time in the past.

PAST CONTINUOUS WITH *WHILE*
While I **was driving** to school, I **was listening** to the radio. I **was listening** to the radio **while** I **was driving** to school.

Note:
Use *while* with the past continuous to show that two actions were happening at the same time.

THE PAST CONTINUOUS AND THE SIMPLE PAST
I **heard** someone in my living room while I **was sleeping**. Boris **was eating** dinner when someone **knocked** at his door.

Note:
The past continuous can describe an action that was interrupted. One action was going on when another action happened.

UNIT 14

Future Time Clauses

STATEMENTS
She **will get** a good job after she **graduates** from college. (main clause) (time clause) After she **graduates** from college, she **will get** a good job. (time clause) (main clause)

Note:
The verb in the main clause is in the future (with *will* or *going to*). The verb in the time clause is in the present.

QUESTIONS
What are you going to do after you graduate? **Where is he going to live** when his company transfers him? Before he starts his new job, **is he going to take a vacation**?

Note:
In a question with a future time clause, use the future question form in the main clause.

APPENDIX B Spelling Rules

Plural Nouns

1. For most nouns, add an *-s*.
   boy – boys   *store – stores*   *student – students*
2. If a noun ends with a consonant and a *y*, change the *y* to *i*, and add *-es*.
   city – cities   *dictionary – dictionaries*   *baby – babies*
3. If a noun ends with *sh*, *ch*, *x*, or *z*, add *-es*.
   box – boxes   *dish – dishes*   *watch – watches*

Present Continuous Verbs

1. For most verbs, add *-ing*.
   walk – walking   *play – playing*   *eat – eating*
2. If a verb ends in *e*, drop the *e* and add *-ing*.
   write – writing   *come – coming*   *drive – driving*
3. If a verb ends in a consonant + vowel + consonant, double the final consonant and add *-ing*.
   sit – sitting   *run – running*   *put – putting*
4. If a verb ends in *w*, *x*, or *y*, do not double the consonant. Add *-ing*.
   play – playing   *relax – relaxing*   *snow – snowing*

Present Verbs: Third Person

1. For most verbs, add *-s*.
   make – makes   *call – calls*   *sleep – sleeps*
2. If a verb ends with a consonant and a *y*, change the *y* to *i*, and add *-es*.
   try – tries   *cry – cries*   *apply – applies*
3. If a verb ends with *sh*, *ch*, *x*, or *z*, add *-es*.
   wash – washes   *watch – watches*   *fix – fixes*
4. These verbs are irregular in the third person.
   have – has   *do – does*

Past Verbs

1. For most verbs, add *-d* or *-ed*.
   save – saved   *rent – rented*
2. If a verb ends in a consonant + *y*, change the *y* to *i* and add *-ed*.
   try – tried   *study – studied*
3. If a verb ends in a consonant + vowel + consonant, double the final consonant and add *-ed*.
   stop – stopped   *rob – robbed*
4. If a verb ends in *w*, *x*, or *y*, do not double the consonant. Add *-ed*.
   play – played   *relax – relaxed*   *snow – snowed*

Comparative Adjectives: *-er*

1. For most adjectives, add *-r* or *-er*.
   large – larger   *short – shorter*   *tall – taller*
2. If a one-syllable adjective ends in a consonant + vowel + consonant, double the final consonant and add *-er*.
   big – bigger   *thin – thinner*   *sad – sadder*
3. If an adjective ends in a consonant + *y*, change the *y* to *i* and add *-er*.
   happy – happier   *heavy – heavier*   *friendly – friendlier*

Superlative Adjectives: *-est*

1. For most adjectives, add *-st* or *-est*.
   large – largest   *short – shortest*   *tall – tallest*
2. If a one-syllable adjective ends in a consonant + vowel + consonant, double the final consonant and add *-est*.
   big – biggest   *thin – thinnest*   *sad – saddest*
3. If an adjective ends in a consonant + *y*, change the *y* to *i* and add *-est*.
   busy – busiest   *noisy – noisiest*   *friendly – friendliest*

APPENDIX C Student to Student

UNIT 2

Student 1: Read the sentences in Set A to Student 2.

Student 2: Read the sentences in Set B to Student 1.

Set A

a. He gets up late.
b. He plays tennis.
c. He studies in the morning.
d. He doesn't pick up his clothes.
e. He makes his bed.
f. He gets up early.

Set B

a. He doesn't get up early.
b. He keeps his things neat.
c. He takes morning classes.
d. He studies at night.
e. He plays basketball.
f. He doesn't make his bed.

UNIT 4

Student 1: Ask your partner about Canada. Complete the chart below.

Student 2: Ask your partner about Mexico. Complete the chart on page 56.

How much tourism is there in Canada?

There is a lot of tourism in Canada.

	Mexico	Canada
Tourism	a lot	
Deserts	two	
Mountains	many	
National parks	67	
Snow	very little	
Ski resorts	one	
Official languages	one	

UNIT 6

Student 1: Read the questions in Set A to Student 2.

Student 2: Read the questions in Set B to Student 1.

Set A

1. How are you feeling?
2. Are you going to need an operation?
3. How long are you going to stay in the hospital?
4. When are you going home?
5. What other tests are you going to need?

Set B

1. What's the problem?
2. When is the doctor going to talk to you?
3. When are they going to take X-rays?
4. When are you going to know the test results?
5. When are you going to return to school?

UNIT 7

Student 1: Read the questions in Set A to Student 2.

Student 2: Read the questions in Set B to Student 1.

Set A

1. Which city is the most populated?
2. Which city has the highest percentage of Hispanics?
3. Which city has the highest median household income?
4. Which city has the least expensive houses?
5. In which city do workers have the longest commute?
6. Which city has the most rainfall?
7. Which city has the fewest sunny days?

Set B

1. Which city has the lowest population?
2. Which city has the lowest unemployment?
3. Which city has the most expensive houses?
4. In which city do workers have the shortest commute?
5. Which city has the lowest median household income?
6. Which city has the least rain?
7. Which city receives the most snow?

APPENDIX D Dictation

UNIT 2

1. The average person wears a seat belt.
2. 10% of people don't wear a seat belt.
3. The average person lives in a house.
4. More than half of Americans own their homes.
5. Many people rent their homes.

UNIT 6

1. A man was in an accident.
2. Another driver hit his car.
3. He stayed in the hospital overnight.
4. He's going to call his insurance company today.
5. He's going to report the accident.
6. He is also going to call his lawyer.
7. He's going to sue the other driver.
8. The accident was the woman's fault.
9. She was talking on her cellphone at the time of the accident.

UNIT 7

1. India is as interesting as China.
2. India isn't as large as China.
3. India is almost as populated as China.
4. India is as diverse as China.
5. Chinese food isn't as spicy as Indian food.

UNIT 8

1. Yolanda's father had a job offer in Florida.
2. He moved his family to Tampa.
3. Yolanda and Diego liked Largo.
4. They lived there for two years.
5. After Yolanda had a baby, they moved back to Tampa.
6. Yolanda needed to go back to work.
7. Diego's job just offered him a promotion.

UNIT 12

Mimi has a difficult time falling asleep at night. She gets in bed and puts her head on the pillow. But as soon as she closes her eyes, she begins to worry—about her job, her health, and her family. So, she now has a routine to relax herself before she goes to sleep. Before she goes into her bedroom, she drinks a cup of hot herbal tea. Then, she brushes her teeth. After she brushes her teeth, she washes her face and puts on her favorite face cream. When she gets into bed, she picks up a magazine and reads for a few minutes. Then, she listens to some quiet music. When she finally turns off her light, she falls asleep more easily.

UNIT 14

1. Maria is going to look for a job before she graduates.
2. Before she looks for a job, she will write her resume.
3. She will send out her resume when she sees a good job posting.
4. If she hears of a job opening, she will call the company.
5. When she goes on an interview, she is going to wear a suit.
6. If she makes a good impression, the company will hire her.

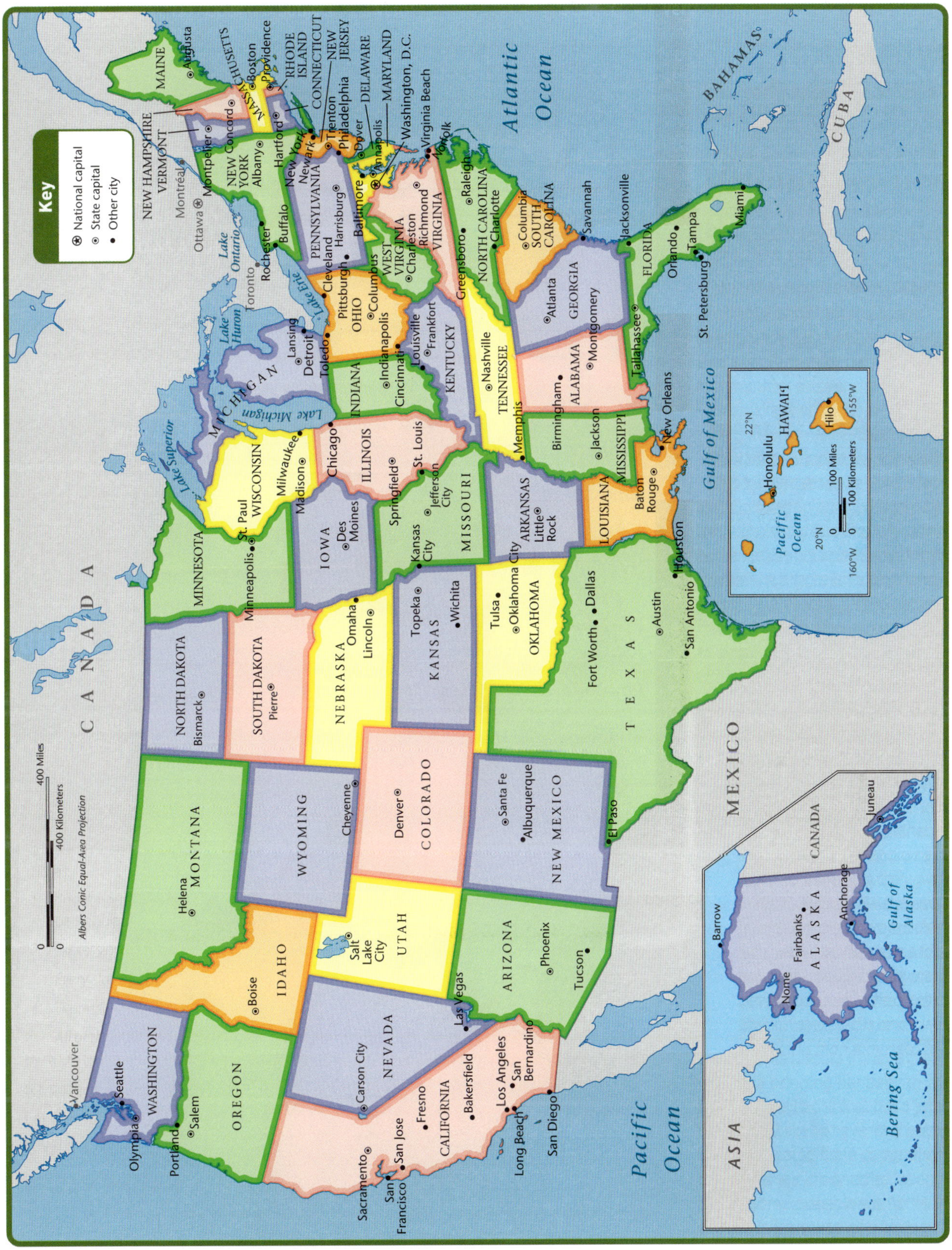
Key
National capital
State capital
Other city
0 400 Miles
0 400 Kilometers
Albers Conic Equal-Area Projection
C A N A D A
Vancouver
Ottawa
Montréal
Toronto
Lake Superior
Lake Michigan
Lake Huron
Lake Ontario
Lake Erie
WASHINGTON
Seattle
Olympia
OREGON
Portland
Salem
CALIFORNIA
Sacramento
San Francisco
San Jose
Fresno
Bakersfield
Los Angeles
Long Beach
San Bernardino
San Diego
NEVADA
Carson City
Las Vegas
IDAHO
Boise
MONTANA
Helena
WYOMING
Cheyenne
UTAH
Salt Lake City
ARIZONA
Phoenix
Tucson
COLORADO
Denver
NEW MEXICO
Santa Fe
Albuquerque
NORTH DAKOTA
Bismarck
SOUTH DAKOTA
Pierre
NEBRASKA
Omaha
Lincoln
KANSAS
Topeka
Wichita
OKLAHOMA
Tulsa
Oklahoma City
T E X A S
El Paso
Fort Worth
Dallas
Austin
San Antonio
Houston
MINNESOTA
Minneapolis
St. Paul
IOWA
Des Moines
MISSOURI
Kansas City
Jefferson City
St. Louis
ARKANSAS
Little Rock
LOUISIANA
Baton Rouge
New Orleans
WISCONSIN
Madison
Milwaukee
ILLINOIS
Springfield
Chicago
MICHIGAN
Lansing
Detroit
INDIANA
Indianapolis
OHIO
Columbus
Toledo
Cleveland
Cincinnati
KENTUCKY
Frankfort
Louisville
TENNESSEE
Nashville
Memphis
MISSISSIPPI
Jackson
ALABAMA
Birmingham
Montgomery
GEORGIA
Atlanta
Savannah
FLORIDA
Tallahassee
Jacksonville
Orlando
Tampa
St. Petersburg
Miami
SOUTH CAROLINA
Columbia
NORTH CAROLINA
Raleigh
Charlotte
Greensboro
VIRGINIA
Richmond
Norfolk
Virginia Beach
WEST VIRGINIA
Charleston
PENNSYLVANIA
Harrisburg
Philadelphia
Pittsburgh
NEW YORK
Albany
Buffalo
Rochester
New York
Newark
Trenton
VERMONT
Montpelier
NEW HAMPSHIRE
Concord
MAINE
Augusta
MASSACHUSETTS
Boston
RHODE ISLAND
Providence
CONNECTICUT
Hartford
NEW JERSEY
DELAWARE
Dover
MARYLAND
Annapolis
Baltimore
Washington, D.C.
Atlantic Ocean
Pacific Ocean
Gulf of Mexico
MEXICO
BAHAMAS
CUBA
ALASKA
Barrow
Fairbanks
Nome
Anchorage
Juneau
CANADA
ASIA
Bering Sea
Gulf of Alaska
HAWAI'I
Honolulu
Hilo
Pacific Ocean
22°N
20°N
160°W
155°W
0 100 Miles
0 100 Kilometers

US Map

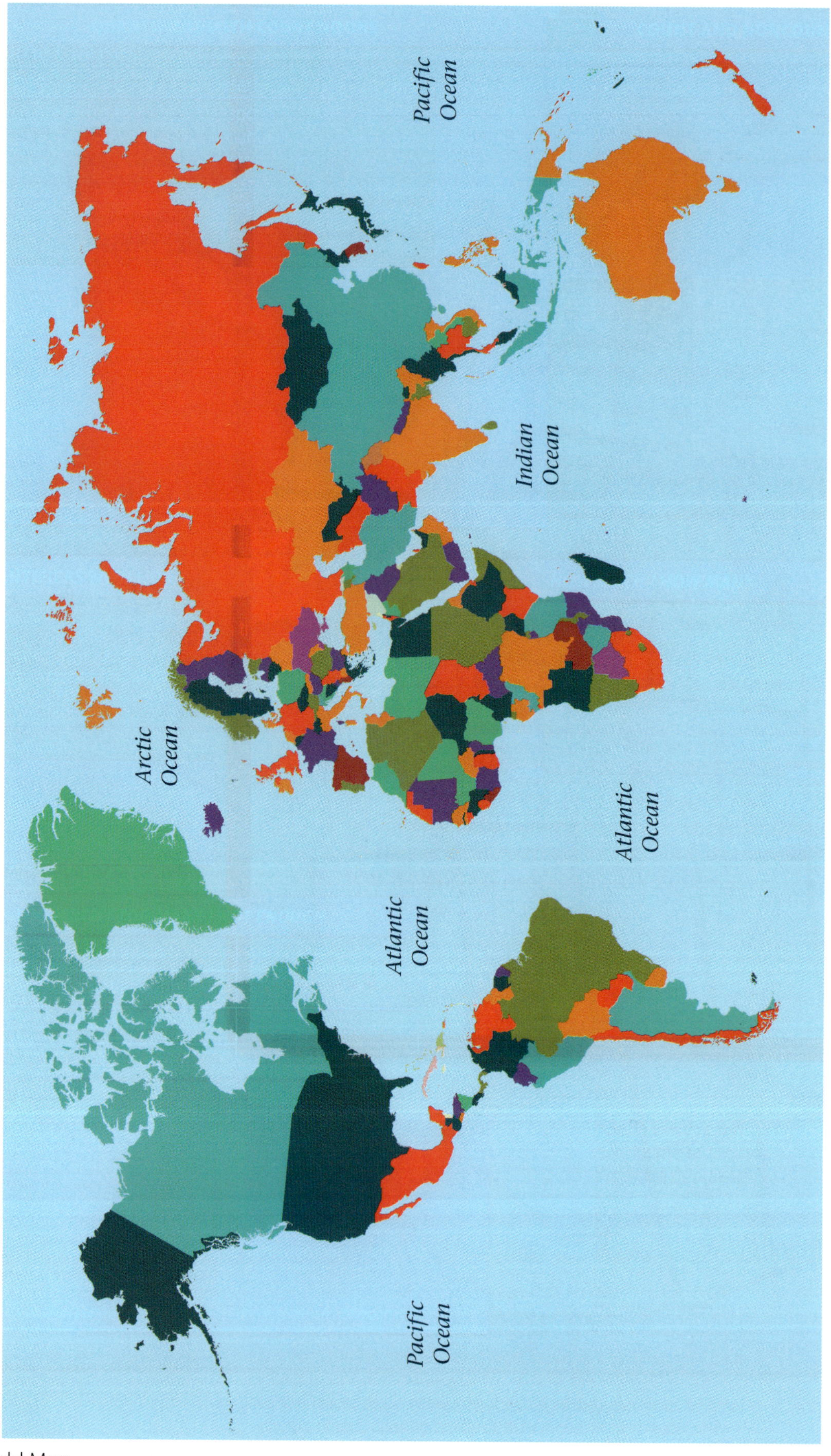
Pacific Ocean
Arctic Ocean
Atlantic Ocean
Atlantic Ocean
Indian Ocean
Pacific Ocean

World Map

PHOTO CREDITS

iv (left) Dick Loek/Getty Images, **iv** (left) Tony Shi Photography/Getty Images, **iv** (left) KAZUHIRO NOGI/Getty Images, **iv** (left) Paul Horsted/Stock Connection/Aurora Photos, **iv** (left) Keystone-France/Getty Images, **iv** (left) Matt Cardy/Getty Images, **iv** (left) Woods Wheatcroft/Aurora Photos, **iv** (left) ©Wolfe House Movers, LLC, **vi** (left) ROBIN UTRECHT/Getty Images, **vi** (left) Jeff Kolodny Photography, **vi** (left) Mike Harrington/Getty Images, **vi** (left) FREDERICK FLORIN/Getty Images, **vi** (left) Lorado/Getty Images, **vi** (left) Caren Brinkema/Getty Images, **2** (left) Siri Stafford/Getty Images, **4** (bottom left) Jetta Productions/Getty Images, **5** (bottom left) Steve Debenport/Getty Images, **5** (bottom right) Jordi Angrill/Getty Images, **10** (bottom) Rawpixel.com/Shutterstock.com, **12** (bottom center) witsanu deetuam/Shutterstock.com, **14** (center right) John Coletti/Getty Images, **17** (center) Tony Shi Photography/Getty Images, **18** (top center) Boston Globe/Getty Images, **28** (bottom center) ©Ken Wolter/Shutterstock, **30** (top center) WIN-Initiative/Getty Images, **33** (center) KAZUHIRO NOGI/Getty Images, **34** (top) Erik Isakson/Getty Images, **36** (top) Phanie/Alamy Stock Photo Stock Photo, **37** (top right) jsmith/Getty Images, **44** (bottom) J. Emilio Flores/The New York Times, **46** (bottom) MirageC/Getty Images, **49** (center) Paul Horsted/Stock Connection/Aurora Photos, **50** (top) Raico Rosenberg/AGE Fotostock, **51** (top right) Clarence Holmes Photography/Alamy Stock Photo, **58** (top) Mike Criss/National Geographic My Shot/National Geographic Creative, **60-61** (top) stevemendenhall/Getty Images, **62** (top) amadeustx/Shutterstock.com, **65** (center) Keystone-France/Getty Images, **66** (top left) Scanrail1/Shutterstock.com, **66** (top center) bfk/Shutterstock.com, **66** (top right) mustafagull/Getty Images, **66** (top left) T3 Magazine/Getty Images, **66** (top left) Howard Kingsnorth/Getty Images, **66** (bottom right) Gargantiopa/Shutterstock.com, **69** (center left) Lyn Alweis/Getty Images, **69** (top left) Andrey_Popov/Shutterstock.com, **71** (top center) Tooga/Getty Images, **71** (top) fizkes/Shutterstock.com, **71** (top) Caroline von Tuempling/Getty Images, **71** (bottom right) Steve Debenport/Getty Images, **74** (top left) PhotoAlto/Odilon Dimier/Getty Images, **74** (top left) Ed Norton/Getty Images, **74** (top center) Jordan Siemens/Getty Images, **74** (center left) quavondo/ E+/Getty Images, **81** (center) Matt Cardy/Getty Images, **82** (top) Portland Press Herald/Getty Images, **82** (top) Joe Raedle/Getty Images, **82** (top) Cultura Creative (RF)/Alamy Stock Photo, **82** (center) Wavebreak Media ltd/Alamy Stock Photo, **84** (top) tab62/Shutterstock.com, **86** (bottom center) Sam Mellish/Getty Images, **87** (bottom) Art Directors & TRIP/Alamy Stock Photo, **92** (center) Melissa Farlow/Aurora Photos, **96** (top right) Don Bartletti/Getty Images, **97** (center) Woods Wheatcroft/Aurora Photos, **98** (top left) maximkabb/Getty Images, **98** (top left) Ian G Dagnall/Alamy Stock Photo, **98** (top left) Andrew Peacock/Aurora Photos, **98** (top left) Alexey Rotanov/Shutterstock.com, **98** (top left) Twin Design/Shutterstock.com, **98** (top left) ZUMA Press, Inc./Alamy Stock Photo, **104** (bottom left) Xiaolu Chu/Getty Images, **104** (bottom right) Soltan Frédéric/Getty Images, **106** (top right) logoboom/Shutterstock.com, **106** (bottom) Eduard Moldoveanu/500px, **107** (bottom center) Paul Giamou/Getty Images, **108** (bottom center) David McNew/Getty Images, **110** (bottom left) Stefano Ravera/Alamy Stock Photo, **112** (bottom center) Planet Observer/UIG/Getty Images, **113** (center) ©Wolfe House Movers, LLC, **114** (top center) Rob Crandall/Shutterstock.com, **115** (bottom center) Klaus Tiedge/Getty Images, **117** (bottom center) Blaine Harrington III/Alamy Stock Photo, **124** (bottom center) Baltimore Sun/Getty Images, **129** (center) ROBIN UTRECHT/Getty Images, **130** (center left) Peter J. Wilson/Shutterstock.com, **130** (center) David Dreambular/Shutterstock.com, **130** (center left) MDay Photography/Shutterstock.com, **130** (center) Cultura RM/Alamy Stock Photo, **130** (bottom) Theo Allofs/Getty Images, **130** (bottom) hepatus/Getty Images, **130** (bottom) eddtoro/Shutterstock.com, **130** (center) Blend Images - REB Images/Getty Images, **130** (center) Tom Wang/Shutterstock.com, **131** (bottom center) Ray Bulson/Getty Images, **134** (bottom) US Army Photo / Alamy Stock Photo, **134** (bottom) macknimal/Shutterstock.com, **136** (bottom) Josh Reynolds/apimages.com, **140** (bottom) Cultura Creative (RF)/Alamy Stock Photo, **142** (bottom) Kevin Horan/Getty Images, **143** (bottom) Ho New/Reuters, **145** (top) Jeff Kolodny Photography, **147** (bottom) Sean Pavone/Shutterstock.com, **151** (bottom) trekandshoot/Shutterstock.com, **154** (center right) STAN HONDA/Getty Images, **156** (top) John Henley/Getty Images, **158** (top) Dua Aftab / EyeEm/Getty Images, **160** (center) Eugenio Marongiu/Shutterstock.com, **160** (center) Studio Intra/Shutterstock.com, **160** (top) Minerva Studio/Shutterstock.com, **160** (center) Olyver Whyte/Shutterstock.com, **161** (center) Mike Harrington/Getty Images, **162** (top center) Reza Estakhrian/Getty Images, **162** (top) Pressmaster/Shutterstock.com, **162** (top) 2p2play/Shutterstock.com, **162** (top left) Mint Images Limited/Alamy Stock Photo, **165** (bottom center) Juan Napurí/Alamy Stock Photo, **172** (bottom) g-stockstudio/Getty Images, **174** (center) Jeff Greenberg/Getty Images, **177** (center) FREDERICK FLORIN/Getty Images, **179** (bottom right) Ariel Skelley/Getty Images, **183** (bottom) Maximilian Stock Ltd./Getty Images, **186** (bottom) Tim Hursley, **191** (center) Lorado/Getty Images, **192** (center) SpeedKingz/Shutterstock.com, **192** (top center) Westend61/Getty Images, **192** (center) Christian Delbert/Shutterstock.com, **192** (center) Adam Gault/Getty Images, **197** (bottom) South_agency/Getty Images, **198** (bottom) Thomas Trutschel/Getty Images, **198** (bottom) Chase Jarvis/Getty Images, **198** (bottom) LightField Studios/Shutterstock.com, **198** (bottom) Mike Focus/Shutterstock.com, **202** (bottom) PNC/Getty Images, **205** (center) Caren Brinkema/Getty Images, **206** (top) Macrovector/Shutterstock.com, **208** (center left) Andrey_Popov/Shutterstock.com, **208** (center) g-stockstudio/Shutterstock.com, **208** (center left) Hero Images/Getty Images, **208** (center) Blend Images - Hill Street Studios/Getty Images, **208** (center) David R. Frazier Photolibrary, Inc./Alamy Stock Photo, **208** (top) anyaivanova/Shutterstock.com, **212** (bottom) Steve Weinrebe/Getty Images, **213** (bottom right) PG Arphexad/Alamy Stock Photo, **216** (bottom left) Agencja Fotograficzna Caro/Alamy Stock Photo Stock Photo, **217** Alex Hinds/Shutterstock.com, **218** (bottom) Spencer Rowell/Getty Images, **241** seeyah panwan/Shutterstock.com, **242** National Geographic Maps

All illustrations Cengage Learning.

AUDIO SCRIPTS

UNIT 1

Track 2, Page 2

Gloria: Hi, Kenji.

Kenji: Hi, Gloria.

Gloria: I'd like to interview you for class.

Kenji: Sure. Go ahead.

Gloria: Kenji, what country are you from?

Kenji: I'm from Japan.

Gloria: How long have you been here in the United States?

Kenji: Six months.

Gloria: Is your family here in the United States?

Kenji: No, my family is in Japan. I came here alone to study English. In Japan, I have my mother and father and one sister.

Gloria: Where do you live?

Kenji: In the student dorms, right here on campus.

Gloria: Are you a new student?

Kenji: Yes. This is my first semester here at school.

Gloria: Do you work?

Kenji: No, I don't.

Gloria: Are you married?

Kenji: No, I'm not. I'm only 21 years old. That's too young to be married.

Gloria: What are your interests?

Kenji: I'm a swimmer. I was on the swim team in high school in my country. They have a great pool here on campus and I swim four or five times a week. And I like photography. I have a good camera and I send a lot of pictures of California back to my family in Japan.

Gloria: What kind of music do you like?

Kenji: I like rock.

Gloria: Do you have a computer?

Kenji: Yes, I have a laptop.

Gloria: Thank you, Kenji.

Track 3, Page 7

1. The cafeteria is on the first floor.
2. The nurse's office is across from the elevator.
3. The bookstore is in the student center.
4. The computer lab is on the third floor.
5. There is a copy machine in the library.
6. The restrooms are next to the stairs.

Track 4, Page 11

1. Students can come to class late.
2. The school gives books to the students; they don't have to buy them.
3. A student can drink coffee in the classroom.
4. Students raise their hands to ask or answer a question.
5. Students speak English in class.
6. It's important to participate in the class.
7. Students are polite and respectful.
8. Students can text their friends during class.
9. There is a quiz or a test every week.
10. There is homework every night.
11. A student can copy another student's homework.
12. I can leave class early every day.

Track 5, Page 12

English Is Frustrating!

Ravi
I work 50 hours a week as a taxi driver, so I talk to people all day. They understand me, but I know I make a lot of mistakes. No one corrects me. My vocabulary is strong. Grammar is my problem. For example, I don't use the simple past. I always say, "I drive him to the office this morning" instead of "I drove him to the office this morning." I'm trying to change little by little.

Maria Luisa
I live in an area where everyone speaks Spanish. I can speak Spanish with my neighbors and friends, at the supermarket, at the bank, and at the post office. I don't work, so it's really difficult to find ways to practice English.

Lian
I understand the grammar and the readings in my class. I think my writing is good, but I'm very nervous when I speak English. I don't want to make any mistakes because people will think that I'm not smart. Also, my pronunciation isn't good. When I speak, people often say, "What? Say that again."

Ketsia
I have been in the United States for one year. I'm studying hard and I'm learning grammar, but the vocabulary is difficult. When I listen, I don't understand many of the words. When I try to read, there are two or three new words in every sentence. I feel bad about it.

UNIT 2

Track 6, Page 19

Hi. My name's Charlie Johnson, and I'm going to tell you a little about myself. I'm 32 years old and I'm single. That's right, I'm not married yet. I'm 6'2" tall and I weigh about 210 pounds. I guess I could lose a little weight. I'm a computer programmer at a large company. I like my job a lot. It's interesting and I can be creative. My hours are long, about 10 hours a day. Sometimes I have to come in on the weekends. But the best part is the salary. I make $70,000 a year. Yeah, it's good. I live in the city, in a one-bedroom apartment. I like it because it's in a good location. It's near public transportation and that's good for me. I don't have a car, but that's okay. I can walk or take a bus to work. And I have a roommate. He spends most of his time sleeping and lying on the couch. He's my cat, Floppy.

Track 7, Page 21

/s/	likes	wants	takes
/z/	owns	drives	studies
/iz/	watches	uses	dances

Track 8, Page 21

1. Lives
2. Walks
3. Drinks
4. Washes
5. Buys
6. Eats
7. Misses
8. Goes
9. Loves

Track 9, Page 26

An American Family

One

This is the Shaw family. Mike Shaw is 42 years old. He is a high school math teacher. Like other public-school teachers, he works nine months a year. His hours are 7:30 a.m. to 3:00 p.m. He earns $60,000 a year and gets excellent benefits. His wife, Maria Shaw, is 39 years old. She is a software engineer. She works at a bank from 9 to 5. She earns $80,000 a year and she has good benefits, too. She's expecting her second child in about a month. She had her first child when she was 31.

Two

Mike Shaw drives to work. It only takes him twenty minutes to get to work. Mrs. Shaw commutes to work. It takes her 40 minutes by train to get to work. At home, she drives a minivan.

Three

The Shaws live in a house with their son, Andy. He's 8 years old. Mr. Shaw's parents also live with them. They're retired. Andy likes living with his grandparents. The Shaws have two pets, a cat and a dog. Their house cost $175,000 and it's old. It has 4 bedrooms, a living room, a kitchen, a family room, and a small yard.

Four

The family eats out every Friday night. They usually eat Chinese or Italian food. After a long, busy week, they like to take a break from cooking.

Five

Every summer, they take a vacation for two weeks. They always go to the beach.

Six

Like many American families, they spend most evenings at home. Maria, Grandma Shaw, and Andy usually sit in the family room and watch TV or a movie. There's another TV upstairs, but everyone likes to sit together in the family room. Grandpa Shaw usually falls asleep in the chair. It's a relaxing evening for everyone except Mike. Mike sits at his desk and corrects his students' homework.

Track 10, Page 28

The Average Community College Student

About 40 percent of all college students in the United States attend community colleges. Community colleges are schools that offer two-year associate degrees and certificates and licenses in a large number of careers, such as paralegal, office assistant, and information technician. The 1,108 community colleges in the United States also train students for new jobs and offer courses in many subjects, including English as a second language.

Most community colleges have open admissions; they accept almost all students who apply. Thirty-six percent of the students are the first ones in their families to attend college. Most students need one or more basic skills courses in reading, writing, or math to prepare them for college-level classes. Sixty-two percent of full-time students work, so full-time schedules are difficult. More than 60 percent of all students attend school part time. The tuition at a community college is more affordable than at a four-year school. The average tuition is $3,520 a year, and more than half of the students receive some financial aid. Many of the students who begin at a community college transfer to a four-year college for their junior and senior years.

Emily is a typical community college student. She attends school part time. As a young woman, she is part of the 56 percent of all community college students who are women. She is 28 years old, the average age of a community college student. Emily's parents and her older brother graduated from high school, but she is the first person in her family to begin college.

Emily works full time in the admissions office in the county hospital. Her goal is to become a registered nurse. She is taking pre-nursing courses and has been accepted to the nursing program. Many of the nurses in the United States receive their degrees from community colleges.

Emily is a second-semester student. During her first semester, she needed to take a course in basic math. This semester, she is taking three courses. In the fall, Emily will attend school full time and work on the weekends. She applied for financial aid and is going to receive $1,500 a semester next year.

Most students take three years or more to complete their degrees at a community college. Emily hopes to have her nursing degree by the time she is 31.

UNIT 3

Track 11, Page 38

A: I don't know where all my money goes.

B: Do you have a budget?

A: No, I don't.

B: Well, have you ever tried to figure out where you spend money?

A: Um, no.

B: Okay. Get a piece of paper. Let's go through your day.

A: Let's see. The first thing I do every morning is stop at the coffee shop. I buy a cup of coffee and a donut there.

B: Alright, how much do you spend there?

A: About $4.

B: And how do you get to work? You only live about a mile from work, right?

A: Well, I usually don't get up in time to walk, so I take the bus. That's $2.

B: Then, what about lunch?

A: I buy my lunch every day. It's about $8 for a sandwich and iced tea.

B: Do you spend any more money on food?

A: Hmm... Just a soda from the vending machine. That's $1.

B: Do you walk home?

A: No, I'm too tired. I pay another $2 for the bus. Oh, and when I get off the bus, I stop and buy a lottery ticket on my way home. That's $1.

B: Well, it's easy to see where all your money goes.

Track 12, Page 42

The Internship

This is Mia, and she is a student at a university in Pennsylvania. She is a junior and is studying design, art, and technology. She wants to design animation for video games. Mia is very excited because she has a summer internship at a company in Washington that produces some of the most popular video games. She knows how to use the necessary software, and she took a couple of courses in computer animation and 3D design. This internship will give her more experience, and maybe the company will hire her after she graduates. Right now, she is excited because her internship is full-time, 40 hours a week, and she will receive $3,200 a month for the three months. She has some financial aid, but tuition at her university is expensive, so the internship will help her pay some of her bills.

It's now six weeks later, and Mia is enjoying her internship. She works with a team of people, and they are designing the characters for a new video game. Mia loves the work, and she is learning how to use different kinds of software and programs. The only problem is her expenses. She knows that she spends too much money, so she has to make some changes. She passes a coffee shop on her way to work and usually buys a cup of coffee. She also buys breakfast and lunch, and little by little, the costs are adding up. At night, Mia wants to relax, so she rents a movie or goes out with the other interns at the company. She loves baseball, so she goes to see the local baseball team, the Seattle Mariners.

Mia needs to save money for next fall's college tuition. To save money, Mia needs to eat breakfast at home. She's trying to think of a few other things that she can do to save money.

Track 13, Page 44

Paying for College

College in the United States is very expensive. However, there are several ways to pay for tuition and fees. To access many of the financial aid opportunities available, students do not need to be US citizens; these opportunities are also open to permanent residents and refugees. High school students can speak with a counselor. People who have finished high school can contact the college that they want to attend. Here are a few options that help students pay for college:

Federal Grants
Many students are eligible for federal grants. Some grants are need-based and help low-income students. Other grants are merit-based and are for students with high grades. Students do not need to pay back grants. They must attend school at least part time. Students can apply for federal grants online.

Scholarships
A scholarship is money that a student receives based on need, high grades, athletic ability, or other criteria. Colleges, local organizations, and businesses give scholarships. Ask the financial aid office or go online to find a list of scholarships that are available.

Tuition Reimbursement
Many businesses help their workers pay for college. In most cases, an employee registers and takes a class at a college. When the employee passes the course, usually with a C grade or better, the employer pays back all or part of the tuition. Check your company's benefits and policies.

Federal Student Loans
The federal government offers student loans with low interest rates. Students do not need to pay back the loan until they finish college. They must pay back the money with interest whether they finish college or not. Students can apply for a federal loan online.

UNIT 4

Track 14, Page 52

1. The Atlantic Ocean
2. The Appalachian Mountains
3. The Mississippi River

Track 15, Page 52

1. Canada
2. Mexico
3. the United States

4. the Rocky Mountains
5. the Grand Canyon
6. Alaska
7. Hawaii
8. the Pacific Ocean
9. Death Valley

Track 16, Page 52

1. There are three countries in North America: Canada, the United States, and Mexico. The United States is in the center. Canada is to the north, and Mexico is to the south.
2. The United States stretches from the Atlantic Ocean on the east to the Pacific Ocean on the west.
3. Many of the major cities in the United States are on the coasts. These cities have excellent seaports.
4. There are two major mountain ranges in the United States; both run from north to south.
5. The Rocky Mountains are very high. Snow covers these mountains most of the year.
6. The Great Lakes are in the northern part of the country.
7. There are many farms and ranches in the central and southern part of the country.
8. The Mississippi River begins in the north and flows south to New Orleans and into the Gulf of Mexico.
9. There are several large deserts in the southwest.
10. There are many beautiful national parks in the west; the Grand Canyon is one of the most popular.

Track 17, Page 57

1. When is it going to rain? It hasn't rained here for two months.
2. Many people are out of work. Stores and factories are closing.
3. Many people don't have a place to live. They are living on the street.
4. That country is very poor. Many people are hungry.
5. It snows and snows. It's snowing again today. When is the snow going to stop?
6. I live in the city. It takes me 30 minutes to drive 5 miles.
7. I don't live in the city. I have to drive to work every day. There aren't any buses in my area.
8. People drink water from plastic bottles. Then, they just throw out the bottles. Most people don't recycle them.

Track 18, Page 58

Montana

Montana is the fourth largest state in the United States. It is located in the northwestern part of the country. On the north, it shares a border with Canada. Montana is divided into two geographic areas. The Rocky Mountains are in the western part of the state. The great plains cover the eastern part. Several important rivers run through Montana. The Missouri river, the second longest river in the United States, begins in Montana.

The western part of Montana receives a lot of rain and snow. Because Montana is so far north, it has very cold winters. There are often heavy snowstorms. In the other seasons, there is a lot of rain. Because the Rocky Mountains are so high, they stop the rain clouds and the eastern part of the state is dry.

With fewer than one million people, Montana has one of the lowest populations in the United States. There are about 50,000 Native Americans living in Montana. Many of the Native Americans live in the state's seven Indian reservations, while others live in small towns and cities throughout the state. Towns and cities are small, and far apart.

Thousands of tourists visit Montana every summer and fall to enjoy the beautiful scenery, to hike in the mountains and to fish in the rivers and lakes. Some tourists stay at the many large horse ranches in the Great Plains. In the winter, skiing is popular in Montana.

Track 19, Page 59

1. How many rivers are there in Montana?
2. How many Native American reservations are there?
3. How much snow is there in the Rocky Mountains?
4. How much industry is there in Montana?
5. How much tourism is there?
6. How much traffic is there in Montana?

Track 20, Page 60

Death Valley

Death Valley National Park is the largest national park in the continental United States. This 3.4 million-acre park in southern California is the lowest, hottest, and driest place in North America. The lowest point is 282 feet (86 meters) below sea level. In the summer, the average temperature is often higher than 120° (49° Celsius), and the highest temperature ever recorded there was 134° (56.6° Celsius). There are some summers when Death Valley receives no rain, and the average yearly precipitation is less than two inches.

The Timbisha Shoshone Tribe of Native Americans has lived in this desert area for hundreds of years.

In 1849, people heard about the discovery of gold in California. Thousands of people began the long trip to the West. This large desert area was so difficult to cross that some travelers looking for gold gave it the name Death Valley.

Today, tourists from all over the United States travel to Death Valley to enjoy its natural beauty. There are over one thousand varieties of plants in this desert, including many kinds of cactuses and flowers. Cactuses, with their interesting and unusual shapes, need very little rain. Their roots are close to the surface of the ground so they can quickly collect any rainfall. A few days after the first rain in the spring, thousands of wildflowers cover the desert.

There are also many animals that have learned to adapt to this hot climate. Most are active at night, sleeping during the day to avoid the hot desert sun. Some animals live their entire lives without drinking any water, getting water from the food they eat.

If you are planning a trip to Death Valley, winter is the best time to visit. The main visitor area has nature exhibits, a museum, and a bookstore. Be sure to watch the informative videos on desert life. After that, you can explore the desert by car, by bike, or on foot. Park rangers offer programs on desert life, the history of Death Valley, and the desert sky at night. If you are planning a trip to Death Valley, don't forget these four essentials: a sun hat, sun block, a lot of water, and a camera.

Track 21, Page 64

I'm going to talk about Tennessee. You spell Tennessee T-E-N-N-E-S-S-E-E. Tennessee is in the southeastern United States. It borders 8 states. On the north, there is Kentucky and Virginia. On the east is North Carolina. On the south, there are three states: Georgia and Alabama, and Mississippi. The Mississippi River is on the west. The two states on the west are Arkansas and Missouri. The capital of Tennessee is Nashville. You spell Nashville N-A-S-H-V-I-L-L-E. The population of Tennessee is 6,300,000. That's 6,300,000 people. Tennessee is a beautiful state to visit and there are many things to do there. If you love music, visit Nashville. Nashville is the capital, but people also call it "Music City, USA." Nashville is the center of the country music industry. You can listen to famous country singers at the Grand Ole Opry House. If you like the outdoors, visit Great Smoky Mountains National Park. More people visit Great Smoky Mountains National Park than any other park in the United States. It's in the eastern part of the state and most of the park is a forest. You can go hiking or fishing or biking or camping. There are several historic areas in the park also. Be careful, there are a lot of bears in the park.

UNIT 5

Track 22, Page 68

1. OK everyone, smile. Say cheese!
2. At the traffic light, turn right onto Main Street.
3. The rain will end this afternoon. We're expecting sunny skies tomorrow with temperatures in the upper 60s.
4. Yes, I'd like a room for three nights. We're arriving on the fourteenth.
5. I'd like a large order of pork fried rice, and a sweet and sour chicken, and two egg rolls.
6. Please tell her that Jake called. That's Jake Parker. My number is 555-7172.
7. I'd like the car for the weekend, March 15th–17th. Do you have a weekend rate? A standard size is fine.

Track 23, Page 69

A: What are you doing?

B: I'm writing a report.

A: What software are you using?

B: I'm using "write now."

A: How's it coming?

B: Very slowly, and it's due tomorrow.

Track 24, Page 70

1. Where is he going?
2. Who are you texting?
3. What is she studying?
4. Who is she calling?
5. What are you listening to?
6. Which game is she playing?
7. What are you ordering?
8. Which site are you using?

Track 25, Page 74

Technology

Technology is changing the way that companies do business. New companies are starting and other companies are losing customers or going out of business. Let's look at four industries and how the internet is changing them.

Airline travel is a good example. In the past, travelers called an airline and made reservations on the phone. Or, they worked with a travel agent to book their flights, their rental car, and their hotel. Today, people are making their own reservations online. They are checking different airlines, dates, and times to find the lowest fares. Before going to the airport, they print their boarding passes or use a phone app to check in.

Movie theaters are still popular, but there are fewer now than there were twenty years ago. People still enjoy watching a movie on a big screen. But, now it's possible to watch a new movie only a few months after it appears in the theater. More people are streaming movies on their computers and tablets. There are no more video rental stores, but some companies now mail movies right to a customer's home.

The taxi business will never be the same. Just a few years ago, people stood on a corner or they called a taxi company on the phone. Now, many people just tap on a phone app and in a few minutes, a ride-sharing driver arrives to pick them up. These drivers have their own cars. Regular taxi companies are losing customers because these new companies offer rides that are cheaper and more convenient. These new companies are also delivering food from local restaurants.

More and more people are shopping online. Sitting at home, people are looking at products, reading reviews, and checking prices. Delivery companies are then bringing the product right to customers' front doors, sometimes later the same day. Each year, the money people spend on online shopping is increasing. How is this affecting stores in towns and malls? Many larger retailers are closing stores in smaller locations. Some companies are going out of business. Other companies are starting online stores.

Technology will continue to change the way we live and the way companies do business. Expect many more changes every year.

Track 26, Page 76

Technology Addiction

"Larry used to be an excellent student. Now, he's falling asleep in class. He's not completing his class work. . . He's always on the computer playing video games. Even at one and two o'clock in the morning, I can hear him playing video games in his room."
—A mother's report

1. An addiction is an activity or a habit that people cannot control and that is harmful to them. Some psychologists are talking about a new kind of addiction—technology addiction. People with a technology addiction can't stop using their electronic devices—checking email and social media, playing video games, chatting, browsing the internet.
2. Do you know any technology addicts? Hours, or even days, pass, and they are still sitting at the computer or looking at their devices. They get upset when someone interrupts them. They feel nervous or depressed when they aren't on the computer, playing a video game, or using the internet. When they finally use their electronic devices again, they feel relieved. They neglect their family and friends.
3. If you think you are becoming addicted to technology, there are steps that you can take to limit your time using electronic devices.
   - Set an alarm for one or two hours. When the alarm goes off, do an offline activity, like reading a book or exercising.
   - Choose a time to disconnect from your electronic devices at night. For example, turn off your computer at 11:00 every night.
   - Do other activities that you enjoy. Go out to lunch with friends, take a class, or exercise.
   - If these ideas don't help, you might need professional help.

UNIT 6

Track 27, Page 83

Surgeon
Cardiologist
Ophthalmologist
Pediatrician
Family doctor
Obstetrician
Dermatologist
Gynecologist
Allergist
Psychiatrist

Track 28, Page 86

D: These are the X-rays, Mr. West. Jimmy has a broken leg. It's a bad break. The nurse is putting ice packs on his leg now because it's swollen quite a lot. We need to wait for the swelling to go down, so we're going to keep him in the hospital for 2 days and then we'll put the cast on.

W: How long is he going to need the cast?

D: For children, it's usually 6 to 8 weeks.

W: He's in a lot of pain.

D: We're going to give him something for the pain in a few minutes. Is he allergic to anything?

W: No, he isn't.

D: He's going to need painkillers for a few days.

W: Can he go to school?

D: Don't worry, he will be back in school next week, but he's going to need crutches.

Track 29, Page 88

1. I'll help you.
2. I'll call her.
3. I'll drive you.
4. I'll make dinner.
5. I'll visit you.
6. I'll take you to the doctor.
7. I'll pick up your prescription.
8. I'll see you tomorrow.

Track 30, Pages 90 & 91

The Accident

There was a bad accident at the intersection of Maple and Central Avenue about ten minutes ago. A woman went past the stop sign and hit another car. A witness who saw the accident immediately called 911. The police and two ambulances were at the scene of the accident a few minutes later.

Luis is lying by the side of the road. His arm is cut very badly. One emergency medical worker is applying a pressure bandage to stop the bleeding. The other technician is talking to him and taking his blood pressure. She's telling Luis that the bleeding is under control. Soon, they're going to take him to the hospital. Luis is going to need thirty or more stitches in his arm.

Two other emergency workers are helping the woman on the stretcher. She is pale and confused. She doesn't know her name and she can't answer any questions. One worker is covering her with a blanket. Because the front windshield of her car is broken, the workers think that she might have a concussion.

A police officer is directing traffic at the scene. Traffic is moving very slowly because everyone wants to look at the accident.

Track 31, Page 92

Asthma

Ricky Garcia is going to play outside with his friends. He is taking out his inhaler and taking two puffs. Five minutes later, he's in the park with his friends, running after a soccer ball. Ricky has asthma, but he knows how to control it.

Asthma is a lung disease. The airways of the lungs become inflamed—that is, red and swollen—making it difficult to breathe normally. A person with asthma may have wheezing, coughing, a tight feeling in the chest, or shortness of breath. Serious breathing problems are called asthma attacks. They can be mild or very serious, requiring immediate medical attention.

Asthma can begin at any age. Childhood asthma, often beginning when a child is younger than ten years old, is one of the most common childhood diseases. Doctors report that the number of young people with asthma is increasing. Over four million children in the US have the disease and the number is growing. It is the number-one cause of absence from school. Asthma is often genetic. If a parent has asthma, the children are more likely to develop the disease. Children with asthma need to be under a doctor's care. They and their parents can learn to understand this disease and to control it.

It is important to find out what "triggers" asthma. In other words, what causes the attack? The most common triggers are exercise, viral infections, stress, and irritants like dust, pollen, or animals. Big cities present added triggers for both children and adults because of air pollution, exhaust from buses and cars, cockroaches, and mold.

There are two kinds of asthma medications—control drugs and quick-relief drugs. Children take control drugs once or twice a day to help prevent asthma attacks. If a child begins to have an asthma attack, he or she needs immediate help, so a quick-relief drug is necessary. This medication is often taken through an inhaler. School-aged children usually carry their inhalers with them. This medication works quickly and children begin to breathe more easily in a few minutes. If a child has a serious asthma attack, he may need emergency care at a hospital or doctor's office.

About half of all children outgrow asthma, and their asthma attacks stop when they are teenagers. However, many people live with the disease into adulthood.

Track 32, Page 96

A: 911. What is your emergency?

B: My daughter ate some of my medication. She's lying on the floor of the bedroom.

A: What is your location?

B: 521 Chestnut Street. In Garfield.

A: Please stay calm. Repeat that address.

B: 521 Chestnut Street, Garfield.

A: Stay on the line. Help is on the way. How old is your daughter?

B: She's four. Oh, my baby.

A: Where is your daughter now?

B: She's on the floor, in my bedroom.

A: Is she breathing?

B: Yes, she's breathing, but she isn't moving.

A: What kind of medicine did she take?

B: It was medication for high blood pressure.

A: How many did she take?

B: I don't know. I don't know.

A: Ma'am, the ambulance is on the way. Is your door unlocked?

B: No, no it's locked.

A: Unlock the door. Do that right now, unlock the door.

B: Yes, I unlocked it.

A: When the medics arrive, give them the bottle of medication.

B: Yes, yes, I will. Oh, the police are here.

A: OK. The ambulance is right behind them. You can hang up now.

UNIT 7

Track 33, Page 99

1. busier than
2. taller than
3. larger than
4. noisier than
5. friendlier than
6. farther than
7. rainier than
8. higher than
9. sunnier than

Track 34, Page 102

1. the busiest
2. the tallest
3. the largest
4. the noisiest
5. the friendliest
6. the farthest
7. the rainiest
8. the highest
9. the sunniest

Track 35, Page 106

Chicago, Illinois; Los Angeles, California; and New York, New York are the three largest cities in the United States. New York is the largest of these three cities, with a population of 8,537,673 residents. New York includes the five boroughs: Manhattan, Brooklyn, Queens, the Bronx, and Staten Island. New York is one of the most diverse cities in the world. Approximately 29% of the residents are of Hispanic origin. Of the three cities, New York had the lowest unemployment in 2010, with an unemployment rate of 4.6%. Household income is the income of all the people living in the same house. The median household income in New York is $55,191. Homes in New York are expensive. If you're looking for a home in New York, plan to spend about $425,000.

Commuting to work takes more than thirty minutes in all three cities. Traveling to work takes the average person 39.9 minutes in New York. Approximately 56.9% of workers in New York drive to work. Although it is very expensive to drive into the city and parking is difficult, less than half of the workers in New York use public transportation.

There is always something to do in New York City. There are more than 115 museums. The Metropolitan Museum of Art is one of the most visited museums in the world. Another popular tourist destination is the Statue of Liberty. The weather in these three cities is very different. New York receives about 49.9 inches of rain a year and about 25.1 inches of snow. It has a lot fewer days of sunshine than Los Angeles. Los Angeles receives about 284 days of sun a year. New York receives about 224 days of sun.

Track 36, Page 108

The Busiest Airports

Three of the busiest airports in the world are in the United States. Los Angeles Airport (LAX) is located in Los Angeles, California. O'Hare Airport (ORD) is in Chicago, Illinois, and Hartsfield Atlanta International Airport (ATL) is in Atlanta, Georgia. These three are the busiest airports in the US because of the large number of passengers that pass through them every year. In addition, these airports move a great deal of cargo (packages, equipment, and so on).

LAX was established in 1928. It is now one of the busiest airports in the world, with 81 passenger and cargo airlines that use the airport. Each year, more than 59 million passengers travel through LAX. About 59,000 employees work at the airport. The employees work at a number of places throughout the airport, including airline counters, coffee shops, bakeries, and the 95 stores where passengers can shop. LAX is a pet-friendly airport with a small pet park where passengers can walk their dogs.

Each year, more than 77 million passengers use O'Hare, another one of the busiest airports in the world, with 70 airlines using its facilities. O'Hare was established in 1945. Today, many frequent fliers know O'Hare because flights often stop in Chicago on the way to other parts of the country or the world. Because so many passengers spend significant time in the airport, O'Hare offers a number of services, such as a hair salon, a children's museum, an athletic club, and a post office. About 52,000 employees operate the airport's 215 restaurants and stores.

Established in 1925, Hartsfield has become the busiest airport in the world. Over 104 million passengers pass through the airport each year. Forty-five passenger and cargo airlines use the airport. More than 63,000 employees work for the airlines and the 263 restaurants and shops. In fact, the airport is the largest employer in Georgia. To help people move from terminal to terminal, or from a terminal to one of the 30,000 parking spaces, the airport has an underground train, which connects all the airport terminals.

UNIT 8

Track 37, Page 116

1. changed
2. rented
3. looked
4. needed
5. liked
6. wanted
7. helped
8. called
9. lived
10. painted
11. signed
12. waited

Track 38, Page 116

1. He lived in a small apartment.
2. He looked at many apartments.
3. He filled out a rental application.
4. He signed a lease.
5. He packed all his things.
6. He borrowed a van.

Track 39, Page 117

Base Form	Past	Base Form	Past
be	was/were	grow	grew
become	became	have	had
begin	began	hear	heard
bite	bit	know	knew
break	broke	leave	left
bring	brought	lose	lost
buy	bought	make	made
come	came	meet	met
cost	cost	pay	paid
do	did	put	put
drink	drank	read	read
drive	drove	ring	rang
eat	ate	run	ran
fall	fell	say	said
feel	felt	see	saw
fight	fought	sell	sold
find	found	send	sent
fly	flew	sit	sat
forget	forgot	sleep	slept
get	got	speak	spoke
give	gave	spend	spent
go	went	steal	stole

Base Form	Past	Base Form	Past
take	took	wake	woke
teach	taught	wear	wore
tell	told	write	wrote
think	thought		

Track 40, Page 120

OK, this is my timeline. I started in 2010 because in that year I graduated from high school and, a few months after that, I found my first job. I worked and I saved money and, in 2012, I bought a car. I already had my license, but I didn't have a car. The next year, that's 2013, I went back to Poland to visit my family and my friends. My grandparents live in Poland and it was my grandmother's 75th birthday, so everyone went back to Poland to celebrate. In 2015, I found another job—a better job—as a store manager. I met Eva, my wife, in 2015 too, and we got married in 2016. After we got married, the next year, in 2017, we moved to Chicago and that's where we live today, in Chicago.

Track 41, Page 122

A: We might move… again! When I was in my country, I lived in the same house for 22 years. I've been in the United States for seven years and I've moved four times. And we might move again.

B: Four times?

A: Yes. Can you believe it? The first move was from Puerto Rico to Florida. My father got a job offer in Florida, in Tampa. My family and I moved to an apartment in Tampa. I met Diego a year later and we got married. We stayed in Tampa and we rented a one-bedroom apartment near my family. Our neighbors were really nice, but we only stayed there for a year.

B: Why did you move?

A: The apartment building was old and it had a lot of problems. The landlord didn't fix things. The air conditioning was always broken. One time in the summer, we didn't have air conditioning for a week. So, we moved to an apartment in Largo. We liked Largo. We were only a few blocks from the beach and for me, it was only twenty minutes to drive to work. We lived there for two years.

B: So, why did you move back to Tampa?

A: That was an easy decision. We had a baby! Ian is three now. I needed to go back to work and we needed someone to take care of the baby. So, we moved back here, to Tampa, closer to my parents. Mom takes care of Ian.

B: So you've been here for three years.

A: Right. But, now we have to decide what to do. Diego's company has offered him a promotion, but it's in Pensacola. It's a big salary increase, so we could buy a house. And I'm pregnant again.

B: You're pregnant! Oh, that's wonderful!

A: Diego wants to move and take the promotion. I can stay home for a few years and go back to work when the kids are in school. But Pensacola is so far from my family, about 500 miles from here. I'm not sure what to do.

B: You have lots of decisions to make.

Track 42, Page 124

Tiny Living

How much space do you need? If you think that you can live in a small, efficient space, maybe a tiny home is right for you. Tiny homes are affordable alternatives to normal-sized homes. There are tiny house communities from California to Texas to Georgia. The American Tiny House Association can give you more information. There are also TV shows about building tiny homes.

Tiny homes come in many styles. Owners can buy and use construction plans or they can customize their tiny homes. Some homes look very modern, but others look like most other homes—just smaller. One thing that tiny homes have in common is that they are very small, but they have the essentials: a place to sleep, a kitchen, a refrigerator, a bathroom, a compact washer/dryer, and an open living space. Others have outdoor space or a balcony. If a person chooses to live in a tiny home, storage space is very important. There is storage everywhere.

There are pros and cons to owning a tiny home. One of the main advantages is the cost. It is cheap to own a tiny home, and the utility bills are lower, especially if the home has solar power. Tiny homes are convenient if an owner decides to move. That is why some tiny homes are on wheels. However, if your home is on wheels, you need a pickup truck to move it. Another advantage is that it takes less time to clean, but you must be organized. A tiny home can be uncomfortable if it is messy. Finally, another pro is that a couple will spend more time together. A con is that you will lose some of your privacy.

In Detroit, Michigan, a program is offering tiny homes to low-income single residents. This program helps individuals who have had hard times because of homelessness, prison, or low income. Any person with a steady job, even at minimum wage, can apply for a new tiny home. Each home has a kitchen, a bathroom, a living room, a backyard, and a washer-dryer. Some homes have separate bedrooms too. The homes cost between $40,000 and $50,000. The residents pay $1 per square foot, so a home of 250 square feet will cost $250 a month. Similar tiny home communities for low-income residents are available in other states.

Track 43, Page 128

Conversation 1

Owner: Hello, Mike Paulis speaking.

Tenant: Hi, Mr. Paulis. This is Sam Jenkins from apartment 205. Our air conditioning isn't working.

Owner: Oh, no… What's your thermostat set at?

Tenant: 75 degrees. It's 82 in here now.

Owner: I see. Will you be home this morning?

Tenant: No, I'm working today.

Owner: Well, tomorrow is Saturday. Will you be home?

Tenant: Yes, I'll be home all day.

Owner: Great. I can come tomorrow morning around 10 o'clock.

Tenant: OK, thanks. See you tomorrow morning.

Conversation 2

Owner: Nora Colwell.

Tenant: Hello, Ms. Colwell. This is Sarah Darmon from apartment 4. I called you yesterday, about the freezer. It isn't working, all the food in the freezer went bad.

Owner: Really? That refrigerator is almost new.

Tenant: Actually, I looked at the date on the side of the door. The refrigerator is 15 years old.

Owner: Hmm. Well, will you be home this morning?

Tenant: Yes, I'll be home.

Owner: I'll come up this morning then.

Tenant: Ms. Colwell, you told me that yesterday and you never came. I had to throw out all the food in the freezer.

Owner: Well, that is a problem. I'll be there today at 9.

Tenant: OK, I'll be waiting.

UNIT 9

Track 44, Page 130

drought
earthquake
flood
forest fire
heat wave
hurricane
snowstorm / blizzard
tornado
volcanic eruption

Track 45, Page 132

1. How deep was the water?
   It was six feet deep.
2. How strong was the wind?
   It was a hundred miles per hour.
3. Were you in Texas during the drought?
   Yes, I was.
4. How long was the drought?
   It was five months long.
5. Was there any rain?
   No, there wasn't.
6. Where were the tornadoes?
   They were in Nebraska.
7. Were you at home?
   No, I wasn't. I was in my car.
8. How many tornadoes were there?
   There were four.
9. When was the earthquake?
   It was last year.
10. How strong was the earthquake?
    Thankfully, it wasn't strong.
11. Were the children in school?
    Yes, they were.
12. Were any children hurt?
    No, they weren't.
13. Where was the forest fire?
    It was in the hills near my town.
14. Was there a lot of snow during the blizzard?
    Yes, there was.
15. Were schools closed for a long time?
    No, they weren't. Schools opened the day after the storm.

Track 46, Page 133

1. Did you see the tornado?
2. Did you watch the storm on TV?
3. Did you evacuate?
4. Did you have any damage?
5. Did you feel the earthquake?
6. Did you lose power?

Track 47, Page 138

A: That was a really bad hurricane you had last month.

B: I know, it was our first hurricane since we moved here to North Carolina. We thought it was terrible, but the old-time residents told us it was just an average one.

A: How much warning did you have?

B: We got nothing but warnings. 24 hours a day, all day for about a week. The radio, the TV, the newspapers—the news was nonstop.

A: So, what did you do to get ready?

B: Well, we had to get everything out of the yard. We put the yard furniture, the barbecue grill, the garbage cans, everything into the garage. If we didn't, they could fly through a window during the hurricane. And, we bought lots of food, canned food, in case we didn't have power for cooking. We had to buy batteries for flashlights and radios, and they told us to buy water, lots and lots of water. And, we filled the bathtub with water too. We also bought a power saw.

A: A power saw?

B: Yes. Hurricanes knock down trees. In a bad hurricane, two or three trees might fall in your yard. Everyone around here has power saws to cut them up.

A: How bad was the hurricane?

B: I thought it was terrible. The rain was so heavy we couldn't see out the windows. The wind was about 80 miles an hour and it reached 100 miles an hour at times. It knocked down the power lines and we didn't have electricity for two days. We were lucky, only one tree came down in the backyard, but our neighbor had a tree come down right through his roof into one of the bedrooms upstairs. He had water all over in all the rooms.

A: So, did you have to evacuate?

B: No, we stayed in the house. For this storm, most people stayed in their homes.

A: Were you scared?

B: I was so scared, most of the time I stayed in the bathroom. I thought any minute something was going to come flying through a window or that a tree was going to fall on our house. My husband was more relaxed, he lit candles and listened to the news. We have a battery-operated radio.

A: So, are you glad you moved to North Carolina?

B: Well, we really like it here but these hurricanes... I don't know, maybe we'll get used to them.

Track 48, Page 140

Tornadoes

A tornado, also called a twister, is a violent, spinning cloud that reaches from the ground up to storm clouds in the sky. Most tornadoes are weak, lasting only a few minutes, and have winds of less than 110 mph. But the strongest tornadoes can last more than an hour and have wind speeds of 200 mph or more. They can destroy houses in seconds, turn over cars, and pull people, trees, and furniture into the air.

The United States has more tornadoes than any other country in the world. In a typical year, there are 800 to 1,000 tornadoes in the United States. Most occur in the middle of the country. Tornadoes form when warm and cool air meet. In the Midwest, the warm air from the Gulf of Mexico often meets the cold air from Canada.

Tornadoes can occur at any time of year, but the usual tornado season is from March through May. Tornadoes form most often in the afternoon and early evening. There is often little warning of a tornado. People who live in the Midwest know the signs of tornado activity. The sky becomes a dark, often greenish color. Dark clouds appear in the sky and there is often large hail. Suddenly, there is a loud sound, like a train or a jet plane. Sometimes, tornadoes occur in groups. Two, three, five, ten, or more tornadoes can form over a large area.

One of the strongest tornadoes in history hit Joplin, Missouri, on May 22, 2011. Twenty minutes before the tornado, sirens rang, warning of the tornado. Some people heard the warnings, but others did not. The tornado was one mile wide and destroyed everything it touched, including homes, businesses, churches, the hospital, and the high school. The tornado killed 158 people and injured 1,150 others. One family ran down into their basement. Twenty minutes later, when they came up from the basement, nothing was left of their house. At the local Home Depot, the tornado lifted off the roof. According to local reports, between twenty-eight and thirty people in the back of the store survived, but the eight people in the front of the store were killed.

The safest place to be during a tornado is in a safety shelter, a small underground room that some people build to protect their families.

Other safe places are basements or a first-floor bathroom, which is often the most solid room in the house.

UNIT 10

Track 49, Page 147

Jack: Cindy, look what came in the mail today. My brother's wedding invitation.

Cindy: What a beautiful invitation!

Jack: I'm really looking forward to the wedding. We haven't seen my family for a while.

Cindy: I know. It's hard. All of them live in Texas and we're here in New York.

Jack: The wedding is in six weeks. We have a lot to do before then.

Cindy: We do! You have the airline reservations, right?

Jack: Yes, that's all set. I also have a ticket for Calli. The airlines said that, although she's only two, she still needs a ticket. By the way, those tickets were expensive. Thankfully, we don't need hotel reservations.

Cindy: Yes, I'm glad we're staying with your sister. Did you rent a car for the week?

Jack: No, I have to do that.

Cindy: Remember, we don't need to rent a car seat. We're bringing one with us.

Jack: How about your dress? Did you find one yet that you like?

Cindy: No! I already bought a dress for Calli, but I still have to find a dress for me.

Jack: Cindy, you only have a few more weeks! And I still have to buy a pair of black dress shoes. What else do we need to do?

Cindy: Let's make a list. I don't want to forget anything, especially for Calli. Number one, we have to remember her favorite blanket. We also need…

Track 50, Page 148

1. They have to pack.
2. She has to bring her dress.
3. They have to leave early.
4. We have to drive to the airport.
5. She has to take her ID.
6. He has to show his boarding pass.

Track 51, Page 148

1. I have to go to the laundromat.
2. She has to work overtime tomorrow.
3. They have to do their homework.
4. I have to pay my phone bill.
5. He has to get gas on the way home.
6. She has to make a doctor's appointment.

Track 52, Page 149

C: Hannah, your life is really going to change after you get married.

H: Change? Of course, it's going to change. It's going to be perfect.

C: You have stars in your eyes.

H: What do you mean?

C: How old are you?

H: I'm 20.

C: And, you live with your mom and dad, right?

H: Until June 15th, our wedding date.

C: Hannah, who cleans the house now?

H: My mom does. But I clean my room.

C: And, what about dinner? Who takes care of it?

H: Well, my Dad cooks and my mom washes the dishes.

C: Ok. Who does the food shopping?

H: Usually my mom does.

C: And who pays the bills?

H: I'm not sure. I guess both my parents pay the bills. I pay my cellphone bill.

C: Hmm. And, who does the laundry?

H: My mom.

C: Does Randy live with his parents too?

H: Yes.

C: And how old is he?

H: He's 21.

C: Do you and Randy ever talk about your life after you get married? Who's going to cook, clean, and do the laundry?

H: No… I'm sure we'll do everything together.

C: Oh, boy. Are you sure you're ready to get married?

H: Of course, we are. We're in love!

Track 53, Page 154

I work as a Transportation Security Officer. Everyone calls us the TSA. It's a US government agency, and we manage the screening at airports. I am a veteran, and I wanted to continue working for the government after I completed my military service, so I decided to apply for this job.

I'm originally from Haiti, but for this job I had to be a US citizen. Luckily, I am a naturalized citizen. I had to complete an application online and answer a lot of questions. After that, I had to pass a medical examination, a background check, a credit check, and a drug screening. I also had to be 18 years old, but that wasn't a problem. I was 30 years old when I applied. Four months after I applied, I got the job.

This is my fifth year as a TSA officer. I like my job because it's different everyday. Sometimes I operate the screening equipment. I have to look at all the bags when they go through the x-ray machine. I have to look for dangerous materials that passengers are not allowed to take on the plane. If I see something, I must tell another agent. That agent must call the passenger and open the bag for inspection. If we find items that are not allowed, like large bottles of shampoo, water, fruit, or dangerous objects, we take them. Sometimes, we have to stop passengers and interview them in a private room. Other times, I watch the passengers go through the metal detector. If I see something, I must use a metal detector wand and search the person. If the passenger is a woman, a female agent must search the passenger.

My favorite job is checking IDs because I can talk to the passengers. I have to be polite and check all IDs carefully. Sometimes, I have to answer a lot of questions. Funny things happen, too. One time, a man took off his belt and came through the metal detector. When he raised his arms, his pants fell down. Everybody had a good laugh that day.

Track 54, page 156

Attending a Wedding

You get a wedding invitation from a friend, and you are excited because this is the first American wedding you will attend. Weddings are different from culture to culture. What are the rules of etiquette for American wedding guests?

First of all, respond to the invitation as soon as possible. The bride and groom have to pay for each guest, so it is important to notify them that you will attend. Most wedding invitations include a response card. If you cannot attend, it is polite to call the couple if you are close friends.

Read the invitation's envelope carefully. Can you take a guest? Maybe your invitation says, "Marianna Lopez and Guest." That means that you can bring only one guest.

What should you wear to the wedding? Check the invitation for details. For a "black tie" wedding, women wear elegant dresses—called evening gowns—and men wear tuxedos. "Semiformal attire" is usually a dress for women and a suit for men. Remember, female guests should not wear white. The guests should be looking at the bride—not at the other guests.

What rules should you follow at the wedding ceremony? The most important rule is to be on time. You should arrive about fifteen minutes before the wedding begins. If you're late, you should enter quietly and find a seat. If something happens during the ceremony that you do not understand, wait until after the ceremony and ask someone to explain.

What kind of gift should you buy? Most guests at American weddings do not have to worry about choosing a gift. Many American couples use a wedding gift registry. The couple goes to a store or online to register for their gifts. They decide what they need and share their registry information with their guests. The guests look at the registry at the store or online, find out which items are still available, and buy their gift for the couple. Then, the store delivers the gift. You don't have to bring the gift to the ceremony. In fact, it is more convenient if you mail the gift.

Couples also appreciate gifts of money. In fact, money is the most popular wedding gift. Place cash or a check in a card that is specially made for money or in a regular greeting card, and put it in an envelope.

Have fun at the wedding!

UNIT 11

Track 55, Page 163

1. Could you please answer the phone?
2. Would you please bring this to the mail department?
3. Would you please make five copies of this form?
4. Could you please repair the printer?

Track 56, Page 169

1. Maybe I'll take a break.
2. I need the number of the technology department. Please look up the number.
3. There's no smoking in this building.
4. Your interview is tomorrow and your hair is too long. You need a haircut.
5. Your license is expired. You need to renew it.
6. Tomorrow is Labor Day. The company is closed.

Track 57, Page 170

One

S: Good morning Carla, Tommy. Carla, how's your mother? Is she still in the hospital?

C: She's much better. Thanks.

S: Glad to hear it. Tommy, could you please work an extra hour today? Carla needs to leave an hour early.

T: Sure!

S: Thank you.

Two

S: Mr. Samuels, we send the lab results to your doctor.

Mr. S: Do I get a copy?

S: No, we don't send you a copy. Let me give you a card. If you would like a copy of your results, you have to call the number on the card. The doctor will have the test results in three days. If the doctor doesn't call you, you should call her.

Three

S: Randy, this is Sharon Taylor at County General. We sent you our weekly order, but I'd like to add two boxes of latex gloves. Yes, five hundred count. Yes. Could you please add two boxes to the order? Thanks.

Four

S: Good morning Ms. Parks, you are here for a blood test, correct? Did you eat anything this morning?

Ms. P: Yes, I just had breakfast. I had a donut and coffee.

S: Oh. Ms. Parks, this is a fasting blood test. You can't eat or drink anything for twelve hours before the test. The doctor didn't tell you?

Ms. P: I don't think so. I don't recall.

S: Don't worry, we can do the test tomorrow. You have to come back tomorrow morning at 8 o'clock and you can't eat or drink anything after 8 o'clock tonight.

Five

S: Ms. Chavan, we have to make a copy of your insurance card. You have Red Lion insurance, so you only have to make a $10 co-pay. Sam, could you please make a copy of this insurance card. Please put it in Ms. Chavan's file.

Sam: Sure!

S: Thank you.

Six

S: Doug, you were good with that little boy. He was really scared about having a blood test, but he came out of your lab smiling.

D: Thanks!

Track 58, Page 172

How to Lose Your Job in 5 Easy Steps

1. Don't worry about time policies. If you have a half hour for lunch, no one is going to say anything if you take an extra ten minutes. If work begins at 8:30, arrive at 8:45. You can always blame the heavy traffic. No one is counting how many breaks you take. If you have two breaks, no one will notice if you take three.
2. Blame your coworkers if you miss a deadline or do a poor job on a project. Be sure that nothing is your fault. If the boss complains about your work, explain to him that "Randy gave me the wrong directions." Or say, "I did my part. Tom didn't do his part."
3. Don't worry about the office dress code. You should wear what you like to work. Be comfortable. You don't need to wear the traditional dress style of the older employees. Shorts, sweatpants, and T-shirts are always appropriate.
4. Post your feelings about work online. You can trust all your friends. No one will share your posts. Your boss and your company don't follow what is happening online. They will never see posts like these:

   "My boss always complains about everyone. But no one ever sees him working."

   "I lied to my boss today. I told her I had a big exam and needed the day off. Hah! She believes anything!"
5. Call other employees by nicknames. Give each employee a funny name based on their personality or their habits. If a coworker eats candy all the time, call him *Jelly Beans*. He'll think it's funny.

UNIT 12

Track 59, Page 178

Henry is a single father with two children. His son, Diego, is 11 and his daughter, Jessica, is 10. He drops his children off at school at 8 o'clock. After he drops off the children, Henry stops at a coffee shop for a large cup of coffee. Then, he drives to work at the bank. His children get home from school at 3:15, but Henry doesn't get out of work until 4. As soon as the children get home from school, they call their father. Henry gets home from work at 4:30. The family eats dinner at 6:00. After they eat dinner, Henry helps the children with their homework. They can watch TV or play video games when they finish their homework. Henry relaxes or watches sports on TV after the kids go to bed. He goes to sleep at 11:30.

Track 60, Page 178

1. After he drops off the children, Henry stops at a coffee shop.
2. As soon as the children get home from school, they call their father.
3. After they eat dinner, Henry helps the children with their homework.
4. When they finish their homework, they can play video games.
5. Before he goes to sleep, Henry watches TV.

Track 61, Page 179

Mark: You get a call every day at 3:15, don't you?

Henry: Yes, that's my son. He's 11. My daughter is 10. They walk home together after school. My son has to call me as soon as they walk in the door.

Mark: Oh, I see. My boys are still little. They stay at daycare until I pick them up at 4:30.

Henry: Big kids, little kids... Childcare is a challenge when you're working.

Track 62, Page 180

I am a stay-at-home mom. My little girl, Emma, is one and a half years old and she keeps me busy all day. I'm planning to stay home until she is two years old. Emma wakes up at 7:00. As soon as she wakes up, she wants a bottle. After her bottle, I give her breakfast. Then, I get her dressed. From 9:00 to 10:30, I clean the house and do laundry. She plays and follows me around the house. At 10:30, we walk to the park. There are lots of other mothers and fathers with their children at the playground. I have a chance to relax and talk to other parents. We are home by 12:00. I give Emma lunch and a bottle. Then, she's ready for her nap. She sleeps from 1:00 to 3:00. At 4:00, I put her in her car seat. We go shopping or I take her to the library. She loves books and I check out five or six books a week. We are home by 5. When we get home, I start dinner. Emma plays on the kitchen floor with the pots and pans. My husband walks in the door at 6 and Emma can't wait to see him. He plays with her until dinner. We have dinner at 7. After dinner, I give Emma a bath. Then, my husband reads her a bedtime story. She's in bed by 8.

Track 63, Page 184

Ava and her husband Matt have two children, Timmy and David. Timmy is three years old and David is five. The mornings are always busy because Ava and Matt are working parents. At 5:45, the alarm clock rings and Matt jumps out of bed. He uses the bathroom first and takes a shower. When he goes back into the bedroom, he wakes up Ava. After Ava gets up, she wakes up the children, then starts to make breakfast. Matt puts on a movie for the boys because they're sleepy and the movie gives them a chance to wake up slowly. Matt gets dressed and eats breakfast. Before he leaves for work, he kisses the children and Ava goodbye. After Matt leaves, Ava eats breakfast with Timmy and David. After breakfast, she gets dressed and gets the boys ready for the day. Then, she takes them out to the car and the boys climb into their car seats. Ava buckles the boys into their seats, then drives to the daycare center which is about fifteen minutes from the house. As soon as she drops off the boys, Ava drives to work. She's a hairstylist. She's often a little late for work, but her customers understand because they are parents, too.

Track 64, Page 186

Before- and After-School Care

Childcare is one of the biggest concerns and biggest expenses for working families today. Most single parents work. In 61% of families with two parents, both parents work. About half of school-age children in the United States need care before and/or after school. There is after-school care for many children, but many others go home to empty houses.

In many families with working parents, grandparents and other family members are the ones who take children to school and pick them up after classes end. This type of care works for families because children are comfortable with their relatives and have time to play, talk, and do homework. This care is often free. In some families, one person with a small child may stay home and watch the children of other family members. In these families, the parents often pay something for the childcare. For other families, neighbors and friends help with after-school care.

About 25% of children attend after-school programs. The majority of these programs are at public schools. The others are at YMCAs, Boys and Girls Clubs, local recreation centers, and religious organizations. For programs at other locations, a van or bus is needed to pick up the children and bring them to the site. When programs do not offer this service, children of working parents do not have the transportation they need.

As of 2018, more than ten million children attend after-school programs, but there are not enough programs. Over nineteen million more children would participate if there were programs in their area.

The cost of an after-school program varies depending on the neighborhood where the program is located and what kinds of activities are provided. Average costs can range between $50 and $100 per week, for one child. Many families qualify for government help to pay for these programs. Also, these programs offer tax advantages for many families when they file their income taxes.

It's not always easy to find information about after-school programs. Parents can ask the child's school about programs in the area, or call their local recreation department because many offer their own programs. Another great resource is the YMCA or Boys and Girls Clubs, which often have activities for middle school and high school students. Parents can also go online to see if any local faith organizations provide care. One of the best sources of information is other parents. Talking to coworkers, neighbors, and the parents of your children's friends can be very helpful.

Good after-school care can help parents relax at work. Most parents are happy with the afterschool programs their children attend. These programs offer snacks, physical activities, help with homework, and STEM (science, technology, engineering, and math) activities. Studies show that children who attend good after-school programs have better school attendance, better behavior, and better grades.

UNIT 13

Track 65, Page 193

Officer: Wow! The robber really made a mess...

Jonathan: Uh, Officer... My apartment always looks like this.

Officer: Oh, excuse me. Now, where were we? What time did you leave this morning?

Jonathan: I left at 8:30.

Officer: Did you lock the door?

Jonathan: Yes, I'm sure I locked the door when I left. I was in a hurry, but I know that I locked the door.

Officer: Did you lock the windows, too? The windows are open now.

Jonathan: Of course, I did. Well, maybe I didn't. I don't remember. I was late for work and it was very hot when I went to bed last night. I opened the windows before I went to bed, but I overslept. Maybe I forgot.

Officer: OK, sir. What time did you come home?

Jonathan: I came home at 6:00 pm.

Officer: When did you notice that something was wrong?

Jonathan: Well, as soon as I walk in the door, I usually put my keys on the table by the door. Well, the table was gone and the keys fell on the floor.

Officer: What else?

Jonathan: I walked into the living room and there was a big empty space where the TV used to be. My TV was gone. It was a new flat-screen TV. My friends were coming over this weekend to watch the soccer game. And my video game system and all my video games are gone.

Officer: Now, we'll have to dust for fingerprints. Did you touch anything else besides the door when you came in?

Jonathan: I opened the refrigerator and my leftover Chinese food was gone, too!

Officer: Are you sure that you didn't eat it?

Jonathan: I'm positive. I was saving that food for dinner tonight.

Officer: I'll call the detectives and they will check for fingerprints. Then you'll have to fill out a report.

Jonathan: Thank you, Officer.

Track 66, Page 194

1. Before I left my house, I locked the door.
2. When we went on vacation, we stopped the mail.
3. She turned on the alarm before she left her apartment.
4. They closed all the windows before they left.
5. I called the police as soon as I saw the broken door.
6. I dialed 911 when I heard a noise downstairs.
7. After someone robbed their house, they bought a dog.

Track 67, Page 194

A: You don't look very happy. What's the matter?

B: When I was at work, someone broke into my house.

A: Really? How did they get in?

B: I forgot to lock the windows before I went to work.

A: Oh. What did they take?

B: They took my computer, the TV, and my camera.

A: Did you call the police?

B: I called the police as soon as I walked in the door.

Track 68, Page 200

1. This is Spike, and he's a burglar. Last night, he tried to rob a jewelry store, but the police caught and arrested him. Spike likes to break into homes, jewelry stores, and cars, but he is not good at his profession.
2. Late last night, Spike and his girlfriend, Tina, drove downtown. While Tina was driving, Spike put on a mask, a black hat, and a pair of gloves.
3. When they arrived at a jewelry store, Tina parked on the side of the store where it was dark. Spike got out of the car.
4. Spike broke a window with a towel and his fist. He didn't make a lot of noise.
5. As soon as he broke the window, he climbed into the store.
6. After he got into the store, he looked around at the jewelry. He decided to take some expensive watches, necklaces, and rings. He put the jewelry into his bag.
7. While he was robbing the store, Tina was waiting in the car. She was watching for the police.
8. Spike was getting ready to leave when he saw some leftover pizza on a table. "I'm a little hungry," he thought. When Spike picked up the pizza, he dropped his bag of jewelry.
9. As soon as the bag fell on the floor, an alarm rang.
10. When Spike heard the alarm, he grabbed the bag and got out of the store. When Tina heard the alarm, she started the car and tried to drive away.
11. When Spike got out of the store, he saw a police car coming down the street and he began to run.
12. As soon as the police saw Spike, one officer got out of the car and chased him. The other officer stayed in the car.
13. The other officer blocked Tina's car before she could drive away.

14. While Spike was running, he took off his mask and hat, but he forgot to take off his gloves.
15. Spike stood on a corner with a group of other men, but as soon as the police officer saw his gloves and the necklace in his pocket, he arrested Spike.
16. The police officers then arrested Tina. They handcuffed both of them and put them in the back of the police car.

Track 69, Page 202

Serving on a Jury

One of the responsibilities of a US citizen is to serve on a jury. A jury is a group of ten to twelve citizens who decide if an accused criminal is guilty or not guilty of a crime. The jury members listen to evidence and make a decision. Someone accused of a crime has the right to a jury trial. This right is written in the United States Constitution, a document of the laws and government of the United States of America.

How does a county select people for jury duty? First, the county sends a summons, or written letter, to a citizen in the mail. There is a random selection of registered voters, licensed drivers, and taxpayers. The citizen must reply to the summons. If the citizen doesn't reply, that citizen will have to pay a fine.

What are the requirements to serve on a jury? First of all, the person must be a US citizen and a resident of the county. The person must be 18 years of age and be physically and mentally able to serve on the jury. The person must not have any criminal convictions, but can still serve if they have traffic violations.

Some people do not want to serve on a jury, but the court will only excuse people for certain reasons, such as if the person is a high school student, the person has to take care of someone who cannot take care of him/herself, or if the person does not understand enough English to follow the trial.

If the court selects you for a jury, there are rules that you must follow:

- Do not discuss the case until you hear all of the evidence.
- Do not investigate the case yourself.
- Do not discuss the case with family members or anyone else.
- Listen to the judge's instructions.

If you are selected to sit on a jury, the average trial is one to three days, but trials may be longer. Also, it is possible that you will report for jury duty, but you will not be selected for a trial. The county calls many people, and only a small number can serve on a trial. If, after one or two days, the court does not call you to trial, your service is complete for at least one year.

UNIT 14

Track 70, Page 213

Jessica is a student at a community college. She's 20 years old, and she lives at home. Right now, she's taking the last level of English classes. She's also taking a math class and a biology class. When she completes these classes, she's going to begin the physical therapy assistant program. School is expensive. Before she begins the program, Jessica is going to apply for financial aid. When she attends classes, Jessica is not going to work. She's going to go to school full time. Her parents are going to help her with her expenses. Jessica plans to complete the program in two years. Before she graduates, Jessica is going to get a lot of experience because all students work in physical therapy practices two afternoons a week. Jessica will apply for a job before she graduates. The college helps all the students find jobs. After she graduates, Jessica will earn about $30,000 a year.

Track 71, Page 214

1. What are you going to do if you win the lottery?
2. What will you do after you finish this class?
3. If she gets a promotion, what is she going to buy?
4. When he finishes college, where will he work?

Track 72, Page 215

A: What are your plans for next year?

B: I'm going to finish my English classes.

A: What are you going to do when you finish your classes?

B: When I finish my English classes, I'm going to enter nursing school.

A: Where are you going to work after you graduate?

B: I'm going to work in the emergency room of a hospital.

Track 73, Page 216

Ronaldo: I don't know what to do. I thought I wanted to become a nurse, but I don't know if I want to be in school for 2 or 3 more years.

Valeria: Do you have to work in a hospital? There are other careers, you know.

Ronaldo: I know, but I worked in a hospital in Brazil, and I liked that. There was always something going on. It was busy, and I like to be busy.

Valeria: Well, how about getting a certificate? My sister is a phlebotomist.

Ronaldo: She draws blood for lab tests, right?

Valeria: Yes. She started at $32,710, and now she's making more.

Ronaldo: What kind of training do you need?

Valeria: Let's go online and check. See? You can do this in less than a year. You need a professional certificate, but some hospitals give on-the-job-training.

Ronaldo: That looks good. The job outlook is high, 25% more jobs in the future. I'm a people person. I like to talk. A phlebotomist has to draw blood and make people feel comfortable. Some people are afraid of needles. I can help people with that. A phlebotomist has to enter patient information into a computer. I have computer experience. This sounds pretty easy.

Valeria: It sounds good for you.

Ronaldo: What other careers are there in a hospital?

Valeria: You like working with people. How about working as an occupational therapy assistant?

Ronaldo: My brother went to an occupational therapist after he got hurt at work. How much education do I need?

Valeria: You need an associate's degree, including 16 weeks of hands-on experience.

Ronaldo: Look. I'll have to take a few semesters of courses. This job requires courses in biology, psychology, a health education course, and others. I took biology and psychology in Brazil. Maybe I could transfer the credit.

Valeria: That's good. You could save some time.

Ronaldo: How much do they make?

Valeria: Oh! An occupational therapist makes about $59,010 on average. And, the job outlook is good, 28%! You're good at teaching people how to do things. Occupational therapy assistants have to teach patients how to use equipment. You would be good at that. And, the assistant has to work closely with the therapist. What do you think? Are you interested in anything else?

Ronaldo: My cousin is a surgical technician. I might be interested in that career. There's a program at the community college in my town. Let's check out the website. According to this site, the salary average is about $45,000. That's good. The outlook is pretty good, too—12%.

Valeria: What does your cousin do?

Ronaldo: He prepares the operating room for surgeries. He has to sterilize the equipment and prepare the patients for surgery.

Valeria: Okay. These all sound good for you. Now, we should talk to my sister and to your cousin.

Track 74, Page 217

1. The salary is the highest of the three.
2. This job requires hands-on experience.
3. This job requires a professional certificate.
4. This person can get the degree at a community college.
5. This job requires the least time at school.
6. The career has the best job outlook.
7. This person talks to patients.

Track 75, Page 218

Automotive Service Technicians and Mechanics

What Automotive Service Technicians and Mechanics Do
Automotive service technicians and mechanics, often called service technicians or service techs, inspect, maintain, and repair cars and light trucks. Basic repairs include changing oil, checking fluid levels, and rotating tires. Service technicians identify problems, often by using computerized equipment. In large shops, automotive technicians specialize in different types of repairs, such as brakes or air conditioning.

Work Environment
Almost 60% of technicians work for automobile dealers or in repair shops. Another 13% are self-employed. Most dealers and shops are well ventilated and well lit. Technicians commonly work with greasy parts and tools, sometimes in uncomfortable positions. Workplace injuries, such as small cuts, sprains, and bruises are common.

How to Become an Automotive Service Technician or Mechanic
High school courses in automotive repair provide a good background, but employers prefer that automotive service technicians and mechanics complete an automotive technology program at a postsecondary institution. Industry certification is usually required once the person is employed.

Pay
The median annual wage for automotive service technicians and mechanics was $39,550 in May 2017. Technicians at automotive dealers usually earn more than technicians at repair shops.

Job Outlook
Employment of automotive service technicians and mechanics is projected to grow 6% from 2016 to 2026, about as fast as the average for all occupations. There should be many job opportunities for qualified technicians.

VIDEO SCRIPTS

UNIT 2

Page 29, Queens, New York: The Most Diverse Neighborhood in the World?

Narrator: In today's global village, multiculturalism is normal, but one neighborhood in particular claims to be one of the most diverse places in the world. Welcome to Queens, New York.

Man 1: How are you doing? What's happening? **(narrating):** We're all immigrants. Who understands an immigrant better than an immigrant?

Narrator: Almost half of the population of Queens was born in another country. Its residents come from 100 different nations, and they speak almost 150 different languages. No racial or ethnic group is a majority here. There may be other neighborhoods with even more foreign-born residents, but only here do we find so many different cultures, nationalities, and ethnicities all in one place.

Woman 1: I know that... you know, I'm from Madras in the southern part of India. My parents lived there, and my grandparents lived there.

Woman 2: My mom's from South Korea and, on my father's side, um, I am German, Irish, English, and I think a little bit of Native American, but that part I'm not sure.

Woman 3: My great-grandfather was Puerto Rican, and his parents were Puerto Rican, and so on and so forth. So, as far as I know we've always been Puerto Rican. And I... I feel connected to that. And I... when I look in the mirror I see that, and I see my grandmother and my great-grandmother. It's something that I cherish, and it's something that I am very protective of.

Woman 4: So, you have Eastern Europeans. You have Hispanics. You have Turkish, Arabic. I like that. I like that very much.

Narrator: A 2001 study measured diversity using a simple idea: How likely is it that two randomly selected people have different backgrounds? In their study, Queens scored highest in the United States. As the most diverse community in the most diverse country in the world, it's a fair claim. But, even if there is no way to prove that it's the most diverse place in the world, Queens, New York is a great example of a melting pot.

UNIT 4

Page 62, Death Valley

This is Death Valley National Park. It's in the Mojave Desert in California. Deserts are very hot and dry. Death Valley is the hottest, driest place in North America. It receives less than two inches of precipitation, or rain, every year. Death Valley also contains the lowest place in North America at 282 feet below sea level. In the summer, temperatures are often in the 90s at night, heating up to around 120 degrees Fahrenheit during the day.

You may think that plants and animals can't live in a place so hot and dry, but Death Valley is actually full of life. Kangaroo rats make nests in between rocks and eat mostly seeds and plants. They don't need to drink water to survive because they get all the water they need from their food. Rattlesnakes also live in Death Valley, but it is rare to see one. During the day, they stay in the shade, but at night, they come out to look for food. Rattlesnakes hunt small birds and animals, like kangaroo rats. Death Valley also has plant life, including many kinds of cactuses. Sometimes, in the spring, wildflowers cover parts of Death Valley if the conditions are right. For wildflowers to grow, there has to be enough rain, warm temperatures, and not too much dry wind. Many tourists come in the spring in hopes of seeing the flowers.

Come visit Death Valley to learn more and see this beautiful place for yourself. Just remember to bring sunscreen, a hat, and a lot of water!

UNIT 8

Page 125, Getaway: Tiny Houses in the Woods

Jon: The housing we have doesn't work very well for the millennial generation. The form's wrong. The function's wrong. The social aspect's wrong. The geography is wrong. We all own all this stuff, or more accurately, all this stuff owns us. Tiny houses are one answer, in that they're small, they're simple, they're affordable. Sixty-eight percent of people who have a tiny house don't have a mortgage. They're an opportunity, personally, for people to find out what's really important and what makes them happy, which, I think, has a lot more to do with how you spend your time and a lot less to do with the stuff you own.

Patrick: Well, we start from the trailer, which is really the only thing that makes this different in construction from a normal house.

Jon: We place these really beautiful, handcrafted tiny houses a short drive from the city so people can go up there for a night, or two, or three, and rent this house, and really just disconnect and find themselves. They are powered by solar electricity. The heat comes from propane. And, we have a composting toilet. So, our tiny houses are completely off-grid.

Patrick: This house took us about a month to build, and then it's done.

Jon: How can we convert our housing stock into something that's more useable for this generation? That's more responsible for the environment? We think this is one small step towards a future where we redefine how we live. Tiny isn't really that tiny. When you're in a small, high-quality space, you can focus on living your life and connecting with people you care about. I think that's the real power in the tiny-house movement.

UNIT 9

Page 141, Hawaii's Kilauea Volcano

Elaine: Good morning. I'm Elaine Quijano. The volcano emergency on Hawaii's big island is far from over. The Kilauea Volcano has been erupting since Thursday, sending lava into neighborhoods and toxic gas into the air. At least nine homes have been destroyed. More cracks opened in the ground this weekend and there are now at least nine active fissures releasing lava. The island has also had more than 200 earthquakes in the past 24 hours. That follows Friday's magnitude 6.9 earthquake, the most powerful quake to hit Hawaii in more than 40 years. Carter Evans is there.

Carter (narrating): The volcanic trail cuts right through the community of Leilani Estates, sitting atop the eastern slope of Kilauea. For four days, the volcano has been spewing molten lava and ash. Large cracks, or fissures, spontaneously erupted in a line through the neighborhood, setting several homes on fire. We watched as smoke engulfed this house.

Sam: It's like a roaring… It's… It's like a goliath. Or like… like a roaring jet engine.

Carter (narrating): Sam Knox lives about 100 yards away from one of the eruptions. **(to Sam):** Did they ask you to evacuate?

Sam: They… told me there was a mandatory evacuation, but by law, I don't have to leave.

Carter: And why did you choose to stay?

Sam: Because this is where I live right here.

Carter (narrating): Two more cracks broke open, bringing the total to nine, with fountains of lava exploding into the night sky, just feet from homes on residential streets. **(to the camera):** Just a few hours ago this street was wide open and now you can see it's covered in about six feet of lava. It cools pretty quickly; you could almost walk on it now, but if you look inside you can see where it's still glowing red. **(narrating):** The lava spread quickly through lava tubes scientists describe as long tunnels underground. It erupts almost as if a hose has been sliced lengthwise.

Female Scientist: The prognosis is for this to continue. We see no slowdown in activity. Our seismic and geodetic data coming from the region still indicate magma accumulating below the general area.

Carter (narrating): That means new eruptive fissures could open up, unleashing more lava and toxic gasses into the community. **(to the camera):** These eruptions have made streets impassible all over this community. You can see where it's blocked the road here. And this isn't the only one. It's one of the reasons they've shut this area down. The concern is that people might get trapped inside and first responders won't be able to reach them. Elaine.

Elaine: Carter, thank you.

VIDEO WORKSHEETS

UNIT 2 – QUEENS, NEW YORK: THE MOST DIVERSE NEIGHBORHOOD IN THE WORLD?

A Complete the sentences.

1. Almost ________________ of the residents of Queens were born in another country.
2. There are residents from ________________ different nations.
3. Almost ________________ different languages are spoken in Queens.
4. In Queens, there are many different ________________, ________________, and ethnicities.
5. Queens, New York, is a great example of a ________________.

B Discuss.

1. Which countries did you hear mentioned in the video?
2. What do you think you will find in Queens since there is so much diversity?
3. Would you like to live in Queens? Why or why not?
4. Do you think that multiculturalism is important? Why?

UNIT 4 – DEATH VALLEY

A Complete the sentences.

1. There are fewer than ________________ inches of precipitation, or rain, each year.
2. The summer temperature averages ________________ degrees Fahrenheit during the day.
3. The summer temperature averages ________________ degrees Fahrenheit during the night.
4. Kangaroo rats eat ______________________ and ______________________.
5. Rattlesnakes eat small ______________________ and ______________________.

B Answer the questions.

1. Where do kangaroo rats find water? ____________________________________
2. What three things do wildflowers need to grow?
   a. ____
   b. ____
   c. ____
3. Why do tourists like to visit Desert Valley in the spring? _______________________

C Circle *True* or *False*.

1.	Death Valley National Park is in the Sonoran Desert.	True	False
2.	It's rare to see rattlesnakes during the day in Death Valley.	True	False
3.	Death Valley is the driest place on Earth.	True	False
4.	Death Valley sits below sea level.	True	False

UNIT 8 – GETAWAY: TINY HOUSES IN THE WOODS

A Answer the questions.

1. What are three advantages of tiny houses?
   Tiny houses are ______________, ______________, and ______________.
2. What percentage of tiny house owners do not have mortgages?
   ____
3. Where do builders construct tiny homes?
   ____
4. Where are some tiny homes located?
   They are located ______________________________.
5. Is this statement true or false? Explain.
   People have to buy tiny houses. ______________________________
6. What type of utilities do tiny homes have?
   ______________ electricity, ______________ heat, and composting ______________
7. How long does it take to build a tiny home?
   It takes about ______________________________.

B Discuss.

1. Why are some environmentalists in favor of tiny homes?

UNIT 9 – HAWAII'S KILAUEA VOLCANO

A Answer the questions about the Kilauea volcano.

1. What did the volcano send into the air?

   ____________________ and ____________________

2. How many homes were destroyed by the volcano?

   ____

3. How many earthquakes did the area experience in 24 hours?

   ____

4. When was the last time that Hawaii experienced such a strong earthquake?

   ____

B Discuss.

1. Why didn't the man evacuate?

   ____

2. Did the law require him to evacuate?

   ____

3. What did you learn about lava?

   ____

4. What did the woman say that she expected to happen?

   ____

5. Why is it dangerous for residents who don't evacuate?

   ____

VIDEO WORKSHEETS ANSWER KEYS

UNIT 2

A.

1. half
2. 100
3. 150
4. cultures; nationalities
5. melting pot

UNIT 4

A.

1. two
2. 120
3. 90
4. seeds; plants
5. birds; animals

B.

1. from their food
2. **a** rain; **b** warm temperatures; **c** not too much dry wind
3. Because they want to see the wildflowers.

C.

1. False
2. True
3. False
4. True

UNIT 8

A.

1. small; simple; affordable
2. 66%
3. on a trailer
4. a short drive from the city
5. False: They can also rent them.
6. Solar electricity; propane heat; composting toilets
7. a month

UNIT 9

A.

1. lava; toxic gas
2. nine
3. more than 200
4. more than 40 years ago

B.

1. He said that he didn't want to evacuate. He lived there.
2. No, it didn't.
3. Answers will vary.
4. She expected no slowdown. More lava and toxic gas was expected.
5. People might get trapped; first responders won't be able to rescue them.

WORKBOOK ANSWER KEY

UNIT 1: THE FIRST WEEK

A.

1. is; study; meet; know; studied; got; use; enroll
2. is; came; didn't study; attend; speak; is
3. is; am; works; live; study; attends; get; talk

B.

1. What country are you from? 2. Where do you live? 3. Is your family here? 4. How long have you been here? 5. Do you have any children? 6. What kind of music do you like?

C.

Answers will vary.

D.

1. are; are 2. study; attends; attends 3. work; have 4. speak; practice 5. like; plays; plays

E.

Answers will vary.

F.

1. enjoy 2. live 3. is 4. play / plays
5. run 6. go 7. like 8. want

G.

Answers will vary.

H.

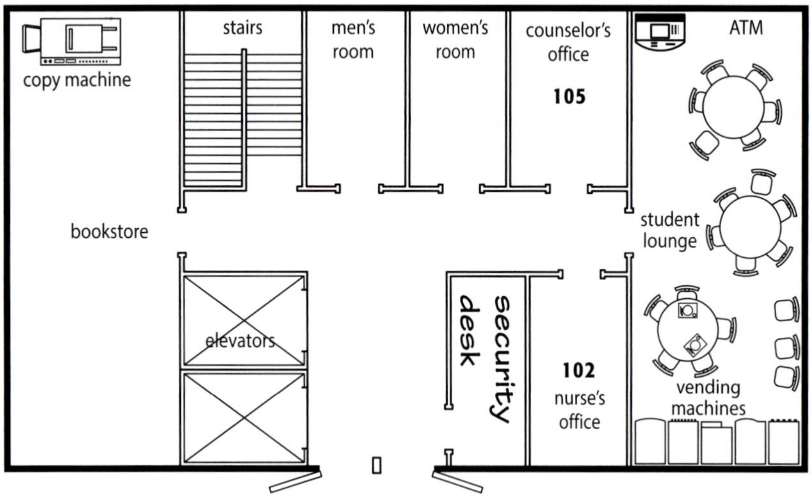

I.

Answers will vary.

J.

1. a 2. b 3. b 4. a 5. b 6. b 7. b 8. a 9. a 10. a 11. a 12. b 13. b

K.

1. No, it isn't. 2. Yes, she did. 3. She doesn't have time to go home. 4. At a fast-food restaurant. / In her car. 5. There is an accident. 6. No, she isn't. 7. She is still wearing her name tag. 8. No, she isn't.

UNIT 2: LIFE IN THE UNITED STATES

A.

1. drive 2. drives 3. doesn't walk 4. don't take 5. like
6. eat 7. have 8. eats 9. come

B.

1. lives 2. don't live 3. moves 4. move 5. don't live
6. doesn't move 7. want 8. live 9. plan

C.

Do you have a computer?

1. has 2. don't have 3. Answers will vary.
4. Answers will vary.

Do high school students work?

1. don't work 2. work 3. Answers will vary.
4. Answers will vary.

Do all children go to kindergarten?

1. go 2. goes 3. don't go 4. Answers will vary.

Do you own a cellphone?

1. owns 2. own 3. Answers will vary. 4. Answers will vary.

D.

1. The average person doesn't / does not sleep nine hours a night.
2. Most Americans don't / do not speak two languages.
3. The average family doesn't / does not have four children.
4. The average American doesn't / does not drink tea for breakfast.
5. Most people don't / do not walk to work.
6. The average American man doesn't / does not exercise every day.
7. The average worker doesn't / does not earn $50,000 a year.

E.

Answers may vary. Possible answers:

1. I am never late for class.
2. They eat out every weekend.
3. I sometimes take the bus to school.
4. We have a test every week.
5. Sometimes I shop online.
6. She eats breakfast every morning.
7. He is / He's hardly ever sick.
8. They take a vacation once a year.
9. We often go dancing.
10. My desk is always organized.

F.

1. have 2. doesn't have / does not have 3. is 4. don't earn / do not earn 5. work 6. votes 7. gets 8. don't volunteer / do not volunteer

G.

Every Thursday after work, Angela, Jackie, and Sara ~~goes~~ ***go*** out to dinner. Every week, the women ~~spends~~ ***spend*** one evening without their husbands or children. They don't ~~talks~~ ***talk*** about problems. They just enjoy an evening out, have a nice dinner, and ~~goes~~ ***go*** to a movie. Each week, a different person ~~choose~~ ***chooses*** the restaurant and the movie. After the movie, at 10:00 or 10:30, the women ~~makes~~ ***make*** plans for the next week.

H.

1. True 2. False 3. False 4. True 5. False 6. True 7. False
8. True

I.

1. Eighty-five percent of workers receive health benefits.
2. Seventy-three percent of workers have paid vacation.
3. The average person likes their job.
4. Most Americans drive to work.
5. About 10 percent of workers belong to unions.
6. The average retirement age is 63.
7. The average worker has thirty minutes for a lunch break.
8. Five percent of Americans work two jobs.

J.

1. T 2. F 3. F 4. F 5. T 6. T 7. T 8. F

K.

Answers will vary.

UNIT 3: WORKING AND SAVING

A.

1. Does; Yes, she does. 2. Does; Yes, she does. 3. Do; Yes, they do. 4. Does; Yes, she does. 5. Do; Yes, they do. 6. Does; No, she doesn't. 7. Do; No, they don't. 8. Does; No, she doesn't. 9. Does; Yes, she does. 10. Do; Yes, they do.

B.

Answers will vary.

C.

1. How often do you receive a paycheck?
2. How much money do you pay in taxes?
3. How much money do you save every week?
4. Does your company pay for your medical benefits?
5. Do you receive your paycheck electronically?

D.

1. does; get up 2. does; go 3. Does; take 4. does; get 5. does; work 6. does; go 7. does; do 8. does; go

E.

Answers will vary. Sample answers:
1. How does Stanley get to school? He takes the bus. 2. What time does he get to school? 3. Where does he work? 4. How many hours does he work? 5. When does he do his homework? 6. How many hours does he study? 7. What time does he go to bed? 8. How many hours does he sleep?

F.

1. Who hates to cook? Jay does.
2. Who eats out every night? Jay does.
3. Who saves $100 a week? Carlos and Amy do.
4. Who has $7,000 in the bank? Carlos and Amy do.
5. Who works next to a coffee shop? Danny does.
6. Who spends $9 a day on coffee? Danny does.
7. Who shops at the mall every weekend? Gina does.
8. Who owes $3,000 on her credit cards? Gina does.

G.

Answers will vary.
1. Do 2. Is 3. Are 4. Is 5. Does 6. Do 7. Does 8. Do 9. Are 10. Is 11. Does 12. Do

H.

1. True 2. True 3. False 4. False 5. True 6. False 7. True 8. True 9. True

I.

1. How many hours a day does he work? 2. Is Tony at home? 3. How many days a week does he work? 4. Does he wear regular clothes at work? 5. Where does Tony work? 6. Is he tired at the end of the day? 7. What does he do? 8. Does he like his job?

J.

1. Fifty-six percent / 56% 2. 21 / twenty-one 3. Forty-one percent / 41% 4. $3,000 / Three thousand dollars

K.

1. False 2. False 3. False 4. True 5. True

UNIT 4: THE STATES

A.

1. cities 2. visitors 3. farm 4. deserts 5. seaports 6. state 7. islands 8. cities; visitors 9. tourist 10. parks

B.

1. is 2. has 3. have 4. run 5. grow 6. is 7. travel 8. receives 9. enter 10. visit 11. supplies 12. lie

C.

1. Yes, there are. 2. Yes, it is. 3. No, there aren't. 4. No, they aren't. 5. Yes, it is. 6. Yes, they are. 7. No, it isn't. 8. Yes, it is. 9. Yes, there are. 10. Yes, there are. 11. No, there isn't. 12. Yes, there is. 13. Yes, it is. 14. No, there aren't. 15. No, it isn't.

D.

1. snow 2. rain 3. boats 4. tourists 5. trees 6. seaports 7. mountains 8. mountain ranges 9. traffic 10. pollution

E.

Answers may vary. Sample answers:
1. there are a lot of 2. there isn't much 3. there are many 4. there are many 5. there aren't many 6. there isn't much 7. there is a lot of 8. there is a lot of 9. there aren't many 10. there are many

F.

Answers may vary.
1. How many cities and towns are there in North Carolina?
2. How many state parks are there in North Carolina?
3. How many public universities are there in North Carolina?
4. How much rain is there in North Carolina?
5. How much tourism is there in North Carolina?
6. How many hurricanes are there in North Carolina every year?
7. How much traffic is there in the large cities?
8. How many miles of coastline are there in North Carolina?
9. How much farming is there in North Carolina?

G.

about 20,984,400 and growing; 22; 16; 19; hot and humid; 82; not very cold; 60; 55; oranges, tomatoes, sugarcane, vegetables, and plants; Florida's largest industry, Disney World, Everglades National Park, Miami Beach

H.

1. c 2. b 3. a 4. b 5. c 6. a 7. a 8. a 9. b 10. c 11. b

I.

1. No, it isn't. 2. Yes, there are. 3. No, there aren't. 4. Yes, it is. 5. No, it isn't. 6. Yes, it is. 7. Yes, it is. 8. Yes, there is. 9. No, there isn't. 10. Yes, it is.

J.

1. Alaska 2. Alaska 3. Hawaii 4. Hawaii 5. Hawaii 6. Alaska 7. Alaska and Hawaii 8. Alaska and Hawaii 9. Answers will vary.

UNIT 5: TECHNOLOGY

A.

1. are planning
2. aren't / 're not / are not asking
3. are / 're making
4. are / 're searching
5. is / 's using
6. is / 's downloading
7. is / 's learning
8. isn't /'s not / is not texting
9. is / 's driving
10. is / 's texting
11. isn't / 's not / is not wearing
12. is / 's following

B.

1. Are the people waiting for the bus? Yes, they are.
2. Is Tomi checking the bus schedule? Yes, he is.
3. Is Sophia reading a book? No, she isn't.
4. Is Jessie listening to music? Yes, she is.
5. Are Diti and Chandi talking? Yes, they are.
6. Is Roberto talking on his cellphone? Yes, he is.
7. Are Mehmet and Lynda standing in line? No, they aren't / 're not.
8. Is the bus coming soon? Yes, it is.

C.

1. is Rosa applying for a loan 2. is Gregor ordering 3. is Joseph paying 4. are your parents moving 5. is talking on the phone 6. are Nelson and Paula eating at 7. is Beata depositing in her bank account 8. are you texting

D.

1. are you doing 2. are you studying 3. are you studying

E.

1. need 2. belongs 3. Are you having 4. forget 5. are looking 6. taste 7. look 8. love 9. am thinking 10. do you prefer

F.

1. works; is working / 's working
2. saves; is saving / 's saving
3. is writing; is writing / 's writing
4. is checking / 's checking; checks
5. pays; is paying / 's paying
6. reads; reads
7. is studying / 's studying; is studying

G.

Answers will vary. Possible answers:

1. He's standing in front of the stove.
2. He's cooking hamburgers and chicken.
3. He's carrying a plate of food.
4. He's going to a table.
5. Anna is making a salad.
6. Anna is using a knife to cut vegetables.
7. Cara is washing dishes.
8. Five people are working in the kitchen.

H.

1. he is 2. they are 3. he does 4. he does 5. he is 6. she is 7. they do 8. she does 9. she is 10. he is 11. he does 12. they do

I.

1. b 2. c 3. four 4. Don't open emails from people and companies you do not know, install software to block junk email, unsubscribe from mailing lists, etc.

UNIT 6: A HEALTHY LIFESTYLE

A.

Sherri – 2, 4, 7; Liz – 3, 5, 9; Manuel – 1, 6, 8

B.

1. She is going to take cool baths.
2. She is going to stay home from school for a week.
3. Her mother is going to apply lotion to Sherri's face and body.
4. She is going to drink tea.
5. She is going to gargle with warm water and salt.
6. He is going to buy a bandage.
7. He is going to put an ice pack on his ankle.

C.

1. Yes, she does. 2. No, she isn't / 's not. 3. Yes, she is. 4. Yes, she does. 5. No, she doesn't. 6. Yes, she is. 7. Yes, she is. 8. No, she isn't / 's not. 9. Yes, she does. 10. Yes, she is.

D.

1. How long / When 2. When 3. How many 4. What kind of / Which 5. How many 6. How long 7. How much / What kind of / Which 8. Which / How many / What kind of 9. How much 10. How high

E.

1. is he going to buy 2. is he going to ride his bicycle 3. is he going to cook 4. is he going to lose

F.

Answers may vary.
1. When are you due 2. What are you going to have 3. What are you going to name him 4. Is your husband going to take any time off from work 5. Are you going to take maternity leave 6. Who will take care of him when you go back to work

G.

Answers will vary.

H.

1. I'll visit her in the hospital. 2. I'll take her to the doctor. 3. I'll send them to Sandra. 4. I'll take it for a week. 5. I'll help them. 6. I'll send him a get-well card. 7. I'll get it for you. 8. I'll need them for a week. 9. I'll call her/him. 10. I'll speak to her/him.

I.

1. This child is getting a vaccine. 2. The child is going to cry. 3. The boy's parents are going to buy him some ice cream. 4. The doctor is taking the man's blood pressure. 5. The man has high blood pressure. 6. The doctor is going to check his cholesterol. 7. This person is reading the eye chart. 8. This person needs reading glasses. 9. The doctor is going to write a prescription for glasses.

J.

1. an allergist 2. cats, dogs, dust, ragweed, strawberries 3. now/late summer 4. strawberries 5. 275 6. 37 7. blood pressure 8. He doesn't eat well; he doesn't exercise; he works 10 hours a day.

K.

Answers will vary.

L.

1. T 2. F 3. T 4. T 5. F 6. T 7. F

UNIT 7: AROUND THE WORLD

A.

1. longer than 2. larger than 3. more popular than 4. larger than 5. smaller than 6. more dangerous than 7. older than 8. hotter than 9. more talkative than

B.

1. there are fewer 2. there are fewer 3. there are fewer 4. there are more 5. there is more 6. there are fewer 7. there is more 8. there are fewer

C.

1. Austin is more populated than Boston. 2. Homes are more expensive in Boston than in Austin. 3. Austin has a higher sales tax than Boston. 4. Boston has more colleges and universities than Austin. 5. Austin has fewer professional sports teams than Boston. 6. Boston has more rainy days than Austin. 7. Austin has warmer weather than Boston.

D.

1. the tallest 2. the largest 3. the busiest 4. the longest 5. the most populated 6. the most beautiful 7. the hottest 8. closest; furthest

E.

1. one of the most beautiful cities 2. one of the largest libraries 3. one of the most crowded cities 4. one of the most famous art museums 5. one of the hottest places 6. one of the most popular sports 7. one of the oldest structures 8. one of the busiest airports

F.

Answers will vary.
1. Is a subway train as fast as a bus? A subway train is faster than a bus. 2. Is walking as healthy as running? 3. Is going to the movies as enjoyable as going to a concert? 4. Is police work as dangerous as military work? 5. Is living in the city as comfortable as living in the suburbs?

G.

1. Dogs are **the** most popular pets in the United States. 2. Birds are **more** popular in China than in the United States. 3. Computer software is the **most** popular item to buy on the internet. 4. France is **as** beautiful as Italy. 5. Arizona is **sunnier** than New York. 6. May is not as hot **as** August. 7. This Thai restaurant serves the ~~most~~ spiciest food in town. 8. Denver International is one of **the** busiest airports in the United States. 9. Soccer is more popular ~~then~~ **than** tennis.

H.

Year Opened – 1904; Number of Stations – 472; Number of lines – 27; Passengers per day – 5,700,000; Cost – $2.75; Hours Open – 24 hours

I.

1. London Tube 2. Moscow Metro 3. New York City Subway 4. New York City Subway 5. Moscow Metro 6. Moscow Metro 7. New York City Subway 8. London

J.

1. the most gold medals 2. the most bottles 3. the most popular kind of exercise 4. the greatest 5. one of the most expensive 6. more movies than 7. the oldest university 8. one of the largest libraries

K.

Year opened – 1852; Number of departments – 12; Visitors per year – four million; Cost – free of charge up to $10.70; Hours open – 10:30 a.m. – 6 or 9 p.m.

UNIT 8: MOVING

A.

1. lived 2. was 3. asked 4. needed 5. was 6. lived 7. agreed 8. arrived 9. were 10. were 11. looked 12. liked 13. applied 14. waited 15. moved

B.

1. He repaired it. 2. He put in a new carpet. 3. He replaced it. 4. He fixed it. 5. He cleaned them. 6. He painted the bedroom. 7. He installed a new lock. 8. He called an exterminator.

C.

1. graduated; found; worked; didn't work 2. changed; became; decorated; learned; decided 3. found; stayed; got 4. opened; was; ordered; were 5. moved; opened; received

D.

1. Stan got his visa in 2016. 2. Stan left Poland in 2017. 3. Stan flew to Chicago. 4. Stan's family / friends met him at the airport.

E.

Answers will vary.

F.

Answers will vary.

G.

1. decided 2. liked 3. was 4. needed 5. looked 6. found 7. saw 8. live 9. moved 10. love 11. has 12. fixes 13. was 14. didn't say 15. hate 16. stand 17. drive 18. comes 19. doesn't feel 20. broke 21. stole 22. feels 23. will look 24. will check

H.

1. came 2. brought 3. found 4. met 5. got 6. lived 7. applied 8. received 9. was 10. didn't 11. studied 12. took 13. didn't 14. got 15. taught 16. paid

I.

1. David 2. David & Maria 3. David 4. Maria 5. David 6. David 7. Maria 8. David 9. Maria 10. Maria

J.

1. They moved last weekend. 2. They moved to Denver, Colorado. 3. Bill's company transferred him there. 4. No, Bill didn't want to move. 5. They lived in Washington, DC. 6. Because Denver is in the mountains and Susan loves to ski. 7. He is going to visit this winter.

K.

1. F 2. T 3. F 4. T 5. T 6. T 7. F 8. F 9. T

UNIT 9: NATURAL DISASTERS

A.

1. was; snowstorm 2. was; heat wave 3. was; earthquake 4. were; were; forest fire 5. was; drought 6. were; hurricane 7. was; tornado 8. was; was; flood

B.

1. How tall 2. How far 3. How deep 4. How difficult 5. How heavy 6. How long 7. How strong 8. How wide

C.

1. did; begin 2. did; get 3. Did; go 4. Did; play 5. Did; shovel 6. did; see 7. Did; have 8. did; hide

D.

1. was 2. was 3. Did 4. did 5. was 6. was 7. were 8. Did 9. did 10. Were 11. did 12. Did 13. were 14. Did 15. Was

E.

1. When did it begin to rain? 2. How many days did it rain? 3. How deep was the water? 4. When did you evacuate? 5. What did you take with you? 6. Did your house have a lot of damage? 7. How long did you stay with your friends?

F.

1. What time did the power go out? 2. Where were you? 3. Did you have a flashlight? 4. How long was the power out? 5. What did you eat? 6. Was the water working? 7. When did you go to bed? / What time did you go to bed?

G.

1. did he take 2. are they going (to go) 3. does she volunteer 4. food and water is she buying 5. smoke alarms did she install in the house 6. is he building 7. took a first aid course last month 8. will your family meet in case of an emergency 9. did he call for (emergency) help 10. do you keep emergency supplies 11. is your fire extinguisher 12. gave the order to evacuate 13. is / 's he looking for 14. did the fire department respond

H.

1. What time did the storm begin? 2. Did the roads flood? 3. Were you late for work? 4. Were a lot of trees down? 5. How long did it take you to get to work? 6. What did your supervisor say? 7. How many workers were out? 8. Was your company closed?

I.

Answers will vary.

J.

1. tornado 2. 5:00 3. basement 4. walls 5. windows 6. table 7. blankets 8. do not stay 9. get out

K.

1. T 2. F 3. T 4. F 5. F 6. T 7. T 8. T 9. F 10. F

UNIT 10: WEDDING PLANS

A.

1. has to hold the flowers 2. has to put a ring on the bride's finger 3. has to perform the ceremony 4. has to take good pictures 5. have to remain quiet during the ceremony 6. has to hold the rings 7. has to play good music 8. have to sit in the front row

B.

1. have to 2. doesn't have to 3. have to 4. don't have to 5. doesn't have to 6. doesn't have to 7. don't have to 8. don't have to

C.

Answers may vary.
1. has to go to the supermarket. 2. doesn't have to fix the lawnmower. He fixed it yesterday. 3. doesn't have to pick up her gown. She picked it up a week ago. 4. has to bake the wedding cake. 5. doesn't have to mow the lawn. He mowed it yesterday afternoon. 6. has to wash the cars. 7. has to vacuum downstairs. 8. don't have to pick up Grandma Grant. They picked her up two days ago. 9. has to take the dog to the neighbor's. 10. don't have to check with the caterer. They checked yesterday. 11. have to set up the tents and chairs. 12. has to decorate the backyard.

D.

Answers will vary.

1. Does the groom have to ask the bride's family for permission first?
   No, he doesn't.
2. Do the families have to exchange gifts?
3. Does the bride have to take her husband's name?
4. Does the couple have to exchange rings?
5. Does the bride's family have to pay for the wedding and reception?

E.

Answers will vary.

F.

Answers will vary.

G.

Answers will vary.

H.

1. Pedro 2. Ricky 3. Mike 4. No one 5. Everyone 6. Ricky 7. Pedro 8. Chris 9. Everyone

I.

1. have to stop 2. don't have to buy 3. should stop to visit sights 4. doesn't have to bring 5. has to help 6. don't have to buy 7. should pack 8. should download

J.

1. Answers will vary. 2. She will often wear red because red is a lucky color in Chinese culture. (paragraph 3) 3. After the older relatives and friends leave, the young people take over the party. There is music, singing, and dancing. The friends of the couple organize many games for the guests and for the bride and groom. The friends of the bride may play funny tricks on the groom. (paragraph 6) 4. They represent the hope that the couple will soon have children, both boys and girls. (paragraph 7)

UNIT 11: AT WORK

A.

1. A landscaper can cut your lawn. 2. An accountant can prepare your taxes. 3. A baker can make your wedding cake. 4. An engineer can design a bridge. 5. A bank teller can cash your paycheck. 6. A photographer can take your wedding pictures. 7. A pharmacist can fill your prescription. 8. A detective can solve a crime.

B.

1. Would you please / Could you please open the window?
2. Would you please / Could you please lend me ten dollars?
3. Would you please / Could you please give me a ride to work?
4. Would you please / Could you please clean the coffee machine?
5. Would you please / Could you please take a message?

C.

1. must 2. can 3. can't / must not 4. can 5. can't / must not 6. must 7. can't / must not; can OR can; can't /must not 8. must not / can't 9. must 10. can't / must not

D.

1. Maybe he will take a vacation. 2. Maybe she will get the job. 3. Maybe I will get a promotion. 4. Maybe my manager will retire. 5. I may / might get a raise. 6. My company may / might close. 7. The economy may / might improve. 8. I may / might change jobs.

E.

Answers will vary.
1. The boss may / might fire him. 2. Ivan may /might get a new job. 3. Kaylee may / might bring the coffee maker back to Young's Appliances. 4. Sandra may / might go home. 5. Jay may / might major in computer science. 6. Beata may / might look for a tutor.

F.

1. has to; might 2. must; might; Could 3. has to; can't; has to 4. has to; might 5. can't; might; has to

G.

1. shouldn't 2. can't / must not 3. do not / don't have to 4. do not / don't have to 5. must not / can't 6. shouldn't

H.

Answers will vary.

I.

1. He might order a hamburger. 2. Could you please bring me a cup of coffee? 3. He has to drive many miles a day. 4. He must not get any speeding tickets. 5. He shouldn't put too much salt in the soup. 6. He can make delicious soup. 7. Could you please check the brakes? 8. He can fix the car.

J.

1. T 2. F 3. T 4. F 5. T 6. T 7. T 8. F 9. F

K.

1. heavy truck driver 2. PV installer 3. medical records technician 4. PV installer 5. heavy truck driver / tractor-trailer driver 6. medical records technician 7. PV installer / heavy truck driver / tractor-trailer driver 8. PV installer 9. Answers will vary. 10. Answers will vary.

UNIT 12: WORKING PARENTS

A.

1. d 2. a 3. f 4. b 5. i 6. c 7. j 8. g 9. e 10. h

B.

Answers will vary.

C.

1. F 2. T 3. F 4. F 5. T 6. F 7. T 8. F

D.

1. after / when 2. When 3. before 4. before 5. after / when 6. When / After 7. after / when 8. Before 9. until 10. When

E.

Answers will vary.

1. Mrs. Butler works late when there is an important project.
2. Mr. Butler stays home and takes care of the children and the house when his wife is at work.
3. Mrs. Butler drops the children off at their schools before she goes to work.
4. Mrs. Butler has a cup of coffee when she gets to work.
5. Mrs. Butler talks with her coworkers, checks her email, and answers her messages before she works on her current project.
6. Mrs. Butler skips lunch or orders a sandwich when she's too busy for lunch.
7. Mrs. Butler leaves work at 6:00 when everything goes well.

F.

Answers may vary.

1. After Mr. Butler finishes the dishes, he does the laundry.
2. As soon as everyone leaves, Mr. Butler does the dishes.
3. Before the twins come home, Mr. Butler reads job ads and sends out resumes.
4. After Mr. Butler makes lunch, he picks up the twins.
5. Mr. Butler feeds the twins when they get home.
6. The twins play in the yard until Mr. Butler calls them inside.
7. When Jessica gets home, Mr. Butler helps her with her homework.
8. When Mr. and Mrs. Butler go out for an evening, Jessica babysits the twins.
9. The family has dinner together when Mrs. Butler gets home at 6:30.

G.

1. she 2. them 3. he 4. them 5. him 6. her 7. me

H.

1. a 2. b 3. b 4. a 5. b 6. a 7. b

I.

Answers may vary.

1. When Ella wakes up, she makes her lunch. 2. Ella takes a shower before the baby wakes up. 3. Ella eats breakfast after she gets dressed. 4. Ella wakes the baby after she eats breakfast. 5. Ella gives Jesse a bottle as soon as he wakes up. 6. Ella plays and talks with Jesse after she changes and dresses him. 7. Ella talks to her mother and has a cup of coffee before she leaves.

J.

1. note 2. progress 3. difficulty 4. needs to come in for extra help 5. extra 6. after school 7. will talk; tomorrow

K.

Answers will vary.

UNIT 13: CRIME

A.

1. After 2. as soon as / when 3. Before 4. When / As soon as / After 5. before 6. as soon as / when 7. when / as soon as

B.

Answers may vary.

1. As soon as I opened the door, I turned off the house alarm.
2. As soon as she got into the car, she locked the doors.
3. After he heard a noise, he called the police.
4. After the robber broke into their apartment, they installed new locks.
5. When the shoplifter tried to leave the store, the security guard stopped him.

C.

Answers may vary.

1. were taking; was watching 2. were sitting; were lighting 3. was looking; was reading 4. was describing; were looking 5. were relaxing; was playing

D.

1. c 2. f 3. d 4. g 5. e 6. h 7. b 8. a

E.

Answers will vary.

F.

Answers will vary.

1. She was reading a magazine when she heard a noise.
2. While she was reading, she heard a noise.
3. His boss was talking when he fell asleep.
4. While his boss was talking, he fell asleep.
5. They were playing when he fell and hurt his arm.
6. While they were playing, he fell and hurt his arm.
7. She was interviewing him when they were interrupted.
8. While she was interviewing him, they were interrupted.
9. They were singing when she brought the cake to the table.
10. While they were singing, she brought the cake to the table.

G.

1. was walking; saw 2. was driving; cut 3. was beeping; stopped 4. stopped; got out 5. were arguing; hit 6. wasn't paying; hit 7. was coming; happened

H.

1. was coming 2. work 3. was pulling 4. driveway 5. open 6. 911 7. asked 8. cellphone 9. driveway 10. name 11. opened 12. house 13. Cecilia 14. was coming 15. mother 16. operator

I.

1. f 2. i 3. h 4. j 5. e 6. b 7. a 8. d 9. g 10. c

UNIT 14: CAREERS

A.

1. after 2. if 3. After 4. If 5. After 6. if 7. before 8. When

B.

1. f 2. h 3. d 4. g 5. a 6. b 7. c 8. e

C.

Answers will vary.

D.

Answers may vary.

1. If it rains, we will come home early.
2. Before I start work, I will check my messages.
3. I will buy a new car when I get a new job.
4. If Bob and Jane have time, they will go to the movies.
5. Before John goes to his interview, he will research the company.
6. Sophia will go back to college if she loses her job.
7. If Rick gets a promotion, he will be very pleased.
8. Maria will give away her winter clothes before she moves to Florida.

E.

Answers may vary.

1. ...is going to take a few courses in digital photography.
2. ...is going to buy a top quality camera and printer.
3. ...is going to develop a business plan.
4. ...is going to choose a name for his business.
5. ...is going to advertise the business.
6. ...he is going to hire a photography assistant.

F.

1. is he going to do; he gets 2. is she going to speak to; she has 3. are you going to study; you go 4. is he going to work; he graduates 5. are they going to hire; they open 6. are you going to wear; you go

G.

Corrected sentences:

1. After Jackie talks to her supervisor, she **will** take a few days off.
2. If Jackie's boss ~~didn't~~ **doesn't** give her time off, she will have a problem.
3. When Pierre gets home from work, he always ~~went~~ **goes** for a long run in the park.
4. He takes a long shower before he ~~is eating~~ **eats** dinner.
5. While Beata was ~~look~~ **looking** for her keys, her son found them in the car.
6. Beata called her husband after she ~~was finding~~ **found** her keys.

H.

1. a 2. b 3. a 4. c 5. b, c 6. c 7. b

I.

1. a 2. b 3. b 4. a 5. b 6. a

J.

1. T 2. T 3. F 4. T 5. F 6. T 7. F 8. F